MAYAMATA

MAYAMATA

An Indian Treatise on Housing, Architecture and Iconography

An Updated Edition With Revised Glossary

Translated by

BRUNO DAGENS

New Age Books

New Delhi (India)

Second English Edition : 2017
Reprint : 1995
First English Edition : 1985

ISBN: 978-81-7822-497-8

Published by
NEW AGE BOOKS
A-44 Naraina Industrial Area, Phase-I
New Delhi (India)-110 028
E-mail: nab@newagebooksindia.com
Website: www.newagebooksindia.com

NAB Cataloging-in-Publication Data
MAYAMATA : *An Indian Treatise on Housing, Architecture and Iconography*
by Bruno Dagens
Includes Introduction, and
revised Glossary.
ISBN 978-81-7822-497-8

Printed by
Anupam Art Printers

CONTENTS

LIST OF FIGURES

FOREWORD

The MAYAMATA and the MĀNASĀRA are the two best known amongst Sanskrit treatises of South India on architecture and iconography. However, unlike the MĀNASĀRA an English version of which by P. K. Acharya was published in 1933, the MAYAMATA has not so far been translated into English. The present book is based upon our edition, with French translation, in the Publication Series of the Institut Français d'Indologie[1]. The Sanskrit text has been omitted so that the book may be of a reasonable size; by the same token we have been able to dispense with most of the footnotes which accompanied the French translation due to the recent publication by the Sitaram Bhartia Institute of Scientific Research, of our book: *Architecture in the Ajitāgama and the Rauravāgama* (New Delhi 1984); the assumption is that the two books will be used together. The glossary is presented in an abridged form; most of the drawings have been retained and some more added but it should be noted that they are meant to be no more than tentative sketches. Lastly, the interpretation of the text has been revised and we are grateful once more to our friend Mary Premila Boseman for her help in the establishing of the English text.

Pondicherry — March 1985

---

1. *Mayamata — traité sanskrit d'architecture*, édition critique, traduction et notes par Bruno Dagens, 2 vols., Pondichéry 1970–1976 (Publications de l'Institut Français d'Indologie no. 40–I & II). For the previous editions of the *Mayamata* see below p. xxxii.

INTRODUCTION

I

THE TECHNICAL LITERATURE AND THE MAYAMATA

The body of Sanskrit literature dealing with architecture and iconography is voluminous but it is scattered and has been insufficiently surveyed; it is matched by a vernacular literature which is even more scattered and even less known.[1] It comprises, first of all, independent works which can be classified under the general heading of "technical treatises" (*śilpaśāstra*) or under the more precise one of "treatises on dwelling" (*vastuśāstra*) or "treatises on dwellings" (*vāstuśāstra*). The use of one or other of these designations in a colophon does not however make for any reliable indication as to the contents of the work or its originality; thus, the *Mānasāra* and the *Mayamata* whose contents are identical, are designated as a *vāstuśāstra* and as a *vastuśāstra*, respectively. The scope of these works, and that of the domain they cover, varies considerably and that goes for the comprehensive treatises as much as for those which confine themselves to limited subjects, such as iconography of Śaivite deities or astrological points bearing upon the founding and the construction of a house. There are few specialized works of importance in this category even so, architecture and iconography being more often dealt with in various works, whether more or less ambitious encyclopaedias or treatises which concentrate upon areas where architecture and iconography are involved. The great purāṇa are to be found in this category, along with encyclopaedias of royal inspiration such as the *Mānasollāsa* or the *Samarāṅgaṇasūtradhāra* and

1. A bibliography on these literature is now in preparation at the Sitaram Bhartia Institute of Scientific Research.

the Śaivite and Vaiṣṇavite āgama of various persuasions, as well as the *Gṛhyasūtra* and the *Arthaśāstra*. These types of works are just those in which the material is most abundant but most scattered and it should be added that a number of small indépendant treatises are nothing more than extracts from much larger works and, as well, that it is hard to be sure whether the *Pūrvakāmikāgama* has borrowed from the *Mayamata* the very great number of passages common to both texts or whether the reverse is the case. That the dispersion is also historical and geographical only complicates the problem still further, and the architecture and iconography, as they appear in a given work, are but the reflection of what was in existence during the time of its drafting in the region where that was done; significant in relation to the described forms, this factor is also apparent in the technical vocabulary which is always more or less marked by regional usage, as well as by borrowings from the vernacular. Then, there is the sectarian bias, whether stressed or not and very apparent in the iconography and also, even if to a lesser degree, in complex architectural forms, if not in their elements envisaged separately. The pretension to universality of many of these texts does nothing to conceal this phenomenon and, whether the regional and sectarian features are more or less emphasized, they are still, usually, obvious. It must also be added that the Indian or, more precisely, the Hindu koiné, is so much the fruit of such a mixture of regional and unitarian trends that each author, or school, may legitimately imagine that its day-to-day reality is nothing but an accurate reflection of the whole Indian world.

In that very extensive and widely disseminated range of works, the *Mayamata* occupies a fairly well defined place. It is a general treatise, a *vastuśāstra*, written in Sanskrit but originating from Dravidian India, most probably from the Tamil area; it is part of the Śaivite agamic literature without the connection being underlined by any pronounced sectarianism and its drafting must have been done during the Cōḻa period, at the time when the architecture it describes had reached the peak of its maturity. Comprising about 3300 verses and divided into 36 chapters, it is identified as a *vastuśāstra*, that is, as a treatise on dwelling, for it defines the *vastu* as "anywhere where immortals or mortals live" (2.1). This definition is followed by specifications which show that the concept of housing is very wide and is divided into four categories: the Earth (considered as original dwelling), buildings vehicles and seats (which last three are nothing but '*vāstu*' deriving from the first '*vastu*', the Earth). Once iconography has been added to this list we have a panorama, brief but inclusive, of the content of the work. Leaving aside here the details of this content which we will analyse further on, we note that the *Mayamata* is arranged in three large sections: the first (Chap. 1–10) deals with dwelling sites, the first *vastu*, the second section with buildings (Chap. 11–30) and the third (Chap. 31–36), with the last two *vastu*, vehicles and seats, and with iconography (Liṅga, images and their pedestals). In these different sections are found entire chapters or significant passages consecrated to particular topics in the sphere of technique or that of the ritual which sets the pace for the construction: system of measurements and quality of the architects (Chap. 5), orientation and laying-out (Chap. 6–7), offerings to the gods of the site (Chap. 8), foundation deposit (Chap. 12), joinery (Chap. 17), rites for the end of the construction of a temple and for the first entry into a house (Chap. 18 and 28) and renovation work and associated rites (Chap. 35).

The work as a whole is coherent in spite of various interpolations which are sometimes, but not always, indicated by changes in the metres. These appear quite frequently in chapters describing temples where they often give information on details of decorative motifs which were evidently mentioned, though not described, in the original text; in the same way the description of a pavilion of the *siddha* type (25.39sq) is interrupted by fourteen verses given over to ritual firepits (*kuṇḍa*); this interpolation would seem to have been entailed by the mention of the fact that the *siddha* pavilion may serve "for all rituals". These interpolations do not seem to give rise to any great internal discrepancy; it is only to be noted that the mention, in a general chapter on temples, of thirteen, fourteen, and sixteen storeyed temples (11.19) seems to be the result of an updating of the text which never otherwise describes temples with more than twelve storeys (cf.22.66sq).

That the *Mayamata* belongs to Śaivasiddhānta literature is demonstrated by the leading place given to Śiva temples, by the chapter given over to the Liṅga and especially by the speculations on the nature of the Liṅga which it contains and, lastly, by the pantheon described in Chapter 36 which is essentially that found in the *śaivāgama*. This being said, the *Mayamata* nevertheless does not appear to be a sectarian work; the list of Śiva's Attendants is followed by a list of those of Viṣṇu (Chap. 23) and Chapter 36 includes descriptions of images of Buddha and Jina which are not usual in agamic literature, no more than are mentions of the temples of these two deities such as are found here in the chapters dealing with villages and foundation deposits (9.70sq and 12.59sq). Ram Raz, who has noted the tolerance shown in the *Mayamata* (and the *Mānasāra*) towards Buddhists and Jains, says however that the locations attributed to the cult places of these two sects were close to those suitable for inferior deities or for malignant spirits (*Essay on the Architecture of the Hindus*, 1834, p.9). This absence of sectarianism is marked in a much more general way by constant references to a very classical society such as is presented in the Dharmaśāstra. The society for which are intended the constructions prescribed by the *Mayamata* is that of the four *varṇa* and the "others", who are installed at a distance and who are responsible for polluting tasks such as refuse collection. If the society of the *Mayamata* is that of the Dharmaśāstra, its political organization is that of the Arthaśāstra; there too the references to classical India are very evident, as well where they concern the hierarchies of towns and villages, as when they give the method of organizing the defence of a kingdom with forts, and the way in which the royal council chamber is to be arranged (cf.Chaps. 9 and 10 and 29.191sq).

It may be said, quite definitively, that the aim of the *Mayamata* is to organize the integration of the external manifestations of Siddhānta Śaivism in a context which could be qualified as "non-sectarian Hindu", so as to avoid the term 'secular' which is not very appropriate when speaking of traditional India.

The South Indian origin of the text cannot be questioned. Aside from the fact that it is virtually inherent in the connection with Śaivasiddhānta, it is brought out still more by the existing evidence of the architecture described. This architecture follows the option characterized by false storeys, which proliferated in Pallava times, and which came to its full flowering in the Cōḻa period, since when it has been perpetuated right up until today. It had already extended to the Krishnā area by the time of the first Cāḷukya, to Ellora under the Rāṣṭrakūṭa and to South East Asia as early as the Preangkorean period of Khmer civilisation. To that may be added a number of details which give evidence of a drafting made in Tamil areas, such as the use of the hybrid *kāyapāda* to designate the struts (16.16sq) or of *saruṣapa* to designate the mustard seed (in place of *sarṣapa* 28.3). The last point to be noted is that the palmleaf manuscripts of the *Mayamata* are in Grantha (Tamil) script or in Telugu or Malayalam script.

The chronological elements at our disposal are mostly sujective. An *ad quem terminus* is given by quotations from the *Mayamata* found in the commentary of the *Śāradātilaka* (a Śākta text) written in 1484 by Raghavabhaṭṭa (cf.comm.ad *Sāradātilaka* 3.21 and 3.53). Our text however must be earlier and may have been written between the definitive elaboration of the false storey option and the appearance of the very big temples of this type, as those of Tanjore or Gaṅgaikondacōlapuram at the beginning of the XIth century. This hypothesis gains weight from the previously noted mention of temples with more than twelve storeys, in what seems to be an interpolation for the sake of updating: the temple of Tanjore has fifteen storeys and it would therefore be 'abnormal' in relation to a treatise which limits the number of storeys to twelve; a mention of Śiva temples with sixteen storeys brings this temple back to the norm however by almost attaining the ideal maximum. In the same way we notice that gateways, according to the *Mayamata*, are not to have more than seven storeys, a maximum which was not achieved till the 12th century with the gateways of the Cidambaram temple. We may therefore establish a chronological bracket which goes from the early 9th century to the late 12th. We may point out, in passing, that the mention of Buddhist and Jain cult places also accords with a drafting in the Cōḻa period, one marked by relative tolerance.

A word remains to be said about the originality of the work. The *Mayamata* forms, as we have seen, a fairly coherent whole and would seem to have been composed all in one piece with some later interpolations and additions. It represents an architectural school well-known throughout South India and its treatment of architecture is not basically very different from that to be found in many other texts, especially in those connected in one way or another with the Śaivasiddhānta tradition. The relationship of these texts to the *Mayamata* may be of diverse kinds and in some cases the *Mayamata* has clearly been used as an authority: in the *Īśānaśivagurudevapaddhati*, which quotes it extensively when dealing with architecture, and in the *Śilparatna*, whose author has borrowed heavily from it. We may even mention here a Singhalese treatise which concentrates upon what is auspicious or inauspicious for a construction and which uses the *Mayamata* to support its own authority.[2] In other texts, however, the direction of the borrowing is less evident and this is especially true of two works which appear to be particularly akin to the *Mayamata*; the *Kāmikāgama* and the *Mānasāra*.

The *Kāmikāgama* is among the most famous of the Śaivāgama; its first part, (*Pūrvakāmikāgama*) is devoted mainly to architecture and is literally crammed with verses, and sometimes even entire passages, which are to be found in the *Mayamata*. It is questionable whether one of these two texts has borrowed from the other or whether both have borrowed

2. Edited and translated into French by J. Liyanaratne under the title: *Le Purāṇa Mayamataya—manuel astrologique singhalais de construction*, Paris 1976 (Pub. Ecole Française d'Extrême-Orient no. 109).

from a third work but it does not seem possible to determine this at the present stage since the editions of the *Pūrvakāmikāgama* in current existence are all at a precritical stage, at best, which does not allow for any assessment of the exact value of the text as we know it.[3] We have personally often been struck by the impression that the composition of the chapters on architecture in this book was often rather incoherent; this would perhaps be explained by the presence of verses and passages borrowed from a well established treatise, such as the *Mayamata*, for the sake of filling in gaps in an ill-preserved text or of adding to information deemed insufficient, or both.

The *Mānasāra* is a comprehensive treatise on architecture and iconography from the same category as the *Mayamata* but, in spite of the numerous parallels between the two works, it would seem that they belong to two slightly different branches of the South India school of architecture. They both have exactly the same overall plan however; even though the *Mānasāra* is longer (5400) verses and has a larger number of chapters (70), these two characteristics would appear to be no more than the effect of a somewhat padded presentation and of a more precise distribution of topics into chapters. P. K. Acharya, the editor, translator and commentator of the *Mānasāra*, assigned an extremely early date to it (Gupta period) and considered it the unique source of all presentations of architecture in purāṇa and āgama as well as in more specialized texts such as the *Bṛhatsaṃhitā* or the *Mayamata*.[4] One of his arguments was that the *Mānasāra* was the most 'complete' of all the texts dealing with architecture, in the sense that all the specific types mentioned in other texts were to be found in it. The early date thus given to the *Mānasāra* has been called into question, notably by T. Bhattacharyya who has pointed out that the argument which we have just cited would rather tend to favour a late dating and to show that the *Mānasāra*, in the state in which we know it, is, at the most, a sort of 'recension

3. See *Kāmikāgamaḥ-pūrvabhāgaḥ*, South India Arcakas' Association Madras 1975.
4. P.K. Acharya, *Indian Architecture according to Mānasāra-Śilpasśāstra* (Oxford 1934, reprint New Delhi 1981), espec. pp. 160–198.

of recensions', which is to say, a late and protracted version drawn from a less 'complete' original and from numerous other sources as well.[5] We tend to agree with this view and would be ready to accept the Ur-*Mānasāra*, if such existed, as a work analogous to, and more or less contemporaneous with, the *Mayamata* for, notwithstanding their differences, both works seem, generally speaking, to refer to an equivalent phase in the development of the school which they represent.

As far as the *Mayamata* is concerned, we may, without over-emphasizing the originality of its teachings, consider it to be a rare and fairly good example of a mediaeval technical text, well preserved in its original form and, as such, worthy to be used as a reference work.

II

THE EARTH AND THE SITES

The first part of the work deals, as has been said, with the first *vastu*, the Earth, in describing the dwelling sites which fall into two categories: natural sites or, more exactly, "primary" sites and towns and villages such as may be established on primary sites and which are designated as "derived" or "secondary" sites. The former, designated by the same words as is the Earth (*bhū*, *bhūmi*, *avani* . . .), are examined, and it is in terms of that examination that they are assessed as suitable or not for a construction or a secondary site; they represent what may be called the natural environment as opposed to towns and villages which are artificial environments, having to be prepared and then modelled according to norms presented in the two chapters on town planning which conclude this first part.

The first chapter lists the contents of the work and ends by speaking of the *Mayamata* as a treatise on "housing" (*vastu*) intended for gods and for men.

5. T. Bhattacharyya, *The Canons of Indian Art* (Calcutta 1963), pp. 183–195.

Chapter 2 begins with the already quoted definition of housing (everywhere where immortals and mortals live), and with an enumeration of its four categories: the Earth, buildings, vehicles and seats. The last three categories however are simply *vāstu*, or derivations from the first, for the Earth is the initial form of dwelling on which the others have appeared. This idea can be most clearly seen in the opposition established between a site chosen specifically for a particular category of inhabitant, that is a secondary type of site (*gauṇa*), and the Earth which is the basic site (*aṅgin*). We return to this question when the different categories of building, vehicle and seat, have been enumerated and it has been indicated that the Earth is first, because she was the first entity to exist and because she is the support of the others and the stabilizing factor of the universe itself. The end of the chapter contains a list of the characteristics appropriate to sites intended for each of the four *varṇa*, to which further allusion is made in the chapter dealing with private houses (cf. 27.5, 46sq).

Sites

Chapters 3 and 4 concern the examination and the taking possession of a site intended for a house, a temple or a settlement. Chapter 3 first lists the favourable and unfavourable features which can be perceived from a superficial examination of the site. Chapter 4 sets out the rituals and empirical procedures which are necessary for taking possession of the site and for the verification of its favourable characteristics. The first rite is the ploughing followed by a sowing to ascertain the site's fertility; this corresponds to the *aṅkurārpaṇa* (germination of shoots) which opens festivals. Next comes a consecration rite combined with a procedure for verifying the permeability of the soil, which should be sufficient but not excessive, and for showing if it is compact enough.[6]

6. See *Architecture in the Ajitāgama and the Rauravāgama*, pp. 30–3.

Measurements

Chapter 5 deals with the system of measurements and with the technicians working on the building. The exposition of the system of measurements (5.1–13) is brief, it enumerates the "formless", (atom to barley seed), and absolute measures in current use (digit, span, various kinds of cubit, pole and rope) giving the specific usage of these latter ones. The only relative measure which is dealt with here is the *mātrāṅgula* or *dehalabdhāṅgula* (digit calculated from the body), used in the ritual and defined as the middle phalanx of the second finger of the officiant. The measurements of distance: (*krośa, gavyūta, yojana*) are defined elsewhere in the work (9.1–2) as are those for areas (*kākaṇī, māṣa, vartanaka, vāṭikā*, 9.2–4) as well as the relative measures in common and current use: module (*daṇḍa* 15.28–29), intercolumniation (*bhakti*, 25.14) utilized for the proportions of pavilions and halls and the digit used in iconography (23.110). Also dealt with elsewhere will be the *āyādi* method with which the auspicious nature of the chosen dimensions is verified (9.18–24, 26.206sq., 32.24, 33.58sq., 36.296–298).[7]

Technicians

Four types of technician (*śilpin* 5.13–25) work on a building. The first is the architect (*sthapati* but also *takṣaka*, see below): the eulogy given here enlarges upon his moral qualities and on his science and it is elsewhere that a more significant definition of his function is to be found (*sthapatiḥ sthāpayet sthiram* 9.128); otherwise he is the master of the work who is responsible for the building until its inauguration (18.199sq., 28.25sq.); he is involved in the various rites which punctuate the construction (12.18 sq., 18.130 sq., 28 passim) as well as in the ceremony which accompanies the extraction of a stone (33.22 sq.); in his religious function he is under the orders of an officiant (*sthāpaka* or *ācārya*). Lastly we note that the term *sthapati* seems equally capable of designating any other artisan (9.95). The *sūtra*-

7. *Ibid.* pp. 18–19.

grahin ("the drawer of the thread") who is responsible for the operation of measuring and of laying-out is the son or the disciple of the architect; we may thus think of him as a foreman, destined to become an architect himself; it is he who is referred to when it is said that, in the case of the architect's death, it is his son or disciple who must bring the work to a satisfactory conclusion (18.160). About the *takṣaka* it is simply said that, as his name indicates, he cuts the stone, wood or brick according to the order of the *sūtragrahin*; as the text unfolds however it becomes evident that the name *takṣaka* may also designate the architect himself (28.10), which designation corresponds to the use of the word *taccaṉ* in Tamil. Lastly the *vardhaki* "fitter" is both a mason and a carpenter. The architect's three assistants rarely appear in the ensuing chapters except in collective formulae such as: "the four of whom the first is the architect" (referring to the distribution of honoraria, 9.130, 10.94; see also 12.22).

Orientation and laying-out

Chapters 6 and 8 deal with the laying-out procedures for buildings and settlements. The orientation of the site is made according to the classic method with a gnomon (*śaṅku*, 6.1–11; fig.1). On this point the text presents the *apacchāyā* (6.11b–13 and 27–28) which is said to be a factor that allows for the rectification of the rough indication furnished by the gnomon; in reality, as Michio Yano recently proved, this development on *apacchāyā*, which is found in the same context in several texts, has nothing to do with the orientation but simply gives a method of expressing the variation of the length of the noon-shadows in a modified linear function, which method would seem to have its far off origin in Babylonia. The unresolved question remains as to how and why this development has been systematically introduced in the orientation rules.[8]

8. M. Yano, *Knowledge of Astronomy in Sanskrit Texts of Architecture—Orientation Methods in the Īśānaśivagurudevapaddhati* (Paper read at the VIth World Sanskrit Conference, Philadelphia 1984).

The layout proper uses stakes and rope (6.14–26); the indications given are not very clear but it would seem that a first line of reference which is called "*pramāṇasūtra*" (measuring line) and which marks the limits of the main body of the building, having been laid down, a second one (*paryantasūtra*, 'line of limit') is drawn which marks the extreme limits of the delineated space. This second line is only mentioned once more in the text (under the name *sīmasūtra*), apropos houses (27.15); the first line, however, appears, under various names (*ājusūtra*, *ṛjusūtra*, *mānasūtra*), as the line from which are determined the projections of elements which are going to be added to the main building as well as the recesses which correspond to the recessed parts of the facades (cf. 15.58–60, 21.223, 22.79–81).

These two lines are evidently used for both edifices and settlements since there are instructions for drawing them in either case (6.21–24). Verses 6.24–26 explain how the lines are drawn from the centre of the house thus allowing for the accurate laying-out of the principal main building of a house with four main buildings (*catuśśāla*) according to the category of its occupants (see as well 27.15 sq.).

Diagrams

The different parts of an assembly going to make up a complex edifice or a group of edifices or a settlement, are positioned with reference to a regular diagram analogous to that used to draw ritual *maṇḍala*. Each of the squares (*pāda*) of the diagram is attributed to a protecting deity by whose name the square is designated. Chapter 7 lists thirty-two of these diagrams, from the single square diagram, to one with one thousand and twenty-two squares (32 × 32) and gives, in detail, the disposition of protective deities on some of them with particular emphasis on those with sixty-four (*maṇḍūka*) and eighty-one squares (*paramaśāyin*) as these are the most often used (7.32 sq., 57–58, figs. 2–6). This chapter gives as well the first example of the use of these diagrams when it describes the body of the Spirit of the building (*vāstupuruṣa*) and indicates the vulnerable points (*marma*) which are not to be touched during the construction (7.49–56; see also 9.86, 27.15–18). Chapter 8 gives details of the offerings to be made to the diagram's protective deities once that diagram has been laid out on the site.

Villages

Chapters 9 and 10 deal respectively with villages (*grāma*) and towns (*nagara*). If the settlements described in Chapter 10 have a largely urban function it would seem that the term *grāma* may be applied as well to villages as such, to sites of villages, and to settlements which may be towns as much as villages. This ambiguity is more marked in Chapter 9 which deals with villages in particular and with towns in general. This chapter begins (9.1–24) with an outline of the dimensions as those dimensions apply, first of all, to *grāma* and *nagara* and goes on to those of five types of settlement where *grāma* and *nagara* reappear, along with *kheṭa*, *kharvaṭa* and *durga* which are described in the following chapter. This exposition begins with indications as to the units for measuring distances and areas and ends with an explanation of the *āyādi* method (see above). Next, the question arises of how many brahmins are to inhabit a village (from 12000 to only one, 9.25–30) and then of the dimensions and names of a village's streets (9.35–39). Eight types of village are defined in terms of the number, of the orientation and of the layout of their streets (9.40–56; fig. 7). The account of the internal organization of villages successively presents the position of doors and of drains and the division of the village into concentric zones (determined on a diagram), each associated with a specific category of inhabitant; it goes on to the disposition of temples and their orientation, to the disposition of public facilities and to the artisans' quarters and then to what is to be set up outside the settlement: the dyers' quarter, the houses of *caṇḍāla* who are to collect the refuse every morning and, lastly, the cremation ground and cemetery. This outline ends with comments on the necessity of keeping to the prescribed plan (9.99–100) and with a note on the foundation deposits of settlements, a subject which recurs in Chapter 12 in connection with temples and houses: the shape of the casket and the composition and position of the foundation deposit for every type of settlement are given (9.101–128).

Towns

Chapter 10 too begins with an exposition of the dimensions of the different types of the towns that it later describes (10.1–12); the drawing of the enclosures is given next and then the dimensions of their walls, the diagrams in use and the width of the streets (10.13–18). The specific descriptions of towns (10.19–51) are more or less detailed and often no more than bare definitions. Successively presented are: *rājadhāni* (capital, see also 29.86), *kheṭa* (inhabited by śūdra), *kharvaṭa* (surrounded by mountains), *pattana* (trading port), *śibira* (fortified camp), *senāmukha* (town provided with a garrisoned fort), *sthānīya* (royal foundation, see also 29.163), *droṇamukha* (commercial city on a river), *viḍamba* (near a village?), *kotmakolaka* (in a forest), *nigama* (artisans' town), *skandhāvāra* (type of fort-town) and *durga* (fort), the description of this last being relatively detailed: different types, necessary qualities, fortified doors and enclosures, inhabitants and gods (10.36–51). The towns as well as the villages may be defined by the number, orientation and plan of their streets, six types of these plans being mentioned (10.52–76). The chapter ends with an exposition of the situating of the various bazaars (*antarāpaṇa*) (see fig. 8) and residential quarters and points out that temples are disposed as in a village.

III

EDIFICES

The second and longest section deals with the architecture itself; it consists first of chapters given over to the precise analysis of the elevation, divided into levels. Next, successively described, are the temples with their enclosures and gateways, the pavilions, halls, residential houses, and the palaces which complex assemblies are more relevant to town planning than to private houses.

Chapter 11 looks at the dimensions and number of storeys in buildings, not otherwise defined, which would seem to be temples as much as dwellings, princely or otherwise. It has already been noted that Śiva temples with sixteen storeys are referred to here, even though the descriptions given in chapters 19–22 on temples do not go above twelve storeys.

Foundation deposit

Chapter 12 deals with the foundation deposit (*garbha* lit. "womb" or "embryo"). This deposit which is essential to the success of the constructions is to be placed in a pit (12.3–5, see also 14.7); its principal element is a casket (*phelā*) with compartments, placed upon a bed of earths, roots and seeds (12.5 sq) in the course of a ceremony conducted by the architect. Next, after a general view has been given, (12.23–32) come the characteristics of the deposits appropriate to temples of the different deities (12.33–70): Śiva, Viṣṇu, Brahmā, Ṣaṇmukha, the Attendants of Śiva (including Sugata-Buddha and Jina) and the Goddesses. Then come deposits for the houses of the members of the different castes, those of the different types of building (*sabhā*, *maṇḍapa*, *raṅga*) and lastly, those of wells and hydraulic works (12.71–100). The descriptions are accompanied by details of the position of the deposit and by some interesting general points: the mixing of the deposit peculiar to a type of building with that peculiar to the occupants of the building (12.83), the relationship between the function of the building and the composition of the deposit (12.88) and finally an interdiction against the placing of the foundation deposit (*garbha*) when the wife of the master of the house is pregnant (*garbhiṇī*, 12.95). Four "first bricks" (*prathameṣṭakā*) are to be placed above the foundation deposit during a ceremony which marks the beginning of the work of construction itself (12.101–114).

Levels of elevation

Chapters 13 to 16 and 18 describe in sequence the different levels (*varga, aṅga*) which may be included in the vertical composition of a building and which will, under all circumstances, be included in that of a temple (*prāsāda*). The structural elements and the decorative levels, to which they correspond on the elevation of the building, are not sharply distinguished and they are designated by the same terms; it is evident though that the descriptions there are, are concerned much more with the appearance of elements and therefore with the decoration than with their structure, a notable exception being the description of the carpentry of the roof in chapter 18.

Socle

Chapter 13 is about the socle (*pīṭha*), an additional level which may be put under the base; after brief indications as to the height and projection determined from those of the base, comes an enumeration of the mouldings and of their proportions for three types of socle with a variation for each type.

Base

The base (*adhiṣṭhāna* . . . etc. cf. 14–40) is really the first level of the elevation, the socle being optional, which explains why Chapter 14, dedicated to it, starts with the method of preparing the ground before construction begins (14.1–10): it must first of all be determined whether the soil is dry (*jāṅgala*) or moist (*ānūpa*) even though both these categories are appropriate; a solid foundation is then established through the digging of a pit, of the dimensions of the projected building, which is then filled with various materials and well tamped; then the foundation deposit is installed; a regulating course (*janma upāna*) is arranged on which the actual base is elevated. The height of the base is determined with regard to the number of the edifice's storeys or to the social class of its occupants (14.11–16, see also 14.47); the projections and recesses of the various mouldings are determined from that height (14.17–18 and (41–44). The proportions of the mouldings of fourteen bases are listed (14.19–37); it is specified however that the proportions given may be slightly modified should need arise (14.39). The chapter ends with some notes on stereobates (*prati, vedi* . . .) which are moulded elements which may be interposed between two major levels (14.45–46, see also 16.51,67).

Pillars

The first part of Chapter 15 (1–61) is given over to the level of the pillars (*stambhavarga*) which rise up between the base and the entablature; this level corresponds to the habitable part of the building and its layout is made along the *pramāṇasūtra* (or *ājusūtra*, cf. 15.57–58 and above chap. 6); in the case of a several storeyed building it is repeated (along with its corresponding entablature) as often as there are upper storeys. In spite of its name it may appear either as a colonnade or as a wall with pilasters or as a plain wall. This chapter, however, scarcely touches upon anything but the description of pillars or of pilasters, the distinction rarely being made (cf. however 15.51); they are designated by an impressive number of synonyms (cf. 15.2). Their dimensions are indicated (15.3–8, 116, 12.55–56), the diameter at the top being of importance since it serves as module (*daṇḍa*) for the whole building (15.28–29). Different types are then defined, either according to their position (15.9–11) or to the shape of their shaft (15.13–27). The crowning elements are the bell capital (*kumbha*), the abacus (*maṇḍi*) and the bracket capital (*potikā*) (15.29–50); but it is only the bracket capital which is indispensable (15.28a). The sole indication as to the composition of facades concerns the intercolumniation which, it is specified, must be regular.

Materials

The second part of Chapter 15 (v.62 sq.) deals with the materials used in construction, especially wood and brick; stones will appear in the chapter on the Liṅga (33.4–36). For wood there are lists of trees well adapted to the construction work (15.64–67, 108b–114, see also 25.182 sq.), followed by observations on their favourable and unfavourable characteristics (15.62–63, 71–76), by a description of the ritual which governs the search for, and the cutting down of, a tree, and by indications as to drying times for the wood (15.81–103). A list of the required characteristics of bricks is then given (15.68–70) and some details of their manufacture (15.115–120). lastly, there are general indications as to the use of materials and the possibility of using one, two or three sorts of materials in a building which is accordingly called "pure" (*śuddha*), "mixed" (*miśra*) or "mingled" (*saṅkīrṇa*).

Entablature

Chapter 16 deals, for the most part, with the third level of elevation, the entablature (*prastara, mañca*) but information is also given on walls and on latticed windows. The height of the entablature is defined according to that of the base or that of the pillars (16.48); it is set on the top of the pillars with a mortar, the composition of which is given (16.41–42, see also 18.92 sq.). It comprises three main parts: first there is, at the bottom, the architrave (*uttara*) surmounted by a sort of fillet (*vājana*) which may be assimilated to an upper fascia (16.2–7); this fascia corresponds structurally to a wall plate which supports, whether directly or not, the beams of the plank floor which are at the level of the entablature (below); it is also surmounted by a decorative element, the *muṣṭibandhana*, made up of lotuses projecting like closed fists, hence its name; these lotuses may be cut directly into the ends of the beams or may be sculpted separately on a moulding which shapes the ends of the beams. Above this lower assembly is a second whose description is very confused and seems to correspond, in fact, to two slightly different systems. The main element of the first would be a sort of pent-roof or dripstone (*gopāna*) whose pronounced projection is held up by several different supports: braces (*pramālikā*) and/or struts (*kāyapāda*) as well as consoles (*daṇḍikā*) (16.7b–18a). The important element in the second system would be a cornice (*kapotapālikā*, *kapota*), rounded and projecting by much less which rests on the upper fascia of the architrave through the intermediary of an historiated frieze or other mouldings (16.18b–24a); the decoration of this cornice comprises false dormer windows (*nāsikā*) placed on its extrados just above a sort of band (*kṣudra?*) which outlines the edge of the cornice. The upper part of the entablature has, as its principal element, a frieze designated by various names (*prati*, *vedi*) which designate as well, in a more general way, the stereobates which make the connection between the various levels and, especially, that found below the attic (*gala*, *kaṇṭha*), that is to say, above the entablature, which duplication does nothing to clarify the description. . . . This frieze is usually historiated but may also be plain; it is placed above a fillet and a groove, which separate it from the cornice and it is surmounted by a fillet (*vājana*) (16.28–35). The beams of the plank floor either rest directly upon the upper element of the architrave (above) or through the intermediary of supports called *valīka*, which seem to be pieces perpendicular to the architrave. Above these beams (*tulā*) come, successively, the joists (*jayantī*), the small joists (*anumārga*) and, lastly, the flooring (or covering) of planks or masonry (16.36–45).

The various types of latticed windows (*jālaka*) are defined by the design of their opening and by the number and arrangement of their transoms and uprights (16.54-62). Lastly the walls which are dealt with at the end of the chapter are obviously light partitions (16.63–66).

Joinery

An examination of the assemblies (*sandhikarma*, Chap. 17) is inserted into the presentation of the levels of the elevation. After giving some information on the procedure (17.1–10) it begins by describing a series of assembled structures defined by the number of pieces of different dimensions which are, in turn, supports and themselves supported (17.15–28); the exact usage of these assemblies is not indicated and the impression is rendered, at least in one case, that the assembly described is not of carpentry work but is a house (17.24–26). On the other hand, there are the much more classical kinds of assemblies which involve vertical pieces such as pillars and horizontal ones such as architraves (16.31–37; figs. 9–10). These assemblies often call for pegs and tenons designated by various synonyms (17.44). The chapter ends with a lengthy exposition of mistakes in assembling and their consequences (17.45 sq.).

Attic and roof

Chapter 18 is much longer than those preceding it and one section deals with the three upper levels of elevation (attic, roof, finial v.1–115) and the rest with the ceremonies which mark the end of the construction of a temple (v.116–216).

The attic, literally the "neck" (*kaṇṭha*, *gala*, *grīva*. . . .) is recessed in relation to the floor it surmounts and to the roof above; a stereobate stands for a base and its entablature is constituted by the edge of the roof (18.2–7).

The description of the roof (*śikhara*, *śiras* . . .) is rather muddled; in contrast to what is given for the other levels, it deals mainly with the structure of the timberwork of the roof. The principal pieces of this structure are the main rafters (*lupā*, but also *raśmi* cf. 25.203 sq.) which are of five types according to whether placed in median positions (*madhya-lupā*), intermediate ones (*madhyakarṇa*, *ākarṇa*, *anukoṭi*) or to whether they are corner rafters (*koṭi*) (18.30–31). A relatively simple geometrical method is given, for calculating the length of these different main rafters when the roof is pyramidal with a height equal to half its width (18.23–36). It depends on the use of a square whose width is half that of the roof and which will be used twice: once to calculate the length of the projection of the rafters on the horizontal plan situated at the level of the wall plate and once to calculate their actual length from that of the projection (fig. 11)[9]. It is to be noted that this method, which involves no trigonometry, may be compared

9. See J. Dumarçay, Les charpentes rayonnantes . . . in *Bull.Ecole Française d'Extrême-Orient*, t.60 (1973), pp. 85 sq and espec. fig. 6.

with that used to draw regular polygons (cf. 25.49 sq.). These rafters support a covering of planks or metal plates (18.46–47 and 65–66); they are joined by various elements such as liernes (*valaya*) but, here again, the detail is not presented in any intelligible way as the text stands. Otherwise, there are indications as to the different shapes of the roof (18.15–16) and to its dimensions (18.7–12).

The finial (*stūpikā*) encloses an axis, fixed to the top of the woodwork; the details of its mouldings are given (with the proportions of the height and width) (18.18–19, 83–90) as well as indications about the axis and about the "vase" which is the main moulding of the finial (18.193 sq.).

Ceremony for the end of the work

The description of the ceremony marking the completion of a temple is preceded by a short note on the mortars used, particularly for the covering and for coatings where there are going to be paintings (18.92–115).

The ceremony at the end of work on the temple (18.116–216) is, to some extent, the counterpart of the foundation rite described in Chapter 12. It is performed on the occasion of the putting in place of the finial above the four 'crowning bricks' (*mūrdhneṣṭakā*) which correspond to the four "first bricks" (*prathameṣṭakā*) and which cover a sacred deposit, which itself corresponds to the foundation deposit. These operations accompany the construction of a building and the opening of the eyes of the images found therein; one of the officiants is the architect who withdraws once the finial has been put in place (18.199 sq.).

Temples

Chapters 19–22 describe temples with up to twelve storeys (*tala*, *bhū*, *bhūmi*) and which have all the six levels of elevation described in the preceding chapters, with the repetition of the level of pillars and entablature when the edifice has more than one storey. The plan of the ground floor may be reduced to one central room, the sanctum (*garbhagṛha, nālīgṛha*) surrounded by a wall; aisles (*alindra, vāra*) may intervene between the sanctum and the exterior wall; the partition wall which surrounds the sanctum is then called *gṛhapiṇḍi* and the exterior wall is often qualified by *hāra*. The entrance to this main building may be preceded by a pavilion (*mukhamaṇḍapa*) which might be said to play the part of a nave. Where the upper levels are concerned, the description of their plan is most often limited to indications as to the arrangement of the aediculae (*kūṭa, koṣṭha, pañjara*) which surround them; these aediculae, which are placed at the top of the storey directly below, are considered as belonging to this storey and not to that which they surround.

Chapter 19 gives the characteristics of temples with one storey (*ekatala*) and some much more general indications. Amongst these latter a description of the pavilion placed in front of the entrance is to be noted (19.4–8, see also 21.18 sq.), as well as a list of synonyms designating temples (19.12–14), the proportions of the finial (19.15–17 cf.chap. 18), those of the door (19.20–22 cf.chap. 30) and the description of the temple's exterior gargoyle (*nāla*); to this is added a classification of buildings according to the differences of plan there may be between their upper levels (attic, roof) and the others (classification *nāgarādi*, 19.35–38, see also 21.99, 35.8); lastly, there is a list of images to be found on the facades of a Śiva temple (19.39–48). The dimensions and proportions of single storey temples are indicated (19.1–3), as well as the various shapes of their plan (19.3–4) and the proportions of their sanctum (19.13–15). The different types of temple are distinguished by their plan and by the presence or absence of aediculae and of foreparts (*bhadra*).

Following on from the proportions and dimensions of temples with two storeys (*dvitala*), Chapter 20 describes fifteen of those temples (fig. 14). Next are given indications for the arrangements of aediculae (20.10–12), for the decorative arches (*toraṇa* 20.36–39, see also 21.29 sq. and 69 sq.) and, lastly, a classification of buildings according to the materials used and the nature, more or less massive, of their structure (classification *sañcitādi* 20.31b–34, see 35.8b–9a).

Chapter 21 gives, in more or less detailed ways, the eight types of three storey temple and, in particular, of the apsidal temple (*hastipṛṣṭha, dvyaśravṛtta*); this description is interrupted by two passages which are probably interpolations and which deal, one with the pavilion placed before the entrance of the temple (21.18–20) and with the position of the aediculae in relation to the *mānasūtra* (21.21–23, cf. Chap. 6) and the other with the *stambhatoraṇa*, a decorative motif on the facades (21.29–33). The chapter ends with general observations on aediculae (*kūṭa, koṣṭha* . . . 21.61–64), on buildings with and without aisles (*anarpita* and *arpita*) (21.64–65, cf. 26.14 and 35.8–9a), on the sanctum, on the stereobates and on the decorative arches (21.68–80).

Chapter 22 is about temples with four to twelve storeys. Whilst the description of four storey temples is relatively detailed (22.2–54, fig. 15), the description of those with five concentrates solely on the division of their elevation (22.55–57). A much simpler method of presentation is used for what follows, which gives only the proportions of the base and of the ground floor, it being understood that the base, as indicated for a temple of six storeys for example, is put in place of that of a five storey temple whose ground floor becomes the second storey of a six storey temple . . . etc. The chapter ends by returning to the subject of aediculae and by giving rules for their arrangement (22.76–92).

Enclosures

The temple is surrounded by an enclosure (*prākāra*), or by several concentric ones, which delimit courts in which various annexes are arranged. Chapter 23 describes these different enclosures, there being five of them at most, and the next describes the corresponding gateways. These enclosures are drawn with the help of nested diagrams (23.2–17). The height and thickness of their walls increase towards the exterior (23.18–25) and galleries (*mālikā*) may be built up against those walls (23.26–31 and 68–73). Amongst annexes installed in the courts, the foremost are the shrines of the Attendants and lists are given, of eight, twelve, sixteen and thirty-two Attendants of Śiva (23.39–58) (fig. 16), as well as lists of those of Viṣṇu (23.98–106). The end of the chapter also gives an iconographic description of the bull (Vṛṣa), principal attendant of Śiva (23.107–131). In the courts beside these shrines are altars and a flagmast (23.74–83, 88–91) as well as various service buildings (23.83–88). The house of the temple priests is in one of the enclosures (23.92) but those of other personnel are outside them (23.96).

The gateways (*gopura*, cf. 24.2) corresponding to these five enclosures increase in size the further they are away from the temple and they may have up to seven storeys (24.2–36); they are very similar to the temples described in the preceding chapters; they are almost always rectangular and have a wagon-roof; the resemblance is emphasized in the specific descriptions (24.36 sq.) by the use of terms, which usually designate the shrine of a temple, to designate here the central passage characteristic to gateways.

Pavilions

Chapter 25 describes the pavilions (*maṇḍapa* 25.1–197) and the halls (*sabhā*, 25.198–237). The pavilion is somewhat the all-purpose building of Indian architecture (cf. the list of its uses given here 25.2b–5). It is usually characterized by a three level elevation (base, 'pillars', entablature 25.25) but it appears in simplified variations which do not comprise a base (*prapā* 25.26–29). The edifice may or may not be hypostyle but in every case the unit of reference for the proportions is the intercolumniation, whether real or supposed (25 13–16). The roof is usually flat but may comprise one or more lanterns (*ūrdhva-kūṭa*) which are generally arranged above areas where the intercolumniation is double or treble what it is elsewhere. The pillars of the *maṇḍapa* are in stone or wood and a list is given of the trees (25.182 sq.) which completes those given in Chapter 15. The descriptions of square and rectangular pavilions rarely go beyond a brief run down of the plan of the edifice. As well, there is the description of a pavilion for water games (25.176–181) and notes on the pavilion in front of the temple (*mukha-maṇḍapa*), on the foundation deposit, on the gallery which may be attached to the facades of a pavilion and on the cloister-like galleries (*mālikā*, 25.188–197). Lastly, the way to draw sacrificial pits (*kuṇḍa*) is inserted into the description of a pavilion such as may be used for sacrifices (25.43–56): especially featured here are simplified methods for drawing regular polygons without recourse to trigonometry.

Halls

The halls (*sabhā*, 25.198 sq.) are hypostyle buildings with a large free space in the centre and with a wagon-roof, hipped or not. The essential matter in the description of this roofing poses the same unresolved problems as do indications of the same type given in Chapter 18.

Dwelling houses

The description of dwelling houses is the subject of Chapters 26 and 27 (Chapter 28 touches only upon the rite of first entry) and it may be said that, roughly speaking, the first gives the different types of plan for the edifice which constitutes the house itself and the second gives the rules relative to the layout and arrangement of this building and of its surroundings, rules which vary according to the social class of the occupants; these two chapters dovetail, however, and it is worth noting that a number of their verses are found mixed into the parallel passages of the *Kāmikāgama* which, in this and in other aspects, comes very close to the *Mayamata*.

Houses appear as the juxtaposition of one or several 'closed' elements (main buildings) and one or several 'open' ones (galleries, verandahs, porchs, courtyards, courts . . .); the number of possible combinations is considerable and some of them are presented in Chapter 26 where houses are classified according to the number of their main buildings (one, two, three, four, seven or ten) and to the arrangement of these main buildings in relation to 'open' elements. It is the term *śālā* which most often designates a main building (hence the expressions *ekaśāla*, *dviśāla*, etc. . . .) but *gṛha*, *vāsa* and *koṣṭha* are used too, and are all ambiguous, even *śālā* being equally applicable to the house as a whole, or to elongated structures situated on the upper storeys, or to a roof shape. A main building is usually an elongated edifice covered with a wagon-roof or a saddle-back roof with a gable at each of its ends; it may consist of a single piece but is more often divided into two or three by one or two partition walls; distinguishable amongst these rooms are one or more chambers (*vāsa*) and the women's apartments (*raṅga*) (fig. 21); when there are only two rooms, then the chamber is the domain of the master of the house, the *raṅga* that of the mistress of the house (27. 133) and the wall separating them is called the 'median wall' or 'wall of Ka' (that is, of Brahmā); it is to pass above the foundation deposit and to be penetrated by a door of the specific type called *kulyābhadvāra* (vaulted door?). When a house comprises several main buildings, these may be attached to each other (*abhinna* or *piṇḍa* modes) or may be separate (*bhinna* mode) but the various arrangements described all seem to correspond to houses with joined main buildings (except perhaps for 26.195). These main buildings are always at right angles to one another, but are joined according to different modes: for example two main buildings may interpenetrate and their ridge beams intersect, or the main buildings may be joined end to end in which case corner rafters will mark the joining of their roofs (figs. 22–31).

The 'open' elements are designated by various terms which are apparently interchangeable (*alindra*, *vāra*, *aṅgaṇa*, *maṇḍapa* . . .) and may all be applied to hypostyle structures or to uncovered areas, whether or not bordered on several sides by constructions; when it comes to the simplest house, with a single main building, the open element is made up of a gallery or a verandah running along one of the sides of the main building (fig. 21); but the arrangement is usually more complex—especially for edifices with multiple main buildings—and the mention, in one description, of various juxtaposed open elements, shows that the vague and interchangeable terms which designate them must correspond to well defined realities which it has not been possible to identify; we note at this point however that the principal open element of the houses with several main buildings is a court within the main buildings where the central pavilion and the altar to Brahmā are to be placed (27.20 sq.).

Secondary elements such as porches, foreparts or outward constructions may eventually be added to these open and closed principal parts (fig.26). Though there are constant mentions of edifices with multiple storeys elsewhere in the text, it should be noted that the only detailed description of such a construction (26.119) is very muddled and it is difficult to understand the arrangement of its (six?) upper storeys.

As shown above, the houses are classified according to the number of the main buildings, each category being again divided into types and variations determined by different factors, such as the way of joining the main buildings, the number and arrangement of open elements and the presence or absence of a particular secondary feature. The text has little to say about the *dviśāla* (or *lāṅgala* "ploughshare shaped") and *triśāla* (or *śūrpa* "winnowing basket shaped") (26.47 sq.; figs. 22–25) nor about the *saptaśāla* and the *dasaśāla* (26.190–193; figs. 30–31) neither are these categories of houses very much dealt with in the rest of the work. It does, on the other hand, describe the many houses with one main building (26. 11–46), and, more than that, those with four (26.64–187) thus concerning itself, in the one case as in the other, with the houses which are most common: basic houses intended for villagers or for citizens of modest means and houses with a central court for the well-to-do (see especially 29.83 sq.).

Dwelling houses are not the only *śālā* to be described by the *Mayamata*; buildings as diverse as the following are put into the same category: monastic buildings (*vihāraśālaka*) stables for horses and for elephants (*aśvaśālā*, *hastiśālā*), to say nothing of buildings for alms (*dānaśālā*) and other edifices of the kind which are frequently mentioned but which are not described (29.188 sq.); *hastiśālā* and *aśvaśālā* are mentioned again in connection with palaces, apropos of which they are described (29.168–187); monastic buildings (26.200) are presented as a specific kind of edifice with several main buildings: these, numbering eleven, are parallel to one another and both the two principal facades of the resulting assembly are constituted by the juxtaposition of eleven gable walls.

Chapter 27 deals, for the most part, with the procedure for laying out a *catuśśālā* along with a list of the appurtenances and dependencies which belong to it and indications as to the positions they are to occupy; in this chapter are to be found the rules, both those general ones which are applicable in all cases, and the specific ones for whichsoever social class. The layout begins with the marking out of the limits of the area in the middle of which the house is to stand, which area is surrounded by a wall (*vaṭabhitti* 27.1 onwards); then a sixty-four square diagram must be drawn on the ground, whose dimensions are those of the house to be built and where the vulnerable points are to be marked (*marma*, 7.49 and 18.15). Then the medians of the four sides of the diagram are drawn and will be used for the layout of the central pavilion and then of the principal main building. The central pavilion is set up right in the centre of the diagram, that is to say in the centre of the inner court of a *catuśśāla* (27.20); its presence is not always mentioned in descriptions of the *catuśśāla* given in Chapter 26 and it is possible that it is often a provisional building, due to vanish when the house has been constructed; whether or not this is the case, it is at the centre of this pavilion that the altar to Brahmā will be built, where will be carried out the daily domestic rites (unless the house is for *śūdra* who have no right to such an altar). The name and position of the principal main building vary according to the category to which the occupants of the house belong, but it is always essential that the median of this main building does not coincide with the corresponding median of the diagram (27.36 and following). If the house is meant for brahmins then this main building is called *sukhālaya* (or *saukhya*) and it is to the north of the central pavilion. If it is for a kṣatriya it is an *annālaya* (or *mahānāsa*) which is to the east and, for vaiśya a *dhānyālaya* to the south and, lastly, for śūdra, a *dhanālaya* is built to the west. These names which correspond to those of the medians of the diagram (*sukhasūtra, annasūtra* . . . etc.) are unexpected (especially where they concern kṣatriya) and the real explanation has yet to be discovered. Another difficulty arises in establishing a relationship between what is indicated here and the rules previously given apropos of sites (chap. 2 verses 10 and following); in fact the position of the principal main building determines, first that of the main building in which is the door of the *catuśśāla*, (to the left of the principal main building from the point of view of one facing towards the centre of the site), and then that of the drain for used water (positioned to the right at the back of the principal main building); otherwise, it is said in Chapter 2 that the site intended for brahmins must slope towards the north and for the other three classes, towards the east; this being the case, if the position of the drain is then well understood when it is in the houses of brahmins (north), kṣatriya (east) and vaiśya (south/south-east), it is on the other hand, hard to see how this works when a house is destined for śūdra, since the drain is placed to the west of this house, that is, at the point which is, theoretically, the most elevated. . . .

Once the principal main building has been set up the position of the foundation deposit must be determined (27.58 and following) as well as those of the master's chamber (*vāsa, svāmisthāna*), of the women's apartments (*raṅga*) (27.133) and of the door (27.71 and following); that done, there remains but the establishing of the different appurtenances and dependencies which are to be found, the former in the main building and the latter, as it would seem, on the periphery of the *catuśśāla*; these elements are listed several times (27.100 and following, 26.112 and following) and their respective positions are indicated in relation to a diagram. Our figure 32 is developed from the information given for a residence (*vastu*) meant for vaiśya (27.112 and following); as far as other castes are concerned the indications are too sparse and incomplete to be capable of giving a minimally coherent graphic representation.

The construction of the house being completed, nothing

remains but to enter it on an auspicious day and according to a well established ritual which is described in classic fashion (Chapter 28).

Royal palaces

The royal palace (Chap. 29) has the form of a cluster of buildings, very diverse and with many large free spaces; the ensemble will be situated within a town or a fortified camp; after the fashion of a temple it is arranged in concentric zones separated from each other by enclosure walls (three or five according to the *Mayamata*). The chapter consecrated to the palace gives a general description of various kinds of palace intended for rulers of different status (29.1–161). Specific descriptions of various edifices which make up part of the palace are given as well (29.168–228) and some notes on the town which surrounds it (29.65 and following, 162 and following), specifications which go to complete the information given in Chapter 10 where the different types of city are described.

Four plans are suggested for palaces and, as with temples or residential houses, their different elements are situated according to diagrams; but, except where the *saubala* palace is concerned (29.108 and following; fig. 34), the names of diagrams corresponding to the different enclosures are not indicated, and it is difficult to be precise about the position of a given building, especially when its relationship to a specific enclosure is not indicated; this is particularly regrettable in that the palace, for which these indications are given with the most exactitude, is just that one which is most cursorily described in its other aspects (fig. 33). These reservations having been made, it is to be emphasized that a certain number of common points can be found in the different arrangements suggested: especially noted will be the position of the *iṣṭadevatā* in the north-east corner of one of the enclosures; the installation, in the same area, of various hydraulic devices is obviously to be taken in conjunction with the fact that Āpa and Āpavatsa rule over a part of the north-east sector of the diagram. Where the area reserved for women is concerned it is to be noted that the main apartments of the queen (situated in the first enclosure) are usually to the south or north and that the greater part of the other female members of the royal entourage are placed to the west, where is located, especially, the *saṅkarālaya* (see 29.35b–37a). The abundance of every kind of storeroom will be noted: things are no different for a palace than for a fort (see 10.46 and following); a palace, like a fort, is to be provided with various defences (see especially 29.158 and following); the walls of the interior enclosures sometimes have moats like that of the outer one (29.87 and following); it is possible that no defensive measures are envisaged but that these moats are simply intended to furnish a supply of water.

The position of the palace within a town varies according to the status of the sovereign who lives there and it is only when it is for an emperor (*viśvanṛpaiśvara*) that it occupies the central part of the town (29.1–3) (see as well 10.71 and following). The town is to be fortified (29.70–72) and its essential function is the sheltering of the royal army (29.65–66 and 161). The city which contains a royal palace is called by different names, depending upon the position it occupies in the country and according to the circumstances under which it was founded: it may, by that token, be a capital (*sthānīya*), a fortified town (*āhuta/agama*), an entrenched camp (*saṅgrāma*) or a town founded to commemorate a victory, most probably on newly conquered territory (*vijaya*) (29.162 and following).

Very few elements of the palace are described in any detail and it is surprising to find no description of the royal apartments nor of devices intended to safeguard the person of the sovereign. The elephant and horse stables are dealt with (29.168 and following), the latter being a *catuśśāla* whose main buildings may possibly be separate. Some other structures described are more typical of a royal dwelling: there is the council chamber, most likely installed in the king's apartments, there is an edifice which is probably meant for the queen's dressing room and there are, in particular, the places for the ceremonies of consecration, of the ritual weighing and of the gold embryo, but, except for these two last, these descriptions are very brief.

Doors

The most interesting part of Chapter 30 (*dvāravidhāna*) is given over to the description of the different parts of the door (30.11–32); otherwise, the chapter deals with dimensions, with the position and with the character, either auspicious or inauspicious, of the doors (ibid. 33–52) and describes different types of gateway (30.53 sq.); as far as these last are concerned, the descriptions given in Chapter 24 (*gopuravidhāna*) are merely repeated and modified slightly. The frame of the door comprises two jambs (*yoga*), an elevated sill (*gulpha*), a lintel (*vimalā*) and a frame (*vājana*) which acts both as lintel and sill. There are one or two leaves (*kavāṭa, talpa*) whose hinges (*hastihasta* ? *vetra*?) turn in a socket (*bhājana*). When there are two leaves, the largest, on the right, supports the rabbet bar (*skandhapaṭṭikā*) and may be penetrated by a wicket door (*āvāra*); the decoration of the leaves may be very varied (30.26–28) and the closing of the door is effected by the horizontal bolts placed inside (*argala*) and outside (*kṣepaṇa*) and by a vertical one (*indrakīla*). The dimensions of a door must accord with those of the corresponding storey of the building and its proportions vary with the status of the occupant of that building.

IV

VEHICLES, SEATS AND ICONOGRAPHY

The third section is the most heterogeneous; it juxtaposes two short chapters on the last two *vastu*, vehicles and seats, with others which are much longer and which deal with the Liṅga, the pedestals, the renovation work and the images.[10]

10. Chapters 35 and 36 are missing in the editions of *Mayamata* prepared by T. Ganapati Sastri (1919, Trivandrum Sanskrit Series n° 65) and by K. S. Subrahmanya Sastri (in Grantha script and with a Tamil translation, 1966–1968, Tanjore Sarasvati Mahal Series no°113-I and II).

Vehicles

Vehicles which are to be carried (31.1–28) are the palanquins (*śibikā*) of which there are three types. The first type has the appearance of a pedestal, hence its name *pīṭha* (or *paiṇḍikā*); it comprises a frame whose pieces (*īṣikā*) have handholds at their ends; above the framework rise latticed sides constituted by alternating slats (*kampa*) and planks; they are surmounted by a handrail (*hasta*) supported by bannisters. Since there is nothing said on the subject it must be assumed that the statues of the *utsavamūrti*, for which the vehicle is evidently intended, are to be placed on the plank floor at the level of the bannisters which support the handrail; the mention, however, of a door in the middle of the front wall of the palanquin allows for the supposition that, in some cases, these images may be placed inside the palanquin. The other two palanquin models have a roof supported by pillars, in such a way as to protect the images without masking them; this roof is in the shape of a *śikhara* (structure with rafters) or of a flat covering like that of a *maṇḍapa*.

Two types of wheeled vehicles are presented successively. The first is a chariot with two wheels to be used in a wide range of ways (31.48–49). Its body (*hāra*) is supported by a frame, made up of an odd number of long beams (*bhāraka*) which are joined to each other by crossbeams (*kampa*) and which rest, through the intermediary of supports (*bhāropadhāna*, "longbeam support") on a beam (*akṣottara*) upon which is fixed the axle (*akṣa*) whose splindles (*akṣāntara*) bear the wheels, which may have spokes or be solid. The pole (*kūbara*) is attached to the median long beams and its end is bent over. The dimensions of the temple chariot, next described, (31.50 sq.) are calculated from those of the shrine; from the brief confused description it is possible to glean that there are three models; the superstructure of the first two has the appearance of a building with several storeys, which may, according to circumstances, be a pavilion (*maṇḍapa*), that is a three level edifice (base, pillars and entablature), or a temple (*prāsāda*) with six (see above); the third type is called "canopy" (*raṅga*) and its superstructure would seem to consist only of pillars supporting a flat covering.

Chapter 32 which deals with beds and seats (*śayanāsana*) is very short and some of the information is repeated, with only slight variations, in the chapter on pedestals (*pīṭha*, chap. 34). Divans (*paryaṅka*) have a simple body whose pieces (*īṣikā*, *adhika*) have attached straps (*paṭṭa*) or a couch of planks; the legs may be straight or made in the shape of animals (32.7 sq.). The regular seats are called *pīṭha*, when square, and *āsana*, when rectangular, and are not distinguished from divans save by their much smaller dimensions (32.10 sq.); the only one where mention is made of a seat back (*uttara*) is the lion throne which must stand on a base, which may itself be supported by a socle (32.13–18 and 34.54–56). The *Mayamata*, like parallel texts, includes amongst *śayanāsana*, the stand for domestic worship (*pūjāpīṭha*, 32.20–23).

Iconography

The god is shown in his shrine in the form of a 'sign' (*liṅga*) which may be 'manifest' (*sakala*, litt. "complete"), 'unmanifest' (*niṣkala*, "incomplete") or 'manifest and unmanifest at once' (*miśra*, "mixed") (33.1–3). The first expression is applied to images (*pratimā*, *bera*) which represent the god anthropomorphically, pseudo-anthropomorphically or theriomorphically, the description of which is the subject of Chapter 36. The term *niṣkala* applies to the god represented by a symbol which may be a part (*kalā*) of himself, like the phallus of Śiva, or may be his characteristic sign, such as the discus of Sudarsana-Cakra, Attendant of Viṣṇu. The third category, that of mixed representations, needs only be touched upon, since the sole known example is the Mukhaliṅga, which is unmanifest by virtue of the Liṅga, which makes up its essential part, and manifest through the faces (or face) of Śiva carved on this Liṅga (36.107 sq.).

Chapter 33 extends itself on the subject of the making of *pauruṣaliṅga*, that is, man-made Liṅga, which may be defined as objects whose nature, as representation of Śiva, is not effective until the Liṅga has been sculpted and installed according to very strict rules which govern as well the materials, the shape, proportions, dimensions and relationship between these dimensions and those of the sanctuary . . . etc. These *pauruṣaliṅga* may be contrasted with *daivaliṅga* ('divine' or 'natural' Liṅga) whose value derives from their origin, the outstanding quality of their appearance or from some other singularity which is not to be submitted to any modification nor elaboration (33.90); the best known amongst the *daivaliṅga* are the 'self generated' Liṅga (*svayambhuliṅga*) (33.87 and following) but the *bāṇaliṅga* is put into the same category (33. 158–9) as well as some *pauruṣaliṅga* which don't conform to the rules (33.88) or which have reappeared after having been lost for an unknown length of time (35.22).

The *pauruṣaliṅga* may be divided into two major categories, that of Liṅga made of ordinary stones and that of those made with other materials (precious stones, earth, wood, metal, 33.153). Those of the second category are less elaborate; it is to be noted, especially, that the presence of "characteristic lines" (*lakṣaṇa*) is not obligatory (33.150–151) and, too, that the triple nature of the Liṅga, (Śiva, Viṣṇu, Brahmā) is not necessarily put into form through a triple section (circular, octagonal and square) because it is sufficient if it is mentally recognized by the faithful (33.156 and following). Stone Liṅga are classified according to various criteria which are: the dimensions (33.48 sq.), the relationship between these dimensions and those of the sanctuary (33.40 sq.), the proportions of the three elements, which may be equal or unequal, in which latter case that of Śiva is always the largest (33.72 sq.) and, lastly, the shape of the uppermost element (*śivabhāga*, *pūjābhāga*) which may be circular or may be polygonal (*dhārāliṅga*) or polygonal and covered with images of Liṅga (*sāhasraliṅga*) (33.82 sq.). The four stages in the making of a Liṅga are as follows: choice and extraction of the stone (33.4–36), cutting the block and putting in the three sections (33.65–71), shaping of the rounded summit (33.92–100) and lastly, the bringing out of the characteristic signs (33.101–142), which operation corresponds to the opening of the eyes of images (18.185 and following) and is to be done at the time when the Liṅga is installed in the sanctuary; these stages are described in detail, and, with respect to the first, the text gives specifications about the different sorts of stone; these specifications go to complete the teachings on materials in the rest of the work.

Theoretically, a pedestal must be made out of the same material as the representation that is to stand on it, but this rule is subject to alteration (34.2–3); if it is in stone it must be monolithic as far as is possible (34.40b–41). Its dimensions are proportionate to those of the sanctuary and those of the image or symbol (34.4 sq.; 51 sq., 56 sq.); square or regular forms are suited to the pedestals of unmanifest images and elongated ones to images (34.10 sq.), and the pedestals invariably have mouldings (34.16–29); their upper face appears as a tank bordered by a rim (*snehavāri*) with a spout (*nāla*). The mortice meant for the tenon of the image, or for the two lower elements of the Liṅga, is in the centre of the pedestal and the fixing is done with mortar (34.64). The pedestal rests on liners (34.44 sq.) and its position varies according to which deity it supports (34.67; 33.37).

Chapter 35 (*anukarmavidhi*, litt. "rules for the final work") deals with two very different subjects, the operations involved in the renovation, in the first place, and the rite of provisional installation in the second. The principle guiding all renovation is simple: the operation must, at the very least, try for a return to the original state but, if possible, there must be an improvement which may mean an extension as much as the use of better quality materials (35.40 sq.). There is a great deal of information on Liṅga in this regard (35.15 sq.) and the idea of renovation encompasses, as well, the purifications after pollution and the rectifications where there have been errors made in making or installing. The rites of foundation should not be repeated in the case of buildings (35.14), a prescription that is similar to the one advising against the placing of the foundation deposit when the mistress of the house is pregnant (12.95): the foundation is an insemination and there cannot be two at the same time.

The provisional installation (35.48 sq.) furnishes a substitute when the shrine or the divine representation which it houses is not able to be used in worship due to specific conditions: during the work of construction of the sanctuary or during the making of an image or a Liṅga or when they have to be renewed; this provisional installation is used as much for moveable images (*utsavamūrti*) as for fixed images placed in a sanctum (35.55). The substitutes may be smaller versions of what they stand for (hence the name *bālasthāpana*) and they must not be in use for more than twelve years, one way to limit the duration of construction or renovation work (35.58).

Chapter 36 deals with images but has very little to say about their making: there is no mention of the materials (but see 33.10–12), the dimensions are only presented in a very general way and the specific proportions are virtually never given (see however 36.69 and 33.107–131). More or less succinct descriptions are found in this chapter: general appearance, posture, attributes, decoration and colours, sometimes with the indication of the reward that is to be hoped for as a result of installing the image. There is no point in looking for any originality in these descriptions which, for the most part appear, almost word for word, in the parallel texts such as the *Kāraṇāgama*. It is perhaps in this area that we can most clearly see the intensive mixing to which the agamic texts were submitted at the time when they were evolving into the versions we now have: their last compilators would have had no hesitation in taking, from the common fund, the developments whose presence was expected. In addition, the lack of originality and precision in the text is shown by the use of certain all-purpose formulae which are not distinguishable as to whether they are genuine elements or simply prosodical padding; thus, *sarvābharaṇasaṃyuktam* (1st or 3rd *pāda* of *anuṣṭubh*) or *sarvābhāraṇasaṃyutam* (2nd and 4th *pāda*).

The deities described are those to be installed in the various temples and shrines (see Chapter 23 passim) and on the facades of these edifices (19.39 sq.). As in the rest of the work, Śaivism is prominent; in fact, on the Vaiṣṇavite side, apart from Viṣṇu as Attendant of Śiva (36.8–12), only Narasiṃha and Anantaśāyin merit any developed description (36.15 sq.). On the other side, sixteen manifestations of Śiva are presented

(36.43 and following) including the Mukhaliṅga which, in other texts, is usually described separately. Amongst secondary deities, important places are given to Sūrya, Kṣetrapāla (or Bhairava), Śāstā and the Seven Mothers whose description is followed by a note on their installation and on certain variations in their positions (36.211 sq.). It may be found surprising that Vṛṣa, Śiva's chief Attendant, does not appear but this image has been presented in detail at the end of the lists of *parivāra* (23.107–131); Buddha and Jina whose shrines are mentioned in Chapters 9 and 12 are the subjects of descriptions which reveal how limited was the knowledge about their sects (36. 281 sq.). The amount of importance given to Jina is probably explained by the relative prominence of the Jain community. Lastly, a number of deities, or series of deities, present problems, for instance the *eight* Marut (36.173b), the *seven* Rohiṇī (36. 194b) or Yakṣiṇī (36.256 sq.) and Saptamātā (36.279–280).

We have regrouped in an Appendix some information related to wells which had been subject to haphazard interpolations in Chapter 36.

V

THEORY AND PRACTICE

The *Mayamata* is just what might be considered a revealed text, it was expressed by Maya, the divine architect, even if of the Asura. Maya, however, introduces himself as a mere intermediary who faithfully transmits the words of the gods (1.15). When he refers to authorities these are the Sages, keepers of divine knowledge, or are the Tantra, that is to say, the *āgama* revealed by Śiva to various intercessors. Being revealed, the *Mayamata* makes no reference to any prior construction or image from which it might have extrapolated the theory it presents. It is immediately apparent that this method differs from that of Vitruvius who had no hesitation in theorizing from actual and precise examples, thus substituting for the irrefutable, but abstract, authority of revelation that of a more concrete antiquity.

That being so, the *Mayamata* is dated, even if approximately, and its theory of architecture has been extrapolated from existing monuments belonging to an easily identifiable school. To the end of developing the theory, these monuments have been carefully analysed and reduced to subsets and then to more or less simple elements which are, nevertheless, simple enough to be able to be combined in a very wide range of compositions. Each of the elements thus separated out is described, according to the single or multiple shapes that it may assume. At the same time a norm is established, governing the conditions of the general use of the given element or those of each of its specific types; these may be defined either by their appearance or by their dimensions or, most often, by both series of factors combined. In the same way a norm is defined for each subset, (itself defined by its constituting elements), and so on. These norms of usage will be considered again but, meanwhile, it is to be emphasized that they answer to greatly diverse constraints which are by no means all to do with technique. To return to the architectural analysis which is the essential step in the elaboration of the theory, the stages of its development remain obscure but it may be assumed that it was constituted progressively, following the elaboration of more and more complex forms and, at the same time, of the vocabulary which allows these forms to be designated as well as described.

It is obvious that, at the time of the drafting of the *Mayamata*, the typological lexicon and the semantic one were both fixed and, for the most part, perfectly adapted to the analysis of those monuments whose construction the text purports to govern. It is significant moreover, that this vocabulary is sufficiently precise and sufficiently flexible to be of use in the synchronic description of all the monuments pertaining to the school, from those built right up to the present day in India south of the Krishnā, to those found in the hindouized kingdoms of South East Asia, to say nothing of such singular phenomenon as the temple "built according to the *āgama*" some years ago in Pittsburgh (U.S.A.). This last reference which justifies the pretension to universality held by the text, pinpoints a weakness in the analysis which has less to do with the internal structures of edifices than with their outward appearance, since that may be nothing but a decoration plated onto a structure to which it corresponds only very approximately, if at all.

Systematic presentations of the results of the analysis are found only with regard to the elevation; its major elements, obligatory or optional depending upon the type of edifice, are described separately one after the other, the full range of possible forms being given for each. The procedure is different when it comes to the plans: it starts with the simplest one for each category of edifice which it then uses as a basis for the more complex compositions. Additionnal elements are introduced progressively in conjunction with the occurrences of the more and more complex types into which they are integrated.

Dimensions and, more than that, proportions occupy a very important place in the presentation of the analysis. The indications of all the possible dimensions, for a given type, allow for a multiplicity of variations and for the duplication of the specifically typological classification by another, pertaining to size; moreover, the procedure allows for the encompassing, by the theory itself, of all its potential and authorized applications.

The systematic usage of proportions strongly indicates that the analysis leads to a modular conception of architecture. Two procedures are followed: the first consists in the employment of units which we will call 'occasional', to divide, for example, the height of a given edifice into *N* parts of which *n* are for the base, *n*' for the level of pillars . . . etc. Besides that there are conventional units set for a whole building and which play the role of modules. Thus, there is the module itself (*daṇḍa*) which is, as mentioned, the diameter of the top of a pillar and which is often used as general reference unit for indicating the value of projections of mouldings or of foreparts. The intercolumniation (*bhakti*) falls into the same category and is for calculating horizontal proportions of hypostyle edifices or pseudo-hypostyle ones. On a more far reaching basis, the width of the main temple is used as a reference unit for calculating the size of the enclosures of the temples. To the use of these various units is added the constant mention of fractional relationship between the different dimensions of an element (door, pillars etc. . .) or of a complex assembly (building, settlement . . .).

To sum up then, all the parts, even the smallest of an assembly, however large it may be, are ultimately connected to one another by an intersecting pattern of different systems of proportions and of modular relationship. This aspect of the analysis goes beyond the architecture since, in temples, the images themselves are integrated into the general system of proportions for which they are even, sometimes, taken as departure point, when the dimensions of a shrine are set according to those of the divine representation it is intended to house.

The analysis of the elevation rests on the postulate that, since the temple (*prāsāda*) is the most perfect of edifices, its elevation will neccessarilycomprise all the elements that are to be found in the elevation of any other category of building, that is to say, the analysis of the elevation of the temple gives the entire vocabulary of forms needed for the description of any elevation whatsoever. This explains why the detailed architectural descriptions begin with that of the levels of elevation of the *prāsāda*, taken one by one. The different categories of edifice being defined by the levels which are comprised in their elevation, their detailed descriptions can then be limited to their specific plans.

The definition of levels gives rise to a general point: the terms employed to designate these levels are the names of the structural elements to which they correspond. This point underlines the fact that the vocabulary used in the analysis has been established on the basis of an architecture whose elements were all structural, and before they had developed into decoration having little or nothing to do with the structure it clothed. It is to be noted that the ambiguity of the vocabulary allows for the descriptions to be applied, as well to that which is no more than a decoration, in the case of temple elevations, as to what is a genuinely structural elevation, in the case of pavilions or houses.

The analysis of plans is given, together with the definitions of the various categories of building, that is: temples (*prāsāda*), gateways (*gopura*), pavilions (*maṇḍapa*), halls (*sabhā*) and houses (*śālā*), to mention only the most important. The temple may be defined as an edifice whose elevation comprises all the six levels and whose plan, in its most simple form, comprises only one room, the sanctum; this basic layout is subject to series of variations in plan as well as in elevation; the edifice may be square, rectangular, apsidal . . . etc. and the exterior, as drawn, may not correspond to the interior drawing of the sanctum, which may be circular in a square edifice, square in an apsidal one . . . etc. Moreover, there may be variations of plan at the different levels, that is to say, a building may have an octagonal or circular superstructure on a square lower part, to give but one example. The variations of the elevation essentially depend upon the number of storeys, that is, on the repetition, or the lack of it, of the pair constituted by the level of the pillars and the entablature and show, as well, in the number and arrangement of aediculae on the entablature. Developed from the basis of the same elementary, one room plan, is another series of variations marked by foreparts or porches built against the facades of the ground floor. The most complex types are extrapolated from the simple layout by concentric additions or by the juxtaposition of the temple proper to a pavilion; both procedures are often used in one and the same edifice. The concentric additions are obtained by the insertion, between the sanctum and the outside of the building, of one or several aisles (*alindra*) separated from each other and from the sanctum by plain walls; the larger plan thus obtained is itself subject to all the elementary type's variations. The extrapolation by juxtaposition entails a pavilion's being added to the entrance of the sanctum; the link between temple and pavilion is made by means of a covered passage (*antarāla*) which is none other than the porch transformed into a corridor; the pavilion conforms to the typological definitions of pavilions, but its proportions are related to those of the temple proper.

The example given for temples applies equally to other categories of building (see for example, above, apropos private houses). The architectural analysis definitively furnishes a catalogue of simple and complex forms which may be used in the context of norms, which are precisely regulated by various constraints amongst which technique is the most often inextricably tied up with the social and religious factors, to the point where it becomes difficult to tell which part belongs to which of these fields. In the social sphere there is, first, the absolute need to conform to the established order in transposing, onto the architectural plan and the built up space, the hierarchy founded upon the *varṇa* and the *jāti*, as much as that deriving from wealth. In the former case there is, naturally and first of all, the organization of the space in such a way that each category has the place suitable for it; but that hierarchy also has to be considered when reserving to (gods and) upper classes, the perfect forms, the greatest dimensions and the best materials, usually bestowing upon them the freedom to use the inferior ones without thereby departing from custom; thus the square sites are reserved for gods and brahmins but they may both use the rectangular sites of other classes, increasingly elongated as one goes down the social scale (cf. Chap. 2 and 3). Similar prescriptions are given for dimensions and materials. In the hierarchy based upon wealth, the most important thing is to avoid disproportion and mediocrity, that is, to confine oneself to the realm of the possible: thus the number of brahmins to be installed in a village may be as small as one, if there is no alternative (9.25 sq.). Elsewhere it is riches by which certain members of lower *varṇa* can be distinguished; a house meant for the well-to-do amongst śūdra (27.125) is referred to, whose description follows directly upon that of another house meant for the powerful amongst *vaiśya* (27.119). This type of hierarchy is connected with the political one established amongst the various 'kings', (that is, kṣatriya) whether with regard to types of town (chap. 10), or to the arrangement of the palace (chap. 29).

Constraints of the religious kind are very diverse and often hard to determine. First to be remembered are those to do with the position of the gods at the top of the social hierarchy and which are nothing but extensions of the constraints already discussed. In the same range of ideas are those pertaining to divine hierarchies, as for example, the organization of the space, the situating of temples, their dimensions and their specific aspects (see, especially, chap. 9); it is worth recalling here the remarks of Ram Raz on the place given to Buddha and to Jina. There are other exigencies arising out of the necessary relationship between the dimensions of a divine representation, whether Liṅga or image, and those of the building which houses it. Lastly, to be included in the religious domain, for want of a more precise alternative, are all the imperatives linked, not only with the ritual but also, in more general fashion, with everything that can be placed under the heading of 'signs'. Ritual is essential to the success of the construction it accompanies: purification of the place, the putting to flight of deities previously established there and of those of the trees and stones that are going to be used, the installation on the diagram of the protective deities of the site, the recognition of the body of the Spirit of the site and the putting in place of the foundation deposit marking the start of the work of construction. There are no particular ritual procedures during the course of the construction itself but special precautions have to be taken in respect of the vulnerable points (*marma*) of the Spirit of the site. At the end of the construction work, fresh ceremonies of consecration of the building and for the installation of its occupants, whether human or divine, assure them, in either case, of a happy life and mark the end of the work and of the architect's responsibility. There are, as well, innumerable constraints connected with 'signs'; the rules relating to choice of site or of materials, for example, clearly show that empirical technique is mixed with divination. In other areas there are speculations relative to the 'gender' of materials and of buildings and to the correspondence, necessary but not always evident, between type and usage. Lastly, there are speculations on more or less auspicious numbers, dealing with the distinguishing of odd and even ones or with the determining, through a complex system of relationships, of whether the dimensions are beneficient and whether they accord with the horoscope of the proprietor or that of the settlement (*āyādi*).

The *Mayamata* confers on the architect the task of putting into practice what it prescribes. In spite of the constraints by which the treatise seems to limit the architecture, it is also true that the architect has considerable latitude at his disposal, as much in the domain of choice of architectural parts as in that of the appearance that constructions may have.

This freedom comes, in the first case, paradoxically enough, from the pretensions of the treatise to universality. The text, seeking to encompass all possible circumstances, envisages them and prepares for them by means of an extended series of specific variations; such being the procedure, it is left to the architect to choose this or that option 'according to circumstances' (*yuktyā*) as is often repeated. Equally the treatise has its limitations which also leave the executant a certain leeway. The first are those of the analysis itself which is not, on the one hand, as precise as it could be and which, on the other, contains, in the area of expression, ambiguities such as those involving the doucine, to take an example already cited. The other limitation is imposed by the written form; descriptive prescriptions are often little other than written transcriptions of graphic representations. From another point of view, the architect who 'knows how to draw' (*citrajña* 5.17) must read and draw simultaneously; this is evident from, for example, the way in which the description of the socle *pratibhadra* is "written"; a literal translation follows (13.12–13a): "With two, one, two and one parts, as well as with two, one, eight, one and one parts and with three parts and one and two, one and two parts are for arrangement of plinth, doucine, fillet and groove, string-course and above a fillet, the dado and above a fillet and a doucine, the cornice, a fillet, a groove, a string-course and fillet". It is clear that the list of dimensions, which follows that of the mouldings to which they belong, is not intelligible unless this description is "rewritten". This rewritting may be a simple gloss but, for a specialist with the responsibility of imposing upon an edifice the form thus described, it is obvious that a drawing made from the reading will be the most appropriate and the most cogent. By the same token, the plans cannot easily be read unless they are transposed to drawings, which the use of regular patterns makes simple. In the realm of elevation the manner of description is curious when, for example, only the proportions of the ground floor are given for a temple of seven storeys, along with indication that it is to be under the bottom of a temple with six storeys; this makes it obvious that the written description is but a written transposition of a drawing and may call for retransposition. In another area, that of iconography, the descriptions, made up of lists of limbs or part of limbs and of proportions, are not intelligible unless the different elements mentioned therein are put together in a drawing.

This necessity, which is due to the nature of the text itself and of its subject, allows the specialist to give an interpretation, whether it be personal or guided by the fashions of the time and place. The monuments, which pertain more or less to the architectural school the *Mayamata* represents, cover a period of fifteen centuries and an area which encompasses a large part of the Indian peninsula as well as of South East Asia. This phenomenon is only possible because, in spite of their doctrinaire character, this treatise and others of the same group, leave to architects the right to originality in the exercise of their art; in other words, the tradition is a guide more than it is a restraint.

Chapter 1
SUMMARY

1.1–2 Having bowed his head before the omniscient God, Lord of the Universe and having listened exclusively to Him, Maya, wise and learned architect (*kartṛ*), proclaims this systematic treatise which is the basis of success for every kind of dwelling (*vastu*) intended for gods and men and which contains the characteristics of dwellings for all.

1.3–11 First (he ordains) the shapes of dwelling sites and the methods of examining and taking possession of them. Then he gives the system of measurements and the method for installing the gnomon. Next (come) the diagrams, the arrangement of the gods (on these last) and the rules relating to offerings. Next (he prescribes) plans for villages and similar settlements as well as the specific characteristics of towns and cities. Then come the rules relating to the number and dimensions of storeys and next the features and arrangement of foundation deposits. Next are given the rules applying to socles, the specific characteristics of bases and of pillars, as well as prescriptions for entablatures. Next come the rules for joinery, the characteristics of roofs and the characteristics of temples with only one storey, with two storeys, with three storeys, with four storeys . . . etc. Next the characteristics of the attendant deities' shrines are given along with those of enclosure walls and of gateways. Next come the rules relating to pavilions and like buildings, the characteristics of *śālā* type houses as well as the disposition of houses and the (rite of first) entry into a house. Next are given the rules relating to palaces as well as the characteristics of doors and their arrangement. Next come the specific characteristics of conveyances and of seats as well as those of Liṅga and pedestals. Next the rules pertaining to repairs are given as well as the particulars and proportions of the images of gods and goddesses; lastly the ritual of the opening of the eyes is indicated. All this is summarized and presented systematically.

1.12 All this has been ordained by the lords of the sages, the immortals, of whom the first is Pitāmaha. All this has been comprehensively set forth by Maya: that is, the characteristics of indestructible dwellings, according to whether they are intended for the pure spirited denizens of the heavens or for men.

Thus ends, in the *Mayamata*, treatise on dwelling, the first chapter: SUMMARY.

Chapter 2

DWELLING SITES

2.1–3 Experts call all places where immortals and mortals dwell, "dwelling sites" (*vastu*). I present their different varieties which are four in number: Earth, buildings, conveyances and seats. The Earth is the principal dwelling place because it is on Her that constructed dwellings (*vāstu*) such as temples have appeared and it is because of Her nature as site and because of (the temples') union with (this) site that the ancients called them "dwelling sites" in this world.

2.4–6a That chosen after a thorough examination of the colour, odour, flavour, form, orientation, sound and tactility, that, once delimited, is what is called the dwelling site; it is different for each caste. It is of two types, the one secondary and the other principal. Villages and the like are secondary but the Earth is the principal site.

2.6b–8 Halls, houses, light buildings (*prapā*) and pavilions with canopies as well as palaces are what are called "buildings". "Conveyances", say the sages, are litters, palanquins, carriages, war chariots and *ānika*(?). Lastly, designated as "seats" are thrones, divans, chairs, aviaries, benches, beds and cradles.

2.9. Of the four categories however it is the Earth which is said to occupy the first place since, for beings, it is She who was before all else and who is the support and stability of the World.

2.10–15a The site suitable for brahmins is square, white, without defects, planted with *udumbara* trees, sloping towards the north, perfect and has an astringent and sweet savour. Such a site is a guarantee of good fortune. The length of the site suitable for kings is one eighth more than its width; it is red in colour and bitter in flavour, it slopes towards the east, is vast and planted with *aśvattha*. Such a site invariably guarantees success. The length of the site suitable for vaiśya is one sixth more than its width; it slopes towards the east, is yellow, of sour taste and planted with *plakṣa*. Such a site is beneficient.

The length of the site suitable for śūdra is a fourth more than its width; it slopes towards the east, is black, has a pungent flavour and is planted with *nyagrodha*. Such a site is a source of abundant riches and grain.

2.15b These are the different types of site suitable for brahmins, kings, vaiśya and other castes. They are all equally suitable for brahmins, gods and kings but for the two other castes the aforementioned rules are to be applied.

Thus ends, in the *Mayamata*, treatise on dwelling, the second chapter: SHAPES OF DWELLING SITES.

Chapter 3

EXAMINATION OF THE SITE

3.1 It is said that rectangular sites too are suitable for gods and for brahmins. The shape of the site must be perfect and it must slope towards the west or south.

3.2–3 It must be filled with the sound of horses, of elephants, of flutes, lutes, water and drums and must be impregnated with the fragrances of *puṃnāga*, jasmine, lotus, grain and *pāṭala*. Its odour is like that of cattle, it is perfect, able to make all seeds grow and of uniform colour. (Its soil) is compact, smooth and pleasing to the touch.

3.4–7a Six kinds of tree grow there: *bilva*, *nimba*, *nirguṇḍin*, *piṇḍita*, *saptaparṇaka* and *sahakāra*. The ground is even; its colour is white, red, yellow or has the shimmer of a pigeon's sheen; it has six flavours: bitter, pungent, astringent, salt, sour and sweet; such a ground is a guarantee of success. The site must be bordered by a water course flowing to the right; it must be of pleasant colour, odour and taste; if a handful (of earth) is taken up it should be pleasing to the sight and to the mind.

3.7b–10a (The ground) is free from potsherds, pebbles, worms, ants and bones; it is free from holes and is covered in white sand. It must be free from charcoal and every sort of pointed object and from sludge, dust, cavities and husks. Such a site is suitable for all castes and brings them success.

3.10b–12 The sages however reject a site which smells like curds, melted butter, honey or oil, blood, carrion, fish or fowl. They equally reject a site which is too near a hall, a sacred place, a palace or a temple. They reject one planted with thorn trees, one which is round, triangular, irregular or shaped like a *vajra* and one (raised in the centre) like a tortoise shell.

3.13–15 They reject too one overshadowed by the dwelling of a caṇḍāla or near the house of a tanner. In the same way they reject one on one, two, three or four roads or near a path smelling of garlic. They reject a site depressed (in the middle) and one in the form of *paṇava* drum, bird, tambourine or fish. They reject those with large trees at the four corners, those planted with sacred trees and those whose four corners are indicated by a wall; in the same way they reject one which is inhabited by a procurer and one where there is a brothel (*saṅkarārāma*?).

3.16–18 So too, they reject a site which is a cremation ground or a place of retreat as well as one in the shape of a porcupine, a monkey or a forest snake and, as well, one which is shaped like a hatchet, a winnowing basket, a mortar, a conch or a stake. So too, they reject one resembling a cat or a lizard, one which is desert or frequented (only) by worms, one in the shape of a house lizard or in any other such shape. The sages condemn too a site to which several roads give access or which is crossed by one road.

3.19 A building erected on such a site, even by mistake, is the source of great misfortune; this is always to be avoided.

3.20 White, (red like) blood, yellow and black, resonant with the trumpeting of elephants and of horses, (endowed with) six flavours, of one colour, perfumed by cattle as well as by grain and lotus, free from pebble and husk, sloping towards the south and the west, bordered by a river in the north or east, equal to the perfect Surabhi, free from sharp objects and bones, such should be the site which, according to the best experts, is suitable for everybody and which does not wither the seeds.

Thus ends, in the *Mayamata*, treatise on dwelling, the third chapter: EXAMINATION OF THE SITE.

Chapter 4

TAKING POSSESSION OF THE SITE

4.1–3 Once he has chosen a piece of land endowed with the prescribed qualities of shape, colour, sound (. . . etc.), the wise architect should begin with an offering to the gods accompanied by exclamations such as "*Svasti*" and cries of good omen such as "*Jaya*". Next he pronounces this formula: "That Spirits, Gods and Demons depart! That they leave this place and go elsewhere for I take possession." Thus possession is taken of the site.

4.4 After ploughing (the architect) must sow seeds of all kinds mixed with cow dung; then, having seen them germinate and reaped the fruits, he puts cows there along with bulls and calves.

4.5–8a In this way (the site) will be stamped down by the cows, sanctified by their breath, purified by the contented lowing of the bulls and consecrated by the froth which flows from the mouths of the calves; it will be bathed by jets of cows' urine, coated with dung and made fertile by the spittle the cows spew out whilst chewing the cud and by their stamping; it will be permeated by their odour and, lastly, will be consecrated by sprinkling of holy water.

4.8b–10a Next, on a lunar day chosen as auspicious according to the configuration of the asterisms, in the favourable half of the day at a moment determined by a wise man, hulled rice and white flowers are to be offered and, if possible, brahmins should pronounce propitious words.

4.10b–15 Next, a square piece of land orientated to the cardinal points must be dug out to the depth of a cubit; this must be done faultlessly so that the pit is not too narrow nor too deep. Next, once he has offered prayers according to the ritual and has consecrated this pit with water of all jewels mixed with sandal and hulled rice, the wise man must fill it with water at nightfall. Then, after purifying himself and concentrating his mind, he lies down on the ground beside the pit facing east and he begins his fast by pronouncing this formula: "Earth, at this site, prosper in riches and in harvests! Be fecund! Salutations to Thee! Be propitious!"

4.16–18a At daybreak the wise architect examines the pit; if he sees a small residue of water he is to consider this as a guarantee of success; if the pit is damp, the building will be destroyed and if it is dry harvests and riches will disappear. When the hole is filled up with its own earth the site is of average quality if the pit is completely full; if it overflows with earth the site will prove excellent and if it is not packed full with earth it is of inferior quality.

4.18b It is after this investigation, carried out in a pit in the centre of the site, that, for the sake of success, the (definitive) choice is to be made of a site which is said to be in the image of Surabhi and which is bordered by a river flowing to the right.

4.19 After recognition of the different types of site, with the help of the precepts given above, he who envisages (establishing) *grāma*, *agrahāra*, *pura*, *pattana*, *kharvaṭa*, *sthānīya*, *kheṭa*, *nigama* or other settlements, must take possession of the site.

Thus ends, in the *Mayamata*, treatise on dwelling, the fourth chapter: TAKING POSSESSION OF THE SITE.

Chapter 5

SYSTEM OF MEASUREMENTS

5.1 All habitations are defined by their dimensions; I am going to present as well, methodically though in few words, the system of measurements.

5.2 The *mānāṅgula* is known to be a multiple of an atom, defined as that which can be perceived by the vision of those who have mastered their senses.

5.3–6a Eight atoms are equal to a speck of dust and, in multiplying each time by eight, we go from a speck of dust to the tip of a hair, then to a nit, to a louse and finally to a grain of barley. Eight barley grains make a digit (*aṅgula*) which is called as well *mātra*. Twelve digits make a span (*vitasti*) twice which is a cubit (*hasta*), called by the learned, as well, *kiṣku*; twenty-five digits make a *prājāpatya*, twenty-six a *dhanurmuṣṭi* and twenty-seven a *dhanurgraha*.

5.6b–11a For vehicles and seats the cubit (is used), for buildings the *dhanurmuṣṭi* and for villages and so on the *dhanurgraha*; the ordinary cubit however may serve for any building; it is also called *ratni*, *aratni*, *bhuja*, *bāhu* and *kara*. Four cubits make a pole, also called *yaṣṭi*; eight poles (*daṇḍa*) make a rope (*rajju*). Villages are to be measured in poles as are *pattana*, towns, *nigama*, *kheṭa*, palaces . . . etc.; but houses are to be in cubits. The sages should employ the span for vehicles and seats, the digit for small (objects) and the barley grain for very small ones. Such is the system of measurements.

5.11b–12 The *mātrāṅgula* is equal to the middle phalanx of the middle finger of the officiating priest; it is (to be used for measurements relating to) sacrifices . . . etc.; that which has just been mentioned is also called "digit taken from the body" (*dehalabdhāṅgula*).

5.13a Knowing all this the architect must measure rigorously.

The Technicians

5.13b–14a Here below, there are four sorts of builders each with their function: the architect (*sthapati*), the *sūtragrāhin*, the *vardhaki* and the *takṣaka*.

5.14b–18a The architect is from a renowned land and he is of mixed caste; a man of quality, he must know how to establish buildings and must be well versed in all the sciences; he must be physically perfect, just, compassionate, disinterested, free from envy, without weakness, handsome, and learned in mathematics; he must know the ancient authors and must be straightforward and master of his senses; he must be able to draw and must know the whole country; he must be generous and not greedy; his health must be good, he must be attentive and free of the seven vices, possessor of a well chosen name and perservering; he must have crossed the ocean of the science of architecture.

5.18b–19 The *sūtragrāhin* is the disciple or the son of the architect and follows his directions; he is skillful in all the arts; he knows how to make the rod and the rope fly and how to measure length, height and proportions.

5.20 The *takṣaka* is so named because he cuts the stone, wood, bricks . . . etc. into small or large pieces.

5.21–22a Versed in masonry, virtuous, capable and cognizant of his trade, he who assembles and correctly erects the pieces cut by the *takṣaka* is the *vardhaki*; it is said that he always works under orders from the *sūtragrāhin*.

5.22b–24 They are active, skillful, pure, strong, compassionate, always respectful towards the master and joyous; they are always faithful to the architect's instructions because, to them, it is Viśvakarman in person who is revealed through his aspect, though without them he can do nothing; that is why the tetrad led by the architect must always be honoured.

5.25 Without these technicians led by the architect nothing beneficial can be embarked upon here below but with them, as with a guru, mortal beings attain deliverance.

Thus ends, in the *Mayamata*, treatise on dwelling,
the fifth chapter: SYSTEM OF MEASUREMENTS.

Chapter 6
ORIENTATION

6.1–2a Now I give the method of determining the cardinal points with the help of a gnomon. (One should proceed) at sunrise during a month when the solar path is towards the north during a bright fortnight when sunrise is beautiful, when there are no spots on the solar disc and when the sun is in the asterism of the appropriate fortnight.

6.2b–3a First of all a piece of ground in the middle of the chosen site should be levelled by the water method; this must be a square of one square pole in the centre of which the gnomon should be set.

The gnomon (fig. 1)

6.3b–5 Herewith the dimensions of the gnomon (*śaṅku*): the largest kind is one cubit long, its diameter is one digit at the top and five at the bottom, it is perfectly circular and without irregularities; one of medium size (has a length of) eighteen digits and a small one a length of twelve or nine digits, their diameter at the top and bottom being (in all cases) proportionate to their length.

6.6–7a The materials prescribed for the making of the gnomon are as follows: ivory, sandalwood, wood of *khadira*, *kadara*, *śamī*, *śāka* or *tinduka* or other hard woods; its tip should be perfectly circular.

6.7b–8a When the gnomon has been made it is set up in the chosen place at sunrise, then a circle is drawn of which the gnomon is the centre and of which the diameter is double the length of the gnomon.

6.8b–11a The line which joins the two points where the shadow (of the gnomon) has touched the circle, in the morning and in the evening, gives the east-west direction. The line which passes through the space between these two points and

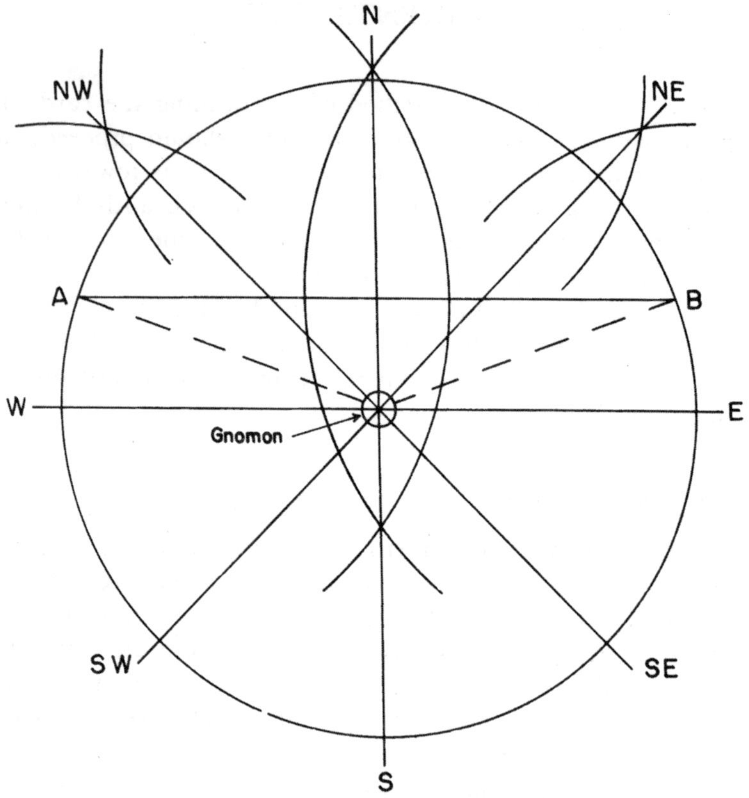

Fig. 1 Orientation (6.3b–11a)

(which is like that which) connects the head and tail of a carp, is the north-south axis; the sage should draw these two lines. Then the circles which have their centres at the east and west points should be drawn.

The *apacchāyā*[1]

6.11b–13 (When the sun) is in Taurus or in Virgo there is no *apacchāyā*; when it is in Aries, Gemini, Leo or Libra the (east-west axis) must be put back two digits; when it is in

1. See Introduction p. xi.

Cancer, Scorpio or Pisces it must be adjusted by four digits, when it is in Sagittarius or Aquarius (it must be adjusted) by six digits and when it is in Capricorn by eight digits. The east-west line is to be fixed after it has been moved to the right or to the left of the shadow.

The rope

6.14–15 The rope measures eight poles and should be made with palm tree or *ketaka* fibres or with strips of cotton or with bark of *nyagrodha* or with *darbha* grass. It has a uniform thickness of one digit at most. For gods, brahmins and kings it is made of three strands but for the other two classes it is made of no more than two.

The stakes

6.16–17 The following woods should be used for stakes: *khadira*, *khādira*, *madhūka*, *kṣīriṇī* or other hard woods. The length of the stakes goes from eleven to twenty-one digits, their diameter is that of a closed fist and their bottom end is pointed.

6.18–19a Grasping the stake in his left hand and holding a pebble in the right, the sage architect, turning to the east or the north, must knock eight successive times at the command of the *sthāpaka*.

Placing the cords

6.19b–21a What is called '*pramāṇa* cord' is determined by the prescribed dimensions (of the intended construction). The *paryanta* cord goes round the outside of the area determined by the *pramāṇa* cord. The cords which establish (certain placings) such as that of the foundation deposit, those which determine the positions of the gods, those with which the diagram is drawn, all are spoken of as "determinating" (*vinyāsa*) cords.

6.21b–22 The foundation deposit for houses is to the south and it is in that direction that the cord must be cast first of all.

Then a stake is set into the ground at a distance from the cord equal to the length of the stake; this is (the limit of) the adjustment layer of an entrance or a wall.

6.23–24a In towns, villages and forts the cord must first of all be cast towards the north-west, then from south to north and east to west, then west to east and north to south.

6.24b–25 (In a house) the cord which goes from the square of Brahmā towards the east is called *trisūtra*, that going west is called *dhana*, that going south *dhānya* and that which goes from the square of Brahmā towards the north is called *sukha*.[1]

6.26 The *pramāṇa* is the cord which gives the dimension of the *sukha(-ālaya)*. For the sake of solidity (the stakes) are to be driven in all around the (central) pavilion at a distance of one, two or three cubits.

The *apacchāyā* (cont.)

6.27 (The east-west line) should be established with adjustments of the following numbers of digits for each ten day period of each month: (Aries) two, one, zero, (Taurus) zero, one, two, (Gemini) two, three, four, (Cancer) four, three, two, (Leo) two, one, zero, (Virgo) zero, one, two, (Libra) two, three, four, (Scorpio) four, five, six, (Sagittarius) six, seven, eight, (Capricorn) eight, seven, six, (Aquarius) six, five, four, (Pisces) four, three, two.

6.28 When the course of the sun has been taken into consideration in relation to the constellations, the indicated adjustment should be made when necessary; this correction once made, the line is drawn from the stake and the ground can be prepared.

Thus ends, in the *Mayamata*, treatise on dwelling,
the sixth chapter: ORIENTATION.

1. These cords correspond to the four main buildings (*śālā*) of a house; see below 27.18sq (p. 238).

Chapter 7
DIAGRAMS

7.1 Now I give the arrangement of the diagrams suitable for all sites.

The thirty-two diagrams

7.2–7 The thirty-two diagrams are: *sakala*, *pecaka*, *pīṭha*, *mahāpīṭha*, *upapīṭha*, *ugrapīṭha*, one called *sthaṇḍila*, *maṇḍūka*, *paramaśāyika*, *āsana*, *sthānīya*, *deśīya*, *ubhayacaṇḍita*, *bhadramahāsana*, *padmagarbha*, *triyuta*, *vratabhoga*, *karṇāṣṭaka*, *gaṇita*, *sūryaviśālaka*, *susaṃhita*, *supratīkānta*, *viśāla*, *vipragarbha*, *viśveśa*, *vipulabhoga*, *vipratikānta*, *viśālākṣa*, *viprabhaktika*, *visveśasāra*, *īśvarakānta* and *indrakānta*.

7.8–21 The *sakala* consists of one square, the *pecaka* of four, the *pīṭha* of nine and the *mahāpīṭha* of sixteen; the *upapīṭha* has twenty-five squares, the *ugrapīṭha* thirty-six, the *sthaṇḍila* forty-nine, the *maṇḍūka* sixty-four and the *paramaśāyin* eighty-one; the *āsana* has one hundred, the *sthānīya* one hundred and twenty-one, the *deśīya* one hundred and forty-four, the *ubhayacaṇḍita* one hundred and sixty-nine, the *bhadramahāsana* one hundred and ninety-six and the *padmagarbha* two hundred and twenty-five; the *triyuta* has two hundred and fifty-six squares, the *vratabhoga* two hundred and eighty-nine and the *karṇāṣṭaka* three hundred and twenty-four; it is known that the *gaṇita* contains three hundred and sixty-one; it is prescribed that there be four hundred squares in the *sūryaviśāla*, four hundred and forty in the *susaṃhita* and four hundred and eighty-four in the *supratikānta*; it is said that the *viśāla* has five hundred and twenty-nine squares, the *vipragarbha* five hundred and seventy-six and the *viśveśa* six hundred and twenty-five; for the *vipulabhoga* six hundred and seventy-six are prescribed, for the *vipratikānta* seven hundred and twenty-nine, for the *visālākṣa* seven hundred and eighty-four and for the *viprabhaktika* eight hundred and forty-one; the *viśveśasāra* consists of nine hundred, the *īśvarakānta* of nine hundred and sixty-one and the *indrakānta* of one thousand and twenty-four. This is prescribed by the ancients versed in Tantra.

The *sakala* diagram

7.22 The basic diagram is the *sakala* consisting of only one square; it is favourable for ascetics and for a fire which consumes a great deal of spread *darbha* grass; it is suitable for sacrifices to Pitṛ and to the immortals as well as for the worship of the guru; the four lines which border it are called: Bhānu, Ārkin, Toya and Śaśin.

The *pecaka* diagram

7.23 In the four squares of the *pecaka* diagram are to be honoured the Paiśāca, Bhūta, Viṣagraha and Rakṣas; it is here that the sages are to install the symbol or the image of Śiva according to the general rules and specific conditions.

The *pīṭha* diagram (fig. 2)

7.24 It is known of the *pīṭha* diagram, which consists of nine squares, that the four Vedas are at the four cardinal points and that Water, Fire, Ether and Wind are (at the intermediate points of which) the first is the north-east; in the centre is Earth.

The *mahāpīṭha* diagram (fig. 3)

7.25–27 The *mahāpīṭha* diagram consists of sixteen squares occupied by twenty-five divinities. The divinities on the periphery are: Īśa, Jayanta, Āditya, Bhṛśa, Agni, Vitatha, Yama, Bhṛṅga, Pitṛ, Sugrīva, Varuṇa, Śoṣa, Marut, Mukhya, Soma and Aditi; those of the interior are Āpavatsa, Ārya, Savitṛ, Vivasvant, Indra, Mitra, Rudraja and Bhūdhara; in the centre is Brahmā, the Lord.

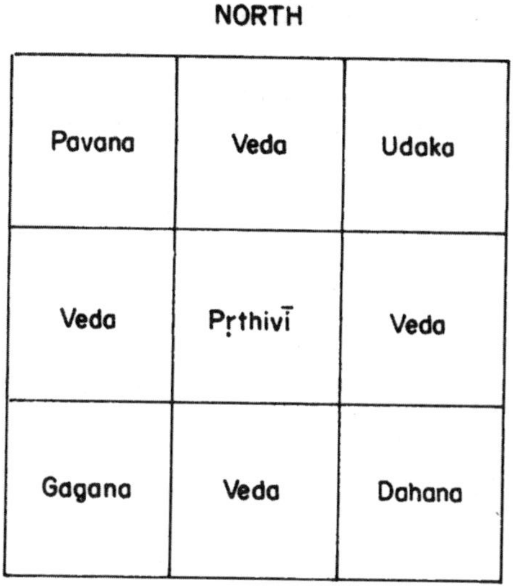

Fig. 2 Pīṭha diagram (7.24)

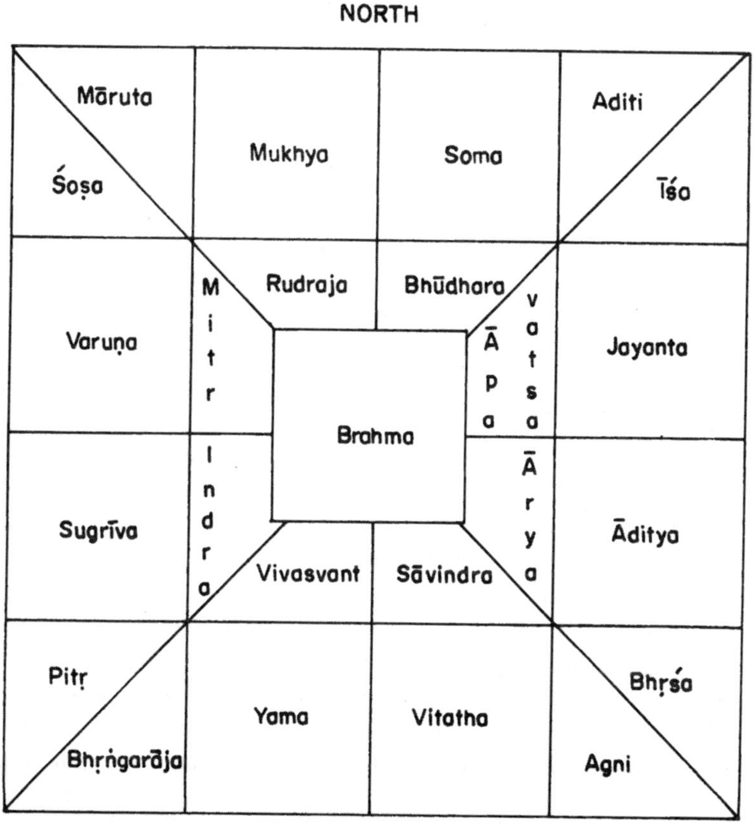

Fig. 3 Mahāpīṭha diagram (7.25–27)

NORTH

Māruta	Mukhya	Soma	Aditi	Īśa
Śoṣa	Rudraja	Bhūdhara	Āpavatsa	Jayanta
Varuṇa	Mitra	Brahmā	Āryaka	Āditya
Sugrīva	Indrarāja	Vivasvant	Sāvindra	Bhṛśa
Pitṛ	Bhṛṅgarāja	Yama	Vitatha	Agni

Fig. 4 Upapīṭha diagram (7.28)

The *upapīṭha* and following diagrams

7.28–29 The *upapīṭha* diagram (*fig. 4*) in which each divinity occupies a square is obtained by adding one unit to both the dimensions of (the *mahāpīṭha* diagram). Thus the sage, adding a unit to each of the dimensions every time, may determine (all the diagrams) up to *indrakānta*.

7.30–32a When the number of squares is even the arrangement should be as that of the sixty-four square diagram; when the number is uneven it must be as that of the eighty-one square diagram. Amongst the diagrams the *maṇḍūka* is the one which should be used for all constructions. That is why, having drawn upon the Tantra, I am going to describe these two diagrams.

7.32b–33a In the sixty-four and eighty-one square diagrams, one being even and the other odd, the gods, of whom the first is Brahmā, are installed on the periphery and in the centre.

Positions of the gods

7.33b–37 Now the gods are presented consecutively starting with (he who rules the) north-east corner: Īśa, Parjanya, Jayanta, Mahendraka, Āditya, Satyaka, Bhṛśa, Antarikṣa, Agni, Pūṣan, Vitatha, Rākṣasa, Yama, Gandharva, Bhṛṅgarāja, Mṛṣa, the Pitṛ deities, Dauvārika, Sugrīva, Puṣpadanta, Jalādhipa, Asura, Śoṣa, Roga, Vāyu, Nāga, Mukhya, Bhallāṭaka, Soma, Mṛga, Aditi and Uditi, these are the thirty-two exterior divinities.

7.38–39 Āpa and Āpavatsa are both inside, at the north-east corner; Savindra and Sāvindra are inside at the south-east; Indra and Indrarāja at the south-west, Rudra and Rudrajaya at the north-west.

7.40 Brahmā is in the centre; he is Śambhu and, facing him, are four gods named Ārya, Vivasvant, Mitra and Bhūdhara.

7.41 The female deities, Carakī, Vidārī, Pūtanā and Pāparākṣasī are on the outside of the four corners and are installed starting from the north-east.

7.42 Such eaters of oblations who have no regular positions are to be placed in those of the other divinities. With twenty lines, twenty-eight intersections, four stakes and four veins (*sirā*), the result is thirty-six, twenty-four, twelve, eight and one squares (?).

The *maṇḍūka* diagram (fig. 5)

7.43–47a There are four squares for Brahmā in the centre of the sixty-four square diagram; the four gods, starting with Ārya, each have a three (square) position and are set up starting from the east; the eight immortals of whom the first

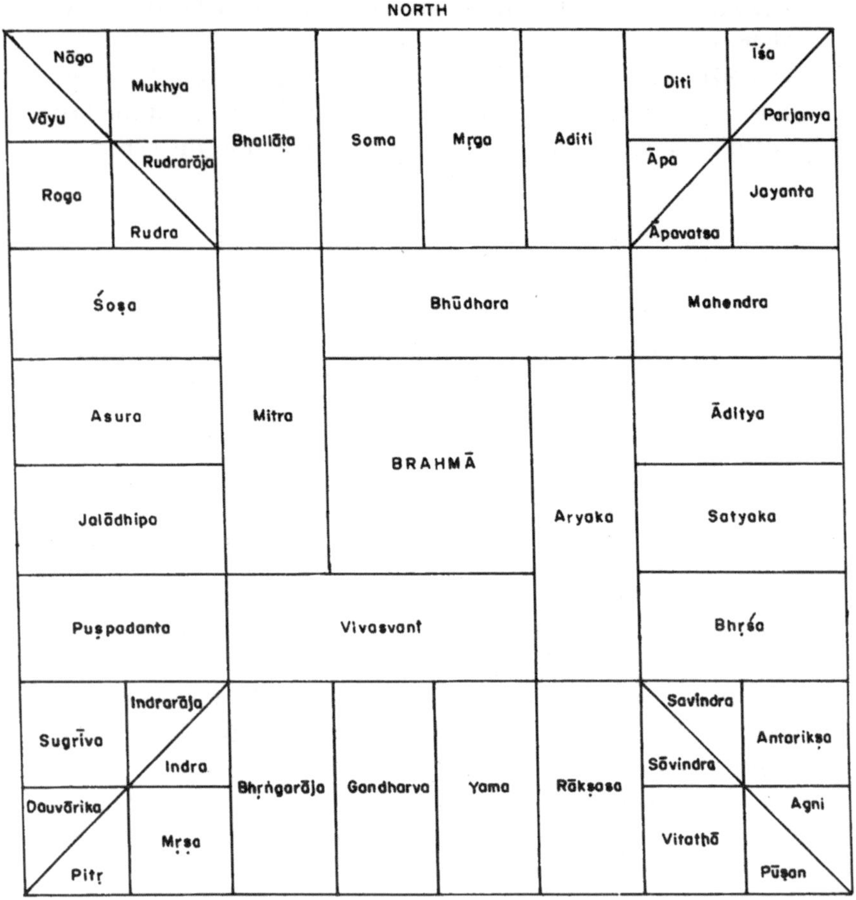

Fig. 5 Maṇḍūka diagram (7.43–47b)

is Āpa are situated in the corners, on a half square; at each cardinal point there are four gods occupying two squares: Mahendra (. . . etc. at the east), Rākṣasa (. . . etc. at the south), Puṣpa-(-danta . . . at the west) and Bhallāṭa (. . . etc. at the north). Jayanta, Antarikṣa, Vitatha, Sugrīva, Roga, Mukhya and Diti each occupy one square; the eight remaining deities, the first of whom is Īsa, rule at the corners, each occupying half a square.

7.47b–48 The site's divinities should be installed in this order on the *maṇḍūka* diagram; it is known that the order for the awarding of places is in accordance with the *pradakṣiṇa*, therefore the immortals are to be installed, each in his place, facing Brahmā.

The Spirit of the building

7.49 It should be known that the Spirit of the building (*vāstupuruṣa*) has six bones, a single heart, four vulnerable points and four vessels, and that he lies upon the ground, his head towards the east.

7.50–54 It is said that the divinity named Ārya is his head, that Savindra is his right arm and Sāvindra his (right) hand, that Āpa and Āpavatsa are his left arm and (left) hand, that Vivasvant is his right side and Mahīdhara his left, that in the middle his trunk is Brahmā, that his testicles are Mitra, that his right foot (and leg) are Indra and Indrarāja and his left foot (and leg) are Rudra and Rudrajaya. He rests with his face to the ground; his six bones, orientated to the east and north, are in the middle of the (central) parts of the site. In the centre of the site are found the vulnerable points and the heart which is Brahmā and it is from there that the veins start. Thus the Spirit is described.

7.55–56 It is known that it is He who, in every human dwelling, is responsible for good and for bad fortune, that is why the wise must avoid tormenting His limbs with the "limbs" of the house for, if not, sorrows innumerable will fall upon the limbs of the owner of the house. Thus the sage must always spare the body of the Spirit (in the course of construction).

The *maṇḍūka* diagram (cont.)

7.57 There are forty-five gods in all in the sacrificial layout named *maṇḍūka*, which consists of sixty-four squares: Ka (occupies) four squares, those facing him three each, sixteen (gods) a half square, eight (gods) one, and sixteen (gods), two.

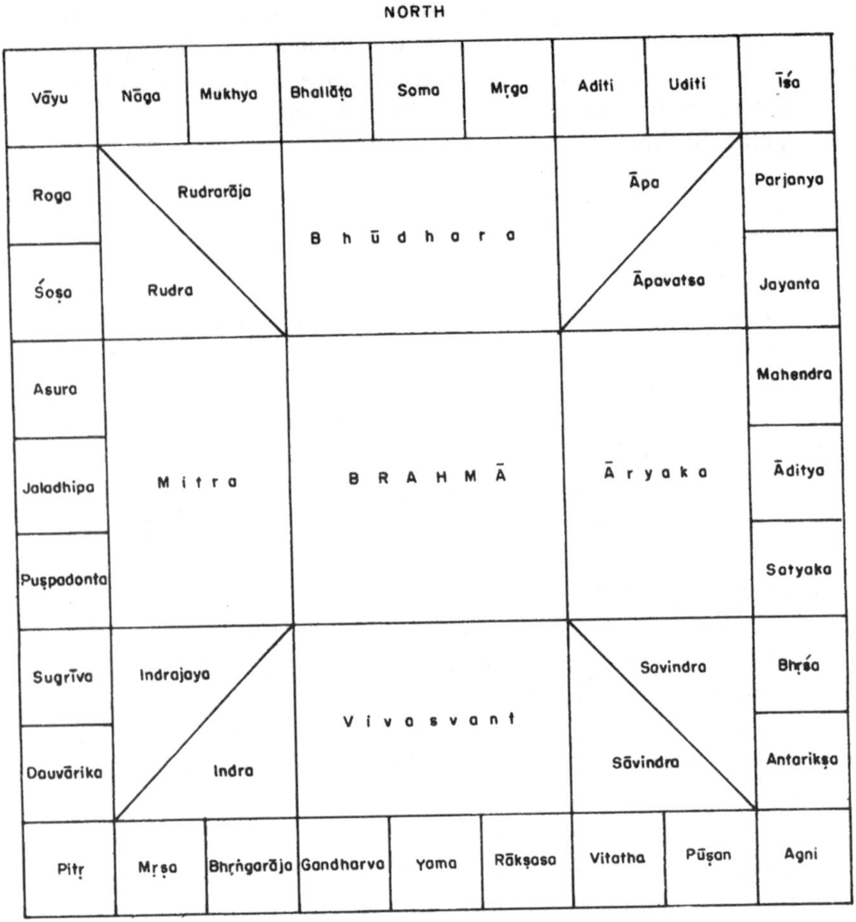

Fig. 6 Paramaśāyika diagram (7.33b–40,58)

The *paramaśāyin* diagram (fig. 6)

7.58 Kamalaja occupies nine squares in the *paramaśāyin* diagram, the four gods facing him, six each, those who hold the intermediate points two, and all those of the periphery, one.

Thus ends, in the *Mayamata*, treatise on dwelling, the seventh chapter: ARRANGEMENT OF THE GODS IN DIAGRAMS.

Chapter 8
OFFERINGS

8.1 It is prescribed that offerings should be made to each god in his own place; individual and common offerings are made starting with that to Brahmā.

Individual offerings

8.2–4a The place of Brahmā is to be honoured with perfumes and garlands, incense, ghee, rice boiled in milk and roasted rice. The offering at the place of Āryaka is a cake of fruits as well as cooked beans and sesame seeds. Curd is prescribed for Vivasvant, *dūrvā* grass for Mitra and for Mahīdhara, milk. These are the offerings to the (gods) of the interior.

8.4b–7 (At the place of) Parjanya the offering should be clarified butter and at that of Aindra, fresh butter and flowers. Entrails and flowers are the offerings for Indra, honey and onions for Bhāskara and, for Satyaka, honey. Fresh butter is offered to Bhṛśa; the offering to Gagana is beans and orpiment, that to Vahni, milk, ghee and *tagara* powder and the offering to Pūṣan is vegetables and milk. An offering of cooked *kaṅku* is prescribed for Vitatha, one of intoxicating juice for Rākṣasa, of vegetables and boiled rice for Yama and, for Gandharva, an offering of pure perfume.

8.8–12 Sea fish is offered to Bhṛṅgarāja and rice with fish to Mṛṣa. A sesame oil cake is offered to Nirṛti and a seed (of sesame) to Dauvārika, a cake is offered to Sugrīva and, to Puṣpadanta, flowers and water. Rice and water is the offering intended for Varuṇa and, for Asura, blood. The offering to Śoṣa should be rice with sesame, to Roga, dried fish, to Vāyu, fat and to Nāga, wine and roasted rice. Flour, curds and ghee should be offered to Mukhya, to Bhallāṭa, cooked rice with molasses and, to Soma, milk rice. Dried meat is to be offered to Mṛga, cake to the Mother of the gods, sesame rice to Uditi and rice and ghee to Īśaka.

8.13–14 Roasted rice is required for Savindra and perfumed water for Sāvindra, for Indra and Indrarāja, goat's fat and flour, for Rudra and Rudrajaya, meat and fat and, for Āpa and Āpavatsa, lotus and the flesh of shellfish and tortoise.

8.15 The offering to Carakī is wine and roasted rice, to Vidārī it is salt, to Pūtanā, *piṣṭa* and, to the last (who is Pāparākṣasī), bean water.

The common offering

8.16–17 All the gods in succession should then be presented with the common offering which consists of pure food with ghee and curds. A young girl or a courtesan should be called to carry the offerings; she will first have purified her mind by means of impositions on limbs and hands.

8.18–19 After each deity has been hailed by name with a formula beginning "OM" and ending "NAMAS" and after water has been offered, the common offering should be made and then that appropriate to each god; next water is again offered. It is thus that the sages proceed at the time of the founding of villages and other settlements, using *maṇḍūka* or *paramaśāyin* diagrams.

8.20 The gods being appeased thus, according to the ritual, they should be dismissed with a formula in order that the layout of the construction may be set up.

8.21–22a Brahmā and the exterior deities are to be installed, each in his place; (their positions) are intended for temples and gateways. The others, and all those without specific positions, are assigned to protect the site.

8.22b The secret ritual pertaining to villages . . . etc. has thus been revealed.

8.23 At dawn, the architect, having fasted, purified his mind and understood all things, must apportion amongst the gods the common and particular offerings according to the rule given above.

Thus ends, in the *Mayamata*, treatise on dwelling, the eighth chapter: RULES FOR OFFERINGS.

Chapter 9

VILLAGES AND OTHER SETTLEMENTS

9.1a Now the dimensions and plans for villages and other settlements are set out according to the rule.

The system of measurements (cont.)

9.1b–2a It is to be known that five hundred poles (*daṇḍa*) make one *krośa* twice of which is half a *gavyūta* and twice that is a *gavyūta*; eight thousand poles are one *yojana*.

9.2b–4a A square, eight poles square, is a *kākaṇī*; four times that is a *māṣa*, four times which is a *vartanaka*; five times one *vartanaka* is a *vātikā* whose quadruple is the area precisely suitable for a family plot in a village. These are area measurements; herewith the dimensions of villages given in poles.

Dimensions of villages

9.4b–5 The largest size for a village is one hundred thousand poles; starting with twenty thousand poles and, with regular increments (of twenty thousand), five dimensions suitable for a village are obtained. The plot intended for a family occupies one twentieth of the village (?).

9.6–7a The smallest size for a village is five hundred poles; by starting with this figure and proceeding to twenty thousand poles by successive increments of five hundred poles, forty dimensions suitable for villages are obtained.

9.7b–8a The width (of a village) is two thousand poles, one thousand five hundred, one thousand, nine hundred, seven hundred, five hundred or three hundred poles.

9.8b–9a The dimensions of a town (*nagara*), given in poles, are from one thousand to two thousand. The largest size for a town is eight thousand poles; (starting with this figure) and reducing it successively by two thousand, four sizes for a town are obtained.

9.10 Village (*grāma*), *kheṭa*, *kharvaṭa*, fort (*durga*) and town (*nagara*): these are the five (settlements) for which I am going to give the dimensions in poles with three variations for each.

9.11–13 The smallest village is said to be sixty-four poles (wide), the medium village is twice that width and the large one triple. A small *kheṭa* is two hundred and sixty-six poles, a medium one three hundred and twenty and a large one three hundred and eighty-four. The respective dimensions of small, medium and large *kharvaṭa* are four hundred and forty-eight, five hundred and twelve and five hundred and seventy-six poles.

9.14–15 A small fort is six hundred and forty poles (wide), a medium one, seven hundred and four and a large one, seven hundred and sixty-eight. Small, medium and large towns are respectively, eight hundred and thirty-two, eight hundred and ninety-six and nine hundred and sixty poles wide.

9.16–17a If sixteen pole increments are used, there are nine more possibilities for each. The length is double the width or three quarters, one half or a quarter (greater) or may be a sixth or eighth (more); otherwise the plan may be square if so desired.

9.17b–18a The basic dimensions (of the settlement) will be taken from that width and length making an odd number of poles; the remainder will belong to the area which is not built up; this is the procedure for all sites such as villages etc. . . .

The *āyādi* system[1]

9.18b–20a (The dimensions given) in poles have to be increased or reduced so as to agree with the *āyādi* series. In order that a perfect result may be achieved (a site) must be selected whose dimensions are not in opposition to the "gains", "losses", "asterisms", "matrices", "ages", "solar days" and "lunar days" nor to the asterisms of the founder nor to his name nor to that of the place itself.

1. See below 26.206sq (p. 233), 33.58sq (p. 313) and *Architecture in the Ajitāgama and the Rauravāgama . . .*, pp. 18–19.

9.20b–22a The sum of the length and the width having been multiplied by eight and by nine and the (product obtained) divided by twelve and ten, the remainders are the "gain" on the one hand and the "loss" on the other. (The sum of the length and the width) having been multiplied by three and (the product) divided by eight, (the remainder) corresponds to one of the eight matrices which are: "flag", "cloud", "lion", "dog", "bull", donkey", "elephant", and "crow"; amongst these "flag", "lion", "bull" and "elephant" are auspicious.

9.22b–23 Next, (the sum of the length and the width) having been multiplied by eight and (the product) divided by twenty-seven, the quotient (*phala*) is the "age" (*vayas*) and the remainder (corresponds) to the asterism; if (the same) product is divided by thirty, (the remainder corresponds to) the solar days, the first of which is Sunday. The entire construction must be made in this knowledge.

9.24 It is auspicious that the "gain" be superior (to the "loss") and totally inauspicious should the "loss" be superior (to the "gain"). As the transgression of these rules leads to failure, nothing should be undertaken prior to deep study (of the subject).

Number of Brahmins

9.25–28 In the largest village of the highest category there are twelve thousand brahmins, in a medium village ten thousand, and eight thousand in a small one. It is prescribed that seven thousand brahmins be installed in a large village of the intermediate category, six thousand in a medium one and five thousand in a small one. Four thousand are prescribed for the largest village in the inferior category, three thousand for the medium and two thousand for the small; the experts ordain that there be a thousand brahmins in the largest village of the last category, seven hundred in the intermediate one and five hundred in a small one.

9.29–30 There are ten varieties of small village which house respectively: one hundred and eight, two hundred and sixteen, three hundred and twenty-four, eighty-four, sixty-four, fifty, thirty-two, twenty-four, twelve and sixteen brahmins. When there is no alternative the gift (of land) is to be given to brahmins in the number of one to ten.

9.31 A village in which there is only one family is a *kuṭika*, also called *ekabhoga*. A *sukhālaya* house should be constructed here and *daṇḍaka* houses elsewhere.[1]

9.32–33a There are two sorts of diagram pertaining to the setting up of all constructions: those consisting of an even number of squares and those where the number is odd. If the number is even, the streets should be drawn along the lines (of the diagram) and, if odd, they should go through the middle of (rows of) squares; any confusion brings misfortune to the inhabitants.

Names of villages

9.33b–34 It is said that there are eight types of village: *daṇḍaka*, *svastika*, *prastara*, *prakīrṇaka*, *nandyāvarta*, *paraga*, *padma* and *śrīpratiṣṭhita*.

Streets

9.35 The street on the periphery of all villages is called *maṅgalavīthi*; the temple or the altar is installed at the centre which is called the place of Brahmā.

9.36–39a The width of a street is two, three, four or five poles but those which traverse (the village) from east to west are six poles (wide) and are called "main streets". The street (which encircles) the middle of the village is called *brahmavīthi* and is the "navel" (of the village). The roads leading to the gates are called *rājavīthi* and those which flank them are the alleys. It is said that all these streets are paved but the *maṅgalavīthi* is said to be the "street for the (temple) chariot". The streets leading to the secondary gates are called *naraca*; those going towards the north are called *kṣudra*, *argala* and *vāmana*.

1. *Sukhālaya*: see 27.40–41 (p. 240); *daṇḍaka*: see 26.22sq (p. 206).

9.39b The street which encircles a village is called *maṅgala-vīthi* and that which encircles a town, *janavīthi*; both are designated as "chariot streets" (*rathya*) but, according to the ancients, this expression applies to all the other streets too.

Types of settlement

9.40 A place where there are only brahmins is called *maṅgala*; that inhabited by princes and merchants is a *pura*; the place inhabited by ordinary people in this world is called *grāma*; a place where ascetics dwell is called *maṭha*.

9.41–42 The sages give the name *daṇḍaka* to a village comprising a road going north and another east; both are rectilinear and cross at right angles to the centre. This village has four gates. *Daṇḍaka* is also the name for a village with one single road, straight as a pole.

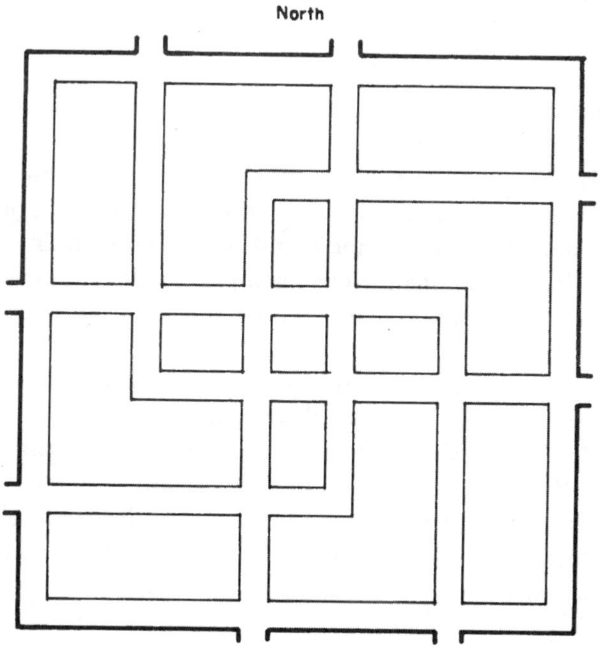

Fig. 7 Svastika village (9.43–45)

9.43–45 A *svastika* village (*fig.* 7) is one whose diagram consists of nine squares; all around is a street drawn outside these (nine) squares. One street starts in the north-east, goes towards the west and ends in the south; one goes from south-east to the north and ends in the west; another goes from the south-west to the east and ends in the north; the last goes from the north-east to the south and ends in the east. This village follows a *svastika* figure and comprises four (main) streets.

9.46 There are five types of *prastara* village; they comprise three streets going from east to west and three, four, five, six or seven starting from north.

9.47 There are five types of *prakīrṇaka* village; they comprise four streets going from east to west and twelve, eleven, ten, nine or eight starting from north.

9.48–50a The *nandyāvarta* village comprises five streets going east-west and thirteen, fourteen, fifteen, sixteen or seventeen coming from the north; it has gates at the four cardinal points. Its plan resembles a *nandyāvarta* figure, the gates being external to the figure, the streets inside it, and there being numerous crossroads; it is said to be in the form of *nandyāvarta*.

9.50b–51a A village with from eighteen to twenty-two streets from the north and six from the east is called *paraga*.

9.51a–52 There are five kinds of *padma* village; they comprise seven streets going east-west, three, four, five, six or seven streets starting from the north and twenty crossroads.

9.53 The *śrīpratiṣṭhita* village comprises eight streets starting in the east and from twenty-eight to thirty-two starting in the north.

9.54a Eight types of village have been described but a *śrīvatsa* or other type of village may also be established.

9.54b–55 In every village the sage begins by laying out the navel. Whether for village or house, only (dimensions in) whole numbers of poles must be used. To draw the plan the sages may use any diagram, from the *sakala* with one square to the *āsana* with one hundred.

9.56 There are four streets in the small village, eight in the medium one and twelve in the large.

Gates[1]

9.57–61a The gateways are established on the squares of Bhallāṭa, Mahendra, Rākṣasa and Puṣpadanta; the four sewage outlets are on the squares of Vitatha, Jayanta, Sugrīva and Mukhya; the eight secondary gates are on the squares of Bhṛśa, Pūṣan, Bhṛṅgarāja, Dauvārika, Śoṣa, Nāga, Diti and Jalada. The breadth of the door is three, five or seven cubits and their height double, one and a half or one and three quarters of that. Every village must be surrounded by a moat and ramparts but the best villages are those located on a river and extending along its south bank.

9.61b–63 In the diagram comprising eighty-one squares and in that with sixty-four, the *brāhma* zone in the centre and the *daiva, mānuṣa* and *paiśāca* zones must be determined, one after the other. The dwellings of brahmins should be in the *daiva* and *mānuṣa* zones and those of the craftsmen in the *paiśāca* zone, or the dwellings of upper classes are there and the temples of the hosts of gods should be placed there too, starting in the east.

Temple locations

9.64–66a At the heart of the village are the temples consecrated by brahmins; the Śiva temple may be here as well or may be outside the village. The temple of Vināyaka should be on the square of Bhṛṅgarāja or that of Pāvaka; the Śiva temple is on the squares of Īśa, Soma or of any other deity and living quarters with the prescribed dimensions are to be constructed around it.

9.66b–73a The positions are now given for the attendant deities of Śiva: the temple of Sura is on the square of Sūrya, that of Kālikā on the square of Agni, the Viṣṇu temple is on the square of Bhṛśa and the Ṣaṇmukha one on the square of Yama. The temple of (Viṣṇu)-Keśava is on the square of

1. See fig. 8 (p. 45).

Bhṛśa, Mṛga or Nirṛti; the Gaṇeśa temple is on the square of Sugrīva or of Puṣpadanta; the Āryaka temple is on the square of Nirṛti. The shrine of Viṣṇu is on the square of Varuṇa; Viṣṇu, in this shrine, may be shown successively standing, seated and reclining, starting from the top floor. Or else, the ground floor is massive and Viṣṇu is shown standing on the top floor. The temple of Sugata is on the Sugala square and that of Jina on the Bhṛṅgarāja square. The shrine of Madirā is on the Vāyu square and that of Kātyāyanī on the square of Mukhya. The shrine of Dhanada and that of the Mothers are on the square of Soma and the Śaṅkara temple on the square of Īśa, Parjanya or Jayanta. Dhanada may be on the square of Soma or on that of Śoṣa where may also be found the Gajānana shrine. By the same token, the shrine of the Mothers may be installed on the Aditi square.

9.73b–75a The Viṣṇu temple is at the centre where should be, as well, the assembly hall, placed on the north-eastern or south-eastern squares of the place of Brahmā, the Hari temple being in its north-western or south-(western) parts. The consequences of constructing upon the five (remaining squares?) will without doubt be disastrous.

9.75b–78 According to whether the diagram is even or odd the place of Brahmā is divided into eight (?) or nine squares. Buildings of the *nalinaka*, *svastika*, *nandyāvarta*, *pralīnaka*, *śrīpratiṣṭhita*, *caturmukha* and *padmāsana* types (?) should be built in each direction, starting from the east and avoiding the Aja square. There should also be a temple of the *viṣṇucchanda* type; it should have from three to twelve storeys. It should be known that the (Viṣṇu) temple may be outside the village and that the (god) should be installed here in standing, seated and reclining positions.

9.79–82 It is laid down that, in the villages, there may be superior, medium, inferior or lowly buildings but that a lowly (building) should not be installed in a superior (village); if prescribed a small shrine may be built in a small village. A temple with three, four or five storeys is to be built in a small (village) and, as well, in a small village there should be a shrine of the same (class). If an inferior temple is built in a village or town of superior class the men there will become inferior and their women will incline towards undesirable conduct; according to this rule a temple should either be equal or superior to (the village). The temple of Harihara and any other building may be as desired (?).

Divinities of the gates

9.83 Caṇḍeśvara, Kumāra, Dhanada, Kālī, Pūtanā, Kālīsuta and Khaḍgin are the divinities of the gates.

Orientation of shrines

9.84–85 In settlements such as villages the temple of Īśa is orientated towards either the east or the west; it is beneficial if turned towards the exterior of the (settlement). The dwelling of Viṣṇu may be orientated in any direction but is beneficial if turned towards the centre of the village. Other (shrines) are orientated towards the east but that of the Mothers is turned towards the north and the entrance of that of Sūrya is in the west. The dwellings of the gods of a city should be built prior to the houses.

Locations to be avoided

9.86 These are the six places where there should be no temples or buildings of that kind: the heart (of the Spirit of the site) and its bones, the stakes, the lines (of the diagram), their intersections and the empty spaces at the corners.

Planning

9.87–91a The cowshed should be to the south, the flower garden to the north and the dwelling of ascetics either near the eastern gate or to the west. A tank or reservoir should be placed everywhere where water is required. The quarter for vaiśya is to the south and that for śūdra on the periphery. The potters' houses are either to the east or to the north, where are found too those of barbers and other artisans; the fishermen's quarter is to the north-west and that of the butchers to the west and, lastly, the oil makers' quarter is to the north.

Houses

9.91b–94 The width of houses should be three, five, seven or, at most, nine poles and the corresponding lengths are obtained by adding successively two poles to the width but should be such as not to exceed twice those widths. The house should then be built with the aid of dimensions calculated in cubits according to the rule. It may be a four main building house called *rucaka*, *svastika*, *nandyāvarta*, *sarvatobhadra* or *vardhamāna* according to its appearance; or else it may be a a *daṇḍaka* house (with one main building) or a *lāṅgala* one (with two) or a *śūrpa* one (with three).[1]

9.95–98 The dwellings of other *sthapati*(?) are to be erected at a distance from the village, to the south-east or to the north-west and a little farther away still are the quarters of the dyers and people of that ilk. Caṇḍāla huts are a *krośa* to the east; the wives of the caṇḍāla wear jewellery in copper, iron and lead; upon entering the village in the morning, caṇḍāla must cleanse it of dirt. Five hundred poles to the north-east is the cremation ground and a little farther on is the cemetery for inferior classes.

Errors in planning

9.99–100 If the houses of caṇḍāla or curriers or the cemetery or well are badly placed or if there is any departure from the rule as regards the arrangement of streets surrounding the temple, the *viśvakoṣṭha* (place for oblations?) and the village itself, then misfortune will result: destruction of the village, loss of the prince and death. Equally, if the temples and bazaars are empty and if heaps of dirt and filth are thrown into the streets the result will be the annihilation of the village.

1. *Rucaka* . . . : see 26.64–187 (pp. 215sq.); *daṇḍaka, lāṅgala, śūrpa*: see 26.11sq. (pp. 205sq.).

Placing the foundation deposit[1]

9.101–103 Now is elucidated the placing of the foundation deposit in villages and in other settlements. If there is a foundation deposit then success is ensured but, if not, failure is inevitable; the greatest care must therefore be taken in the laying of a comprehensive deposit including earths, roots, grains, (grains represented in) metals, colouring substances and precious stones such as *indranīla* sapphire. The elements chosen for a deposit should be flawless and are to have been purchased.

9.104–106 Having filled the (foundation) pit with water, the sage puts the elements in place beginning with the earths; above the grains a flawless copper casket must be put, for which there are five (possible) widths which are: fourteen, twelve, ten, eight or four digits, the height being equal to the width. The casket may be either square or circular and it has twenty-five or nine compartments.

9.107–112a If the container is in accordance with the *upapīṭha* diagram (and thus has twenty-five compartments) then the gods will be placed there as follows: Vajrin in gold and a silver bull in (the compartment corresponding to) Sūrya, Yamarāja in copper and a gold elephant in the compartment of Yama, Jalādhipa in silver and a gold lion in that of Varuṇa, Dvijarāja in silver(?) and a silver horse in that of Soma. In the compartment of Īśa there should be mercury, in that of Anala tin, in that of Nirṛti lead and in that of Samīraṇa gold. In the compartment of Jayanta there is cinnabar, in that of Bhṛśa orpiment, in that of Vitatha red arsenic, in that of Bhṛṅgarāja pyrites, in that of Sukhandara lapis, in that of Śoṣa red chalk, in that of Gaṇamukhya antimony and in that of Aditi red copper. This is to be properly understood and the elements arranged in order.

9.112b–113 The lords of the cardinal points are installed facing the centre (of the casket) and in four compartments; their images are six, five, four, three or two digits high and their mounts half that height; they are either standing or seated.

1. For a more detailed account see chapter 12.

9.114–117a There is a pearl in the compartment of Āpavatsa, coral in that of Marīci, a topaz in that of Savitṛ, a tiger's eye gem in that of Vivasvant, a diamond in that of Indrarāja, an *indranīla* sapphire in that of Mitraka, a *mahānīla* sapphire in that of Rudrarāja and an emerald in that of Mahīdhara; a ruby is placed in the centre. The responsibility for the arranging of precious stones and colouring substances should devolve upon those well acquainted with their nature and with the placing of gods.

9.117b–119 *Svastika* in gold, iron, copper and silver should be set at the four cardinal points. Around the compartment of Brahmā and exterior to it, the following grains should be placed, starting from the east and in the given order: *śāli* in gold, *vrīhi* in silver, *kodrava* in iron, *kaṅku* in tin, *māṣa* in lead, *tila* in mercury, *mudga* in iron and *kulattha* in copper.

9.120–122a When an offering has been made to the casket everything should be arranged (in it). The length (of the board which is to cover the casket) is greater by one digit than its width and may be twelve digits to thirty-two by successive increments of five. Above is a perfectly circular stake in *khadira* wood which should be laid in place on top of the casket by those who know the rules relating to foundation deposits.

9.122b–126a In *sthānīya*, *droṇamukha*, *kharvaṭa*, in towns of all types, in villages and in *nigama*, *kheṭa*, *pattana* and *kotmakolaka*, the foundation deposit may be at the place of Brahmā, that of Ārya, that of Arka or those of Vivasvant, Yama, Mitra, Varuṇa, Soma or Pṛthivīdhara or, again it may be to the right of the gates situated at the places of Puṣpadanta, Bhallāṭa, Mahendra or Gṛhakṣata or it may be placed beneath the temples of Viṣṇu, Śrī or Skanda in order that the protection of the village may be guaranteed and all wishes accomplished.

9.126b–127 Once the foundation deposit is in place an image is set up above it, in a pit lined with stones and bricks and the size of two cupped hands. (Images) (?) of all the gods not mentioned should be placed in the squares (of the diagram) starting with Aja.

9.128 The architect must install a solid (construction) well protected by the corresponding foundation deposit(?); he may look in the chapter dealing with foundation deposits for what is not given here.

9.129 Thus have been expounded the dimensions of sites suitable for gods and superior and inferior castes as well as the dimensions, street layouts and embellishments to settlements such as villages; this has been taken from the Tantra.

9.130 The prince is obliged to offer land and cows to the tetrad who are led by the architect and who are skilful in measuring. He who does this without reservation will gain riches in abundance and his kingdom will extend to the moon and stars as long as the world shall endure.

Thus ends, in the *Mayamata*, treatise on dwelling,
the ninth chapter: VILLAGE PLANNING.

Chapter 10
TOWNS

10.1a Now I give the dimensions of towns followed by their plans.

Dimensions of towns

10.1b–3 Going from three hundred poles up to eight thousand by successive increments of one hundred poles, seventy-eight widths are obtained for towns (*nagara*). Going from a hundred poles up to three hundred by successive increments of ten poles, twenty-one (widths) for very small towns are obtained.

10.4 The surrounding wall of the largest capital city measures sixteen thousand poles; diminishing to four thousand poles by successive reductions of five hundred poles gives twenty-five (possible perimeters for capitals).

10.5–11a Going from three hundred poles to four hundred by successive increments of twenty poles, gives the widths of the six types of *kheṭa*: two superior, two medium and two inferior. From (four hundred poles) to four hundred and ninety-six there are six (possible) widths for *droṇamukha*. From two hundred poles to four hundred by successive increments of fifty poles there are five possible widths for *kharvaṭa*. From two hundred poles to three hundred and forty by successive increments of ten poles gives fifteen possible widths for *nigama*. From one hundred to five hundred poles by successive increments of one hundred poles gives five (possible) widths for *kotmakolaka* and, according to the sages, these widths apply to the *pura* as well. The width of *viḍamba* goes from two hundred to five hundred poles giving seven possible widths with a difference of fifty poles between each.

10.11b–12 The dimensions having been indicated, here are the proportions: the length is double the width or one and a quarter times it, otherwise the length exceeds the width by a sixth or an eighth.

The surrounding wall

10.13–14 Square, rectangular, round, elliptical or perfectly circular, such are the five layouts for the walls. Their lengths may be seven tenths, six eighths, five sevenths, four fifths or three fourths of the perimeter (of the town?).

10.15–16a The thickness of the (bottom of the) wall is two, three or four cubits; its height is seven, ten or eleven cubits: its thickness at the top is two thirds what it is at the bottom. There is a moat all around the exterior and inside are the temples ... etc.

Places to be avoided

10.16b–17a Diagrams such as *pecaka* (with four squares) or *āsana* (with a hundred squares) or those between them should be used; the sage must avoid (building) on their lines and on other forbidden places.

Streets

10.17b–18 A street should be planned there, or wherever desired, but starting at the north (or at the) east and according to the rules. From one pole to seven by successive increments of half a pole, there are thirteen (possible) breadths for the streets.

The royal capital

10.19 A heavily populated town situated in the middle of the kingdom and beside a river is an "ordinary" (*kevala*) town though if there is a royal palace there it is a "royal capital" (*rājadhāni*).

10.20–21a A town is called "ordinary" when it has fortified gates at the four cardinal points and very large ramparts, when it contains shops as well as dwellings for all classes of people and temples for all the gods.

10.21b–26a A town called "royal capital" is impregnable at the north and at the east; it is encircled by a wall beyond which is a glacis of earth; beyond that is a moat and, lastly, farther away is a fortified garrison keeping watch in all directions, the royal guard facing to the east and to the south. This town has high gateways, various types of gallery (*mālikā*) and temples to all the gods. It is frequented by all sorts of courtesans and has a number of gardens. Elephants, horses, war-chariots and foot soldiers abound. People of all classes (live there). It has gates and posterns and contains a great number of dwelling houses as well as the king's palace. It is called *pura* or *nagara* when it is situated in forested country and when it contains houses for all classes, and shops.

Definitions

10.26b–27 A *kheṭa* is inhabited by śūdra; it is situated in the vicinity of a river or of a mountain. A *kharvaṭa* is surrounded by mountains and is inhabited by people of all classes. A *janasthānakubja* is heavily populated and situated between a *kheṭa* and a *kharvaṭa*.

10.28–29a A *pattana* is a town where products from other countries are to be found; it is inhabited by people of all classes; there are shops and an abundance of merchandise such as precious stones, grains, fine cloth and perfumes; it is situated by the sea and extends along the coast.

10.29b–30a Sages say that a *śibira* is situated in proximity to the realm of an enemy prince; it is provided with everything necessary for war and it accommodates the army and the commander-in-chief.

10.30b–31a According to the sages a *senāmukha* is a place where people of all classes are mixed; it contains a royal palace and is provided with a well fortified garrison.

10.31b–32a A *sthānīya* is a town founded by the king and situated beside a river or near to a mountain; it comprises a royal palace and a large garrison.

10.32b–33a A town which extends (both) along the right and left banks of a river and which is frequented by traders of all sorts and inhabited by people of all classes is a *droṇamukha*.

10.33b–34a An inhabited place in the vicinity of a village is a *viḍamba*. An inhabited place in the middle of a forest is a *kotmakolaka*.

10.34b–35a A *nigama* is a town where the four castes are gathered, where people of all classes live together and where there are a number of artisans.

10.35b–36a A *skandhāvāra* is near a forested region or a river; it is heavily populated and comprises a royal palace; that which is found next to it is a *cerikā*.

Forts

10.36b–38 There are seven types of fort: the mountain fort, the forest fort, the water fort, the earth fort, the desert fort, the natural fort and the mixed fort. The mountain fort is built amidst mountains or on the side of a mountain or at its summit. The forest fort is situated in a dry place, hidden in a forest. The mixed fort unites the characteristics of the two preceding ones. The natural fort has only natural defences; the earth fort has (ramparts) of earth. The water fort is in the middle of a river or is in the sea. The desert fort is (situated in a place) devoid of trees and of water.

10.39–40a A fort should contain reserves of water, of food and of weapons; the ramparts are to be very big, very high and extremely thick; it should be impregnable at all points by virtue of its surrounding walls and it is guarded on all sides. Beyond the ramparts is a path, hidden in a forest, which is not waterlogged and is difficult of access.

10.40b–42a There are fortified gates with stairways, some visible and others secret. Their doors have double leaves and are provided with four bars, with bolts and with a one cubit high clamp. (These gatehouses) are provided with a kind of bretesse (*minṭhaka*) which rests in the centre on a pillar and access (to which) is by a secret stairway. These gateways are in the form of pavilion, hall or *śālā*.

10.42b–43 The enclosure walls may be built according to one of twelve layouts: square, circular, rectangular, elliptical, *nandyāvarta* shaped or shaped like a cock or like the temporal bone of an elephant or like a coiled snake or square with curved sides, triangular, octagonal or semi-circular.

10.44–46a Brick ramparts are at least twelve cubits high and are twice as high as thick; the wall has a passable road at its base; inside the ramparts are all kinds of war machines set up at elevated points. All around is a moat and on its earthen bank are towers connected (with the wall); and beyond, and all around this, is a camp.

10.46b–48a The fort is inhabited by people of diverse classes and contains the palace of the king. Present here are numerous elephants, horses, war-chariots and foot soldiers. It is abundantly provided with grain, oil and molasses, as with salt, medicaments, perfumes and poisons and with metals, charcoal, gut, ivory, bamboo and combustibles such as fodder and with leather, vegetables, barks and hard woods.

10.48b–49a A fort must be inaccessible, proof against attack and impregnable; it is constructed for defence and victory and must be impenetrable by enemies.

10.49b–50 Indra, Vāsudeva, Guha, Jayanta, Vaiśravaṇa, the Aśvin, Śrī and Madirā, Śiva, Durgā and Sarasvatī: these are the deities who are to be honoured within the walls and who should be borne in mind when a fort is built.

10.51a Such is the organization of forts as prescribed by the sages of old.

Town planning

10.51b I now present the plans of all (towns) one after another.

10.52–53 Streets which go from east to west number twelve, ten, eight, six, four or two and the same numbers are suitable for those which go from north to south. In odd numbers there are eleven, nine, seven, five, three or one streets (in each direction). According to whether the diagram is in even or odd numbers, the number of squares for Aja is two, three or one (?).

10.54–61 Streets are now indicated for all towns and cities. When there is one single street which is straight this is a *daṇḍaka* plan; if (this street), at its centre, crosses another coming from the north, this is a *kartaridaṇḍaka* plan. If there are two paved streets starting from the east, this is a *bāhudaṇḍaka* plan. If there are gates at the four cardinal points and a large number of paved streets on either side of the main street this is a *kuṭikāmu-khadaṇḍaka* plan which is otherwise as above. When there are three streets towards the east and three towards the north the sages say this is a *kalakābandhadaṇḍaka* plan. If there are three streets towards the east separated from each other by several alleys this is a *vedibhadra* plan suitable for all types of town. It should be known that the *svastika* plan is the same as for villages of that name; it comprises however, at most, six streets going east and six going north and, as has been mentioned above, the layout of the principal roads is that of a *svastika*.

10.62 When there are four streets going north, one around the place of Brahmā, and three paved streets towards the east it is a *bhadraka* plan which is suitable for all types of town.

10.63–70 When there are five streets going east and as many north as well as a large number of alleys this is a *bhadramukha* plan; when there are six streets going east and as many north as well as a large number of alleys this is a *bhadrakalyāṇa* plan. When there are seven streets from east to west and as many proceeding from the north, the rest being as above, this is a *mahābhadra* plan. When there are eight streets going east, eight north, twelve other streets and a great number of cul-de-sacs and alleys this is said to be a *vastusubhadra* plan. If a town comprises nine streets going east and nine north as well as gates, posterns, alleys and cul-de-sacs and a royal palace it is called *jayāṅga*. A town which comprises ten streets proceeding from the east and as many from the north, which contains a royal palace and where there are numerous alleys arranged according to the specific circumstances, such a town is named *vijaya* by the sages.

10.71–75a (In the *sarvatobhadra* plan) there are eleven streets from the east and eleven from the north; the king's palace is to be found, as is convenient, to the west of the place of Brahmā;

in front of it is a huge empty yard; the queen's dwelling (*antaḥpura*) is in the chosen place and all that remains is arranged as expedient. Streets which proceed (from the place of Brahmā in the centre) towards the north and east are the royal streets; on either side of these are *mālikā* houses intended for the royal retinue; beyond these (*mālikā*) and on both sides is the quarter of the merchants and to the south of that the quarter of the weavers whilst that of the potters is to the north and, beside this, the quarters for each of the lower castes. The rest is to be as ordained above; this is the *sarvatobhadra* disposition.

10.75b–76 Such are the sixteen varieties of town prescribed by the sages of old. A street should not be interrupted nor a crossroads established at the centre of a town plan. Anything which has not been laid down should be carried out by the sages in accordance with the wishes of the king.

Bazaars (fig. 8)

10.77–79 Now I lay down the disposition for inhabited quarters and for bazaars (*antarāpaṇa*) appropriate to all types of towns. On the periphery is the chariot road and inside it is the merchants' quarter; to the south of this is the weavers' quarter and to the north that of the potters; a great many other artisans are installed along that road.

10.80–86a A street encircles the place of Brahmā and it is there that the bazaar for betel and similar produce, for fruits and for articles of value should be installed. Between the square of Īśa and the Mahendra gate is the bazaar for meat, fish, (dried) products and for vegetables; between the Mahendra gate and the square of Agni is the bazaar for solid and liquid foods; the ironmongers are between the Agni square and that of Gṛhakṣata; between this last and that of Nirṛti are the coppersmiths; between the square of Pitṛ and that of Puṣpadanta is the clothing bazaar; between this last and the square of Samīraṇa is the bazaar for grains, rice and fodder. Between the square of Vāyu and that of Bhallāṭa is the bazaar for fabrics and materials of that kind and there is too the bazaar for foodstuffs such as salt and oil; between this and the square of Īśa is

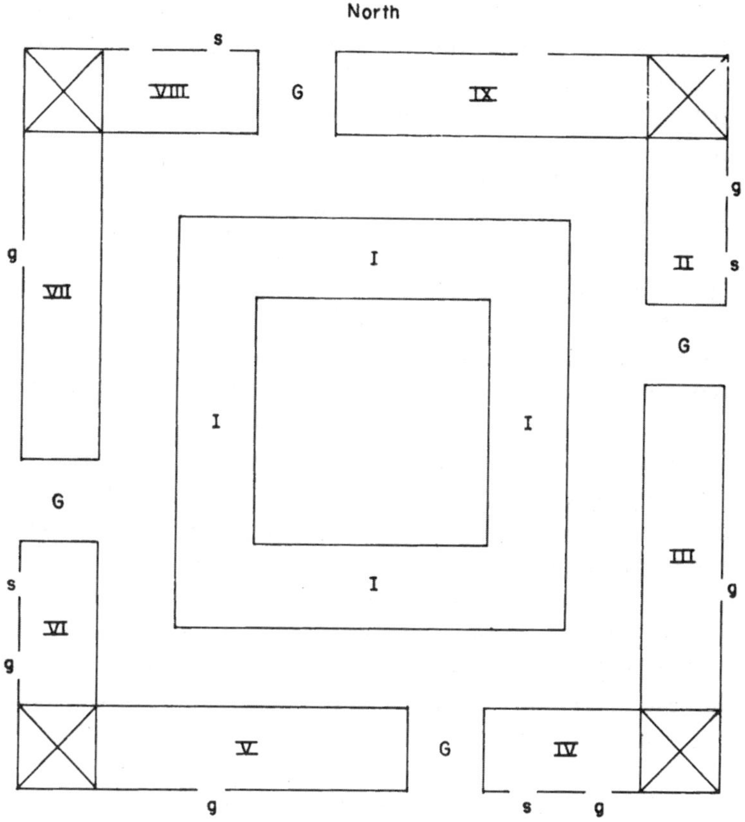

Fig. 8 Town layout (9.57 *et sq.* and 10.80 *et sq.*)

G: gates; *g*: small gates; *s*: sewage outlets.
Bazaars: I: betel, fruits and valuables; II: meat, fish and vegetables; III: solid and liquid foodstuff; IV: ironmongers; V: coppersmiths; VI: clothings; VII: grains, rice and fodder; VIII: fabrics, salt, oil . . . ; IX: flowers.

the bazaar for perfumes, flowers . . . etc. Such are the nine bazaars established in the centre and on the periphery (of the town).

10.86b–87 Along the streets leading to the centre is the bazaar where are found gems, gold, clothes, madder, black pepper, peepul seed and orpiment as well as honey, ghee, oil and medicaments.

10.88–90 Śāstṛ, Durgā and Lakṣmī should be worshipped

at the places, (respectively), of Ārya, Vivasvant, Mitra and Pṛthivīdhara. Beyond this the temples are placed all around as in a village. Houses for people of all castes are installed a little farther away. The caṇḍāla and kolika huts must be two hundred poles beyond the town to the east and south-west.

10.91 Everything not indicated here should be arranged as has been prescribed for villages. A *pattana* has one straight road where no bazaars are to be found; for all other (towns) the bazaars should be established according to each specific case.

10.92 *Sthānīya*, *durga*, *pura*, *pattana*, *kotmakolaka*, *droṇamukha*, *nigama* as well as *kheṭa*, *grāma* and *kharvaṭa*: these are the ten types of settlement established according to circumstance and they have been described by the sages of old.

10.93 The measurements, plans and streets suitable for villages and other settlements are described according to the Tantra. These are intended for the classes, the first of which is the brahmin class, and for inferior castes.

10.94 The generous prince gives land and cows to the tetrad led by the architect and practised in work such as measurement. If he does this without reservation, riches in abundance will be his and his realm will stretch to the moon and stars as long as the world shall endure.

Thus ends, in the *Mayamata*, treatise on dwelling, the tenth chapter: RULES FOR TOWNS.

Chapter 11

THE NUMBER OF STOREYS AND THE DIMENSIONS

11.1–3a Now I give in full, and systematically, the rules relating to the number of storeys. There are differences (between the buildings) due to the layout of the plan, according to whether it is square, rectangular, round, elliptical, octagonal, hexagonal or apsidal. (Other variations) are due to increases or diminutions (in the number of storeys) and this is called *bhūmilamba*.

11.3b–7a There are four (possible) widths for single storeyed buildings, starting from three or four cubits and increasing successively by two cubits. For two storeyed buildings there are four (possible) widths, from five or six cubits to eleven or twelve with successive increments of two cubits. There are five possible widths for three storeyed buildings, from seven or eight cubits to fifteen or sixteen by successive increments of two cubits. Going from nine or ten cubits to fifteen or sixteen there are four (possible) widths for four and five storeyed buildings and so on. Lastly, it is stated that a very small single storeyed building measures one or two cubits.

11.7b–8a Some say that in houses, divine or human, the measurements may be given in an odd or even number of cubits and that half a cubit may be added to or subtracted from (that prescribed number).

11.8b–9 The height is ten sevenths, nine sixths, eight fifths, seven fourths or six thirds the width (according to whether the buildings are of) *śāntika*, *pauṣṭika*, *jayada*, *adbhuta* or *sārvakāmika* (category); or, equally, the height may be double or one and a half times or one and a quarter times the width.

11.10–11 Buildings which are less than fifteen cubits wide are the "small" buildings. Going from seventeen or eighteen cubits to seventy by successive increments of two cubits, twenty-seven possible (widths) are obtained for buildings of four to twelve storeys with three (varieties for each of them).

11.12–13 Going from twenty-three or twenty-four cubits to one hundred by successive increments of three cubits, twenty-seven corresponding heights are obtained. This goes for the larger buildings of which there are three varieties: superior, medium and inferior.

11.14–16a Going from thirteen or fourteen cubits to sixty-five by successive increments of two cubits, the same number (of widths) as above is obtained for four to twelve storey buildings. Going from seventeen or eighteen cubits to ninety-five or ninety-six by successive increments of two cubits, the corresponding number of heights is obtained. There are three varieties (of each of these buildings which are medium sized): the superior, the medium and the inferior.

11.16b–17 Going from nine or ten cubits to fifty-five or fifty-six by successive increments of two cubits, twenty-four (possible) widths are obtained for buildings of five to twelve storeys (of inferior size).

11.18–19 He who is well versed in calculating proportions should construct buildings of (ten) to twelve storeys, with the aid of the proportions given for those which have seven, eight, or nine storeys. Temples with twelve, thirteen or, at most, sixteen storeys are, respectively, thirty-six, forty-two and fifty cubits wide and are consecrated to Śiva.

11.20 The width is to be measured along the exterior face of the pillars and the height from the base up to the finial, yet some say that the height is measured (only) up to the top of the roof.

11.21–22a The heights of large buildings have been given in cubits and they should be ten sevenths the corresponding widths. Where small buildings are concerned the rule to be followed is that their height is double their width.

11.22b–25 It is stated that buildings of up to twelve storeys are suitable for Sārvabhauma gods, those with eleven (at most) are for Rākṣasa, Gandharva and Yakṣa, those which have nine or ten (at most) are suitable for brahmins; fifthly, buildings with seven storeys are suitable for crown-princes and for kings; those which have from (seven) to eleven storeys are for universal monarchs; those which have three or four storeys are suitable for merchants and śūdra and, lastly, those with five storeys are for officers (*paṭṭabhṛt*).

11.26 Those who are knowers of the subject never plan constructions of more than one hundred cubits in height and seventy cubits in width.

11.27 I have expounded the different heights and widths fitting for very small, small, medium and large buildings according to the ancients; I have expressed these dimensions in different numbers of cubits and I have indicated for whom these buildings are intended according to the rule: that is, for the lords of the immortals of whom the first is Aja, and for men.

Thus ends, in the *Mayamata*, treatise on dwelling, the eleventh chapter: RULES FOR THE NUMBER OF STOREYS.

Chapter 12

THE FOUNDATION DEPOSIT

12.1–3a In few words, but precisely, I present the rules relating to the placing of the foundation deposit in the temples of gods and in the houses of brahmins and (other) classes. A foundation deposit provided with all the components prescribed is a source of success; an incomplete deposit or the absence of any one element leads to failure; this is why the foundation deposit should be set in place with the utmost care and without error.

12.3b–5 The depth of the pit (containing) the deposit must be equal to the height of the base of the building concerned. (The pit) is square and lined with bricks and stones. After it has been filled with water its bottom should be covered with every sort of earth: from a river, from a pond, from a wheat field, from a mountain, an anthill, a crab's hole, from the ploughshare, from the horn of a bull or of a buffalo and from an elephant's tusk.

12.6–8 Next should be arranged on that: a root of *padma* in the middle, one of *utpala* in the east, one of *kumuda* in the south, one of *saugandhi* in the west and one of *nīlaloha* in the north. The eight grains are placed above that: *śāli*, *vrīhi*, *kodrava*, *kaṅku*, *mudga*, *māṣa*, *kulattha* and *tila*; the arrangement is made according to the *pradakṣiṇa* taking *śāli* in the north-east as the starting point.

The casket

12.9–12 Over that is placed a copper casket; there are twelve possible widths for this receptacle, from three or four digits to twenty-five or twenty-six digits by successive increments of two digits. Its height is equal to its width, or less by an eighth, sixth or fifth. (These twelve sets of dimensions) are suitable for buildings of, respectively, one to twelve storeys. (Otherwise) the width of the casket is a third the height of the pillar of the building concerned or it is equal to the diameter of this pillar or to seven eighths or three quarters of that diameter; regarding the height (it is always calculated) as above.

12.13–15a The casket is shaped like a pavilion with three levels of elevation. It is circular or square and comprises twenty-five or nine compartments; the height of the partitions dividing (these last) is half or one third that of the casket; their thickness should be two, three or four barley grains' (*yava*). If it corresponds to the *upapīṭha* diagram then twenty-five gods are honoured therein.

Rites

12.15b–17 On the eve (of the day of the setting in place of the foundation deposit), the ground around the pit should be perfumed and incensed and lamps should be (arranged there). The casket should be washed in the mixture of the five products of the cow and it should be covered by braided threads. Then, when a *caṇḍita*—also called *maṇḍūka*—diagram has been drawn on the sacrificial ground which is covered with an even coat of rice, unhusked and pure, the gods, starting with Brahmā, are installed with an offering of hulled white rice.

12.18–19 Then the architect, in a whisper, invokes the Lord of the World, having propitiated Him with offerings of flowers, perfumes . . . etc. Pitchers are arranged next, all of them covered with linen, filled with pleasantly perfumed water, surrounded by fragrant flowers and not pierced or sullied and arranged five to a line.

12.20–21 On the diagram drawn with perfumed rice upon the sacrificial area, after flowers, perfumes . . . etc. have been scattered, an offering is made to the casket in a clockwise direction and according to rule. The casket is then wrapped in white cloth and the sage places it upon white linen on a spread of *darbha* grass.

12.22 Finally, after drinking pure water and fasting, the learned architect, the sage, honoured by the *sūtragrāhin* and his other assistants, settles himself for the night.

12.23–25a (Next day the architect) arranges the components in the casket, starting with the grains: the *śāli*, figured in gold, the *vrīhi* in silver, the *kulattha* in copper, the *kaṅku* in tin, the *māṣa* in lead, the *mudga* in iron, the *kodrava* in iron and the *tila* in mercury; the placing of the grains is to be done with care in the given order to the eight directions beginning with that of Īśa (in the north-east).

12.25b–27a (Next) cinnabar is put on the square of Jayanta, on that of Bhṛśa orpiment, on that of Vitatha red arsenic, on that of Bhṛṅgarāja red chalk, on that of Sugrīva lapis lazuli, on that of Śoṣa hematite, on that of Gaṇamukhya antimony and on that of Uditi red copper.

12.27b–29 In the centre should be a ruby, on the square of Marīci coral, on that of Savindra a topaz, on that of Vivasvant a tiger's eye; a diamond is prescribed for the square of Indrajaya, for that of Mitraka an *indranīla* sapphire, for that of Rudrarāja a *mahānīla* sapphire, for that of Mahīdhara an emerald, and a pearl for that of Āpavatsa; these are all to be placed in the inner (squares of the diagram) starting at the centre and proceeding towards the east . . . etc.

12.30–32a On (the eight squares corresponding to the cardinal and intermediate directions), beginning with that of Īśa, the medicinal plants are arranged: *viṣṇukrāntā*, *triśūlā*, *śrī*, *sahā*, *dūrvā*, *bhṛṅgaka*, *apāmārga* and *ekapatrābja*. Then, on the (squares of the gods) beginning with Jayanta the eight fragrant plants are arranged: sandalwood, bdellium, camphor, clove, cardamon, *latāphala*, *takkola* and *inā*. Lastly, *svastika*, in gold, iron, copper and silver, should be placed at the cardinal points.

12.32b What has been given is fitting for all gods but each one has his specific attributes (which will now be presented).

Foundation deposit for the Śiva temple

12.33–35 (The following attributes) should be placed in the main directions beginning with the east: skull, trident, *khaṭvāṅga*, axe, bull, bow, gazelle and noose. The eight auspicious objects in gold should be placed according to the same disposition: mirror, vase of abundance, bull, double fly-whisk, *śrīvatsa*, *svastika*, conch and lamp; the wise architect arranges these eight divine objects according to the directions of the *sthāpaka*.

12.36–41a Then, the perfect and solid casket having been closed with a lid, propitiatory offerings of perfumes and other things having been made, the lid should be purified with water from the pitchers. Next, whilst the brahmins whisper the Veda, whilst conches and drums sound and cries of joy and victory are raised, the architect, accompanied by the *sthāpaka*, the five parts of his body adorned with flowers, ear-rings, necklace, bracelets and rings, having donned the sacred thread of gold, dressed in new clothes, anointed with white (paste), head covered with white flowers, and purified, must first meditate upon the surface of the Earth in Her wholeness, for it is She who supports the elephants who are lords of the cardinal points and who, together with the ocean and the lords of the mountains, rests upon Ananta; then, in a murmur he invokes the Lord of the World, responsible for creation, preservation and destruction.

12.41b–43a The deposit is placed according to rule in a hole beneath a pillar to the right of the door (of the shrines) of Brahmā and other gods and goddesses; it must be under the *homastambha* and below the plinth or under the *pratistambha* and below the stereobate (*prati*); if it is placed too high or too low in relation (to plinth or stereobate) it will be a source of misfortune.

12.43b–46a Above the casket a slab should be set, made of wood or stone, twice as wide as the casket, five digits thick and bearing images. Above this is installed a pillar held up by four bricks, ornamented with precious stones and plants and decorated with fabrics, flowers . . . etc. The foundation deposit of (the temple of) Īśa having been described, those (of the shrines) of other divinities will now be given.

Deposit for the temple of Viṣṇu

12.46b–48a The deposit for the Viṣṇu shrine comprises a discus in gold in the centre as well as a conch, a bow, a mace and a sword, (all) in gold; the bow and the conch are to the left, the sword and the mace to the right; Vainateya in gold should be placed in the front.

Deposit for the shrine of Brahmā

12.48b–51 There is a sacrificial thread, Om, *svastika*, and an image of Fire, all in gold, as well as a lotus, a flask and a rosary of *darbha*, (these last) in copper. At the centre the lotus should be set down at the place of Brahmā's throne and, in its centre, Om encircled by the sacrificial thread; the *svastika* are at the cardinal points, the flask and the rosary of *kuśa* to the left and the burning fire is in front. Such is the deposit for Brahmā to be put at the place of Brahmā.

Deposit for Ṣaṇmukha

12.52–53 The foundation deposit for the dwelling of Ṣaṇmukha comprises *svastika*, rosary, spear, discus, cock and peacock in gold; the spear, in iron, is in the middle, the cock to the left. the peacock to the right and the rosary in front.

Deposits for other Attendants

12.54–58 The foundation deposit for the temple of Savitṛ (i.e. Sūrya) (comprises) an *ambuja*, an elephant goad, a noose and a lion. That for the temple of Vajrin (Indra) comprises a thunderbolt, an elephant, a sword, a discus and a fly-whisk. That for the shrine of Pāvaka (Agni) comprises a ram in Jambu gold and a spear; that of Yama, a water buffalo in iron and a noose in gold; the deposit for the shrine of Nirṛti comprises a sword in iron; that of Varuṇa a *makara* in copper and a noose in gold; a black gazelle in gold should be placed for Vāyu and a *vyāla* for the consort of Tārā (i.e. Bṛhaspati). The image of a man is prescribed for the temple of Naravāha (i.e. Kubera) and that of a *makara* for the shrine of Madana. For the dwelling of Vighneśa there should be an axe and an ivory rosary; for Āryaka (i.e. Hariharaputra) there should be Om and a crooked stick (*vakradaṇḍa*) in gold.

12.59–60 The foundation deposit for the shrine of Sugata (i.e. Buddha) comprises an *aśvattha*, a vase, a lion and an umbrella in gold; the *aśvattha* should be in front, the umbrella above it, the vase to the left and the lion to the right.

12.61–63 The deposit for the shrine of Jina comprises a *śrīvatsa*, an *aśoka*, a lion, a flask, a rosary, a peacock's tail in gold, a triple umbrella, a *karaka* vase and a gold fan; the (*aśoka*) tree must be in front and the umbrella above (it), the tail (of the peacock) to the right and the rosary together with the flask to the left; in the centre is the *śrīrūpa* and the lion; the *karaka* vase and the fan are to the left.

12.64–66 The sage must arrange the deposit for the shrine of Durgā in the following way: a parrot and a discus in gold, a lion and a conch in silver, a gazelle in copper and an iron sword. For Kṣetrapāla there are *khaṭvaṅga*, sword, and spear in gold. For Lakṣmī there should be a *padma*, for Sarasvatī Om in three letters. In the deposit for the shrine of Jyeṣṭhā there should be a standard featuring a crow, and an *utpala* in gold.

12.67–69 In the Kālī temple should be placed (images of) *preta* as well as a skull, a trident and a bell. In the shrine of the Mothers there should be gold images of *haṃsa*, bull, peacock, Garuḍa, lion, elephant and *preta*. The deposit for the shrine of Rohiṇī comprises a rosary and a lamp and it is known that in the shrine of Pārvatī there must be a mirror and a rosary and, in that of Mohinī, a lotus rosary and a vase of abundance.

12.70 For gods and goddesses who have not been mentioned, the foundation deposit is to comprise umbrellas, standards and emblems with the attributes of the gods and images of their mounts.

Specific deposits for human dwellings

12.71–73 Now the specific foundation deposits are given for castes, brahmins and others. The deposit fitting for brahmins comprises a *karaka* vase and a tooth stick, one in copper, the other in gold, as well as a sacred thread, the sacrificial fire and the utensils for sacrifice, all in silver. The thread is in the centre, the utensils to the right and the vase to the left; the tooth-stick and the fire are in front and there are *svastika* at the cardinal points.

12.74–77 (The deposit proper to kṣatriya) should comprise a gold discus in the centre, to the left a silver conch and copper bow, to the right a gold mace and iron sword; four elephants are in the four directions in, respectively, gold, iron, copper and silver; there is (as well) in the middle a gold *śrīrūpa* and regalia at the four cardinal points: umbrella, standard, emblem and sceptre. This deposit should be put in place at the royal gate (if for a king); for other people it should be placed where suitable. If it is a deposit pertaining to Pārṣṇeyaka it must be to the right (or to the south) of the Vijaya gate.

12.78–80a For vaiśya a ploughshare is prescribed, a conch in iron, a small copper crab, the five weapons (of Viṣṇu) and a bean in lead; there is a horse, an elephant, a bull and a lion on the squares of Arka, Agni, Varuṇa and Indu, respectively; four silver cows are disposed at the cardinal points and a bull in the east.

12.80b–82 The deposit proper to śūdra is equally suitable for vaiśya; it comprises a seed bowl, a gold plough and a copper yoke but it should be known that there is a silver cow at each of the cardinal points and, in the centre, a bull in front of which is the yoke. The plough is to the right with the seed bowl and the seeds are in gold.

12.83–84 The foundation deposit proper to (each) of the main buildings of a house and that proper to the caste must be mixed. The dwellings with several storeys . . . (?).[1] In the four main buildings (of a house) starting with that in the north, the foundation deposit must be on the squares of Puṣpadanta, Bhallāṭaka, Mahendra and Gṛhakṣata, under the wall of the facade to the right of the door.

12.85–87 In a *mahānasa* (i.e. *annālaya*)[2] an earthenware vase with its lid should be put, either beneath the pillar to the right of the door or under the right jamb, and with it *dārvika*, rice, a plane, a sieve, a tooth stick and an iron image of the fire. The deposit of the building located in the south (i.e. *dhānyālaya*) is

1. The half-verse 83b seems to be out of place.
2. See below 27.18sq (p. 238).

a ladle filled with cooked rice. The deposit of the *dhanasadman* (i.e. *dhanālaya*) must be a key and a bolt. The *sukhālaya* deposit is to comprise a bed, a lamp and a seat.

12.88 It is the activity performed in a building which is to determine the deposit peculiar to that building and it is objects characteristic of that activity which are to be put here.

12.89–90 In a hall (*sabhā*), in a light building (*prapā*) and in a pavilion, the foundation deposit is placed beneath the corner to the south or beneath the second pillar to the right of the door or beneath the right door jamb. It comprises an iron elephant and a grain of *kodrava*; in the centre of the container gold images of Lakṣmī and Sarasvatī should be placed.

12.91–92a The foundation deposit for a theatre (*raṅga*) is placed beneath the apse (*kuṭikā*) or at the base of the *maṇḍita-stambha* (?) or in both places; it consists of all kinds of instruments in every type of metal.

12.92b–95a The deposit for the hall intended for the *hemagarbha* ceremony should comprise a *śrīvatsa*, a lotus and a vase of abundance in gold; it must be inserted beneath the door jamb or beneath the corner pillar, as given above, and this goes as well for the *tulābhāra* pavilion. The deposit appropriate for dwellings of members of a heterodox sect is constituted of the attributes of that sect and, for all inferior castes, it is that by which each is characterized which makes up the foundation deposit.

12.95b If the wife of the master of the house is pregnant (*garbhiṇī*) the foundation deposit (*garbha*) should not be laid in place.

12.96–97 Precious stones and other elements must be arranged in a smaller container by those who are well acquainted with the position of the gods (in diagrams). If the deposit is to the right of the door, or of the bedroom of the house-owner, it must face inwards; if in the centre it must be orientated towards the exterior.

Formula for foundation ceremony

12.98 The architect must install the foundation deposit correctly according to the rules given above and after pronouncing the following formula, facing east or north. Here is the formula:

"Glory to the formulae and to the deities which are their letters! Glory to the Lord of all Jewels! Homage to supreme Prajāpati giver of all truth! Homage to Śrī! Homage to Sarasvatī! Homage to Vaivasvata! Homage to Vajrapāṇi! Homage to the eternally youthful Destroyer of all obstacles! Glory and Homage to Vahni!"

Deposits for wells . . . etc.

12.99–100 In the case of a reservoir, well, tank, pond or bridge there should be disposed, to the north or to the east, in a hole the size of two cupped hands, a bowl and a fish as well as a frog, a crab, a snake, and a *makara* in gold.

The first bricks

12.101–104a The foundation deposit should be laid in place in the evening at a favourable moment, during an auspicious conjunction, at the time and part of the day appropriate, and the four first bricks during the day. In every place where there is a foundation deposit there must be four first bricks. These have to be put in place with earths, roots, grains, (grains figured in) metals, colouring (substances), gems, medicinal plants, fragrant plants and specific elements (*bīja*). In a stone house (the first bricks) are to be stones whilst bricks are suitable for a brick house. Each one should be as wide as the foundation deposit casket, twice as long as wide and half as thick as wide.

12.104b–108a No matter what the building, there are at least four first bricks but if it is medium or large there must be eight or twelve. A male (brick) has rectilinear sides the length of which is an odd number of digits and, in the case of a female brick, this number is even; a neuter brick has curved sides. These bricks must be pleasant to the touch and well baked; they must give off a pleasing sound and be of attractive appearance. They should be used in male, female and neuter buildings respectively and should, in the case of a restoration, be of the same nature as those that were previously there. The first stones must be flawless, without rough patches and without grooves.

12.108b–110 To start with, the first of the four bricks should be placed beneath the *jhaṣāla(-stambha)* but in a temple (*vimāna*) it should be placed beneath the *nikhātāṅgri* and on top of the foundation deposit.[1] For gods and brahmins the architect is to install the first brick to the south-east and then proceed clockwise to the other corners.

12.111 Some say that the first brick is to be placed in a pit lined with bricks (etc. . .) the depth of which is not to exceed two fifths (of the width?); it is to be put in the appropriate place by one clad in new clothes as mentioned above.

12.112 When all is auspicious: the day, the fortnight, the planets, the time and the moment, the sage first of all arranges in the casket the images, the medicinal plants, the glittering gems, the eight metals such as gold (. . . etc.), the eight colouring substances such as antimony. Then, at night, the earths, the roots and the eight grains are installed at the bottom of the pit. Then, in the morning, after making an offering to the casket according to the rituals, he installs the foundation deposit in water.

12.113–114 After the foundation deposit has been laid in place, at daybreak, complete and in conformity with the ritual, at the bottom of a pillar or of a door jamb, depending on whether a divine or human dwelling is involved, the pillar or the jamb should be installed exactly above the foundation deposit and in conformity with the rule. They must be perfect and strong. The architect is to put the jamb or the pillar in place after they have been purified with water from twenty-five vases covered with new cloth and with (paste) of white sandal and provided with all the beneficent objects.

Thus ends, in the *Mayamata*, treatise on dwelling, the twelfth chapter: PLACING THE FOUNDATION DEPOSIT.

1. *Jhaṣālastambha, nikhātāṅghri*: see below 15.9–11a (p. 71).

Chapter 13
THE SOCLE

13.1–3 The socle (*pīṭha*) is to be placed beneath the base to make (the building) higher, more solid and more beautiful. Its height depends on that set for the base; it is equal to the latter or is three quarters, half or two fifths of it or it may be one and a half, one and three quarters or twice it.

13.4–5 The projection of the socle in relation to the plinth of the base may be from one to five tenths of its height or it may be one module (*daṇḍa*) or one and a half or two or three modules or it may be equal to the projection of the plinth of the base in relation to the pillars (of the ground floor of the building). There are three categories of socle (given as) *vedibhadra*, *pratibhadra* and *subhadra*.

Vedibhadra socles

13.6–8 The height (of the socle) is divided into twelve (equal) parts: the plinth takes up two parts, a doucine one and the fillet which tops this (doucine) one half, the dado five, a fillet one half and a doucine one; the remainder is for the upper string-course and the fillet (which surmounts it). Such a socle has eight mouldings, or six if the upper and lower doucines are omitted. There are thus two sorts of *vedibhadra* socle suitable for all buildings.

Pratibhadra socles

13.9–11 The height (of the first *pratibhadra* socle) from plinth to string-course is divided into twenty-seven (equal) parts. The plinth takes up two parts, a doucine two, a fillet one, the dado twelve, (the fillet) which tops the dado one, a doucine one, the dripstone three, and a fillet and a groove one each; the upper string-course takes up two parts and its top-fillet one.

A socle like this, furnished with all these mouldings, is called *pratibhadra*.

13.12–14 (The height of) the second *pratibhadra* socle (is divided into) one part more (than the height of the first one). The plinth takes up two parts, the doucine three, a fillet one, and a groove one; the (lower) string-course takes up two parts, a fillet one, the dado eight and the (fillet) which tops it one; a doucine takes up one part, a dripstone three, a fillet one, a groove one, a fillet one, the (upper) string-course two and the fillet which tops it one.

Subhadra socles

13.15–17a The height (of the socle) is divided into twenty-one (equal) parts: the plinth takes up two, as does the doucine (which surmounts it); a groove takes up one half, a doucine one half, the string-course two; a doucine takes up one half, as does the fillet which tops it; the dado takes up eight parts, the (fillet) which surmounts it one, a doucine half a part, the dripstone three and the top fillet one half. This is a *subhadra* socle.

13.17b–19a The second type of *subhadra* socle should have the following mouldings: a plinth with a height of two parts, a doucine of three parts, a groove of one part, a string-course of two parts and a fillet of one; the dado should have a height of eight parts, a fillet of one, the superior string-course two and the top fillet one.

13.19b–20 In all buildings, whether or not provided with an aisle, the face of the string-course (*prati*) is to be decorated with lions, elephants, *makara*, *vyāla*, dwarves, leaves (etc.) or with fish on whose heads ride infants.

13.21 The sages say that (the dimensions) of all the mouldings of the socle should be increased or diminished to bring them into proportion with those of the base.

13.22 The height of the socle is double or one and half times that of the base or is equal to it, or it is half, three quarters or two fifths, two thirds or one third of it. If however the socle is surmounted by a stereobate (its height) is equal to that of the base and the socle is to comprise a large upper string-course. In order that the socle be stable the wise man builds it upon all the proper elements.

Thus ends, in the *Mayamata*, treatise on dwelling, the thirteenth chapter: RULES FOR SOCLES.

Chapter 14
THE BASE

Preparing the ground

14.1–4a For the building of houses of gods, brahmins and (other) classes there are two sorts of ground suitable, dry (*jāṅgala*) and moist (*ānūpa*). "Dry" terrain is well supplied with gravel, hard to dig and (when it is dug) rich in water clear as the moon. The terrain is "moist" when the foundations, dug to the dimensions of the projected building, reveal open blue lotuses and withered cucumbers along with white sand.

14.4b–8 After water has been reached the trench should be filled with bricks, earth and fine sand and packed tight so that there are no gaps, then, when this has been stamped down by the trampling of elephants as well as with large logs of hard wood, the sage, after having filled up the (remaining) hollow with water which, (if the enterprise is) to be successful, it will retain, must verify the horizontality of the ground with this water. Next the foundation deposit should be laid down according to rule and, lastly, the adjustment slab (*homa*) should be set in place; this is two or three times as wide as a pillar and its thickness is half its width. Above this slab (*upāna*) is a lotus and a secondary slab, the proportions of which are imposed upon the sage by the harmony.

14.9–11a The regulating course (*upāna*) called "origin" (*janman*) should be laid down after the original ground has been raised one cubit and has been rendered compact. Directly above this is the base (*adhiṣṭhāna*) unless there is a socle (beneath it); above the base is the (so-called) "level of the pillars" (*jaṅghāvarga*) which is made up of pillars or of a wall. The height of (the ground floor) is the same as that of the stereobate which is above the dripstone (of the base).

14.11b–16 The base is that upon which buildings such as temples rest. Its height may be determined in two ways, according to the number of the storeys (of the building) or to the caste. For the gods that height is four cubits, for brahmins it is three and a half cubits, for kings three cubits, for crown princes two and a half, for merchants two and, lastly, for śūdra, one cubit. Such are the heights of the base according to caste. Herewith these, (calculated) according to the number of storeys, starting with a height of one pole (i.e. four cubits) for the base of a building with twelve storeys and decreasing by six digits (for each storey less) down to buildings with three storeys, the largest of which have a base one and three quarter cubits high. Another method of calculating the height of the base is indicated by the sages for smaller buildings: this height should be equal to half that of the corresponding pillar less a sixth or an eighth. Such is the height of the base calculated according to the number of the storeys of the building.

14.17–18a The sage will make the projection of the plinth (of the base) one third less than the projection of the regulating course; the projection of the torus and the string-course and the recess of the dado are equal (to the projection of the plinth).

14.18b The number of parts into which the given height (of a base) should be divided and how they should be distributed is now indicated.

Pādabandha base

14.19–20 The height (of the base) is divided into twenty-four parts: the plinth takes up eight parts, the torus seven, a fillet one, the dado three, a fillet one, the upper string-course three and its two flanking fillets one. Such is the *pādabandha* base which is prescribed by the sages for buildings intended for brahmins, kings, vaiśya and śūdra.

Uragabandha base

14.21–22 (The height of the base) is divided into eighteen

1. The description of this base starts from the top and not from the bottom as is usual.

equal parts: the top-fillet takes up one part, the upper string-course two, a champfered fillet one, a talon (?) three, the well rounded torus six and the plinth five. This is an *uragabandha* base which, furnished as it is with two string-courses, resembles a serpent's mouth (?); it is suitable for the palaces of gods, brahmins and kings.

Pratikrama base

14.23–24 The height of the base is divided into twenty-one (equal) parts: the false plinth takes up one part, a doucine one and a half and a fillet one half; the main plinth takes up seven parts, the torus six, its talon one, and two flanking fillets one each; the upper string-course takes up two parts and its fillet, decorated with lotuses, one. Such a base, decorated with images, elephants, *makara*, *vyāla* (. . . etc.), is called *pratikrama* and is appropriate for temples and, when decorated with foliage and creepers, is suitable for the houses of brahmins and kings, bringing happiness, prosperity and victory.

Padmakesara base

14.25–26 (The height of the base) is divided into twenty-six (equal) parts: the (first) plinth takes up one part, a doucine two, a (second) plinth one, a (second) doucine six, a groove one, a (third) doucine one, a reed one, a (fourth) doucine four, a fillet one and a groove one; a string-course takes up two parts, a fifth doucine one, the upper string-course two, a (sixth) doucine one and the top fillet one. Such is the *padmakesara* base which is furnished with fillets, string-courses and doucines as well as with torus, plinth and grooves; it is prescribed for the temple of Śambhu.

Puṣpapuṣkala base

14.27–28 The height of the base is divided into nineteen parts: the (false) plinth takes up one part, the (main) plinth five, a doucine one, a groove one half, a doucine one half, the torus which comes next four; then, a doucine takes up half a part, a fillet one half, a small dado two, a fillet one half, a doucine one half, a string-course two and the row of leaves which surmounts it one half and, lastly, the top-fillet takes up half a part. Such a base, furnished with several doucines, is called *puṣpapuṣkala* and is prescribed by the foremost amongst the artisans for medium and large temples.

Śrībandha base

14.29–30 The height (of the base) is divided into thirty-two parts: the false plinth takes up two parts, a doucine one, the main plinth seven, a (second) doucine one, a third (doucine) one, a (fourth) doucine four, a groove one, a talon (*dhara*) one, a dado three, a fillet one, a row of leaves one, the dripstone four and each or the two fillets which flank it one; the upper string-course takes up two parts and the top-fillet one. This base, furnished with several doucines, is called *śrībandha.* It must be established by an able *vardhaki*, is suitable for the palaces of gods and kings and brings good health and prosperity.

Mañcabandha base

14.31 The height of the base is divided into twenty-six equal parts: the false plinth (*khura*) takes up one part and the main plinth six, a doucine above that takes up five parts, a fillet one, the dado three, another fillet one, a doucine one, the dripstone three and the groove topping it one and a fillet one; the upper string-course (*vaktra*) and the two top-fillets take up one part. Such is the *mañcabandha* base which should be used for the palaces of gods and of kings.

Śrīkānta base

14.32 When the base is furnished with a projecting fillet together with a groove and an (upper) string-course (?) which has no top-fillet, it is called *śrīkānta*; its torus is octagonal or rounded and it is suitable for the denizens of the sky.

Śreṇībandha base

14.33 The height of the base is divided into twenty-six (equal) parts: the small plinth takes up one part, a doucine two and a fillet one; the main plinth above that takes up six parts, the torus four, a fillet one, a groove two, a fillet one, a doucine two, a fillet one, a groove two, a fillet one, a doucine one and a half and the top fillet one. This *śreṇībandha* base is appropriate only for gods.

Padmabandha base

14.34 The height of the base is divided into eighteen (equal) parts: the plinth takes up one and a half parts, a small (fillet) one half, a doucine five, a talon one, a doucine three, a reed one, a doucine one and a fillet, above that, one. Then, a fillet which is below (the string-course) takes up one part, the upper string-course two and the top fillet one. Such is the *padmabandha* base which should be used by the sages for the houses of the principal gods without there being any error.

Vaprabandha base

14.35 (The height of the base) is divided into twenty-two equal parts: the small plinth takes up two parts, a doucine and the fillet which tops it one each. The main plinth takes up five parts, the torus four, a doucine one, a fillet one, a recessed strip two, a fillet one, a doucine one, the upper string-course two and the fillet which tops it one. Such is the *vaprabandha* base.

Kapotabandha base

14.36a When the torus is well rounded and when there is a dripstone at the top of the base it is a *kapotabandha* base.

Pratibandha base

14.36b When the upper string-course and the top fillet

together take up four parts and when the torus resembles a champfered string-course the base is called *pratibandha*.

Kalaśa base

14.37 (The height of the base) is divided into twenty-four (equal) parts: the plinth (*khura*) takes up one part, a doucine two, a fillet one, the dado three, another fillet one, a (second) doucine two, a (third) fillet one, a (third) doucine two, a groove one, a fourth doucine one, a reed two, a row of leaves one, a groove one and each of the fillets which flank it one; the upper string-course takes up two parts and the top fillet one. Such a base is called *kalaśa*.

Characteristics common to all bases

14.38–39 Such, with their characteristics, are the fourteen varieties of base prescribed by the sages. If expedient, any one of them may be provided with small pillars and false dormer-windows and the elements which I have indicated may be reinforced. In order to make the base more solid the wise man should add or subtract (to the proportions indicated) one part or half, three quarters or one quarter of a part, or (he should add or subtract) two digits, one and a half digits or one half or one quarter of a digit. If the whole is to be harmonious it is essential that the proportions of the base be related to those of the building, whether it is large, medium, small or very small; thus affirm the ancients who had mastered their passions, whose intelligence was unrivalled and who were well versed in the Tantra.

Synonyms

14.40 *Masūraka*, *adhiṣṭhāna*, *vastvādhāra*, *dharātala*, *tala*, *kuṭṭima* and *ādyaṅga* are synonyms (whose meaning is base).

Dimensions of projections

14.41–44 The projection of the torus (*kumuda*) is as great as that of the plinth (*jagati*); that of doucines is always equal to their height; that of the top of the row of leaves is a quarter or an eighth of the row's height; that of the string-course is equal to its height or to three quarters of it. The projection and recess of all mouldings are to be calculated according to the rule which has been given above or according to the appearance and solidity sought.

Rule for the interruption of the stereobate

14.45–46 In no case should the sage interrupt the stereobate (*prati*) (which tops the base). If the stereobate is interrupted for the sake of establishing a door, the door will be inauspicious but, if necessary, the *pādabandha* base may be interrupted above any one of its five (main) mouldings from the plinth onwards. This is not to be done however on a base comprising a stereobate.

14.46½ The wise man will place where prescribed that which is prescribed.

14.47 The height of the base is half that of the pillars or it is equal to that half, less a sixth, seventh or eighth. Such is to be the height of the base for all types of building; it is precisely this that was prescribed by Śambhu in ancient times.

Thus ends, in the *Mayamata* treatise on dwelling, the fourteenth chapter: RULES FOR BASES.

Chapter 15

DIMENSIONS OF PILLARS AND CHOICE OF MATERIALS

PILLARS

15.1 I now present, along the lines of the other treatises but fully and in ordered fashion, the heights of the pillars, their diameter, form, decoration . . . etc.

15.2 *Sthāṇu*, *sthūṇa*, *pāda*, *jaṅghā*, *caraṇa*, *aṅghrika*, *stambha*, *talipa* and *kampa* are all synonymous (and designate pillars).

Dimensions of pillars

15.3–5a The ground floor pillars of a twelve storey building are eight and a half cubits high; by subtracting one span for each storey a height of three cubits is obtained for the pillars of the top storey. The height of a pillar may otherwise be calculated from a given height: it is double that of the corresponding base but the Svayambhū(-āgama) ordains that the height of a pillar be more than double that (of the base).[1]

15.5b–8 The diameter of the ground floor pillars (of a twelve storey building) is twenty-eight digits; by subtracting two digits for each storey six digits are obtained (for the diameter of the pillars of) the top-storey. The diameter of a pillar may otherwise be one tenth, one ninth, or one eighth of its height; that of the pilaster is half, two thirds or three quarters (that of the pillar). It is said, as well, that the thickness of the wall is twice or three, four, five or six times (the diameter of the pilaster). It is said that the *homa* (?) which are above the plinth project all around the pillars (which rest on them) (?)

1. The *Svāyambhuvāgama* is one of the main canonical texts (*mūlāgama*) of the śaiva school.

Different types of pillars

15.9 The *pratistambha* rises from the stereobate, (which tops the base), up to the architrave. The part of the (*nikhāta*)-*stambha* above the plinth (of the base and below its summit) is equal to a third of the height of the pillar.

15.10a After a deep excavation has been made the nature of the soil should be determined (?).

15.10b–11a It is said that a "pillar (whose bottom) is concealed" (*nikhātastambha*) rises from the plinth of the base up to the architrave. It is said that a *jhaṣālastambha* rises from the base up to the architrave.

15.11b–12 The diameter of a pillar at its summit is from a sixth to a twelfth less than at its bottom. (It is also said) that the diameter of a ground floor pillar of a twelve storey building is a sixth of the height of that pillar and that the same relation exists between the height and the diameter of the pillars (of the) upper (storeys).

15.13–16 A pillar whose section is square (from) top (to bottom) and which is provided with a bell capital and an abacus is called *brahmakānta*; if it is octagonal it is called *viṣṇukānta*; if it is hexagonal it is called *indrakānta* and if it is sixteen sided, *saumya*. If a pillar is double section, square at the bottom and octagonal, sixteen sided or circular above, it is called *pūrvāśra* (but) it is called *rudrakānta* if it has a bell capital and an abacus and if it is completely circular. If the median part is twice as high as it is wide and is octagonal section, if (the upper and lower parts) are square and if there is neither bell capital nor abacus it is referred to as a pillar "octagonal in the middle".

15.17a The *rudracchanda* pillar comprises three equal parts, one square, one octagonal and one circular.

15.17b–19 The width of a lotiform base of pillar is one and a half or two modules or twice its height. The upper part (of a *bhadraka* pillar) is of whatsoever form desired or it comprises an abacus (and is) decorated with *cakravāka* (birds); it has a lotiform base at the bottom and projecting elements on its median part; this is a *bhadraka* (pillar) which may be without an abacus.

15.20–22a A pillar which, no matter what the form of its upper part, is decorated from the bottom up with *vyāla* or elephants, lions, dwarves (etc. . . .), bears the name of its decoration. Correspondingly then, that decorated throughout its height with protomes of elephants and which is provided with bell capital and abacus is called 'pillar with protomes' (*śuṇḍapāda*), that decorated with pearls throughout its height is called *piṇḍipāda*.

15.22b–26a A pillar of the *citrakhaṇḍa* type has a square element at the top two modules high beneath which is an octagonal element with a doucine-like profile half a module high; beneath that again is a sixteen sided element one module high and next a (second) doucine profile, as above, then a square section median band one module high, then a (third) doucine profile and a (second) sixteen sided element as above; at the bottom, the remaining part of the height is occupied by a square element. If the median band is octagonal section then the pillar is called *śrīkhaṇḍa* and if it is sixteen sided the pillar is called *śrīvajra*.

15.26b–27a If the upper part of the pillar is square section and if there is a projecting triple band the pillar is known as a *kṣepaṇastambha* and its triple band is decorated with leaves etc. . . .

15.27b At the summit and at the bottom of the pillar is a tenon a third or a quarter as wide (as the pillar).

15.28a All pillars are provided with a bracket capital and ornamented with various images.

Definition of the module

15.28b–29a The module (*daṇḍa*) is the width of the top of the pillar and it is according to this module that all the measurements of every element of a building are to be taken.

Bell capital

15.29b–30 Herewith, in order, the names of the (various)

bell capitals (with their heights): *śrīkara* is one and a quarter (modules) high, *candrakānta* one and a half, *saumukhya* one and three quarters and *priyadarśana* one half.

15.31 Starting at the top of the pillar, there are successively: the bracket capital (*potikā*), the dye (featuring a human figure), the abacus (*maṇḍī*), the bell capital (*kumbha*), the support (*skandha*), the doucine and the band ornamented with garlands (*mālāsthāna*).

15.32–34a The height of the bell capital being divided into nine parts, the astragal (*dṛk?*) takes up one part, the bell four, a groove one, a band with masks one, a doucine one, a reed half a one and the double *hīra*(?) half a one. The diameter of the double *hīra* is the same as that of the pillar and that of the band with masks is double that; the diameter of the bell is double (that of the pillar).

15.34b–39a The diameter of the abacus is double (that of the pillar) or can be four, three and a half or three modules. (The abacus) is three modules high and its height is divided into three (equal) parts: the upper connecting element occupies one, as do the reed and the inverted doucine; this abacus is in the form of a serpent's jaws; from the reed (downwards) its form is that of the pillar. The dye featuring a human figure is a support (?), its width is the same as that of the pillar and it is always square section no matter what the pillar. The support is a quarter the height of the dye (or may be) one module high; the doucine below it is half that height and the band ornamented with garlands is one module high and one module (wide) (?).

Bracket capital

15.39b–42 The bracket capital (*potikā*) is the width of the pillar and is as high as wide; the largest is five modules long and the smallest three; the medium is four or three and a quarter modules long or four and three quarter modules. These measurements multiplied by four give (the total height) of pillars comprising an abacus and a bell capital whilst, multiplied by three, they give the height of pillars lacking these elements. The selected height should be used for all the pillars (of any one storey of a building).

15.43–47 The top of the bracket capital is a string-course a third or a quarter its height and whose overhang is half, two thirds or three quarters (its width). The height of that part of the bracket capital which is decorated with waves is a third or a quarter (that of the bracket capital); this element is provided with a median band, slightly projecting and decorated with foliage; the height of the waves is invariably constant but they grow progressively narrower (starting from the centre). (The element which is decorated with the waves) has, at its ends, a projection, half or one third of its width, which is in the form of the tail of a *makara* and surmounts a fist-like decoration (*muṣṭi-bandha*); it may have, (at both ends), a gargoyle or a *matala* (?) or a dançing figure and, at the top, a decoration of dwarves, elephants, *makara* or *vyāla*. The median band of the bracket capital is the same width on both sides of the pillar.

15.48–50 (The bracket capital) is called *citrapotikā* if decorated with foliage and (garlands) of jewels or if its upper string-course is decorated in various colours; it is called *patra-potikā* if decorated with foliage. If it is decorated with waves like those of the Ocean it is then called *taraṅgiṇi*. These waves number four, six, eight, ten, twelve or even more; they are equal (in height) and become progressively wider (from the sides inwards).

Further features of pillars

15.51 According to whether (its section) is square, octagonal or circular a pilaster's projection will be a quarter, a half or three quarters its width.

15.52–54 The intercolumniation should be from two to four cubits which, if six digits are added each time, gives nine possibilities. After a suitable intercolumniation has been chosen it is to be used for all the pillars of any one building no matter what its type. If the disposition of the pillars is irregular this will bring destruction upon the building and upon its site but, if the whole arrangement is true to the principle, success will ensue.

15.55–56 The diameter of a stone pillar is the same as that of a wooden one or may be half as much again or double; such a pillar is appropriate for buildings intended for gods but not for those intended for men. According to the ancients, the pillars may be (of) brick, stone or wood but should be homogeneous (in any one building) and their number, which may be either even or odd for gods, must be odd for men.

15.57–58a The measuring line (*ājusūtra*)[1] goes along the inside or the outside of the row of pillars (which surrounds the building) but, in houses or *śālā*, it is along the median axis and in temples exterior to their pillars and, in bedrooms, on their axis (?).

15.58b–59a According to some sages the height of a building of any type is measured from the plinth (of the base) to the roof but, according to others, it is measured from plinth to finial.

15.59b–61a In assembly halls and pavilions (the measuring line) goes along the axis of the pillars or along their exterior. The (measuring line) (*mānasūtra*) should therefore, depending upon the case, go along the interior, the exterior or the median axis (of walls and pillars); this is a source of good fortune but failure is certain if there is any deviation from the rules, as is affirmed by the treatises.

CHOICE OF BUILDING MATERIALS

15.61b Wood, stone and brick are the materials to be used for (vertical) elements such as pillars and (horizontal) elements such as architraves.

Trees

15.62–63 The chosen trees must be perfect, hard and vigorous; they should neither be old nor should they be saplings; they should not be crooked and should be undamaged; they

1. *Ājusūtra*, *mānasūtra*: see above 6.19sq (p. 13).

should be growing in a holy place, mountain, wood or river-bank and they should be pleasing to eye and to mind. It is a certainty that such trees are conducive to prosperity and good fortune.

15.64–67a Herewith the trees suitable for the shafts of pillars: *puruṣa, khadira, śāla, madhūka, campaka, śiṃśapa, arjuna, ajakarṇin, kṣīriṇī, padma, candana, piśita, dhanvana, piṇḍī, siṃha, rājādana, śamī* and *tilaka*. Equally suitable are *nimba, āsana, śirīṣa, eka, kāla, kaṭphala, ṭimisa, likuca, panasa, saptaparṇaka, bhaumā* (?) and *gavākṣīn*.

Stone[1]

15.67b–68a Suitable stones are of even colour and are hard, perfect, pleasing to the touch and are embedded in the earth with an eastward or northward orientation.

Bricks

15.68b–70 Bricks are female, male or neuter and must be without flaw, compact and uniformly baked; they should, as well, give off an harmonious sound. Male, female and neuter bricks must be free from fissures (?) and cracks. It is well known that a building constructed out of such materials is conducive to the growth of Dharma, Artha and Kāma.

Trees to be avoided

15.71–76 The (chosen) trees should not be close to a temple and should not have been struck by lightning nor scorched by any conflagration; they should not be growing in a place inhabited by spirits nor beside a major roadway nor in a village and they should not have been sprinkled with the water from the ritual (and thus be objects of cult worship); they should not be frequented by birds nor by wild animals nor should they have been bent by wind nor by elephants; they should

1. For a more detailed account, see below 33.4sq (p. 307).

not be dead nor be serving as shelter for caṇḍāla nor for men of any caste whatsoever; they should not be entangled with each other nor should they be twisted; they should not harbour white ants nor be strangled by liana nor be bound; they should not be hollow nor have empty veins (?), there should be no twigs whatsoever on their branches; they must not have been damaged by wild bees nor by worms nor should they bear fruit out of season; they should not be propped up and should not grow near a cemetery nor assembly hall nor holy ground; they must not belong to any god or deity nor should they be found near a tank, well, pond or like place.

15.77 Materials from a forbidden locality give rise to all sorts of misfortune and the correct materials should therefore be chosen with the utmost care.

15.78–79a Stones should be used for temples and for the dwellings of brahmins and of the king as well as for heterodox (shrines) but they are inappropriate for vaiśya and śūdra and such a building so constructed will bring about the disappearance of Dharma, Artha and Kāma.

15.79b–80 A building constructed out of only one material is said to be 'pure' whilst with two materials it is called 'mixed' and with three, 'mingled'. Success emanates from houses built according to the above mentioned principles.

Search for trees

15.81–82a One who wishes to look for materials should go into a forest, under a constellation favourable to the enterprise and during a bright fortnight; he must previously have accomplished the solemn preliminary rites and it is essential that the portents and omens be auspicious and that sounds of good omen accompany him (on his expedition).

15.82b–83 To begin with, the chosen trees are to be propitiated, as also the forest deities, with the aid of perfumes, flowers and fumigations and with offerings of meat, boiled rice with sesame, rice with water and fish and with food of all kinds.

15.84–86 Once bloody offerings have been made to the

Spirits, the tree suitable for the (projected) work should be selected. A tree which is straight, cylindrical from root to top and which has plenty of branches is called 'male' whereas it is 'female' when broad at the bottom and thin at the top, and neuter when it is broad at the top and thin at the bottom. A tree intended for a *muhūrtastambha*[1] should be male, but male, female and neuter trees are suitable for every part of a building.

15.87–88 The architect, purified and wise, is to spend the night on a spread of *darbha* to the east of the tree having first placed his axe beside him to the right. Then in the morning, after drinking pure water and facing to the west, the perfect architect, clad in white and with axe in hand, pronounces this formula:

15.89–90 Herewith the formula: "Let Spirits, Divinities and Demons disperse! On you O trees let Soma bestow power! May It be propitious for you O sons of Earth! Divinities and Demons I shall accomplish this act and you must change your dwelling place".

15.91–93 The pure architect, having done this and having paid homage to the tree, whets the edge of the axe suitably with milk, oil and ghee and then embarks upon the cutting down of the selected tree. Having left one cubit at the base, he knocks three times and begins his examination; if water flows out this will bring about an increase in fortune and if milk-white sap (the house owner) will have many sons but if there is blood-red sap this will mean the death of the owner (of the house) and the greatest care should be taken to avoid such a tree.

15.94 If the cries of lions, tigers or elephants are heard at the moment when the tree falls this is a good omen but the sages condemn tears, laughter, shrieks and whispers (heard at that moment).

15.95–98 It is auspicious that the tree should fall to the north or the east and it augurs badly if the fall is to any other direction. It is lucky if it falls onto *sāla*, *aśmari* or *ajakarṇin* trees but if the tree falls upside down this will cause the death of the relatives and servants (of the householder). If, by falling

1. *Muhūrtastambha*: see 27.66sq (p. 243).

amongst surrounding trees, the tree remains in place once cut this presages death, if it is held back at the top, and illness, if it is held back at the bottom. If the trunk of the tree is broken this heralds the death of the wood-cutter and if its top is broken this will mean the disappearance of his line; preparation must thus be made for the fall of the tree, at its top and its base (?).

15.99–100 The tree is to be cut at both its extremities and, if a *muhūrtastambha* is wanted, it is squared off then covered with white cloth and hoisted onto a litter. The well advised man will, however, have it transported by chariot if it is intended for a god, a brahmin, a king or a vaiśya though for a śūdra he will have it carried on a man's back.

15.101–102 The tree is laid on its side and then hoisted into the chariot. Once the tree selected by the architect has been taken into the workshop through the door prescribed, it is installed by being drawn up onto the sand with its top towards the east or the north. The tree is to be kept without being moved for six months, until it is dry.

15.103–104a In the same way all the nails should be stowed away with great care along with the other metal pieces and all these things should point in the same direction (?).

15.104b–108 These are the other trees which may be used for *muhūrtastambha*, for the gods as well as for the higher castes: *kārtamāla*, *khadira*, *khādira*, *madhūka* and *rājādana*. Herewith the figures for the dimensions (of the *muhūrtastambha*), the height and diameter: the height is twelve, eleven, ten or nine spans and the diameter that same number of digits although, at the summit, this diameter is less by one tenth; the concealed part (at the bottom) is five, four and a half, four or three spans. The heights and widths prescribed above and calculated according to the number of storeys may also be used. In the case of a *jhaṣālāṅghri* the bottom of the pillar should never be hidden.

15.109–114 *Aśvattha*, *udumbara*, *plakṣa*, *vaṭavṛkṣa*, *saptaparṇa*, *bilva*, *palāśa*, *kuṭaja*, *pīlu*, *śleṣmātakin*, *lodhra*, *kadamba*, *pārijātaka*, *śirīṣa*, *kovidāra*, *tintriṇīka*, *mahādruma* (?), *śilīndhra*, *sarpamāra*, *śalmalī*, *sarala*, *kiṃśuka*, *arimeda*, *abhaya*, *akṣa*, *amalaka*, *kapittha*, *kaṇṭaka*, *putrajīva*, *ḍuṇḍuka*, *kāraskara*, *karañja*, *varaṇa*, *aśvamāraka*, *badara*, *vakula*, *piṇḍin*, *padmaka*, *tilaka*, *pāṭali*, *agaru* and *karpūra*, these trees must not be used in constructing houses for, though they are all proper to gods, they bring misfortune to men; care should therefore be taken to avoid using them in human dwellings.

The making of bricks

15.115–116a Salty, off-white, black and uniform, red and swollen, these are the four kinds of earth from which red and swollen earth should be taken. Earth suitable for making bricks, tiles . . . etc. will be free from gravel, pebbles, roots and bones and will be mixed with white sand; its colour will be homogeneous and it will be pleasing to the touch.

15.116b–119 Clods of earth are put into a knee-deep hole filled with water then, when (the earth and water) have been mixed, this mixture should be crushed by foot and without a pause, forty consecutive times; next it is soaked in the sap of *kṣīra*, *kadamba*, *amra*, *abhaya*, *akṣa* and the three myrobolans and kneaded three times, after which the bricks are fashioned. These bricks are four, five, six or eight digits wide and twice as long as wide, their thickness in the middle, as at both ends, is a quarter or a third their width. Once they are completely dry these bricks are baked in the usual manner.

15.120 Subsequently, when one, two, three or four months have gone by, the knowledgeable man immerses the bricks carefully in water and then takes them out; those which are not damp when they come out are to be used for a brick construction.

15.121 After the wood, bricks and stones have been chosen according to these principles, the sages in charge of the construction will erect a building which will be a success but the use of any proscribed material or of any material taken from another building will, say the ancients, cause the ruin of the building and will bring misfortune.

Thus ends, in the *Mayamata*, treatise on dwelling, the fifteenth chapter: DIMENSIONS OF PILLARS AND CHOICE OF MATERIALS.

Chapter 16
ENTABLATURE

16.1 I now describe the components of the entablature, suitable for all types of building, starting from its architrave (*uttara*) up to its frieze (*vṛti*).

The architrave and its upper fascia

16.2–3 There are three kinds of architrave: the *khaṇḍottara* type whose width is equal to one module and which is as high as wide, the *patrabandha* type whose height is three quarters of its width and the *rūpottara* type the height of which is half the width; the width (of the last two types) is one module. The projection (of the architrave) at the corners is three quarters, half or a quarter its width (?).

16.4 The disposition (of the components), from architrave to frieze (*prati*), is called *svastika*, *vardhamāna*, "in *nandyāvarta* form" or *sarvatobhadravṛtti* (?).

16.5–7a The height and projection of the architrave's upper fascia (*vājana*) are a third or a quarter (of a module? of the height of the architrave?) and its upper part is decorated with foliage. Above is the "fist-moulding" (*muṣṭibandhana*), cut out from the (ends of the) beams or made up separately on the top of the upper fascia; it is a string-course (decorated with protruding) lotuses; it is half a module high and has a projection half as great as its height; it has a gargoyle lower down which projects by one module in relation to the upper fascia.

The braces

16.7b–9a Above this are the braces (*pramālikā*) provided with tenons at top and bottom; their height is one module and their diameter a quarter or a third their height; they are topped by a bell-capital and an abacus; they are curved like an elephant's trunk and they project as much as do the consoles.

The consoles

16.9b–10a The consoles (*daṇḍikā*) are next above this; their width is equal to one module, their thickness to a quarter of (their width) and their projection is half that of the rim (of the dripstone); they resemble the ("fists" of the) fist-moulding unless they are square section.

Lierne and dripstone

16.10b–11a Above these is either the lierne (*valaya*) or the dripstone (*gopāna*). The height and the width of the lierne vary according to circumstances and its thickness is proportional to its height.

16.11b–12 There is a band (*paṭṭikā*) whose height is to be equal to the width of the (fists of the) fist-moulding (?); once protruding lotuses (*kṣepaṇāmbuja*) have been cut out (on it), the remaining parts (between the lotuses?) are to be arranged on the consoles. On the top of it the sage should arrange the dripstone, cut to the required dimensions (?).

16.13 The sage so disposes the dripstone that its overhang extends down to the level of the top of the architrave or, if the particular circumstance and appearance so dictate, to the top of the upper fascia or to just above the beams.

16.14 It is said that the distance between the (rim of the dripstone) and the wall is the same as that between (the wall) and the extremities of the beams. If the dripstone is just above the consoles its overhang extends down to the upper fascia.

16.15 The width of the dripstone is half a module and its thickness half that width (?). The sloping dwarf-rafters (*kampa*) (of the dripstone) are to be regularly spaced and are to be provided with an inside hole for the lierne.

The struts

16.16 The struts (*kāyapāda*), the proportions of which are

given here, should be placed between the consoles and the upper fascia. They are as wide as the pillars and their projection is a quarter (of their width); there is a band at their summit.

16.17–18a The intervals between the struts are to be closed by planks in hard woods. The sloping cover above is made up of planks with a thickness equal to an eighth (of a module?); above the dripstone however there should be a roofing of metal or bricks.

The cornice

16.18b–20a (Or else) (?) there may be a cornice (*kapotapālikā*) of which the height and projection is two or three modules or may be one or two cubits according to whether it is for a large or a small building. In order to give a pleasing appearance a foliage decoration (*pālikā*) is put at the corners on (the extrados of) the cornice or else it is placed in the centre; it is set into the stone or into the stucco coating.

16.20b–22a Above the upper fascia there may be a frieze of dwarves, *haṃsa* . . . etc.; it is one module or three quarters of a module high and the upper fascia is as above. The overhang of the cornice (extends) to that (frieze) or is one module or half a module. The projection and the height of the cornice are (then) from one and a half to three modules.

16.22b–23a (Or else) a *vasantaka* (?) or a *nidrā* (?) may also be arranged above the upper fascia; their height is three quarters (that of the fascia) and the height of the cornice above is as already given.

16.23b–24a (The cornice) is thus to be made solid; the sages should arrange it so that it is sturdy as to its materials, stone or brick, and according to the particular circumstance.

16.24b–27 The projection of the *kṣudra* (eave of the cornice?) is a third or a quarter the height of the cornice. On the cornice the false dormer-windows (*nāsikā*) rise (like) *karṇikā* (?) above the edge of the rim; they are a module and a quarter, a module and a half or two modules wide and high; their top, which is in the form of a lion's ear, rises up to the fillet (*āliṅga*) or to the frieze or to the top part of the frieze; they must be in *svastika* form (?) and a false dormer-window ought to be above a false dormer-window (?). The proportions of their hollow part and of their tip may also be in accordance with the appearance required. These false dormer-windows must not rise above the upper part of the frieze.

Top of the entablature

16.28–29a (Above the cornice or the dripstone) there is a fillet (*āliṅga*) of which the height is a quarter of a module (?) and the projection (also) a quarter of a module (?); above there is a groove (*antarita*) of which the recess is equal to the projection (of the fillet). A triple band at the top is as high as a pillar and stands on and between the pillars (?).

16.29b–32a Above this is the frieze (*prati*) with a height of one module or three quarters or half a module and with a projection three quarters or half its height. Or else, the projection of the front of the frieze is one module, one module and a quarter or one module and a half and its height should be that indicated above. This frieze is ornamented with *vyāla*, lions or elephants or it may be bare. (Above) there is a fillet (*vājana*) of which the height and projection is a third or a quarter that (of the frieze).

16.32b–35 There are three types of frieze: *samakara*, *citrakhaṇḍa*, and *nāgavaktra*. The upper part of the *nāgavaktra* has the auspicious form (?) of a snake's hood. The *samakara* is fitting for gods and brahmins; it has a square profile and is crowned by a *makara*. The *citrakhaṇḍa* is suitable for princes, merchants and śūdra; (its profile) is semicircular and its face has a decoration of elephants; the form of its upper part may vary so it is called, accordingly, *kakara*, *karkaṭa*, *bandha* or by some other name (?).

Arrangement of the beams

16.36–39a The beams must be arranged above the upper

fascia (of the architrave) or above the *valīka* (?).[1] These *valīka* are one module or three quarters of a module high, their width is half their height and their length three, four or five modules. They end in a gargoyle or in a *vyāla* or in a form resembling a wave (*taraṅga*), resting on side elements (?). Such are *valīka*, above which a "decorative band" (*varṇapaṭṭikā*) should be placed, a quarter of a module in height and width (?). The space between them is to be closed up by planks.

16.39b Strong beams, one module high and with a width three quarters their height, are placed next above; to be properly arranged their orientation should be the same as that of the door.

16.40–41a Above the beams are the joists whose width and height are equal to the width of the beams, unless their height makes up half a module. Above the joists are the small joists and above those are the planks whose thickness is a sixth or an eighth (of a module).

16.41b–42a The assembling of the entablature and pillars is to be done with a mixture of bricks and lime to which are added *karāla*, *mudgī*, *gulmāṣa*, *kalka* and *cikkaṇa*.

16.42b–44a The architrave and its upper fascia are to be placed perpendicular (to the axis of the door). The beams must have the same orientation as the door and the joists are perpendicular (to them); the small joists above lie in the same direction (as the door does); this is auspicious. For gods and kings however the beams may be perpendicular to the door.

16.44b–45 The intervals between beams and those between *valīka* are of two or three modules; the joists are separated one from the other, by two, two and a half or one and a half modules; between the small joists are spaces of one module each and (the roofing) above them is to be unbroken.

16.46–47 The entablature is made up of elements that may or may not be decorated. The beams and other elements, of small (buildings), are calculated with a view to solidity. There may or may not be images on any one of these elements. Above

1. *Valīka*: this term may designate a kind of corbel.

the framework there is a ceiling of planks or of bricks, (in which case) the procedure is still as above.

Height of the entablature

16.48 The height of the entablature is equal to that of the base, less a tenth or an eighth or it is half the height of the pillars. The height of the entablature should be so calculated that it is solid, in proportion to the whole (building) and of pleasant appearance; it is in this manner that the well-advised proceed.

Preparation of the coating

16.49 (To make the coating) the following are used: honey, ghee, curds, milk, bean water, (scraps of) leather, bananas, molasses, juice of the fruits of the three myrobolans and coconut milk; these products, in prescribed proportions, are added to lime and a hundred parts of this mixture are mixed with twice that quantity of gravel.

Even and odd measurements

16.50a In the houses of men, cubits, pillars, beams and other elements of that type are of odd numbers but, in those of gods, the numbers may be even or odd.

The door

16.50b There is no error in placing the door of a building meant for gods, brahmins or kings in the middle of the facade, but for all other categories an auspicious door is placed to one side of the middle of the facade.

The stereobate

16.51 Above the frieze (*prati*) (of the entablature) is the stereobate (*vedi*) of the attic the height of which is one and a half, one and three quarters or twice (that of the frieze).

16.52 It has two, four or six horizontal mouldings (? *kampa*) whose thickness is equal to a quarter of a module; these mouldings are ornamented with leaves of lotus, of *śaivala* or of other plants.

16.53 Dwarf pillars are arranged above these mouldings; at the top and bottom are, respectively, a string-course with lotus decorations and an *agrabandhana* (?) with the same profile as the horizontal mouldings.

Latticed windows

16.54–55a The sages are to place the latticed windows (*jālaka*) above a stereobate in such a way that they don't (coincide) with the middle of the wall or the axis of a pillar. Their width is from two to four modules and their height twice the chosen width or else it may be one and a half or one and three quarters that width.

16.55b–56a The construction of a window with a median mullion is to be avoided. The latticed windows have, vertically, an even or odd number of uprights as do the transoms, arranged according to width.

16.56b–57a According to circumstances the following types of window may be made: *gavākṣa*, *kuñjarākṣa*, *nandyāvarta*, *ṛjukriya*, *puṣpakhaṇḍa*, *sakarṇa*.

16.57b–60a *Gavākṣa* is the name of the one whose polygonal embrasure comprises an odd number of sides. That whose polygonal embrasure comprises an even number of sides is called *kuñjarākṣa*. That whose embrasure is delimited by five lines which, clockwise, determine a *nandyāvarta* figure is called *nandyāvarta*. That with uprights and transoms crossing at right angles is called *ṛjukriya*. The *puṣpakhaṇḍa* and *svastika* types resemble the *nandyāvarta* type.

16.60b–61 The two jambs (of the window) do not coincide with the middle of the wall and they have shutters, either one or two shutters, that can be opened and closed. The windows are at the level of the pillars or at that of the attic.

16.62 The circular windows have an embrasure in the form of the sun; (there are three types): *svastika*, *vardhamāna* and *sarvatobhadra*.

Walls

16.63 According to the specific case, the well advised man builds (the walls) of wood, stone or bricks. There are three sorts of wall: latticed wall, plank wall and brick wall.

16.64–66 The latticed wall is provided with latticed windows. The brick wall is of bricks. The plank wall is of planks and comprises a median upright; at top and bottom the assembly of the (plank) wall is made up of a band with lotus decoration (?); the thickness of the planks is equal to a quarter, a sixth or an eighth (of the diameter) of the pillars or else the plank wall may, according to the case in question (?) resemble the side of a palanquin; such is to be the plank wall, there, where prescribed by the sages versed in the science of architecture.

Envoi

16.67 According to the wise, those are the rules relating to the entablature, to the elements of the stereobate of the attic, to the latticed windows and to the three types of wall. A stereobate must not be interrupted by the installation of a window. In no case should a moulding of a stereobate be interrupted.

Thus ends in the *Mayamata*, treatise on dwelling, the sixteenth chapter: RULES FOR ENTABLATURES.

Chapter 17
JOINERY

17.1 Now the assembling of oblique, vertical and horizontal pieces is explained. A single construction (is made) with many pieces (and results) from their being assembled.

17.2 Weakness (being the characteristic) of the tops of trees the solidity increases with distance from it. It is prescribed that assemblies should be made with wood of good quality and of uniform type.

Varieties of assembly

17.3 There are six sorts of assembly: *mallalīla*, *brahmarāja*, *veṇuparvaka*, *pūkaparva*, *devasandhi* and *daṇḍikā*.

Rules for assembling

17.4–7a The architect, standing outside, at the four cardinal points, should first examine the house. Then he is to assemble, to the right and to the left, what is long and what is short, respectively. If his intention is to make an assembly at the centre and to the right, then he assembles a very long piece in the centre and long and short ones as before. Otherwise, pieces of uniform size should be assembled to left and right with a longer one in the middle; but, if there is no middle piece, then the pieces of equal size are assembled to left and right. This is the way assemblies are done, exterior (to the house).

17.7b–8a The following procedure is described for the interior: the architect, standing at the heart of the house, should examine it towards the four directions and then assemble, as indicated above, long, short and equally sized pieces.

17.8b–10a It is said that the pieces must be assembled with the awareness that one will support and the other be supported. The bottom (of a piece) should not be put together with the bottom (of another one) nor top with top. An assembly is marked for success when it unites the bottom (of a piece) with the top (of another); the bottom should be arranged below and the top above.

Assemblies: *mallalīla* . . . etc.

17.10b–12a *Mallalīla* is the name of a single assembly which unites two pieces. A *brahmarāja* assembly occurs where three pieces are united by two assemblies. When there are four or five pieces and, accordingly, three or four assemblies, this is a *veṇuparva* suitable for the houses of both gods and men.

17.12b–13a Six or seven pieces and, accordingly, five or six assemblies, make up a *pūkaparva* said to bring riches.

17.13b–14a When there are eight or nine pieces and seven or eight assemblies, this is a *devasandhi* suitable for all dwellings.

17.14b–15a When there are many assemblies and many pieces, the long and the short being assembled as above, this is a *daṇḍikā* which bestows riches and happiness.

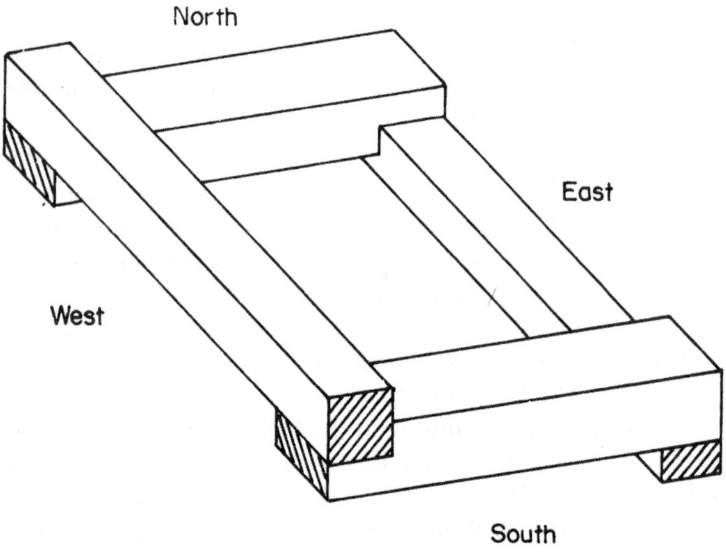

Fig. 9 Sarvatobhadra assembly (17.15b–18)

Sarvatobhadra assembly (fig. 9)

17.15b–18 The bottom of the (first) piece should be in the south-east (corner) and its top in the north-east; their assemblies are now given: the first supporting piece is on the eastern side and its bottom and top are cut (on their upper face); it is on them that the tops of the south and north pieces should rest; their bottoms are cut on the upper face and (on them rest) the western piece, the top and bottom of which are cut on its lower face and which is a supported piece. Such an assembly is called *sarvatobhadra* and it must be carried out with the south as the starting point.

Nandyāvarta assembly

17.19–21a The *nandyāvarta* assembly is made in the form of a *nandyāvarta* figure. One long piece stretching from north to south has a projection at its southern (end); another long piece, stretching from east to west has a projection in the west; a (third) long piece, stretching from south to north, has a projection in the north and a long west-east piece has a projection in the east.

17.21b–22a The assembling of these pieces starts in the east and one is considered as supporting and the other as supported each time. This is the *nandyāvarta* assembly which may equally have its starting point in the south.

Svastibandha assembly

17.22b–23 When there is a long piece with its top at the north-east (joined) to several pieces on either side, when there is a perpendicular piece (joined) by tenons to two or more pieces and when all this is arranged in *svasti*(*-ka*), the assembly is called *svastibandhana*.

Vardhamāna assembly

17.24–26a When there are a number of pieces all around

and as many within, when there is a courtyard(-like space) at the centre with forepart(-like projections) outside, according to circumstances, when east and west foreparts extend north and south, when these foreparts are correctly placed after the rooms have been properly put together, the result is known as a *vardhamāna* assembly (?).[1]

17.26b–27a The assemblies are to be made, on every upper floor of the building, just as they are made on the ground floor. Any deviation from this rule leads to certain failure according to the Treatises.

17.27b–28 The pieces of a whole, whether long or short, must be assembled with a view to the obtaining of a solid ensemble adapted to the needs of the case in question. The skilled will proceed thus and a building realized in this way gives promise of success.

Assemblies for pillars and for horizontal elements

17.29 It is said that there are five types of assembly suitable for pillars: these are *meṣayuddha*, *trikhaṇḍa*, *saubhadra*, *ardhapāṇi* and *mahāvṛtta*.

17.30 These are the five types of assembly suitable for horizontal elements: *ṣaṭśikhā*, *jhaṣadanta*, *sūkaraghrāṇa*, *saṅkīrṇakīla* and *vajrābha*.

Assembling the pillars

17.31 When there is a central tenon (with a width) a third (that of the pillar) and a length twice or two and a half times its width, this is a *meṣayuddha* (mortice-and-tenon) assembly.

17.32 In the *trikhaṇḍaka* assembly, there are three mortices and three tenons arranged as a *svasti*(-*ka*). The assembly called *saubhadra* comprises four peripheral tenons.

17.33 An assembly is called *ardhapāṇi* (scarf joint) when

1. It is not clear if this *vardhamāna* assembly corresponds to the arrangement of some specific timber work or to that of a house with four main buildings (*catuśśāla*).

half the lower and half the upper pieces are cut to size according to the thickness chosen (for the pillar) (*fig. 10*).

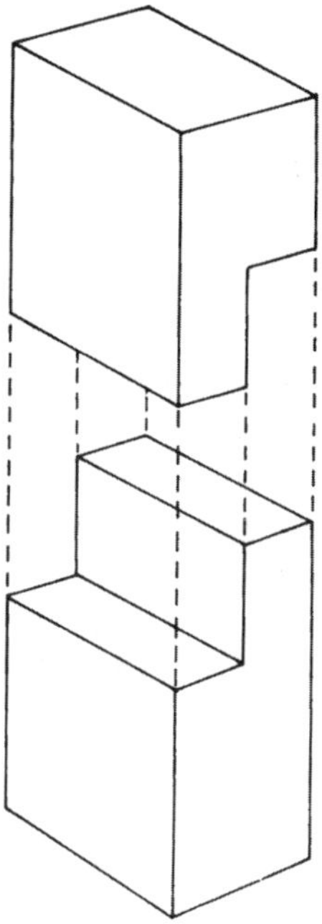

Fig. 10 Ardhapāṇi assembly (17.33)

17.34 When there is a semi-circular section tenon at the centre the assembly is called *mahāvṛtta*; the well advised man employs this for circular section pillars.

17.35–36 The assembling of (the different parts of) a pillar should be done below the middle and any assembling done above will be a source of failure; (however) the assembly which brings together the bell-capital and the abacus gives the certainty of success. When a stone pillar, with its decoration, (is to be assembled) this should be done according to the specific case.

17.37 It should be known that the assembling of vertical pieces is done according to the disposition of the different parts of the tree; if the bottom is above and the top below, all chance of success is lost.

Assembling the horizontal elements

17.38 An assembly is called *ṣaṭśikhā* when six ploughshare shaped tenons are arranged on both sides of an *ardhapāṇi* (assembly) and, in the middle of its thickness, a pin.

17.39 The *jhaṣadanta* assembly comprises several tenons on the upper and lower pieces; they are arranged perpendicular to the assembly plan and their number is determined by the solidity required in the specific instance.

17.40 The *sūkaraghrāṇa* assembly is like the snout of a boar; it comprises tenons of various sizes according to the solidity required and the specific case.

17.41 The *saṅkīrṇakīla* assembly must be made with pegs of various sizes. The *vajrasannibha* (dovetail) assembly comprises one tenon in the form of a *vajra*.

17.42 (For a given construction) only one out of this series of assemblies is to be used, from top to bottom; any deviation will lead to failure.

17.43 Where lateral pieces are concerned, the bottom is always placed inside and the top outside; if the top is within and the bottom without this will mean the death of the householder.

Tenons and pegs

17.44 *Śikhā*, *danta*, *śūla* and *viddha* are synonyms (which designate "tenon"); *śalya*, *śaṅku*, *āṇi* and *kīla* are synonyms (designating "peg").

17.45a The width of a tenon or of a peg is an eighth, seventh or sixth the (width of the) pillar.

Errors in assembling

17.45b–46 One who is very wise must make the side of the peg flush with the centre of the pillar. If the extremity of the pillar coincides with that of the tenon this causes death and the same is true if the extremity of the tenon coincides with the middle of the pillar. If the end of the pillar coincides with the middle of the assembly this will be a source of grief and if the middle of the assembly coincides with the middle of the pillar this will mean death.

17.47–49 It is essential that assembling on the squares of the gods presiding at the cardinal and intermediate points and at the doors be avoided. The squares of Arka, Ārkin, Varuṇa and Indu are those of the cardinal points; the squares of Agni, Rākṣasa, Vāyu, and Īśa are those of the intermediate points and those of Gṛhakṣata, Puṣpākhya, Bhallāṭa and Mahendra those of the doors; no assembling should be done there. Pegs and tenons are not to be placed in the locations indicated above.

17.50–51a In the same way, the sage, in assembling, must avoid the (points which are at the) middle or (at) the (first and third) quarters (of the length of the pieces); a tenon is to be placed to the left or right of the median line of a piece; a tenon placed in the middle of a piece brings about sudden death.

17.51b–52 A tenon placed in the hole intended for a nail or vice-versa will bring about the final collapse of Dharma, Artha and Kāma and of happiness. The joining on the right, of what is to be joined on the left, is to be avoided at all costs.

17.53a A (peg) placed between the length of a piece and the width of another (?) is called *kalpyaśalya* (?).

17.53b–54 If an assembly is made as mentioned above, in the middle of a piece or in any forbidden place, this, whether done in ignorance or haste, will mean the end of happiness for people of any class.

17.55–56 Old pieces should not be joined with new material nor new pieces with old material. The assembling of new pieces is to be done with new material and that of old pieces with old material. When pieces are assembled according to these precepts this will always guarantee success whereas deviation entails failure.

17.57–58a All the elements above (the pillars), such as the architrave, are to be assembled as indicated above, with or without tenons as the case demands, but this assembly is to be directly above the pillars and not above the intervals (between them).

17.58b–59 Pieces are not to be assembled above the place of Brahmā for that would be a source of misfortune. A pillar set at the place of Brahmā leads to the death of the house owner but no error is made if upper pieces, such as beams, go above that place.

17.60 When assembling male, female or neuter woods, those which are male should be joined (with those that are male) and, in the same way, female (with female); on no account should one type be joined with the other. The assembling of neutral ones is to be done with only one of the other types if it is to be a success; it may also be done according to the rules (for male and female ones) given above.

17.61 It is according to these principles that the assembling of the elements should be done, in a divine or human house; what is joined according to them brings success whereas that which does not accord with them is the ruin of success.

17.62 The best and exceedingly wise architect is advised to make a small but deep hole; the peg must be of wood, stone or ivory; the mortice (is cut in) a baked brick and the brick is to be made even around its circumference with mortar. Anything that has not been given must be as above and (the architect) must make the assembly so that it will bring perfection to the mind.

Thus ends, in the *Mayamata*, treatise on dwelling,
the seventeenth chapter: RULES FOR JOINERY.

Chapter 18

UPPER LEVELS OF ELEVATION AND THE CONSECRATION CEREMONY

UPPER LEVELS OF ELEVATION

18.1 I now present the decorative elements of the attic, the shapes of the roof, the proportions of the rafters and the characteristics of the finial.

The attic

18.2 The attic proper is twice as high as its stereobate and the height of the roof is double or triple that of the attic. The attic may however be the same height as its stereobate.

18.3–5a The projection of the pilasters placed against the stereobate, in relation to the pilasters (of the attic), is a third (the thickness of) the wall of the sanctum (at the level of the attic?); the recess of the attic is the same (in relation to its stereobate) whether a divine or a human dwelling is being dealt with but the projection of the pilasters of the stereobate may also be equal to a fifth or a quarter of the thickness of the wall and it will then be the same for the recess of the attic. The attic is to be calculated with precision, according to one of these three sets of proportions.

18.5b–7a The decorative elements of the attic are the architrave and its upper fascia, the fist-moulding (*muṣṭibandha*), the braces (*mṛṇālikā*), the consoles (*daṇḍikā*) and the lierne (*valaya*). Above the fist-moulding are *vyāla* and dancing figures attached (to the upper elements) from the top down. The arrangement of the consoles depends upon the shape of the roof just above them.

Different types of roof

18.7b–11a The height of the roof may be determined in the manner given above but may also be proportional to the distance between consoles: it is two fifths, three sevenths, four ninths, five elevenths, six thirteenths, seven fifteenths, eight seventeenths or a half of it; these are the eight possible heights for the roof and here are the corresponding names, as are known to learned ones: *pāñcāla*, *vaideha*, *māgadha*, *kaurava*, *kausala*, *śaurasena*, *gāndhāra* and *āvantika*.

18.11b–12a With the exception of the smallest, all these types are suitable for gods and, save for that (whose height) is equal to half (of the distance between the consoles), for men.

18.12b–14 The eight heights for rafter work (*lupodaya*) corresponding to these roofs, the first of which is *āvantika*, go from eleven tenths to eighteen seventeenths (of the height of the roof proper). Here are the names which correspond to these eight heights of rafter works, the first being *vyāmiśra*: *vyāmiśra*, *kaliṅga*, *kauśika*, *varāṭa*, *drāviḍa*, *barbara*, *kollaka* and *śauṇḍika*.

Roof shapes

18.15–16 The roofs (of buildings) intended for gods and for heterodox sects may be in the following shapes: square, circular, hexagonal, octagonal, dodecagonal, sixteen-sided or in the shape of a lotus bud or of a myrobolan fruit or they may be elliptic or spheric.

18.17 The roofs of palaces have at least eight sides and eight faces but roofs may also have from six to sixty faces (?).

Height of the finial

18.18–19 The height of the lotus (which is at the summit of the roof) is a quarter or a fifth that of the roof. Above is the finial, whose height is equal to that of the lotus or to a third of it. In the case of a very small (building) however the height of the finial is half or a third that of the roof. The elements of the finial will be briefly indicated below.

Number of rafters

18.20 There may be five, (seven, nine or) eleven rafters (*lupā*) or there may be four, (six, eight or) ten; these are the four numbers possible for divine and human dwellings.

Puṣkara (?)

18.21–22 The interior height given above is that of the *puṣkara* (?) named *vyāmiśra*. *Puṣkara* are set above or below the middle (of the roof? of the rafters?). Starting with a half (of that height?) and proceeding up to the maximum height, they are to be set upward and downward (?). This is a secret which has been disclosed.

Dimensions of rafters (fig. 11)

18.23 A square area is marked out, the width of which is half of the distance between consoles (*daṇḍikā*) and which is delimited by lines called *ka*, *uṣṇiṣa*, *āsana* and *sīma*.

18.24 Below the *āsana* line a parallel one is drawn at a distance equal to the projection of the consoles in relation to the architrave (of the attic). Points are placed on the *āsana* line, which divide (it) into four (five, six, seven, eight, nine or) ten parts (according to the number of rafters?).

18.25–26 Starting from the intersection of *ka* and *uṣṇiṣa* and passing through these points, lines are drawn up to the limit of the overhanging eave (*chāyā*) (which is marked by the parallel traced below the *āsana* line). Next, the distances up to the eave (?) are drawn on the *āsana* line starting from (the end of this line which goes plumb to) the base of the *ka* line; this gives the positions of the extremities of consoles. The length of each rafter is the distance between the intersection of *ka* and *uṣṇiṣa* and the extreme point (corresponding to this rafter).

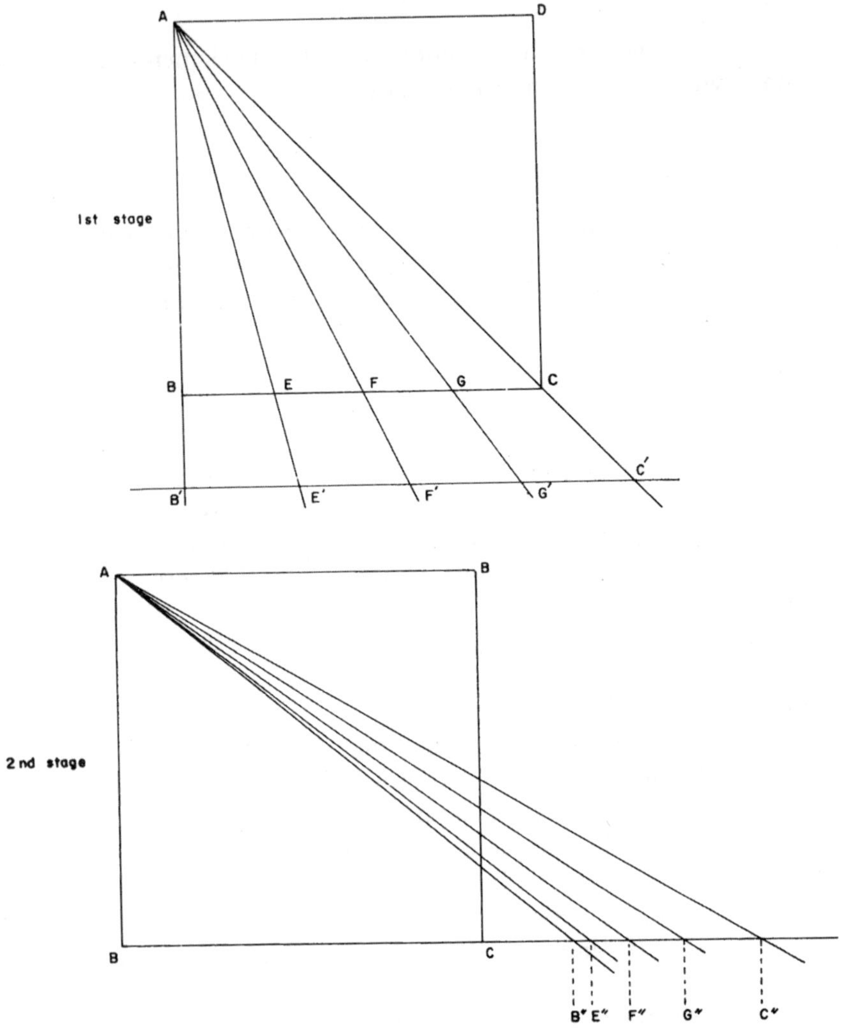

Fig. 11 Calculating the rafters (18.23 *et sq.*)

AB = Ka line; *BC* = Asana line; *CD* = Sīma line; *DA* = Uṣṇiṣa line.
1st stage: Calculating the projection of rafters onto a horizontal plane; *A* being the center of the roof, the distance *AB* is half the width of the frame on which rest the rafters and *AB′* half the total width of the roof; *AB′* is the projection of the median rafter, *AC′* that of the corner rafter; *AE′*, *AF′* and *AG′* are the respective projections of the intermediate rafters (*madhyakarṇa*, *ākarṇa*, *anukoṭi*, see 18.30).
2nd stage: Calculating the length of rafters.

A being the top of the roof, *AB* is its height; *BB″*, *EE″*, *FF″*, *GG″* and *CC″* are the lengths of the projection of the rafters (= *AB′*, *AE′*, *AF′*, *AG′*, *AC′*). *AB″*, *AE″*, *AF″*, *AG″* and *AC″* are the total lengths of the rafters.

18.27–28a Each of the extreme distances (?) is then drawn again on the *ka* line (?) and all (?) should be measured with the corresponding hypotenuse going up to the eave (?). Each of these extreme lines corresponds to the extremity of a *malla* (?).

18.28b–29 Thus the dimensions (?) of the median rafter are increased according to the number of the other rafters (?). When this has been done, the lengths of the corresponding *malla* are obtained by a process of increase and decrease; it is known that these *malla* are taken from the corresponding *puṣkara* (?).

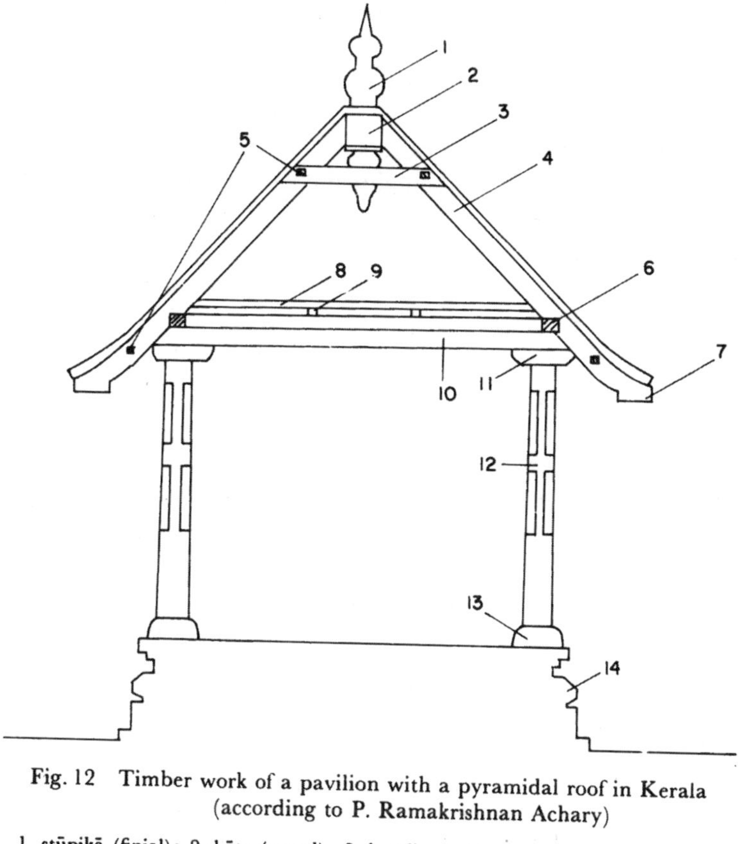

Fig. 12 Timber work of a pavilion with a pyramidal roof in Kerala (according to P. Ramakrishnan Achary)

1. stūpikā (finial); 2. kūṭa (newel); 3. bandha (collar beam); 4. lupā (rafter); 5. valaya (lierne); 6. kṣudrottara (wall plate); 7. nīvra (eave); 8. phalaka (plank floor); 9. tulā (beam); 10. uttara (architrave); 11. potikā (corbel capital); 12. stambha (pillar shaft); 13. stambhapīṭha (pillar base); 14. adhiṣṭhāna (base).

The five categories of rafters

18.30–31 Rafters are arranged in the centre or off-centre. Five specific rafters are called, in order: median (*madhya*), *madhyakarṇa*, *ākarṇa*, *anukoṭi* and corner-rafter (*koṭilupā*). (The *āsana line*) is divided into an even number of parts when their number is odd and into an odd number when it is even.

18.32–35 [*This deals with the way to install rafters for a saddle-back roof (or for a wagon-roof?), between a ridge beam* (pṛṣṭha-vaṃśa) *and a wall plate (?)*]

18.36–37 [*This deals with the newel* (kūṭa) *of a pyramid roof and with other elements such as* cūlikā *(?) and* jānu *(?).*]

Dimensions of roof elements[1]

18.38 The width of the rafters is one, one and a quarter or one and a half modules; their thickness is a third, a quarter or a fifth their width.

18.39–40 The width of the *jānu* is half that of the architrave or a quarter that of the *cūlikā* (?); their thickness is equal to the length of the consoles (*daṇḍikā*) or it is three quarters or half of it. The lierne (*valaya*) and the edge of the *jānu* make up more than half the length of the consoles. . . . ? . . . the overhang of the *jānu*. . . ?

18.41–45 [*This deals with various elements and mentions a* kuṭhārikālalāṭa *which seems to be the gable of a porch (?)*].

Roofing

18.46–47a . . . ? . . . Roofing is done with planks and metal sheets or with tiles, the choice being made according to the degree of solidity required; planks are laid above the rafters with *aṣṭabandha* mortar above and below (?).

1. We have not been able to understand the exact meaning of several of the technical terms found here. For the sake of comparison figures 12 and 13 give the vocabulary used by a traditional architect from Kerala to describe the timber work of a pavilion and that of a temple gateway.

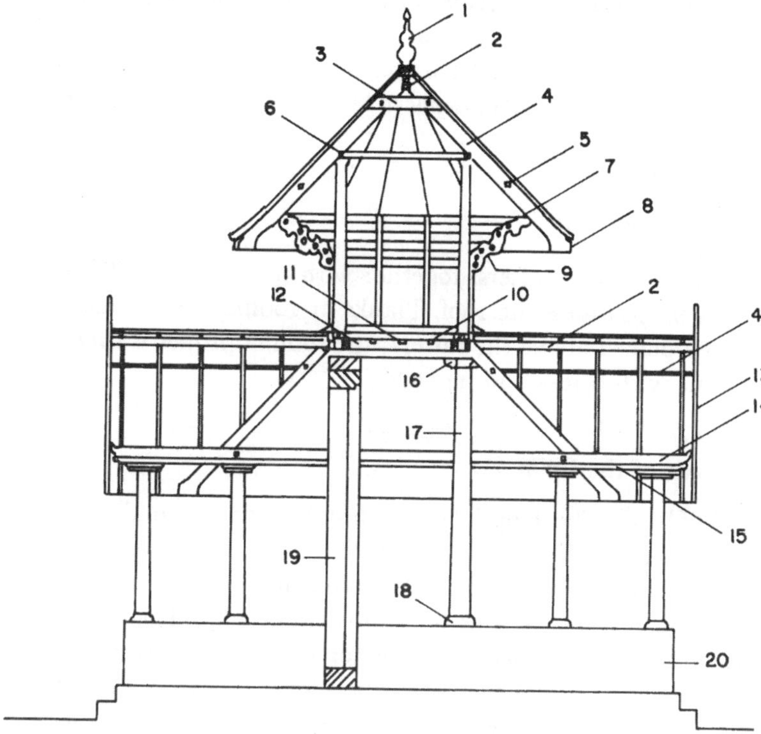

Fig. 13 Timber work of a temple gateway in Kerala (according to P. Ramakrishnan Achary)

1. stūpikā (finial); 2. vaṃśa (ridge beam); 3. bandha (collar beam); 4. lupā (main rafter); 5. valaya (lierne); 6. uttara (wall plate); 7. viṣkambhottara (secondary wall plate supported by braces); 8. nīvra (eave); 9. viṣkambha (brace); 10. phalaka (plank floor); 11. jayanti (joist); 12. tulā (beam); 13. mukhaphalaka (gable); 14. kṣudrottara (secondary wall plate); 15. uttara (wall plate); 16. potikā (bracket capital); 17. stambha (pillar); 18. stambhapīṭha (pillar base); 19. *dvāra*-stambha (doorpost); 20. adhisthāṇa (base).

Fixing of the lierne

18.47b–48a The holes for the lierne (*valaya*) are pierced below the middle of the rafters. To do this, sixteen *paralekhā* (?) are to be prepared (?).

18.48b–55 [*This deals with the drawing of* paralekhā *which should be done on the same square figure as the drawing of the rafters (see above)*].

18.56–64 [*This deals with several elements amongst which is the* ghaṭikā *a square piece which seems to be placed in relation to the lierne and the gable*].

Roofing (cont.)

18.65–66a The rafters, together with the *valayakṣa* (?)[1] are put in place inside the roof. Planks or roofing strips (*kampa*) may be placed above the rafters; the roofing proper is then to be done with bricks and mortar.

The axis of the finial

18.66b–67 The length of the finial's axis is equal to the height of the pillar (of the upper floor ?); its diameter, at the top, is a quarter (of a module) and is one module at the bottom. The mortice on which its bottom is (to be placed) goes from the bottom of the *śaṅku* (?) to the top of the roof (? *muṇḍa*).

18.68–77 [*This deals with the setting up of the finial's axis, then with the internal arrangement of the roof and probably with some decorative features*].

Decoration of the porch gable (?)

18.78–79 Above (the gable of the porch) are square and elongated aediculae, as on the temple itself. (The pediment) is made up of transoms and uprights or else it comprises a central arch in the middle of which Lakṣmī (is figured) seated, sprinkled (by elephants) and holding lotuses. The gable (*lalāṭa*) is to be decorated as given here or in some other fashion.

18.80–81 The *kuṭhārikā* (?) is to be put in place; it is stren-

1. *Valayakṣa* appears in descriptions of *sabhā* where its meaning is no clearer than here (see 25.208sq, p. 201).

gthened by a one module wide tenon that pierces the beam (?) of the gable. At its corners are overhanging decorations of foliage and *makara* or else these are at its center or halfway between the centre and the corners, according to circumstance and to the appearance desired.

The finial[1]

18.82 The (crowning) bricks are on the upper assembly of intersecting rafters (?); above, and piercing them, should be the finial's axis.

18.83–87a The dimensions of the finial having been given, its mouldings are now presented. The height (of the finial) is to be divided into twenty-two parts, distributed as follows, (starting from the base): one and a half for the lotiform base, a half for the (first) fillet above that, a half for the first reed, a half for the (second) fillet, one for a lotus-like element, five for the vase next above that, one for another lotus-like element, half a one for the (third) fillet, one for a supporting element, half a one for the (fourth) fillet, one for the (second) reed, half a one for the (fifth) fillet, one for another supporting element, half a one for the (sixth) fillet, half a one for a lotus-like element, one for a slab, half a one for a lotus-like element, half a one for the (third) reed and four and a half for the lotus bud.

18.87b–89a The respective widths of these elements, starting from the lotiform base, are as follows: seven, two, three, two, five, nine, five, three, three, three, four, three, two, three, five, six, five, two, three (twenty-seconds of the total height). To enhance the appearance, (the dimensions of) the lotus bud may be increased by one or one half part.

18.89b–90 In the same way as for that which supports it, this bud may be square, octagonal, sixteen-sided or circular or its form may be the same as that of the roof unless it accords with the decorative effect (required). These forms are suitable for gods, kings, brahmins and vaiśya.

18.91 Once this finial, suitable for gods, kings, brahmins

1. See 19.15b sq (p. 119).

and vaiśya, but not for śūdra, has been assembled, the mast for the flag is raised over it.

18.92a A temple built with these features is a guarantee of success.

Coatings and mortars

18.92b–93a *Karāla, mudgi, gulmāṣa, kalka*, and *cikkaṇa*, mixed with lime are, all five, suitable for every kind of work.

18.93b–94a *Karāla* is gravel stones the size of *abhaya* or *akṣa* fruits. *Mudgi* is gravel the size of a bean.

18.94b–95 What is called *gulmāṣa* is composed (of one part) of grains of sand (which are) one and a half, one and three quarters or twice the size of a lotus fibre, and (of one part) each of lime, gravel and shells. *Karāla* and *mudgi* are also prepared in this way.

18.96 To make *kalka*, grains of sand of the dimensions indicated above and (morsels) of lime the size of a chickpea should be crushed together. *Cikkaṇa* must be an homogeneous (liquid).

18.97–98a These five products are used separately to join bricks securely together without gaps and as prescribed; the proper one should be chosen for each usage.

18.98b–101a First, each of the above (substances) is crushed with pure water then (they are ground) anew with sap from *kṣīradruma, kadamba*, mango, *abhaya* and *akṣa* as well as with juice of the fruits of the three myrobolans and water of broad bean; next, after the gravel, shells and lime have been mixed with well water, the mixture should be pounded by horses' hooves, then filtered through fine linen; this is how well advised people impart viscosity to *kalka* and *cikkaṇa*.

18.101b–103 That called *bandhodaka* is prepared by the masons, using curds, milk, bean water, molasses, clarified butter, bananas, coconut milk and mango juice. After the wall has been washed with clear water the *bandhodaka* is used as a coating if images of any sort are to be placed there.

18.104–105 Above the dripstone and according to prescription, well advised people place tiles, baked or unbaked or in metal, and cover them (with coating); the *karāla* layer is one digit thick as are those of *mudgi* and *gulmāṣa*; *kalka* is half as thick and the thickness of *cikkaṇa* is half that (of *kalka*).

18.106 However, in the case of a gutter, the thickness is chosen according (to the specific circumstance).

18.107 It takes six months to obtain a perfect result, four for an average one and two for a mediocre one; then, the materials having been moistened with *bandhodaka*, the procedure is as has been given above.

18.108 A bed of bricks is then arranged above the rafters and lime (?) is put on it. It is known that the (brick) roofing must be completely covered with coating to the thickness indicated above.

Paintings

18.109 On the (walls) of the houses of gods and brahmins, inside as outside, the well advised man will always put paintings which are suitable for them.

18.110–112a Representations of joyous scenes and religious images are proper for the houses of brahmins, and of other castes too, where they bring success. Battle scenes and images of death and misfortune should not appear there nor representations of combat between gods and demons, neither pictures of naked mendicants, of the love play of ascetics nor of suffering people. In the houses of others one may do otherwise if one so wishes.

18.112b–114 There must be five parts of bean water, nine of molasses, eight of curds, nine of clarified butter, seven of sap, six of leather (?), ten of juice of the three myrobolans, four of coconut milk, one of honey and three of bananas. To obtain a good mortar, all these elements should be mixed with a hundred parts of lime. It is said that there should be more of molasses, honey and milk than of any other ingredients (?).

18.115 To a hundred parts of lime are added two parts of a mixture made of two parts each of lime, *karāla*, honey, clarified butter, bananas, coconut (milk), bean (water), tamarind (water) (?) milk, curds, molasses and juice of the three myrobolans; in this way a mortar is obtained which sages, versed in the Tantra, say is rock-like.

The crowning bricks

18.116–118 Next, four crowning bricks are placed at the top of the dwellings of gods, brahmins, kings and vaiśya; these are their characteristics: they are perfect and evenly baked, they give a pleasant sound and are of pleasing appearance, they are male or female and have neither fissures nor holes, their width, length and thickness are the same as those of the first bricks.

18.119–120 In a stone building the "bricks" are to be flawless stones; the bricks used at the start and finish of construction must be auspicious and must be of the same nature as the materials used from base to roof.

18.121a (The bricks) at the top of a "male" building should however be of the same nature as the materials of the upper parts; here is revealed a secret.

Axis of the finial

18.121b–122 A wood or metal axis is prescribed for the finial. Its width at the bottom and its height are equal to those of a pillar of the upper storey and it tapers progressively towards the top which is one digit wide.

18.123–124 The lowest third (of the axis) is square section and above that it is circular; at the bottom is disposed the "peacock's foot" the length of which is three times its width and whose width and height are equal to the diameter of a pillar; it is solid as if on the ground (?) and decorated with five images (?).

18.125–126a Otherwise, the length of the axis is double that of the finial and its width half, one third or a quarter the diameter of a pillar; in that case the diameter at the top is half a digit and the peacock's foot is calculated in terms of the degree of stability required.

18.126b–127a The axis of the finial may be in the shape of

a pin, nail, or Liṅga; these are the three shapes the sages prescribe.

CONSECRATION CEREMONY

Laying in place of the crowning bricks

18.127b–129 A pavilion is to be constructed next to the building and to the north; the sacrificial area, where there are four lamps, is covered with cloth and endowed with all the auspicious objects; a *caṇḍita* (diagram), also called *maṇḍūka*, should be drawn on a propitious layer of pure unhusked rice; then the gods should be arranged, starting with Brahmā, with an offering of husked white rice.

18.130–132a After propitiating the Lord of the World with perfumes and flowers, the architects, in a murmur, invoke Him. An offering is then made to the gods (by calling them) each by name and according to the ritual. Next, twenty-five identical pitchers are set out, filled with perfumed water and surrounded by the five jewels as well as by braids, herbs and gold pieces; these pitchers are provided with covers.

18.132b–133a Then, when each of the gods of the *upapīṭha* diagram has been called by name in a (formula) beginning with OM and ending with *namas*, they are propitiated with flowers, perfumes etc. . . . .

18.133b–134a When bricks and axis have been washed with the five products of the cow as well as with water of *kuśa* and of the nine gems, they are covered with a cloth.

18.134b–136a To the right of each vase, upon the sacrificial area of pure unhusked rice, an offering is made to the gods according to the ritual after they have been appeased with flowers and perfumes; the bricks and the axis are then wrapped in cloth and arranged on a spread of *darbha*.

18.136b–137a This must be done by the pure minded architect who must be clad in fine clothes and garlanded with white flowers; his upper clothing is covered by a white cloth and he holds a piece of gold in his hand.

18.137b–138a After drinking pure water and undergoing

a fast, with his mind at peace, he settles down for the night on a white cloth to the north of the vases.

18.138b–141a (In the morning), the sun being without spots, during an auspicious lunar month and fortnight, under a favourable conjunction, the architect must follow the directions of the *sthāpaka*; the five parts of his body are adorned with flowers, ear-rings, necklaces, bracelets and rings; he must be covered with gold jewellery, wear a gold sacrificial thread, be clad in new clothes, anointed with white paste and he must be crowned with white flowers; his mind must be pure.

18.141b–142 He must first meditate upon the Earth's surface in its totality, She who supports the Lords of the cardinal points and of the continents and who, along with the Ocean and the Lords of the mountains, rests upon Ananta; then, in a whisper, he invokes the Lord of the World who is responsible for Creation, Existence and Death.

18.143 It is now that the bricks and the axis are washed with water from the vases, as described above, and the architect propitiates the gods with flowers, perfumes and incense and with the lighting of the lamps.

18.144–145a After making an offering according to the ritual, with auspicious cries such as "Jaya", and after the brahmins have murmured the Veda and, once conches and drums have sounded, the architect lays the bricks in place starting from the south-east.

18.145b–146 He arranges them half way up the height of the roof of the building or between the *gagra* and the *patra* (?) or at a third or a quarter the height of the roof or under the lotus (surmounting the roof), it is there that the axis of the finial is elevated, its length depending upon the height of that finial.

18.147a The position of the bricks has been consolidated beforehand and any holes found there have been filled in.

18.147b–150 The nine precious stones are placed in the middle (of the four bricks): emerald to the east, tiger's eye to the south-east, *indranīla* sapphire to the south, pearl to the south-west, crystal to the west, *mahānīla* sapphire to the north-west, diamond to the north and coral to the north-east. In the very centre are a ruby and gold along with simples, (the grains figured) in metal, (colouring) substances, *bīja* and grains.

18.151–153a The axis of the finial is placed above this in such a way as to be stable and straight. From that axis is suspended a long banner going down to the ground floor; it should be attached with beautiful braids of linen or cotton and should hang towards the north-east; if it touches the ground at the north-east this increases the good fortune of all living beings.

18.153b–154 Next, the building and the axis of the finial are to be covered with strips of white cloth; then a cow and her calf are installed at each of the four cardinal points and the door is decorated with cloth of various colours.

Honoraria for officiating priests

18.155–156 The donor of the sacrifice, whose mind is pure, bows his head before the Lord, then, with a joyous heart he gives to the architect the cloth that has been adorning the doors, pillars, finial and temple and he gives, as well, grains, money and cows, with their calves, and he honours other assisting people with his devotion.

The placing of the deposit

18.157–158 This is the way in which to proceed, according to the best of sages: in temples, (the deposit should be placed) at their summit, in palaces, on the lateral walls (at the bottom of which is the foundation deposit) and between the storeys; in pavilions it is in the centre, in halls and similar buildings it is placed under the lotus (which surmounts the roof) and in gateways it is at the summit, as in temples.

The completion of the work

18.159–161 That which is done according to the ritual is a source of success. He who constructs a building, from beginning to end, gains an overflow of happiness, pleasure and well-being but, if he should die (before the work is finished) his son or his pupil must draw on a piece of cloth (the image) of his master and bring the undertaking to a successful conclusion according to the rules expounded by his master; the building which, due to ignorance or haste, is completed according to other rules, will bring about the rapid and certain death of its owner.

18.162 If someone embarks upon something in a particular way, he must finish it in the same way; otherwise, if he alters that way, this will bring about unfortunate changes in (the life of) the house owner.

18.163 The characteristics of the attic have been given, the shapes of *puṣkara*, the dimensions of *malla* and the ornamentation of the summit (of the building); (also indicated) has been the correct method of binding all the elements with a mortar such as *karāla*, as well as that of placing the crowning bricks.

Wood for the axis of the finial

18.164 *Khadira*, *sarala*, *sāla*, *stambaka*, *aśoka*, *panasa*, *timisa*, *nimba*, *saptaparṇa*: all these trees as well as *puruṣa*, *vakula*, *vahni*, *kṣīriṇī* and other similar trees are suitable for making the axes of finials strong, without flaws, solid and perfect.

Consecration rites

18.165 Once the building is finished, the donor, as well as the master and the *vardhaki* must perform the rite of consecration by water and they must do so during the (auspicious) fortnight of a favourable lunar month, in the period when the sun's path is to the north.

The pavilion for the preparatory rites

18.166–167 For nine, six, three or five nights, the *aṅkurārpaṇa* is celebrated according to the ritual: a beautiful consecration pavilion is built to the north or the east of the building; it is to be square, nine, seven or five cubits wide and provided with eight pillars; it is decorated with new cloth and (inside) is a canopy covered with fine fabrics, decorated with white flowers and of pleasing appearance.

18.168–170a In the middle of the pavilion a sacrificial area is laid out with unhusked rice; it is one pole wide. A diagram is drawn there with sixty-four squares, where the guardians of the site are arranged, starting with Brahmā; they are represented by husked white rice and propitiated with flowers, perfumes, incense and lamps; the offerings are made to them according to the ritual.

18.170b–172 Next, twenty-five pitchers are placed above this, adorned with cloth and surrounded by jewels, gold and braids; they have lids, are flawless and are without holes; they are filled with *hāṭaka* water. They are arranged according to the *upapīṭha* diagram, once (each of the gods of the diagram) has been invoked by the pronouncing of his name in a formula beginning with OM and ending with *namas*.

18.173–174 Then the architect whose mind is pure, whose soul is stainless and who is faithful to his vow, drinks pure water, undertakes a fast and settles himself to the north of the vases on a spread of *darbha* surrounded by four lamps and a complement of auspicious objects.

18.175–176a In front of the temple a sacrificial pavilion is to be built according to rule; it has four doors, each adorned with an arch, and it is decorated with cloth, garlands of *darbha* and crowns of flowers.

18.176b–178a An altar is established in the middle; its width is a third that of the pavilion; at the four cardinal points are square fire pits whilst those at the intermediate directions are shaped like peepul leaves; lastly, half way between the place of Surendra and that of Īśa, is one octagonal one; they are all provided with one or three levels of steps.

Putting the *mūrtikumbha* in place

18.178b–179 The *sthāpaka* accompanied by the "guardians of the images" is to perform the oblations according to the ritual; this sage, after establishing a sacrificial area of unhusked rice in the middle of the altar disposes there the *mūrtikumbha* (vase of the god), bearing the basic formula in mind.

18.180 Then the *sthāpaka* puts fire in circular fire pits at the four cardinal points of the temple.

18.181 Then the temple is to be "dressed" in cloth from base to finial whilst the finial's axis is adorned with new cloth interwoven with *kuśa*.

Offerings to the divinities of the site

18.182–184 The *sthāpaka* must then select the food for the offering: milk rice, cooked beans and barley, sesame rice, white (rice) with molasses, yellow (rice), black and red (rice); he lays all this before the god in a gold vessel with curds, milk, ghee, honey, gems, flowers, rice and water; in the evening, carrying this vessel and a banana, and accompanied by his assistant, he makes an offering to the gods, protectors of the site, with these liquids.

The opening of the eyes

18.185–187a Later, one morning, the sun being without spots, during the auspicious lunar month and fortnight, dressed in fine clothes, adorned on the five parts of his body, wearing a thread of gold and white ointment, his head wrapped in a turban and covered with white flowers, wearing clothes that have never been washed, the architect, following the ritual, performs the ceremony of the opening of the eyes. (He must do it) for the divine images who are at the cardinal points and for the others.

18.187b–188 He must first bathe (the image) in water from the vases and pay it homage with perfumes and flowers. Next, with a gold point, he draws the first circle of the eye and then, with a sharp point he draws the other three.

Consecration

18.189–190a Subsequently, having covered the piles of

grains for the brahmins with new cloth and having displayed in turn, a cow, her calf and a maiden, the architect, at the command of the *sthāpaka* goes once more (to the summit) of the temple.

18.190b–191 To the sound of conches, drums and other musical instruments, whilst cries of good omen are raised, he hangs great banners at the four cardinal points which reach from the tip of the finial to the ground and which are hung, by braids of linen or cotton, from (the image of) a man.

18.192–193a Then the wise architect makes a libation, sprinkling the sap of sandalwood and agalloche, perfumed water of all fragrances, as well as the liquid contained in the pitchers and *kuśa* water; in doing this he invokes the Master of the World.

The vase of the finial

18.193b–194 The vase of the finial of a temple is made with the five elements mixed together or with gold, silver or copper, stone, bricks or stucco; it should be conceived in relation to the axis.

18.195 After the vase has been solidly placed, (the architect) consecrates it with perfumed water then, coming down from the roof, he consecrates the sanctum and the pavilion (in front of it); at the end he stands before the god and, bowing, says this:

18.196 "O guard this house against collapse, against deluges of rain, against blows from elephants, against attacking winds, against burning fire and the crimes of thieves. Be favourable to me!"

18.197 "In good health, happy, rich, renowned, glorious, full of marvels and great exploits, eternal place of rites that are not inauspicious, let the Earth live ever in the ways of Dharma!"

18.198 "May Brahmā, Viṣṇu, Śaṅkara and all the gods as well as Kṣoṇī, Lakṣmī, Vāgvadhū, Siṃhaketu, Jyeṣṭhā and all the goddesses bestow upon creatures, happiness, well being, absence of passion and health!"

18.199 These words being pronounced, the architect's work is accomplished.

18.200–201 The *sthāpaka* now does the purification according to the rule and with the aid of rites such as sacrifice; after making a libation with liquids from the vases, the five products of the cow and with *kuśa* water, he must give thanks with perfumes, flowers and offerings of food. It is then that he imposes "*prasāda*", the principal formula on He who is the chief deity of the temple.

Honoraria

18.202–203a It is then that the donor, standing in front of the temple with a serene mind, takes responsibility, with a joyous heart and following the instructions of the *sthāpaka*, for the fruits, beneficent or not, (of the work) of the architect.

18.203b–204 Then he must honour the *sthāpaka* and architect to the utmost; in company with his sons, his brother and his wife, this donor joyously showers them with money, grains, cattle, clothes and land.

18.205 As for the other craftsmen of the construction, such as the *takṣaka*, they will be satisfied with pieces of gold and fine clothes.

18.206 It is with great pleasure that he presents the architect with the decorations of the temple, finial, pillars and pavilion as well as with the cloth, the banner and the cow.

The necessity for the consecration ritual

18.207–208 A building where the procedure is thus will prosper (beyond) the Yuga and the donor will derive outstanding rewards in this world and the next. If he proceeds otherwise there is no reward and only Bhūta, Piśāca and Rākṣasa will inhabit the building.

18.209–210 A consecration should always be carried out in a temple once it is finished and this is so for pavilion, hall, theatre, monastery (*vihāraśālaka*), for pavilions for the *hema-*

garbha and *tulābhāra* ceremonies, for *viśvakoṣṭha*, for storeroom and for kitchen.

18.211–212 The architect performs that consecration according to the ritual, once he has made an offering to the gods who protect the site; his soul and his thoughts must be pure, the five parts of his body adorned and his upper and lower garments new. He performs the consecration by water to the accompaniment of cries of good omen.

The time for the consecration

18.213 It is an excellent thing to perform the consecration in a month when the solar course is to the north, though it may also be done when the solar course is to the south if there is any urgency.

18.214 If the building is perfectly finished, three days or one day (after its completion) or on the very day (of that completion), he who is responsible and who wishes to benefit considerably must install the deity.

The putting in place of the vases

18.215a Depending on whether there are one, three or five vases, (the temple has one, three or five) principal deities and there must be one, three or five images.

18.215b Each vase is arranged whilst the formula fitting to the corresponding deity is pronounced and after precious stones and gold have been placed underneath.

18.216 This is how a building is happily finished, such as will increase the fortunes of the owner, his family, his people and his cows. If these rules are broken, if an unfinished building is entered, if the tutelary deities are deprived of their offerings, nothing is gained but misfortune.

Thus ends, in the *Mayamata*, treatise on dwelling, the eighteenth chapter: Rules for the making of roofs and for the end of the building work.

Chapter 19

ONE STOREYED TEMPLES

19.1–3a Here, briefly and in accordance with the treatises, I present one storeyed temples (for which) there are four series of possible dimensions; their width goes from three to nine cubits or from four to ten. Their height may be ten sevenths their width or one and a half, one and three quarters or twice it; these four types of proportions are called *śāntika*, *pauṣṭika*, *jayada* and *adbhuta*.

19.3b–4a Their plan may be square, circular, rectangular or elliptic, apsidal, hexagonal or octagonal and the same plans are suitable for their roofs.

The pavilion in front of the shrine[1]

19.4b–5 The pavilion in front of the shrine (*mukhamaṇḍapa*) is the same (width) as the shrine or it is three quarters or half (that width). If there is a covered passage (linking pavilion and temple) and a porch, the pavilion is then the same (width) as the (temple). The pavilion is provided with an even number of pillars arranged symmetrically and it comprises all the prescribed elements.

19.6–7 The width of the covered passage is one or two cubits or it is proportional to the dimensions of the temple; it is two modules long; if it comprises a porch, the width of that porch is two or three cubits and there is, on the side, a stairway decorated with an elephant's trunk serving as handrail.

19.8 The thickness of the walls (of the pavilion) and covered passage is equal to that of the walls of the shrine or is three quarters or half that width. The sage is to establish a porch, with two or three modules (of projection), on the side and on the front of the pavilion.

1. See 25.188sq. (p. 198).

19.9 When calculating the width, height and length in cubits a distance of less than a cubit may be subtracted, (that is) three quarters, half or a quarter of a cubit but the procedure, in that case, is as for the (main) building; some treatises forbid any increase or diminution.

Synonyms designating buildings

19.10–12 *Vimāna*, *bhavana*, *harmya*, *saudha*, *dhāman*, *niketana*, *prāsāda*, *sadana*, *sadman*, *geha*, *āvāsanaka*, *gṛha*, *ālaya*, *nilaya*, *vāsa*, *āspada*, *vastu*, *vāstuka*, *kṣetra*, *āyatana*, *veśman*, *mandira*, *dhiṣṇyaka*, *pada*, *laya*, *kṣaya*, *agāra*, *udavasita*, and *sthāna*, these terms are synonyms according to the sages.

Dimensions of the sanctum

19.13–15a Here are all the possible widths for the sanctum calculated from the width of the temple: one third, three fifths, four sevenths, five ninths, six elevenths, seven thirteenths, eight fifteenths, nine seventeenths or one half.

Proportions of the finial

19.15b–16a The diameter of the lotus (which is at the bottom of the finial) is two tenths that of the top of the roof. It is prescribed that the diameter of the vase (of the finial) be a third that of this lotus.

19.16b–17 The diameter of the recessed part under the vase is a third that of the vase; that of the groove which is above the vase is a third that of the recessed part; that of the slab (above) is triple that of the groove and that of the lotus bud is a third that of the slab.

19.18–19a The projection of the large false dormer windows (set in the roof) is equal (to their width) or is three quarters or half of it; their height goes up to the recessed part (of the finial) and is two thirds or three quarters their width and it is said, too, that the height (of the pole) for the standard is half or three quarters their height.

19.19b The height of the stereobate of the attic is a third that of the attic itself and the width of the small false dormer windows (which decorate it) is a module and a half or two modules.

The door

19.20 The height of the door is nine tenths, eight ninths or seven eighths that of the pillars and its width is half its height. The door is situated in the middle (of the facade wall) of the royal palace.

19.21 The width of the door jambs is equal to the width of the pillars or to that width increased by a quarter; the thickness (of the door jambs) is half or three quarters their width. On the outside is a string course decorated with lotuses (of which the width) is three quarters of the thickness (of the door jambs) (?).

19.22 The thickness being divided into twelve parts, the middle of the door sill is at a distance (from the exterior face) equal to five parts, the middle of the door jamb is at the same distance (from the other face) and the middle of the wall must be equidistant from these two points; thus do the sages prescribe.

The gargoyle

19.23–24 Whatever the type of temple, its (interior) floor should be at one of these five levels: (lower) plinth, (upper) plinth, doucine, dado or stereobate. There must be a duct through the wall and a gargoyle positioned on the exterior whose (height) extends above and below (floor level).

19.25–28 Starting with twelve digits and proceeding to twenty-four by successive increments of three digits, five (possible) lengths are obtained; the five corresponding widths go from eight to sixteen digits by successive increments of two digits; the thickness is equal to the width or is three quarters or half of it. In the middle (of the gargoyle) is a duct, three, four, five or six digits wide and as deep as wide. The width (of the gargoyle) at its extremity is three fifths what it is at the beginning; this extremity is provided with a spout fashioned in the form of a lion's mouth and is slightly lower than the departure point.

19.29 A gargoyle like this is to be installed in the middle of the left facade of the temple; it may also be in the position, on the exterior, that the spout of the pedestal occupies inside.

General appearance of temple

19.30 All the elements which are to be used in conjunction (in a building), with their widths, lengths and heights, have been given briefly and in order. The over-all look of the building will now be indicated.

19.31–32 If the roof and the attic are circular then this is a temple of the *vaijayanta* type; if there are corner aediculae it is *śrībhoga*, if there is a forepart (in the middle of the facade) this is *śrīviśāla* and if the roof is octagonal it is *svastibandha* but if it is square it is said to be *śrīkara*. If the plan is square but comprises an apse it is *hastipṛṣṭha*; if the roof is hexagonal it is *skandakānta*. These names are equally applicable (to plans which are similar) but elongated.

19.33–34 The *kesara* comprises a forepart in the middle of its facade. There are aediculae at the level of the roof, some at the corners and others in the middle; there is a false dormer window above the foreparts. The attic and roof are circular or square; (the width and the projection of) the median foreparts are respectively three and two fifths, three and two sixths or three and two sevenths (the width of the building).

Classification of buildings

19.35–38 There are three classes of buildings: *nāgara*, *drāviḍa* and *vesara*[1]. The square or rectangular building is called *nāgara*, the hexagonal or octagonal one, whether regular or elongated, is called *drāviḍa* and the circular, elliptic or apsidal one is called *vesara*. The building which is square up to the finial is also called *nāgara*, that which is octagonal from

1. See also 21.99 (p. 137) and 35.8–9 (p. 335).

the attic *drāviḍa* and the one which is circular from the attic *vesara.*

Images on the temples

19.39–40 (Images) of the gods are arranged at the cardinal points on each storey of the temple. On the ground floor, in the east, are the two guardians of the door, Nandi and Kāla; in the south Dakṣiṇāmūrti, in the west Acyuta or Liṅgasambhūta and in the north Pitāmaha.

19.41–42a Vināyaka is at the centre of the facade of the pavilion which is before the shrine or he is to the south (of this pavilion); Nṛttarūpa is placed to the left or to the right of Vināyaka (on the southern face of the pavilion) and in the north there is Kātyāyanī or Kṣetrapāla.

19.42b–43 The prudent man places seated or standing images at the cardinal points; these images may either be isolated or set up in historiated panels. The prescription for the ground floor is thus; what is suitable for the upper storeys, is now indicated.

19.44–45a Those to be installed on the second floor are Purandara or Subrahmaṇya in the east, in the south Vīrabhadra, in the west Nārasiṁha and in the north Vidhātṛ or Dhanada.

19.45b–46 On the third floor is the group of the Marut. On each floor there are the Amara, the Siddha, the Gandharva and the Muni; every (upper storey) must have sixteen images.

19.47–48a At each corner of the base of the attic is (the image) of a bull; the mounts of each of the gods represented are to be placed to the right of the corresponding god.

19.48b–49 A shrine with all these characteristics is a guarantee of success. I have described the dwelling of gods in this chapter; it may or may not be provided with corner aediculae, with false dormer windows, with arcatures or with median foreparts; it is decorated with all essential elements and all types of base, pillar, stereobate . . . etc.

Thus ends, in the *Mayamata*, treatise on dwelling, the nineteenth chapter: RULES FOR ONE STOREYED TEMPLES.

Chapter 20
TWO STOREYED TEMPLES

20.1–2a Now, in brief, I present the five possible sizes for two storeyed temples: their width is from five or six cubits to thirteen or fourteen by successive increments of two cubits; their height is calculated as above.

20.2b–3a The width (of the ground floor) is divided into six or seven equal parts; there is one for the width (of each) of the corner aediculae, two or three for the length of the median aediculae and the rest are for the recesses (which separate them) and in which are the niches.

20.3b–5 The height of the temple is divided into twenty-eight parts: three for the base, six for the ground floor, three for its entablature, five for the storey and two for its entablature, one for the stereobate of the attic and two for the attic itself, four and a half for the roof and one and a half for the finial; such must be the disposition from the bottom upwards.

Svastika temple (fig. 14)

20.6–7 The base is square and so are the attic and the roof; there are four corner aediculae and four more (in the middle of the facades); above are eight small size false dormer windows and forty-eight others which are very small; there are four large niches in the roof.

20.8–9a On the wall, in the middle of the recesses are creepers coming up out of vases. A temple like this, provided with arcatures, socle (etc. . . .) in various forms, is suitable for all the gods and is called *svastika.*

Vipulasundara temple

20.9b–10a However, if corner aediculae are lower than median ones and if there is a socle (beneath the latter) this is a *vipulasundara.*

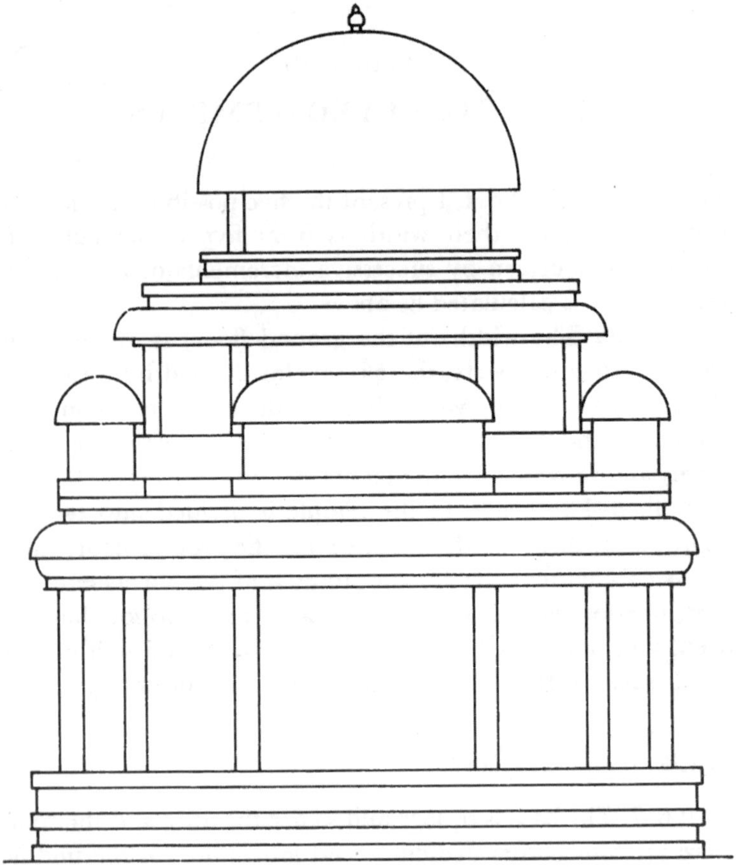

Fig. 14 Two storey temple: svastika type (20.6–7)

Aediculae

20.10b–12a For temples with two storeys or more, the height of the stereobate which supports the aediculae is a tenth that of the pillars (of the corresponding storey): the height of the body (of these aediculae) is three tenths, that of their entablature one and three quarter tenths, that of their attic one and a quarter tenths and that of their roof three tenths. The corner and median aediculae (may be) elevated by a socle.

Kailāsa and other temples

20.12b–13a If median aediculae are lower than corner ones however and if there is a socle (beneath these latter) this is said to be a *kailāsa*.

20.13b–16a Or, if the stereobate of attic, the attic, roof and finial are all circular, if there are eight corner aediculae and four median ones, if there are fifty-six false dormer windows, if the projection of the median aediculae is of two or three modules in relation to the corner aediculae, if the attic and the roof are the same height (as above), if there are both corner and median aediculae, the temple is called *parvata* and is suitable in all cases; a base and pillars of any types may be used.

20.16b–18a Again, if there are four elongated aediculae set into the roof which is square plan, if there are four corner aediculae and forty-eight small false dormer windows, if there is a base of whatsoever type desired, this is said to be *svastibandha* for which all types of elements are suitable.

20.18b–19 Or again, if corner and median aediculae are on socles and if (consequently) the recess niches are much lower, if there are sixty-two false dormer windows, this is a *kalyāṇa* for which all types of decoration are suitable.

20.20 Or, if there are no aediculae set into the roof but there are four false dormer windows, this is said to be *pāñcāla*.

20.21 If the stereobate of attic, the attic, roof and finial are octagonal and if there are eight false dormer windows on the roof, this is said to be *viṣṇukānta*.

20.22–23 If there are no socles under the corner or median aediculae, if the plan is rectangular with a length a quarter more (than its width), if stereobate, attic and roof are rectangular and if there is a triple finial, this is said to be *sumaṅgala*.

20.24 If stereobate, attic and roof are elliptical and if all the elements prescribed above are present this is a *gāndhāra*.

20.25–26 Or, if the plan is rectangular with a length a quarter more than its width, if the roof comprises an apse, if there is one elongated aedicula on the facade, this is said to be *hastipṛṣṭha* type; its base may equally be apsidal.

20.27a (Or again), if the plan of the base is square whilst that of the sanctum is circular and if the elements prescribed (above) are all present, this is a *manohara*.

20.27b–28a If the plan is circular from the plinth (of the base) to the finial, within and without, and if everything else is as above this is *īśvarakānta* type.

20.28b–29a If the sanctum is square and the base circular and if the plan is circular from base to finial, this is a *vṛttaharmya*.

20.29b–30a Or, if the base is rectangular, the attic and roof hexagonal and everything else as above, this is said to be a *kuberakānta*.

20.30b–31a There are five possible dimensions for the fifteen types of two storeyed temple which the expert is to construct as has been prescribed.

New classification of buildings

20.31b–34 There are three kinds (of building) called *sañcita*, *asañcita* and *upasañcita* and it is said that these are male, female and neuter. The *sañcita* building is made out of stone or bricks; it is massive from entablature to roof and is said to be male. That which is of bricks or wood and which comprises inaccessible hollow (*bhoga*) parts is *asañcita* or female. That which is hollow in places and massive elsewhere is called neuter or *upasañcita*.

Engaged structures

20.35 According to the ancients the proportions of the engaged structures (*khaṇḍabhavana*) are as follows: the height of their finial is one seventh the height of the pillars of the upper storey; the height of their roof is three sevenths (that of the height of the pillars), that of their pillars two sevenths, and that of their base below, one seventh.

Arcatures

20.36 The height of the colonettes (of arcatures) is seven

tenths, six ninths or five eights that of the pillar (of the corresponding storey); the rest (of that height) is occupied by the (lintel decorated) with *makara*. The width of the arch is half the height (of the colonettes) or it is one sixth, one fifth or a quarter of it.

20.37 The niche's height is equal to its width; the diameter of the colonette is three quarters that of its base (?). Decorative arcatures should be placed in the recesses, in the middle of the facade of the building, on corner aediculae and on elongated ones.

20.38–39 (The arcatures are) to surround the door, or to be placed beside it or in the middle of the facades. The niches for the guardians of the door are elevated up to the architrave, or else the arch which surrounds it is elevated up to the dye with human figure or up to the bracket capital (of the ground floor pillars). These niches are to be disposed according to the arrangement of the entrance peculiar to each building.

Thus ends in the *Mayamata*, treatise on dwelling, the twentieth chapter: RULES FOR TWO STOREYED TEMPLES.

Chapter 21
THREE STOREYED TEMPLES

21.1–2a Now I briefly present three storeyed temples for which there are five series of possible dimensions; their width is from seven or eight cubits to fifteen or sixteen by successive increments of two cubits; their height (is calculated) as above.

Svastika temple

21.2b–3 If the (width of the ground floor) is seven, eight or nine cubits it is to be divided into seven or eight parts; the width of the corner aediculae (topping its entablature) takes up one part, the length of the median ones two or three, the width of the projecting niches half a part and the recesses (which separate these different elements) the same.

21.4 The second storey must be six parts in width, the width of the corner aediculae taking up one part and the length of the median aediculae twice that and the recesses being one part wide.

21.5 The third storey is three parts wide and comprises a median part to which the sage gives a projection of one module, one and a half or two modules.

21.6–8 As for the height of the temple, the sage is to divide it into twenty-four parts: three for the base, four for the body (of the ground floor), two for its entablature, three and three quarters for the body (of the second storey), one and a half for its entablature, three and a half for the body (of the third storey), one and a quarter for its entablature, one half for the attic and its stereobate, three and a half for the roof and one for the finial.

21.9–10 There are eight corner aediculae, eight niches and eight median aediculae; the plan is square from base to finial; on the upper storey are sixteen small niches as well as ninety-six small false dormer windows. Base, pillars, stereobate of the attic and all other elements may be of any type. On the roof are eight large niches; the median aediculae are equal one to another and are more elevated than the corner aediculae. This then is the dwelling of Śambhu; it has three storeys and is called *svastika*.

Vimalākṛti temple

21.11–13 When the width is divided into seven or nine parts, each corner aedicula makes up one part, the elongated aediculae one or two (in length) and the recesses one in width. There are eight corner aediculae, twelve elongated aediculae, eight niches and one hundred and twenty small false dormer windows. The roof and the attic and its stereobate are octagonal and there are eight niches (in the roof). This building, ever fitting as dwelling for Śambhu, is called *vimalākṛti*.

21.14 When the width is seven or nine cubits it is to be divided into seven or nine parts; the width of the corner aediculae makes up one part and there are eight of these; there are twelve median aediculae, eight niches and, in the attic, eight (more) niches; there are one hundred and twenty small (false dormer windows). This is a *vimalākṛti* building.

Hastipṛṣṭha temple

21.15–18a For a building provided with an apse and which is eleven cubits wide it is prescribed that the length be greater than the width by four eights of that width. The base is to be rounded at one extremity as are the attic and the roof; this rounded part is to be drawn with (a radius equal to) half the width of the building. Starting from the front, the two sides and the back are to be divided into twice times twelve parts; the width of the square aediculae, that of the elongated ones and that of the niches make up one part; the length of the elongated aediculae makes up two and the width of the recesses one.

The pavilion in front of the shrine

21.18b The pavilion that comes before the shrine is of the same width as the shrine or (its width) is three quarters or half that.

21.19–20 The upper part of the pavilion is decorated in the same way as that of the shrine; in all temples the pavilion is to have corner aediculae, elongated aediculae . . . etc. Otherwise it may comprise (only) three levels of elevation and is, in that case, decorated with arcatures . . . etc. The pavilion is on the same plan (as the shrine) but if there is a covered passage this is on a lower level.

21.21–23a All elements such as the corner and elongated aediculae project in relation to the *mānasūtra*, which projection is equal to half or a quarter their width or it is one module, one module and a half, two modules and a half or three modules, this being the projection in relation to the *mānasūtra*. A building organized according to this principle invariably guarantees success. A straight line should indicate the extremity (of the projecting elements) for, if this line is broken, that is a source of misfortune.

Hastipṛṣṭha temple (cont.)

21.23b–24a Above, the width (of the second storey) is six (eighths that of the ground floor). By dividing the two sides, starting at the rear, into twice twelve parts, the same proportions as above are set for the square aediculae, those which are elongated . . . etc.

21.24b–25 The width of the last storey is four (eighths that of the ground floor) and the different elements are to be placed according to the demands of the specific case. On the gable of the roof on the front of the building are two false dormer windows shaped like elongated aediculae and crowned (?) by square aediculae surrounded by small pillars.

21.26–29a Square and elongated aediculae are arranged so as to give a pleasant effect and there are thirty niches with colonettes on the roof. There are eight square aediculae and as many elongated ones; there are twelve niches and, in the recesses, twenty-four small false dormer windows. All types of base, pillar, stereobate of attic (etc.) are suitable for the decoration (of such a temple); its base may or may not have a socle. This is said to be *hastipṛṣṭha* and is fitting for all gods.

Stambhatoraṇa

21.29b–32 The pilaster (of the *stambhatoraṇa*), two thirds as high as the pillars (of the corresponding storey), is provided with all the necessary elements; it has no bracket-capital but comprises an abacus which surmounts the dye with a human figure. Above is an architrave and its upper fascia and then a band with lotuses, a groove and a fillet; above that is an arched piece featuring a *makara*, decorated with foliage and, in its inner part, ornamented with lotus stems. Provided with all these elements (such a motif) is called *stambhatoraṇa*; in all types of building it is to be placed between the pillars, in the recesses, in the middle of the corner aediculae and on the covered passage.

21.33 On a pillar provided with all (prescribed) elements is to be placed, above the historiated dye and at the same height on both sides, an architrave crowned by an upper fascia, a lotiform cornice and an arcature, which last is decorated with *makara*, flowers or some other motif; this arcature, which surmounts an isolated pillar, is to be placed either on a temple, on a pavilion, on a house or on any other construction.

Hastipṛṣṭha temple (cont.)

21.34–36a Or else, when the base is rectangular the width makes up eight parts and the length ten. The square and elongated aediculae as well as the niches are one part wide, as are the recesses.

21.36b–39 The second storey is six parts wide and the third four parts and their length is two parts more than their width. Stereobate, attic and roof are rectangular but have a rounded extremity; square and elongated aediculae etc. should be arranged in the same way as above. All types of base are suitable (for this temple) and, as well, all types of pillar may decorate it. Above the pillars are *svastibandha* false dormer windows. The sage must construct this building to be solid and well adapted (to its use); the ancients call it *gajapṛṣṭha*.

21.40a A wise man should calculate for a temple with an even number (of cubits) whatever its type.

Bhadrakoṣṭha temple

21.40b–43a When the width is thirteen cubits it should be divided into nine parts: the width of the sanctum takes up three, the thickness of its walls one, the width of the aisle one and that of the exterior walls one. The width of the square and elongated aediculae and the length of the elongated ones is three parts; the width of the niches is half a part and what remains is for the recesses. In the middle of each elongated aedicula is a niche with a projection of three modules.

21.43b–44a Above, the width (of the second storey) is six (ninths that of the ground floor); the square aediculae here are one part wide and the length of the others is twice as much; the recesses take up one part of the width and they have niches.

21.44b The upper storey has a width three (ninths that of the ground floor) and the central part of its facade projects by three modules.

21.45–48a The base (of this building) is square, its attic and roof octagonal. The aediculae at the four corners of the first floor have a square roof, the roof of those of the second storey being octagonal. There are eight of these aediculae and as many niches, elongated aediculae and small niches; on the attic are sixty-four *svastika* false dormer windows. This type of building is called *bhadrakoṣṭha*.

Vṛttakūṭa type

21.48b–49 If the aediculae on each of the storeys are circular however and if the roof of these aediculae, also circular, is broken by four false dormer windows (this building) is said to be *vṛttakūṭa* which is suitable for gods under any circumstances.

Sumaṅgala temple

21.50–51 Again, if the temple is rectangular, its length an eighth more than (its width), if the oblong corner aediculae have an elliptical roof, if there are neither median aediculae nor projecting parts and if (everything else) is as above, this is called *sumaṅgala* and is to be endowed with a triple finial.

Gāndhāra temple

21.52–54a When the width is fifteen cubits it is divided into fifteen parts, the sanctum taking up four parts of the width, the thickness of the wall (around it) one, the aisle one and the (wall with) engaged structures arranged all around, one. There are corner and median aediculae with niches between them; all these elements are one part wide but the median aediculae are two parts long. This is what the sages prescribe.

21.54b–55a On the second storey whose width is six (tenths that of the ground floor) there are corner aediculae with a width of one part; median aediculae, two parts long, are arranged here too, as well as the niches which make up one part of the width.

21.55b–59 The (width of the) last storey is four (tenths that of the ground floor); the central element (of its facades) is two parts wide and projects by one module, one module and a half or two modules. The base is square as are the attic and the roof. There are eight corner aediculae, as many median ones and there are niches; higher up there are eight projecting niches and a gutter. *Svastika* false dormer windows are all around. Every type of base, pillar, stereobate, window and arcature are suitable (for such an edifice). If its corner and median aediculae are elevated they have a stereobate (at their base). (Such a temple) is called *gāndhāra*; both its attic and its roof may be octagonal.

Śrībhoga temple

21.60 If stereobate, attic and roof are circular however, the temple, which is as above in other respects, is called *śrībhoga*.

Aediculae

21.61–62a (The plan) being circular, elliptic, apsidal, octagonal or hexagonal, it has corner and median aediculae and niches on each storey. Square and elongated aediculae and niches should also decorate engaged pavilions.

21.62b–64a If the plan is circular or apsidal the procedure is the same as when the plan has rectilinear sides, the proportions may be rather smaller or may be exactly the same. The upper part will be smaller than the lower part by an eighth or a tenth (?). The sensible man proceeds according to the appearance, the degree of solidity and the goal sought.

New classification of buildings

21.64b–65 There are two sorts of temple: *arpita* and *anarpita*. An *arpita* temple has no aisle but an *anarpita* does have one. It is like this that the sage arranges all (temples) even the small ones (?).

Sanctum

21.66 The width of the sanctum is a third, three fifths, four sevenths, five ninths, six elevenths, seven thirteenths, eight fifteenths, nine seventeenths or half that of the temple to which it belongs.

Stereobate

21.67 The stereobate is placed beneath the attic and beneath elements of the temple such as corner and median aediculae. This stereobate may or may not be present in the recesses where there are niches or small false dormer windows.

Decorative elements: arcatures . . . etc.

21.68–72 We now give the decoration for three types of arcature named: *patratoraṇa*, *makara*(*-toraṇa*) and *citratoraṇa*. The *patratoraṇa* is in the shape of a crescent moon and is decorated with foliage. The arcature, in the middle of which Purin-Śiva stands on the snouts of two *makara*, is called *makara-toraṇa* and is decorated with liana of various kinds. *Citratoraṇa* is where Purin, placed at the centre, is flanked by two *makara* which he holds by the trunks; from their mouths pour Vidyādhara, dwarves, lions, *vyāla*, *haṃsa*, infants as well as garlands and festoons and cascades of jewels, ornaments for this arcature which is perfectly proper for gods and for kings.

21.73–79 In the niches (under the arcatures) there are statues. These arcatures comprise two colonettes and the well advised arranges them beneath the architrave. The height of the (corresponding) pillars of the building being divided into five, six or seven parts, two will be for the upper part of the arcature and the rest for the colonettes; these are square or octagonal section and are provided with bell-capital, abacus . . . etc. They may not have bracket-capitals however. Above these, or above the dye with human figure, should be placed the lintel, its fillet, the lotiform cornice and a small fillet. The sloping part in the form of a *makara* is elevated to the upper joint (of the pillars of the building). The arcature is half as wide as high (or) its height is equal to that of the door and the width to the intercolumniation. The upper part, which surmounts the lintel and which is in *makara* form, has the eight beneficent objects upon it: on the gable is Pañcavaktra (i.e. Śiva) and above, the trident, parasol, flag, standard, *śrīvatsa*, drum, vase, lamp and *nandyāvarta*, for these are the eight beneficent objects which bring happiness to all.

21.80a Thus presented are the four types of arcature suitable for gods and others.

21.80b–81 Above a lotiform base a beautiful liana inclines in relation to the vase; above, a pilaster is decorated with intermingled foliage and creepers; above, (again), a lotus which crowns the abacus forms the summit of the *kumbhalatā* (?). Such is the *padmakumbhalatā*.

21.82–83 This may be done otherwise: above the upper joint (of the pilaster) is placed a dye ornamented with a human image; it is then a *stambhakumbhalatā* whose upper part is like that of a *stambhatoraṇa*. This motif is to be placed in the recesses of the walls of divine and human dwellings.

21.84–86a The *vṛttasphuṭita* is as high as the colonettes of the arcature; its width is six, eight, ten, twelve or fourteen digits; its projection is half, two thirds or one third its width; the upper part is rounded and it comprises a dado ornamented with a *śukanāsī*. It is the ornament of divine dwellings.

Stairs

21.86b–88a The sensible man puts a stairway between two storeys. Three sections are possible for the stairwell: square, circular and rectangular. There are four types of stairs: *trikhaṇḍa*, *śaṅkhamaṇḍala*, *vallīmaṇḍala* and *ardhagomūtra*.

21.88b–90 The *śaṅkhamaṇḍala* diminishes in width from bottom to top. The *vallīmaṇḍala* is like a liana which climbs by curling round a tree. Starting from the first step and going up, the navel is to the right. The width of the stairs is from two to seven modules, that of the bottom step is from two to four times that of the stairway.

21.91–92 The height of the steps of steep stairways is a quarter, half or three quarters their depth. But for the sake of elephants, children and the aged, their steps should be in regular succession; their depth is sixteen or eighteen digits and their height makes up the sixteenth of it. A well constructed stairway must be like this.

21.93–95 The width of the strings is two modules and their thickness is a quarter of that, steps and risers are to be solidly fixed on them. A stairway comprises an uneven number (of steps), it may or may not be concealed (in the wall). In the case of pavilions, the projection (made by the stairway) on the outside is equal to one intercolumniation. For all castes, the ascent of the stairs should be effected turning to the right. If these prescriptions are not complied with, the result will be death.

21.96–97 For ascending the base (or the body of the ground floor or its entablature) there must be a staircase on the facade or at the sides. The rail goes from the first step to the landing (*phalaka*). The height (of this stairway) is the same as those of the base, the body of the building and the entablature. A stairway conceived according to these principles is a guarantee of success.

21.98 The arcatures which are suitable, depending on circumstances, for divine and human dwellings, have been described; also described in this chapter are the different forms of stairway and their various types, and this has been done following the prescriptions of the sages well versed in the science of architecture.

21.99 There are three kinds: *nāgara*, *drāviḍa* and *vesara* (corresponding) respectively to *sattva*, *rajas* and *tamas*, that is, to brahmins, kings and vaiśya whose respective tutelary deities are Hari, Vidhātṛ and Hara.

Thus ends, in the *Mayamata*, treatise on dwelling, the twenty-first chapter: RULES FOR THREE STOREYED TEMPLES.

Chapter 22

TEMPLES WITH FOUR OR MORE STOREYS

Four storeyed temples

22.1–2 Now, briefly presented, are temples with four storeys for which there are five series of possible dimensions: their width goes from thirteen or fourteen cubits to twenty-one or twenty-two by successive increments of two cubits; their height is calculated as has been previously indicated. I now lay down the proportions of the width and of the height of these temples.

Subhadraka temple (fig. 15)

22.3–4 If the width is thirteen cubits it is to be divided into eight equal parts: the width of the corner aediculae makes up one part of the length and the width of the niches one part. The width of the second storey is also divided into eight; the corner and median aediculae are arranged as in the preceding case and above those of the ground floor.

22.5–6a The width of the third storey is six (eighths that of the ground floor): the corner aediculae are one part wide, the median ones two parts long and the niches half a part wide. Above that, (the width of the fourth storey) is three (eighths that of the ground floor) and a third of it, in the middle, projects by one module.

22.6b–10 The craftsman divides the height (of this temple) into twenty-nine parts: two and a half for the base, five for the body (of the first storey) and half that for its entablature; above, the body (of the second storey) makes up four and three quarters and its entablature two and a quarter; this last number, doubled, is the height of the body (of the third storey) whose entablature makes up two parts of the height. The body (of the fourth storey) makes up four and a quarter parts and

Fig. 15 Four storey temple: subhadraka type (22.3 *et sq.*)

its entablature one and a quarter; the stereobate of the attic makes one and the attic itself two, the roof four and a half and the (two parts) which remain are for the finial. The plan is square from the base.

22.11–12 There are twelve corner aediculae and the same number of median ones, and of niches, and there are four niches in the roof. It is decorated with small niches and *svastika* false dormer windows. The base is as has been given above and so are the pillars, the ornaments and the arcatures. Such a building, supplied with all the ornaments, is called *subhadraka*.

Śrīviśāla temple

22.13–14 This building is called *śrīviśāla* however when, the aediculae being placed at the corners or in the middle depending upon circumstance, the roof is circular; the roof of the corner aediculae is also circular. The sanctum occupies half the width of the building, the thickness of the interior wall one third of the remainder and the same goes for the aisle and the exterior wall. All types of base, pillar, stereobate (. . . etc.) are suitable for this temple.

Bhadrakoṣṭha temple

22.15–16 If the width is fifteen cubits it must be divided into nine equal parts: three for the width of the sanctum and, (on each side), one for the thickness of the interior wall, one for the width of the aisle and one for that of the (exterior wall with) engaged structures.

22.17–18 The width of the corner and elongated aediculae and of the niches is one part; the length (of the elongated aediculae) is triple their width, which is equal to their projection; these aediculae comprise a large central niche whose width and depth made up one part. Between corner aediculae, median aediculae and niches, are recesses half a part wide.

22.19–20a The width of the second storey is eight (ninths) that of the ground floor; the width of the aediculae is to be one part and so is that of the median aediculae whose length is twice that; the width of the niches which are to be disposed between corner and median aediculae is one part.

22.20b–21 Above this, the width (of the third storey) is six (ninths that of the ground floor); the corner aediculae are one part wide as are the median aediculae whose length is double their width; between these are niches half a part wide. Above, (the width of the top storey) is four (ninths that of the ground floor) and it projects in the middle by one module.

22.22–24a The corner aediculae (of this temple) are octagonal and the median ones cruciform. The large sized roof is octagonal and decorated with eight niches. The total number of aediculae and niches is the same as above. The distribution of the elevation is to be made according to what has already been said, The name of this four storeyed temple is *bhadrakoṣṭha*.

Jayāvaha temple

22.24b–25 When the width is seventeen cubits it is to be divided into ten equal parts: four for the sanctum and, (on each side), one for the interior wall as for the aisle and the (exterior wall with) engaged structures.

22.26–27a The width of the corner aediculae, of the large niches and of the median aediculae is one part; the length of the median aediculae is double their width and what is left is for the recesses with their niches.

22.27b–28a Above this, when a place has been left for the gutter, there remain eight (tenths of the width of the ground floor) for the width of the first storey; the corner aediculae are one part wide and the median ones are twice as long as that; the recesses and overhanging niches which separate them also make up one part.

22.28b–29 Above this, (the width of the third storey) is six (tenths that of the ground floor); the width of the corner aediculae is one part, the length of the median ones two and, (between them), are recesses with small niches in them. Next above, (the width of the fourth storey) is three (tenths that of the ground floor) and it projects by one module, at its middle.

22.30–34a The base (of this temple) is square, its attic and its roof are octagonal; it has twelve median aediculae and as many corner ones as well as eight niches and sixteen small false dormer windows; there are eight other niches. The median aediculae are slightly elevated. All kinds of base, pillar, stereobate, window, arcature and ornamentation are appropriate for this building. It is decorated in various colours. Its base may or may not be on a socle. All around, (on the entablature), is a decoration of *svastika* false former windows. The vertical disposition of elements is the same as in the preceding case. This type is called *jayāvaha*.

Bhadrakūṭa temple

22.34b–36 When the width is nineteen cubits it is to be divided into ten (equal parts): four for the width of the sanctum and, (on each side), one for the thickness of the interior wall, one for the width of the aisle and one for the width of the (exterior wall with) engaged structures surrounding it. The width of the corner and median aediculae and of the niches takes up one part, the length of the median aediculae two, and there are one part wide recesses.

Kapotapañjara

22.37–40 The width of a niche set into the middle of a corner aedicula is two fifths the width of the latter and its depth one fifth. (This niche) is flanked by two colonettes and is provided with socle, base, entablature, stereobate, attic and roof and with all necessary decoration. It extends from the level of the base (of the aedicula) to its architrave. Its height being divided into nine parts, its socle makes up one part, its base two, its pillars twice that, its entablature one and a half and the stereobate of its attic a half; the height of its attic is equal to the distance between architrave and cornice.

22.41–42 It is shaped like a cage and recessed in relation to the cornice. According to circumstance and to appearance desired, it may be surmounted by a pole. This *kapotapañjara* is appropriate for all types of temple and should be placed at the centre of recesses or of aediculae.

Bhadrakūṭa temple (cont.)

22.43–44a The corner and median aediculae and the niches are as above. Above that, leaving aside the space for the gutter, there remain eight (tenths of the width of the ground floor for that of the second storey); the corner aediculae are one part wide and the length of the median ones twice that; there are niches set between them.

22. 44b–46a Above, (the width of the third storey) is six (tenths that of the ground floor); the corner and median aediculae are as has been given above. For the fourth storey the procedure is as has been prescribed for the *vijaya* (i.e. *jayāvaha*?) type. It should be known that the number of all elements such as aediculae is as given above but that there are sixteen large niches too. This type is called *bhadrakūṭa*.

22.46b–47a If the decoration is different however, comprising elongated aediculae with median projection, and if the roof and the attic are circular plan, this is said to be a *manohara* building.

Āvantika type

22.47b–48 Or again, if the decoration is different and if the roof and the attic are square plan, this is said to be *āvantika*; all types of base, pillar, stereobate (etc. . . .) are fitting for it and it is considered a perfect abode for Śambhu.

Sukhāvaha type

22.49–50a When the width is twenty-one cubits, it is to be divided into ten parts; four for the width of the sanctum and, (on each side), one for the thickness of the interior wall, one for the width of the aisle and one for the thickness of the outside wall. The corner aediculae, the niches and the median aediculae are one part wide; the length of these median aediculae is double (their width) and the recesses are one part wide. The decoration comprises windows and *makaratoraṇa*.

22.50b–52a Above, again, the space for the gutter having been set aside, there remain eight (tenths of the width of the ground floor for that of the second storey). The corner and median aediculae and the niches are one part wide, whilst the length of the median aediculae is double that. Above this, (the width of the third storey) is six (tenths that of the ground floor); the corner aediculae are one part wide, the median aediculae twice as long and the niches are one part wide. Above again, (the width of the fourth storey) is four (tenths that of the ground floor); its middle part occupies half the width and projects by one module; there is a false dormer window above this projection.

22.52a–52b The attic niches are two and a half digits wide. The attic, its stereobate and the roof are circular plan; there are eight big engaged niches and eight small ones (in the roof).

22.53–54a On the first storey, the corner and median aediculae and the niches are elevated by a stereobate. Above this, it is the median aediculae which are elevated and, higher up, it is the corner aediculae, which are circular plan although their roof is octagonal (?) on the median (storey). On the first storey, however, the roof of the corner aediculae is square plan and there is a false dormer window above it without an opening (?).

22.54b The name of this divine palace is *sukhāvaha*; it may have any sort of base, pillar and decoration.

Five storeyed temples

22.55–57a The height of a five storeyed temple is to be divided into forty-eight equal parts: two and three quarters for the base, five and a half for the body (of the first storey), two and a half for its entablature, five and a quarter for the body (of the second storey) and two and a half for its entablature; five for the height of the body (of the third storey) and two and a quarter for its entablature, four and three quarters for the body (of the fourth floor) and two for its entablature; four and a half for the body (of the fifth storey) and one and three quarters for its entablature; one for the stereobate of the attic, two for the attic itself, four and a quarter for the roof and two for the finial.

22.57b The width (of a five storey temple) is to be divided into nine, ten or eleven equal parts.

Temples with six to eleven storeys

22.58 If (a storey is added), below the elevation (thus obtained), whose body makes six parts and whose base three, a six storey temple results, the width of which is of the same proportions as those given above.

22.59–60a If (another storey is added) below that, with a body of six and a half parts and a base of three and a half, whilst its width is divided into eleven or twelve parts, the result is a seven storey temple, fitting under any circumstances.

22.60b–61 If (another storey is added) below that, whose body is seven parts and base three and a half and whose width is divided into ten, eleven, twelve or thirteen parts, an eight storey temple is obtained according to the leading experts.

22.62–63a If (yet another storey is added) below that, with a body of seven and a half parts and a base three and three quarter parts and whose width is of the same proportions as given above, the result is a nine storey temple.

22.63b–64a For a ten storey temple (there is added) below (another body) of eight parts on a base of four; the proportions of its width are as given above or else it may be divided into fourteen parts.

22.64b–66a If, (once again, a storey is added) below, whose body is eight and a half parts and base four and a quarter and the proportions of whose width are as given above, if not divided into fifteen, sixteen or seventeen, the result is an eleven storey temple.

Twelve storeyed temples

22.66b–67a Next, as regards a twelve storey temple: (a storey should be added) below, whose body is nine parts and base four and a half and whose width may be divided into from sixteen to twenty-four parts.

22.67b–69a Starting with the sanctum and proceeding towards the exterior up to the limits of the building, the interior wall, aisle and exterior wall should be arranged successively. Here are their proportions: the sanctum is two, three, four or six parts in width if its proportions are not the same as those previously indicated; the aisle is one or one and a half parts wide and the remainder is for the walls.

22.69b–70a There are those, though, who say that the width of a twelve storey temple is to be divided into twenty-seven parts, of which six are for the walls and five for the aisle.

22.70b–71a There is a decoration of corner aediculae (etc. . . .) on the exterior. The corner and elongated aediculae, the niches and small aediculae which extend like elephants' trunks should be arranged by the expert, according to appearance desired and to what is decorative.

22.71b (The dimensions of temples) may be calculated in an even or odd number of cubits, as is preferred.

22.72 The width of the corner aediculae is two parts if the number of these, (in the total width), is even; the length of the elongated aediculae is twice as much, or else (the width of the corner aediculae) may be four parts; at all events, it is to be understood that (this width) must be expressed in an even number if the total number of parts is even.

22.73 The expert, eminent amongst architects, must proceed according to these rules or to the different proportions and arrangements prescribed by the great sages.

Engaged structures

22.74–75 If the temple is four-storeyed, the engaged structures should be elevated to the height of the first storey; if it is five, six or seven-storeyed, to the second storey; if it is eight, nine or ten-storeyed, to the third; lastly, if it is eleven storeyed, they go up to the fourth storey and if twelve storeyed, to the fifth one.

Aediculae

22.76–78a Whosoever wishes to arrange elements such as aediculae, starting from the first storey, must reduce their proportions appropriately, storey by storey. All elements such as square and elongated aediculae may be arranged on each storey as indicated above. The kinds of square and elongated aediculae and niches (etc. ....) used (on engaged structures) should be the same as those proper to the building itself which have been previously indicated.

22.78b–79a Square aediculae should be placed at the corners of two to twelve storey temples, elongated ones in the middle, and niches between them.

22.79b–81 These elements are to project in relation to the *mānasūtra*; this projection is equal to half or a quarter their width or it is one, two or three digits. The *mānasūtra* is not to extend into the interior of the diagram; a straight line marks the extremity (of the projecting elements); if it is broken this will be a source of misfortune; as well, all elements such as aediculae should be outside the *mānasūtra* (?).

22.82–83 The roof of corner aediculae is square, octagonal or circular plan or is sixteen sided and it has a finial; at the centre is a niche; it has (small) half-moon dormer windows and a gable (*mukhapaṭṭikā*) and is surmounted by a pole.

22.84–85 The elongated aedicula has several finials and it is in the middle. If it is behind it is shaped like an elephant's back but in front its shape should be that of an clongated building. The sensible man places niches between these different aediculae. Or else, (the aedicula), open at the side, may be decorated with an elephant's trunk (?).

22.86–89 This is the disposition that corresponds to the *jāti* mode. If there are elongated aediculae at the corners and a square one in the middle with, between these, a decoration consisting of small elongated aediculae and other similar elements, this is *chanda* mode. When either the square aediculae or the elongated ones are on a stereobate and, consequently, some are higher than others, this is *vikalpa* mode. The *ābhāsa* mode can be identified when these two arrangements are employed together and is suitable for very small buildings, small, medium and large ones. An edifice envisaged along the lines of any of these systems, the first being *jāti*, guarantees success whilst the transgression of any of these rules will bring about certain death.

22.90–92a According to whether (the aedicula) is hexagonal or octagonal or comprises an apse, an eighth, ninth or tenth of its width must be added to the exterior . . . ?

22.92b–93a If the dimensions of the house are in whole numbers, the earth will be very abundant (in riches), that is why the sage must draw everything with the greatest of care.

22.93b–94 Thus have the characteristics of temples been laid out in succession; next indicated are the dimensions, in cubits, and the proportions of the height and width of buildings of from one to twelve storeys; the arrangements of elements such as aediculae have been indicated as well as names and types (of temples). Maya has accurately made statement of all that has been prescribed by the great seers, of whom the premier is Brahmā, for the construction of temples of various kinds, perfect and without flaw.

Thus ends, in the *Mayamata*, treatise on dwelling, the twenty-second chapter: RULES FOR TEMPLES WITH SEVERAL STOREYS STARTING WITH THOSE WITH FOUR STOREYS.

Chapter 23

ENCLOSURES AND ATTENDANTS' SHRINES

Enclosure

23.1 Now the sanctuary enclosures are prescribed just as they have been given by the experts. They are intended to protect and embellish the temple and to contain the Attendants' shrines as well.

Dimensions of enclosures

23.2–3 (The diagram for) the main temple is drawn up with four squares: that for the first enclosure is the *mahāpīṭha* consisting of sixteen squares, that for the second is the *maṇḍūka* (64 squares), that for the median enclosure, the *bhadramahāsana* (136 squares), that for the fourth enclosure, the *supratīkānta* (484 squares) and that for the fifth the *indrakānta* (1024 squares).

23.4–5 This is the procedure with diagrams which are even; now that for those which are odd is given. The (main) temple occupies only one square; the diagram for the first enclosure is the *pīṭha* (9 squares), that for the second is the *sthaṇḍila* (49 squares), that for the median one the *ubhaya-caṇḍita* (169 squares), that for the fourth the *susaṃhita* (441 squares) and that for the fifth the *īśakānta* (961 squares).

23.6–7 On the quadrangular area thus obtained, the length of the front facade is to be calculated as has been given above. It is one and a half, one and three quarters, twice, two and a half, three or four times (the width of the temple). In this way the front length of each enclosure is calculated.

23.8–10a Where the smallest of small temples are concerned, the *antarmaṇḍala* is built at a distance (from the temple) of one and a half times the (temple's) width and the second enclosure at the same distance, augmented by three cubits; the third is five cubits farther than that, the fourth seven cubits beyond (the third) and the fifth nine beyond (the fourth).

23.10b–12 For the medium category of (small sized) temples the *antarmaṇḍala* is built at a distance equal to half their width, the second enclosure is five cubits farther, the third seven more than that, the fourth nine, and the fifth eleven more.

23.13–15a For the superior class (of small sized temples) the first enclosure is at a distance equal to half the temple's width, the second is seven cubits farther, the third nine and, beyond that, the fourth is eleven more cubits away and the fifth thirteen more.

23.15b–16 These are the prescriptions for small sized buildings of low, medium or high category; it is according either to this method or to that previously indicated, that the sage is to establish the surrounding enclosures and is to calculate, as above, the length of their front facade.

23.17 The expert on measurements takes the dimensions from the interior face of the walls; some specialists, however, prescribe they be taken from the middle (of their thickness) or from their exterior face.

Enclosure walls

23.18–20a The thickness of the *antarmaṇḍala* wall is a cubit and a half; (for the other enclosures) three digits are added to this figure (per enclosure), up to two cubits; thus is the thickness of the five enclosure walls determined. The height of each wall is three or four times its thickness and the thickness at the top is seven eighths (that at the bottom).

23.20b–21 The walls are elevated up to the height of the architrave, the bell-capital or the abacus (of the pillars of the main temple). They are provided with various elements such as a base and are decorated with flanking structures or they are bare; their top has rounded or semi-circular merlons (?).

23.22 Measured in cubits, the thickness of the enclosure walls of the smallest temple goes from one cubit to one and a half by the same increase as given above (i.e. by three digits).

23.23–25 The coping of the enclosure wall comprises an architrave, an upper fascia and a cap-stone; its height is equal to the width of the wall or to that width augmented by a quarter or by a half; this height is divided into eleven parts: three for the architrave, three for the fascia, two for a doucine and three for the cap-stone. The wall (on its exterior face) may be bare or it may have flanking structures (on its interior face); these comprise (all necessary elements), beginning with a base, and their projection is (equal to) their height.

Cloister-like gallery

23.26–28a (Or else) a cloister-like gallery (*āvṛtamaṇḍapa*) with one, two or three storeys, may be arranged on the interior face of the wall, the exterior face being bare. The height of the top storey (of this gallery) may be two thirds of its ground floor or it may be three quarters or seven eighths of it, or the height (of the gallery) is the same as that of the wall on its exterior face. This gallery may be *mālikā*-shaped or may have a long verandah.

23.28b–29 The greatest heights (that may be attained) by the exterior walls are the following: that of the floor of the bottom storey of the main temple, that of its architrave, of its engaged structures or of its roof.

23.30–31 A gallery with one or two storeys may be built all around; it is provided with a base (etc. ...) whose height is equal to the base of the wall or is three quarters or six eighths of it; the height of the pillars of this gallery is double (that of its base) or may be (double) less a sixth or an eighth.

Decoration of wall coping

23.32a Images of bulls and dwarves should be arranged on the coping of the wall.

Height of bases

23.32b–34 The base of the central (temple) exceeds by one

cubit (that) of the first enclosure; with the other enclosures this difference diminishes by six digits for each one; this is suitable for a small temple and, for a medium one (the difference) is eighteen digits, diminishing by four digits for each enclosure up to the fifth. The architect should proceed in this way, according to this progression.

Attendants' shrines

23.35–36a The sanctum of an Attendant's shrine takes up half its width, which width is a third, a half or three quarters that of the main temple; it is also said that the width of these edifices is three, four, five, six or seven cubits.

23.36b–38 According to the sages well acquainted with the treatises, there are eight, twelve, sixteen or thirty-two Attendants. The (heights) (of the images) of the Attendants placed in these shrines are to be determined according to rule; the well advised one will choose dimensions as prescribed for a manifest image; endowed with all their distinctive signs, these images may be standing or seated.

The eight Attendants

23.39–40a When the sanctuary is small, there are eight Attendants and a single enclosure; if it follows the *pīṭha* diagram, they are placed starting on Āryaka's square, (in the following order): Ṛṣabha, Gaṇādhipa, Kamalaja, the Mothers, Guha, Ārya, Acyuta and Caṇḍeśa.

The twelve Attendants

23.40b–42a If the diagram is *upapīṭha*, the Attendants to be put there are twelve: in the first place there are Vṛṣa, Kamalaja, Guha and Hari who are arranged as above beginning at Āryaka's square and, in the second place, Ravi, Gajavadana, Yama, the Mothers, Jaleśa, Durgā, Dhanada and Caṇḍa who are installed from the square of Sūrya and going round to the right.

The sixteen Attendants

23.42b–45a If the diagram is *ugrapīṭha*, sixteen Attendants are installed. Vṛṣabha and the others are inside as in the preceding case, on the squares of Ārya etc. . . . . Then follow Caṇḍa at Īśa's square, Candra at Jayanta's, Sūrya at Bhṛśa's, Gajavadana at Agni's, Śrī at Vitatha's, Sarasvatī at Bhṛṅganṛpa's, the Mothers at Pitṛ's, Śukra at Sugala's, Jīva at Śoṣa's, Durgā at Vāyu's, Diti at Mukhya's and Uditi at Uditi's.

The thirty-two Attendants (fig. 16)

23.45b–52 If the diagram is the one named *sthaṇḍila*, thirty-two Attendants are installed; around the nine squares of Brahmā's place are these divinities: in the first place Śrī at Sāvindra's square, Jyeṣṭhā at Indrajaya's, Umā at Rudrajaya's and Sarasvatī at Āpavatsa's; in the second place, Vṛṣabha and the others at Āryaka's square . . . etc. as in the preceding case; then Īśa is installed at Īśa's square, Śaśi at Parjanya's Nandikeśvara at Mahendra's, Surapati at Bhānu's, Mahākāla at Satya's, Dinakara at Antarikṣa's, Vahni at Anala's Bṛhaspati at Pūṣan's, Gajavadana at Gṛhakṣata's, Yama at Ārkin's, Bhṛṅgiriṭi at Gandharva's, Cāmuṇḍā at Mṛṣa's, Nirṛti at Pitṛ's, Agastya at Bodhana's Viśvakarman at Puṣpadanta's, Jalapati at Varuṇa's, Sage Bhṛgu at Asura's, Prajāpati at Yakṣa's, Vāyu at Samīraṇa's, Durgā at Nāga's, Vīrabhadra at Ballāṭa's, Dhanada at Soma's, Caṇḍeśvara at Mṛga's and Śukra at Uditi's. This is the arrangement on the *sthaṇḍila* diagram, according to the consensus of the learned.

23.53a According to whether the diagrams are even or odd, Attendants' shrines are built up against the wall of the enclosure or are detached and installed in the middle of the diagram's squares.

23.53b–54a Where there are three or five enclosures, the arrangement is as above: the first eight Attendants are to be found, (according to circumstances), in the *antarhāra* or in the *madhyahāra*.

23.54b–56a If the main temple is orientated towards the

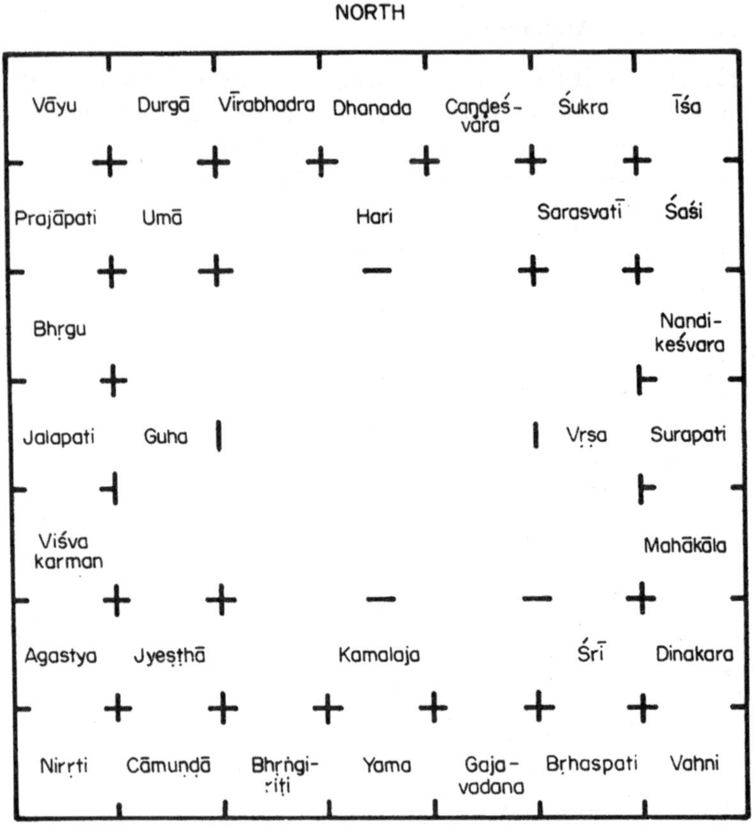

Fig. 16 Śiva's Attendants (23.45b–52)

west, Vṛṣabha is at Mitra's square whilst Kamalaja, Guha and Hari are at those of Bhūdhara, Ārya and Vivasvant respectively; their orientation should be the same as that of the shrine of Īśvara but the others must face the temple from the positions mentioned above.

23.56b–57a According to whether the temple is orientated towards the west or the east, Vṛṣa either faces God or has his back to Him. Lastly, it is said that Caṇḍeśa and Ibhānana must be orientated to the south and north respectively.

23.57b–58a The shrines of Attendants are to have the appearance of temples, pavilions, halls (*sabhā*) or houses (*śālā*) and are each to be provided with all prescribed elements.

Storeyed galleries

23.58b–59a In the *madhya*(*-hāra*) and in the *antarhāra*, a row of storeyed galleries (*mālikā*) should be built with one, two, three, four or five storeys.

23.59b–60a A wall should be built above a wall and a pillar above a pillar; pillars may be installed above walls but walls should not be above pillars.

23.60b–61a (*Mālikā*) have square and elongated aediculae (etc. . . .) or they have latticed walls, they may also resemble pavilions, houses or halls.

23.61b–67a Their proportions are now indicated and the dimensions of their pillars: the distance between the top of the base of the main temple and its architrave being divided into seven equal parts, the base (of the *mālikā*) makes up two parts of the height and the pillars five; the pillars have the full order. Or else, the height of the pillars (of the temple) being divided into nine parts, the base (of the *mālikā*) makes up two parts of the height and the remainder is for the height of its pillars, for which there are fifteen possible heights, from two and a half cubits to six by successive increments of six digits; their diameter is equal to the thickness of the wall and their intercolumniation is in proportion, this being true both for large and small buildings; it is also said that the diameter of the pillars may be from six to twenty digits by successive increments of one digit.

23.67b–69 The height of the base (of a *mālikā*) is half that of its pillars or is half, less a sixth or an eighth or else it is a third or a quarter the height of the pillars; the base is to be *pādabandha* or *carubandha* type. (A *mālikā*) is ornamented with an entablature, the total height of the elements of which is a quarter less (than that of the base); here the principles given above are to be applied and adapted.

Annexes

23.70–71a Annexes (*khalūrikā*) built around houses meant for men are like (the *mālikā* around the temple). They are found all around in the first, (second) and third enclosures; their doors, which are orientated in whichsoever direction desired, are to conform to the principles given for mortals.

23.71b–72a The Attendants' shrines are arranged in the prescribed positions of which the first is Ārya's, and are orientated towards the temple as given above.

23.72b–73 Outside and in front of these shrines are the pavilion for the dance, the altars etc. . . . The pavilion for ablutions and that for dance may also be between these shrines and have the same proportions.

Altars

23.74–76 The height and width of the two altars are equal to half (the width) of the sanctum of the temple. The *balivisṭara*, however, may also have a height and width of one, two or three cubits. The (*paiśāca-*) *pīṭha* is exterior to the temple at a distance equal to half (the width) (?) of the temple; the distance between the *balivisṭara* (and the gateway) is the same or is three quarters that. The *paiśācapīṭha* is exterior to the five enclosures in front (of the temple) and the *balivisṭara* is between the *paiśācapīṭha* and the temple.

23.77–78 The height of the altar is divided into sixteen equal parts: the first plinth makes up one, the second four, the torus three, the listel which comes above one, the dado three and the listel surmounting it one, the fillet two and the crowning fillet one.

23.79–80a Above this is a lotus with a diameter half or three quarters the width (of the altar) and, also above, in the centre (of the lotus), is its receptacle whose width is three quarters that of the lotus; the height of the lotus is three quarters (its width) or is half the height of the receptacle.

23.80b–81 The altar may or may not have a median projection; it may be on a socle. According to the specific case it may be shaped as one or other of the bases. Such are the features of altars as they have been given by the greatest sages of old.

The flag mast

23.82–83a In front of Vṛṣabha, half way from the temple, is the place for the flag mast with the trident in front of it; all (three), beginning with Vṛṣa, are inside (the enclosure) and to the left, on the way from gateway (to temple).

Buildings within the enclosures

23.83b–84 The building for oblations is built against the wall of the *maryādi* enclosure in the south-east corner, with the treasury between this corner and the (eastern) gateway, whilst the pavilion for ablutions is on Yama's square (in the south) where too is the pavilion for flowers.

23.85 The pavilion for the gods' weapons should be close to the south-west corner whilst the dormitories are to be at the squares of Varuṇa and Vāyu.

23.86 The pavilion for religious discourse is at Soma's square, the well at that of Īśa and the tank encompasses that of Āpavatsa.

23.87–88a The pavilion for musical instruments is between the north-east corner and the (eastern) gateway; the *vimāna* (?) is next to Īśa's square unless it is the shrine of Caṇḍeśvara which is there; but this may otherwise be at the position previously indicated by the sages.

The flag mast (cont.)

23.88b–91 The flag mast in front of the altar is to be in proportion to the temple; for the very small temples its height is twice theirs, for small ones, equal, for medium ones it is three quarters or half and for big ones a quarter or a half. The pole itself is a cubit wide or is sixteen, twelve or ten digits; it is endowed with bell-capital and abacus and, above the latter, is an image of a dwarf or of a bull; it is in stone or in wood and its section is circular, octagonal or sixteen sided.

Other buildings

23.92 The house (of the head priest), the well, the tank, the garden and the pond may each be placed in any position as may the *maṭha* and the dining hall.

23.93–94a If a sanctuary has only one enclosure it is not the *antarmaṇḍala* but the *antarhāra*; if three, they are *antarhāra*, *madyamahāra* and *maryādabhitti*; if there are five enclosures, the five types described should be used.

23.94b There are images of bulls along the entire length of the top of the enclosure walls.

23.95 To the east, and at a distance from the flag mast of the goddess equal to three, four or five times the width of the main temple, are houses of courtesans on both sides of which are places for masseuses.

23.96–97a All around, outside the enclosures, are the habitations of the servants (of the temple) but these houses may otherwise be to the east; the hermitage of the Master is in the south or in the east but opens to the south.

23.97b All that which has not been described is to be done at the behest of the prince.

Attendants of Viṣṇu

23.89–100a The Attendants to be arranged around the Viṣṇu temple are now presented: Vainateya is at the east and the shrine of Gajamukha is at the position of Vahni; Pitāmaha is at Yama's position and the Mothers at that of Pitṛ; Guha is at Jaleśa's, Durgā at Vāyu's and Dhanādhipa at Soma's; lastly, Senāpati is at Īśa's. For altars (etc. . . . .) the procedure is as above and it is like this that things are to be done when there is only one enclosure.

23.100b–102 Directions are now given as to the procedure for twelve Attendants. Cakra is in front of Viṣṇu, Garuḍa a little to the south and Śaṅkha to the north; they face the exterior and are to be represented in manifest images. Sūrya and Candramas are on each side of the gateway facing the interior; the oblations pavilion is at the position of Vahni and the rest is as above.

23.103–105a When there are sixteen Attendants they are installed in the *antarhāra* and in the *madyahāra*; Pakṣirāja and the altar are in front of the main temple's pavilion; the Lords of the cardinal points are to be each in his place with the exception of Śiva (Īśa). Installed as well are Āditya, Bhṛgu, the two Aśvin, Sarasvatī, Padmā, Pṛthivī as well as the Sages and Saciva: all these deities must be in the space between the (corners) and the *dvārapāla* who are in the middle.

23.105½ When there are thirty-two Attendants they are to be arranged according to the specific circumstance.

23.106 Caṇḍa, Pracaṇḍa, Rathanemi, and Pāñcajanya, Durgā, Gaṇeśa, Ravi, Candra: these great gods, as well as Sarveśvara and Surapati are, all ten to be installed on the facades of the gateways of the five enclosures.

Characteristics of (the image of) Vṛṣa.

23.107–110a The characteristics of the image of Vṛṣa are now briefly described. When the image is large-sized, its height is equal to that of the door or to that of the Liṅga; when it is of medium size then it is three quarters that height and, if it is small, two thirds. (Or else), the small sized image will be equal to half the height of the sanctum and the large size one equal to the total of that height. The difference between these two dimensions divided into eight parts yields nine possible heights, or else, from one cubit to nine there are three heights for each category beginning with the small images.

23.110b–113a The digit is equal to a fiftieth part of the image's height. The length is forty digits and these are the proportions: (from the top) of the head to the top of the neck there are ten digits; the height of the neck is eight digits and there are sixteen digits (from the neck) to the top of the rear thigh; this is six digits long and the dimension of the knee is two digits; the foot is six digits long and it is said that the hoof is two double digits.

23.113b–116 The space between the horns is two digits whilst their own length is two double digits; their diameter at the bottom is three digits and, at the top, two. The frontal is nine digits, the width and height of the muzzle is five digits; the eyes are two digits long and one and a half wide; the distance between muzzle and eyeline is eight digits, from nape to the neck itself, six digits and the height of the frontal from the eyeline is half a digit.

23.117–118a The distance between eyes and ears is equal to the length of the ears, that is, five digits; at the bottom, the ears are two digits wide, in the middle two digits wide, as at the top; their thickness is half a digit.

23.118b–119 The muzzle is a digit and a half long and the open part is a digit high and the mouth five digits long; the upper lip is three digits high and the lower two.

23.120a The tongue is three digits long, two wide and one thick.

23.120b–121a The diameter of the neck is ten digits but is twelve at its lower part; at the nape, the thickness of the neck is eight digits at the withers and six at the bottom of the head.

23.121b–122a The hump is six digits wide, its height half its width and it is two digits at the withers.

23.122b–123a The height of the flanks at the level of the hump is eighteen digits; that of the spine is fourteen; the width of the body is twelve digits.

23.123b–125a The width of the hind thighs is ten, eight and then four digits; their length is five digits and the knee is two; the hind feet are five digits long and three wide; the height of the hooves is three digits.

23.125b At its start, the tail has a diameter of three digits and at its end, one and a half; it hangs down to the foot.

23.126 The testicles are three digits long and two wide; the length of the penis is three digits and its diameter at the beginning is one digit.

23.127a The space between the thighs is four digits high and that between the hocks two.

23.127b–129a The remainder may be determined relative to the specific circumstance; the image may be standing or stretched out, depending upon which is most convenient and, also in relation to circumstance, it may be made in stucco, metal or other materials; if in metal, it may be hollow or solid.

23.129b–130 Vṛṣa's height is to be in proportion to the height of the manifest image (of Śiva); even the smallest increase or diminution causes sorrow without end and this is why the prudent man endows this image with all characteristics prescribed.

23.131 According to the best of sages, Vṛṣa may have one of three heights: the largest is equal to that of the door or to that of the Liṅga, the medium is three quarters that and the smallest two thirds.

Thus ends, in the *Mayamata*, treatise on dwelling,
the twenty-third chapter: RULES FOR THE
THE ENCLOSURES AND FOR THE
ATTENDANTS' SHRINES.

Chapter 24
GATEWAYS

24.1 I now give the characteristics of gateways which are to be proportionate to the (main) temple according to whether it is very small, small, medium or large.

Dimensions of the five gateways

24.2–3a The width of the *dvāraśobhā* (gateway of the first enclosure) is six sevenths that of the main temple; those (of the gateways of the second, third and fourth enclosures) are, respectively, seven eighths, eight ninths and nine tenths (that of the main temple) and that of the (gateway of the fifth enclosure), called *gopura,* is ten elevenths that of the main temple. This applies when the main temple is small or very small.

24.3b–5 These are the prescriptions for temples of medium size: the five gateways, from *dvāraśobhā* to *gopura,* have respective widths equal to three quarters, four fifths, five sixths, six sevenths and seven eighths (that of the central temple).

24.6–7a These are the prescriptions for large sized temples: the five gateways, from *dvāraśobhā* to *gopura,* have respective widths equal to a third, a half, two thirds, three quarters or four fifths (that of the central temple).

24.7b–10 These widths are now given in cubits. If the main temple is small or very small, there are three possible widths for each of the five gateways, the first of which is the (*dvāra*)-*śobhā*: they go from two cubits to sixteen by successive increments of one. (If the temple is of medium size), the three series of widths for the five gates, the first of which is the *dvāraśobhā,* begin with three cubits and go up to thirty-one by increments of two cubits. (If the temple is big), fifteen dimensions are obtained by starting with nine cubits and going up to thirty-seven by successive increments of two cubits, which dimensions are the widths of the five gateways, the first being (*dvāra*)-*śobhā*.

The five gateways

24.11 *Dvāraśobhā*, *dvāraśālā*, *dvāraprāsāda*, (*dvāra*)-*harmya* and *gopura*: these are the respective names of (the gateways of the five enclosures) the first of which is *dvāraśobhā*.

24.12–18a Their widths may also be measured in cubits (in the following way): the five possible widths (of the main temple) being three, five, seven, nine or eleven cubits, two cubits are added to make up (the widths corresponding to) the first of the five (gateways). Thus, the five widths of the *dvāraśobhā*, which is on the first enclosure, are five, seven, nine, eleven or thirteen cubits; the width of the *dvāraśālā* is from fifteen to twenty-three cubits; the five widths of the *dvāra-prāsāda* are from twenty-five to thirty-three cubits; in the same way, the five widths of the *dvāraharmya* go from thirty-five to forty-three cubits and, similarly, the sages say that the five widths of the *gopura* go from forty-five to fifty-three cubits. The procedure is the same for the palaces of great universal kings.

24.18b–19a The length of the five gateways, the first of which is (*dvāra*)-*śobhā* are, respectively, one and a half, (one and three quarters), two and a third and two and two thirds (their width).

24.19b–21a Here are their respective heights calculated from their widths: ten sevenths, six quarters, seven quarters, nine fifths and double. The heights of gateways are calculated thus.

24.21b–22 The projection of the gateways in relation to the outside of the enclosure walls is a third, a quarter or two fifths of their width.

Dimensions of doors

24.23–25 Here are the calculations for the width of the doors according to whether (the gateway) is small, medium or large; if it is small that width will go from one and a half (cubits) to five by successive increments of six digits; (if medium) it will go from two to seven cubits by increments of nine digits; (if it is large) it will go from two to nine cubits by increments of twelve digits. Thus there are fifteen dimensions possible in each instance.

24.25b–26 Now the corresponding heights for the doors of the five gateways are indicated; they are respectively: seven fifths, ten sevenths, double, double and a quarter, and double and a half their width.

Dimensions of bases etc. . . .

24.27–28 The heights of the pillars and of the base (of gateways) are to be calculated in relation to the main building. The height of the base is three quarters, four fifths, five sixths, six sevenths, seven eighths, eight ninths, nine tenths, ten elevenths or eleven thirteenths that of the base of the main temple; the part remaining each time is for the socle. The base is *pādabandha* type.

24.29–31a The height of the gateway's pillars is the same as that of those of the main building or may be seven eighths, eight ninths or nine tenths of it; they are sunk, at the bottom, into the base right down to the regulating course (*homa*). The door rises to the architrave and has a width half its height. The foundation deposit is beneath the wall which rises to the south of the entrance.

Types of gateway

24.31b–34a *Śrīkara*, *ratikānta*, *kāntavijaya*, *vijayaśālaka*, *viśālālaya*, *vipratīkāntā*, *śrīkānta*, *śrīkeśa*, *keśaviśālaka*, *svastika*, *diśāsvastika*, *mardala*, *mātrākāṇḍa*, *śrīviśāla* and *caturmukha*: these are the names given to the fifteen types of gateway.

24.34b–35 For small temples, the five gateways, beginning with (*dvāra*)-*śobhā*, have from one to five storeys respectively, for medium temples, they have from two to six storeys and for large ones from three to seven.

24.36 The base is on a socle and the height of the body

rises to the architrave. The proportions of the remainder, up to the finial, are now given.

Single storeyed gateways

24.36½–38a (The height) of single-storeyed gateways from architrave to finial is to be divided into six equal parts: one and a half for the entablature, one for the attic, two and three quarters for the roof and the remainder for the finial.

Two storeyed gateways

24.38b–40 Here are the proportions for when there are two storeys. The distance between the first storey's architrave and the finial is divided into nine equal parts: one and a quarter for the entablature (of the first storey), two and a half for the body (of the second) and one for its entablature, one for the attic, two and a half for the roof and the remainder for the finial. This is the way in which a two storey building should be set up.

Three storeyed gateways

24.41–43a These are the proportions when there are three storeys: the height from the architrave (of the first storey) to the finial is divided into twelve parts: one and a quarter for the entablature (of the first floor), two and a half for the body (of the second) and one for its entablature, two for the body (of the third) and three quarters for its entablature, one for the attic and two and a half for the roof; what remains is the height of the finial. This is the procedure when there are three storeys.

Four storeyed gateways

24.43b–46a Now the procedure for when there are four storeys is indicated. The height, from architrave (of the ground floor) to finial, is divided into eighteen parts: one and three quarters for the entablature (of the ground floor), three for the body (of the second storey) and one and a half for its entablature, two and a half for the body (of the third) and one and a quarter for its entablature, two for the body (of the fourth), one for the attic and three for the roof, the remainder being the height of the finial.

Five storeyed gateways

24.46b–49 These are the proportions for when there are five storeys: the height from architrave (of the first storey) to finial is divided into twenty-three parts: two for the entablature (of the first storey), three and a half for the body (of the second) and one and three quarters for its entablature, three for the body (of the third), one and a half for its entablature, two and a half for the body (of the fourth) and one and a quarter for its entablature, two for the body (of the fifth) and one for its entablature, one for the attic and two and a half for the roof; what remains is the height of the finial.

Six storeyed gateways

24.50–54a (When there are six storeys) the height between the architrave (of the first storey) and the finial is to be divided into twenty-nine parts: two for the entablature (of the first storey), four for the body (of the second) and one and three quarters for its entablature, three and a half for the body (of the third) and one and three quarters for its entablature, three (for the body of the fourth) and one and a half for its entablature, two and a half for the body (of the fifth) and one and a quarter for its entablature, two for the body of the top storey and one for its entablature, one for the attic and two and a half for the roof; what is left is the height of the finial. This is the way to proceed where six-storeyed buildings are concerned.

Seven storeyed gateways

24.54b–58 Now the procedure for seven is shown. The

height between architrave (of the ground floor) and finial is to be divided into thirty-six parts: two and a quarter for the entablature (of the first storey), four and a half for the body (of the second) and two for its entablature, four for the body (of the third) and one and three quarters for its entablature, three and a half for the body (of the fourth) and one and three quarters for its entablature, three for the body (of the fifth) and one and a half for its entablature, two and a half for the body (of the sixth) and one and a quarter for its entablature, two for the last storey and one for its entablature, one for the attic, two and three quarters for the roof; what remains is the height of the finial.

24.59a These are the elevations of the gateways in relation to the number of their storeys.

Horizontal proportions of gateways

24.59b–60a The width of a single storeyed gateway is divided into five parts: three for the median passage and the rest for the thickness of the walls.

24.60b–62 (If there are two storeys) the width is divided into seven parts: four for the median passage and the rest for the thickness of the walls. The corner aediculae are one part wide; the length of the median aediculae is three parts on the width of the building and five on its length; between these aediculae are decorative niches. This is the procedure when there are two storeys.

24.63–64a If there are three storeys, the width is divided into nine parts: three for the median passage and one (on each side) for the interior wall, one for the aisle and one for the exterior wall. All elements such as corner aediculae are to be arranged as previously given.

24.64b The rest is for the thickness of the walls; the corner aediculae make up one part of the width (?).

24.65–66a The median aediculae are three parts long, the projecting niches make up one part of the width and the recesses half a part; the median aediculae on the long facade are five or six parts in length.

24.66b–68a Above, the width is seven (ninths that of the ground floor), the width of the corner aediculae makes up one part of the width and the length of the median ones two; on the two-part wide recesses are small niches half a part wide; the median aediculae on the long facade are five parts long. This is the procedure when there are three storeys and all else should conform to the experts' prescriptions.

24.68b–70 (If there are four storeys) the width is to be divided into ten parts: three for the median passage and, (on each side), one and a half for the thickness of the (interior) wall, one for the aisle and one for the (exterior wall with its) engaged structures, the aediculae being arranged as given above; the big median aediculae in front and behind are five or six parts long. It is through the arrangement of all these prescribed elements that the most perfect of four storeyed (gateways) is arrived at.

24.71–72a When there are five storeys the width is divided into eleven parts: three for the median passage and, (on each side), two for the thickness of the (interior) wall, one for the aisle and one for the (exterior wall with its) engaged structures. The rest is arranged as given above.

24.72b–74a This is what is to be done when there are six storeys. The width is divided into twelve parts: four for the median passage and, (on each side), two for the thickness of the (interior) wall, one for the aisle and one for the (exterior wall with its) engaged structures. The rest, that is the aediculae and so on, should be arranged as previously given.

24.74b–77 (When there are seven storeys) the width is divided into sixteen parts: four for the median passage and, (on each side), two and a half for the thickness of the (interior) wall, one for the aisle and one for the (exterior wall with) engaged structures. The aediculae and similar elements are arranged as given above; the big median aediculae, both in front and behind, are six parts long; there are niches, aediculae provided with an apse, and elongated aediculae on the sides (?). All types of base, pillar, stereobate, window and architrave are suitable. This is how a seven storeyed gateway is made in whatsoever circumstance.

Doors and stairways

24.78–79a The width of the doors (of upper storeys) is less by a fifth or a quarter than that of the ground floor; a door with its jambs and lintel is to be placed in the centre of each storey.

24.79b–80 The stairway leading to the upper storeys rises from the median passage; it begins on a square platform and is arranged by the well advised according to specific circumstance and appearance desired.

Specific arrangements

24.81–84a Now the different types of gateways are presented one after the other and with their particular arrangement. The *dvāraśobhā* should be shaped like a pavilion and the *dvāraśālā* like an elongated *śālā*; the sages say that the *dvāraprāsāda* looks like a *prāsāda*, the *dvāraharmya* like a *mālikā* and that the *dvāragopura* resembles a building with a number of *śālā*. The arrangement of a gateway always conforms to the specific circumstance.

Dvāraśobhā: śrīkara type

24.84b–86 Here is, first of all, the arrangement of the *śrīkara* type: its length is double its width or equal to one and a half times that width. Its width is divided into five, seven or nine parts and its proportions in length are calculated from its proportions in width. It has one, two or three storeys and is endowed with all elements prescribed.

24.87–88 There are niches all around of *svastika* type. There is a large niche both in front and behind, and on either side, a gable niche. The roof resembles a cruciform aedicula and it is surmounted by an even number of finials. It may have a rafter frame or may be in the shape of a pavilion.

Ratikānta type

24.89–91a Here are the characteristics of the *ratikānta* type:

its length is one and a half times its width and all elements such as aediculae are to be arranged as given above. Its roof is wagon shaped; there are six niches in front and six behind and false dormer windows of the *ardhakoṭi* type. The number of finials is even. Inside are vestibules with pillars and architraves.

Kāntavijaya type

24.91b–92a Here are the characteristics of the *kāntavijaya* type: its length is two thirds its width and the proportions of its storeys and arrangements of elements such as aediculae are as given above.

24.92b–93 Inside there are pillars and architraves as well as various decorative elements. On the front and back of the roof are six niches and, on the sides, two; (this roof) is a hipped roof (*sabhākara*) which has an uneven number of finials.

24.94a There are three types of *dvāraśobhā*: the door itself is to be decorated on its exterior.

Dvāraśālā: *vijayaviśāla* type

24.94b–95 Here are the characteristics of the *vijayaviśāla* type: its length is double its width or is one and a quarter, one and a half or one and three quarter times it. (Its width) is to be divided into seven, nine or eleven parts and there are one, two, three or four storeys.

24.96–97 If there are three or four storeys there is an aisle and four *mukhapaṭṭikā* (?). There is a large projecting false dormer window of the *ardhakoṭi* type at front and back of the roof and there are several niches on the sides. The wagon roof has an uneven number of finials. This (gateway) is provided with all prescribed elements.

Viśālālaya type

24.98 Here are the characteristics of the *viśālālaya* type. Its length is one and three quarters (its width) and its proportions and the arrangement of its elements are the same as given above.

24.99–100a (On the roof), front and back, are projecting niches with *ardhakoṭi* type false dormer windows and there are four niches on each side; this wagon roof has an odd number of finials and all else is as given above.

Vipratīkānta type

24.100b–102 Here are the characteristics of the *vipratīkānta* type. Its length is greater than (its width) by two thirds. All elements such as aediculae are to be arranged as given above and the proportions too are the same as in the preceding case. There is a projection on each of the four facades and four niches on the roof, the roof itself being provided with projections. There are pillars and architraves inside. The number of finials is uneven.

24.103a These are the three types of *dvāraśālā* all of whose elements are decorated.

Dvāraprāsāda: śrīkānta type

24.103b–104a Here are the characteristics of the *śrīkānta* type. Its length is one and a half times its width and its width is to be divided into nine, ten or eleven parts; there are three, four or five storeys.

24.104b–106a Inside is an aisle (?) as well as pillars and architraves. There are inner vestibules with projections above the door. There is a big niche in front and at the back. There is a wagon roof and, on it, *ardhakoṭi* type false dormer windows as well as four niches.

Śrīkeśa type

24.106b–107 Here are the characteristics of the *śrīkeśa* type. Its length is triple its width and the proportions of its storeys are as given above. Its base projects at the entrance. There is a median passage and all prescribed elements: aediculae etc. . .

24.108a All types of base, of pillars, of stereobate (etc. . .) are appropriate. Inside are pillars, architraves and vestibules.

24.108b–110 There are big niches at front and back (of the roof), which is wagon shaped, and four niches on its sides. All necessary elements should be put in place. There are false dormer windows of the *svastika* type all around. Such a building should be embellished with latticed windows of the *gavākṣa*, *nandyāvarta* or other (varieties).

Keśaviśāla type

24.111 Here are the characteristics of the *keśaviśāla* type. Its length is one and a half times its width. The storey proportions are the same as above and there are vestibules.

24.112–113a The aediculae etc. . . . . are to be arranged as previously. There are four large niches behind, in front and on the sides of the hipped roof; behind, in front and on the side. . . . (?) There is an uneven number of finials.

24.113b These are the three types of *dvāraprāsāda*.

Dvāraharmya: *svastika* type

24.114 Here are the characteristics of the *svastika* type. Its length is double its width which is to be divided into ten, eleven or twelve parts. It has four, five or six storeys.

24.115 Inside are pillars and architraves. Storey proportions are as above. All elements such as aediculae are present and there is an aisle.

24.116 There is a hipped roof and a decoration of false dormer windows of the *svastika* type. There are eight niches on the hipped (roof) and an odd number of finials.

Diśāsvastika type

24.117 Here are the characteristics of the *diśāsvastika* type. Its length is double its width and its proportions and the arrangement of its aediculae (etc. . . .) are as above.

24.118 It comprises an interior wall, an aisle and an exterior wall with engaged structures. There is a large forepart both in front and behind.

24.119–120a Its elliptical roof comprises four big niches and four others. There are pillars and architraves inside. All prescribed elements are to be present and anything not mentioned here is to be implemented as given above. The number of its finials is uneven.

Mardala type

24.120b–121a Here are the characteristics of the *mardala* type. Its length is double its width, the proportions of its storeys and the arrangement of elements such as aediculae being as above.

24.121b There are *sabhā* shaped foreparts in front and behind and their projection is a third the length (of the building).

24.122–123a The roof is wagon shaped and has small false dormer windows; there is a big niche however as well as four others at front and back. Inside are pillars and architraves. Such are the three types of *dvāraharmya*.

Dvāragopura: *mātrakaṇḍa* type

24.123b–124 Here are the characteristics of the *mātrakaṇḍa* type. Its length is double its width which is to be divided into eleven, twelve or thirteen parts. It has five, six or seven storeys. The storeys' proportions are as above and so are elements such as aediculae.

24.125 Inside are pillars and architraves. This gateway has four foreparts and comprises an interior wall, an aisle and an exterior wall with engaged structures.

24.126 Its roof is wagon shaped with a large niche in front and at the back, and small niches should be arranged on the sides according to specific circumstance.

Śrīviśāla type

24.127 Here are the characteristics of the *śrīviśāla* type. Its length is two fifths its width and its proportions are as given above. It is cruciform plan from bottom up.

24.128–129 It has a cross wagon-roof (*krakarakoṣṭha*) or a hipped roof. All types of base, pillar, stereobate (etc. ...) are suitable for it. At each of the four directions there is a large niche decorated with small dormer windows and all the way around there is a decoration of false dormer windows of the *svastika* type.

Caturmukha type

24.130 Here are the characteristics of the *caturmukha* type. Its length is greater than its width by a quarter; the proportions of its storeys are as above. There are foreparts on each facade.

24.131 *Kumbhalatā* are to be placed in the centre of the recesses, up against the wall, and there is a decoration of arcatures, latticed windows, *vṛttasphuṭita* etc. . .

24.132–133 There are corner aediculae, niches and median aediculae as well as small elongated ones. It comprises an interior wall, an aisle and an (exterior wall) with engaged structures. It has a hipped roof or a wagon roof with four (large) niches and two others on each side.

24.134 There are corner aediculae (etc. ...) on each storey as well as all prescribed elements and there is a stairway inside. These are the three types of *dvāragopura*.

24.135 (The gateways), starting with the *śrīkara* type, may or may not have gutters according to circumstance. Their elements may be massive or hollow.

24.136–137 Fifteen types have been described for the (five) gateways of which the first is the *dvāraśobhā*; they are fitting for the shrines of great gods. Their bases, pillars and elements are of various types. They each have their own particular characteristics. They have socles of various kinds, they are decorated and may or may not have foreparts. They are massive or hollow (structures). They have one to seven storeys depending upon the circumstance. Their roofs may be in the form of *sabhā* (hipped roof), *śālā* (wagon roof) or *maṇḍapa* (flat roof?).

Thus ends, in the *Mayamata*, treatise on dwelling, the twenty-fourth chapter: RULES FOR GATEWAYS.

Chapter 25
PAVILIONS AND HALLS

PAVILIONS

25.1 Now the pavilions are given, such as are suitable for gods or brahmins, kings, vaiśya or śūdra.

Position of pavilions

25.2–3a They are in front of shrines, in places of pilgrimage and of retreat, and they are in pleasant spots; in settlements such as villages (they are placed) in the middle and at the cardinal and intermediate points; in houses they may be inside or outside, in the centre or in front.

Functions of pavilions

25.3b–4 There is the pavilion as habitation, the sacrificial pavilion, the pavilion for consecrations and ceremonies of that sort, the pavilion for the dance, the wedding pavilion, that for alliances and that for the *upanayana* ceremony.

25.5 There is also the audience pavilion, that for military reviews and that where negotiations take place. There is the pavilion for hair-cutting and that for meals and for entertainment.

Names of pavilions

25.6a Here are the names prescribed for these pavilions, systematically presented:

25.6b–8a The sixteen square plan pavilions appropriate for gods, brahmins and kings are *meruka*, *vijaya*, *siddha*, *padmaka*, *bhadraka*, *śiva*, *veda*, *alaṅkṛta*, *darbha*, *kauśika*, *kuladhāriṇa*, *sukhāṅga*, *saukhyaka*, *garbha*, *mālya* and *mālyādbhuta*.

25.8b–11a The eight rectangular plan pavilions appropriate for gods and (for brahmins) as well as for kings, are *dhana*, *subhūṣaṇa*, *āhalya*, *srugaka*, *koṇa*, *kharvaṭa*, *śrīrūpa* and *maṅgala*. The eight pavilions intended for vaiśya and śūdra are *mārga*, *saubhadra*, *sundara*, *sadhāraṇa*, *saukhya*, *īśvarakānta*, *śrībhadra* and *sarvatobhadra*.

25.11b–12 Now, here are their proportions, the height and diameter of their pillars, (the types of) their bases and socles and, here too, are described the light buildings (*prapā*) and the canopy (*raṅga*) which is in the centre (of a pavilion), their decoration, the arrangement of their pillars and their overall appearance.

Proportions

25.13–16 From one and a half to five cubits by successive increments of six digits, there are fifteen possible values for the intercolumniation and the length is to be calculated from the width, as calculated with these (values as) units (*bhakti*); the length, calculated from the width divided into one, two, three, four or five, is one part more. Up to a cubit may otherwise be added, by increments of three digits to each unit of the width calculated in units, the result being eight possible sizes for the long side of the pavilion. This system of measurement is always to be employed and (the proportions) of rectangular pavilions are invariably determined in this way.

Pillar dimensions

25.17–18a There are twenty-three possible heights for pillars, from two and a half to eight cubits by successive increments of three digits.

25.18b–20a The corresponding diameters go from eight to nineteen digits by successive increments of half a digit; the bottom of the pillar may otherwise have a diameter an eleventh, tenth, ninth, or eighth of its height whilst, at the top, it is ten elevenths, nine tenths or eight ninths what it is at the bottom.

Height of base

25.20b–21 It is common to all these buildings that the height of the base is half that of the pillars but the height of the base (of pavilions) may be two fifths or a third that of the pillars.

Height of socle

25.22–23 The base may or may not rest on a socle with a height equal to its own or double or triple it, but the height of the socle may also be that indicated in the chapter on socles and it is, anyway, to be adapted to circumstance and to the appearance sought.

25.24 The decoration of socle, base, pillars and entablature is as has been given above but everything else is to be adapted to meet the particular case.

Definition

25.25 What is called a 'pavilion' has three levels of elevations: base, pillars and entablature, and is provided with a frieze (*prati*) above the cornice.

Etymology of the term *maṇḍapa*

25.26a The *maṇḍapa* is so called because it protects (*pati*) the *maṇḍa*, that is: the decoration.

Light buildings

25.26b–28a I now describe the light buildings (*prapā*) suitable for all classes of society: their pillars rise from the ground; above the architrave there are main rafters, purlins and common rafters; these buildings are covered with coconut palms and the like.

25.28b–29 The height of their pillars will be as indicated above and their diameter four, six, eight or ten digits; these dimensions are appropriate to hard wood and may also be used for bamboo.

The canopy

25.30–31 The height of the central platform (*vedikā*) is a tenth, ninth, eighth, seventh, sixth or fifth that of the pillars. A canopy should be set up in its centre: the height of its base is a quarter the height of the (building's) pillars, that of its own pillars half of that and that of its entablature a quarter.

25.32–33a According to whether the plan (of the building is even or odd), the length of the canopy is two units or one and it comprises eight or four pillars; however, it is said as well that a canopy may be like a light building (that is to say without base).

25.33b–34 The canopy is to be provided with all necessary elements and built with various materials. The centre of a house, hall, light building or pavilion: these are the four positions possible for a canopy which may be of three (different) dimensions.

Mālikāmaṇḍapa

25.35–36a A pavilion with storeys is a *mālikāmaṇḍapa*. If a pavilion has two storeys it is covered by a *śikhara*. That which divides the two storeys is called the "median stereobate".

Meruka type

25.36b–37a The *meruka* pavilion is square and one unit wide; it has four pillars and has eight false dormer windows (on its entablature). This is said to be the seat of Brahmā.

Vijaya type

25.37b–39a A *vijaya* pavilion is square and is two units wide with eight pillars and eight false dormer windows; it has the (three) levels of elevation starting from the base and there is no central pillar. For a wedding however it should be a light building with nine pillars.

Siddha type

25.39b–40 Square and three units wide, it has sixteen pillars and sixteen false dormer windows. In the middle is a court which may or may not be covered by a lantern (*kūṭa*).

25.41 There is a door at each of the cardinal points and an ornamental archway in front of each door. It is suitable for rites such as sacrifice, performed by gods, brahmins and kings. It is called *siddha* and is fitting for all rituals.

The sacrificial pavilion

25.42 The wise man, after dividing the inside of the building into eighty-one parts, installs the altar on the nine central squares; then, in the middle of the three rows of squares that surround (the altar), starting in the east, he sets out firepits which, in sequence, are in the shape of a square, a vulva, a semicircle, a triangle, a circle, a hexagon, a lotus and an octagon.

Firepits (fig. 17)

25.43–44 The quadrangular (firepit) is a cubit wide and one deep; three lines (are drawn) on its four faces if there are three levels of steps and two if there are two. These step levels are seven, five or three digits high and their respective widths are four, three and two digits. A vulva is to be made in the east, in the shape of an elephant's trunk, its width, length and depth being respectively four, six and one digits; this vulva is arranged so as to lie in the direction of the fire.

25.45 The levels of steps may, equally, have a height and depth of four, three or two digits or there may be only one, one span high. A firepit should however always have a vulva which is not to be at a corner.

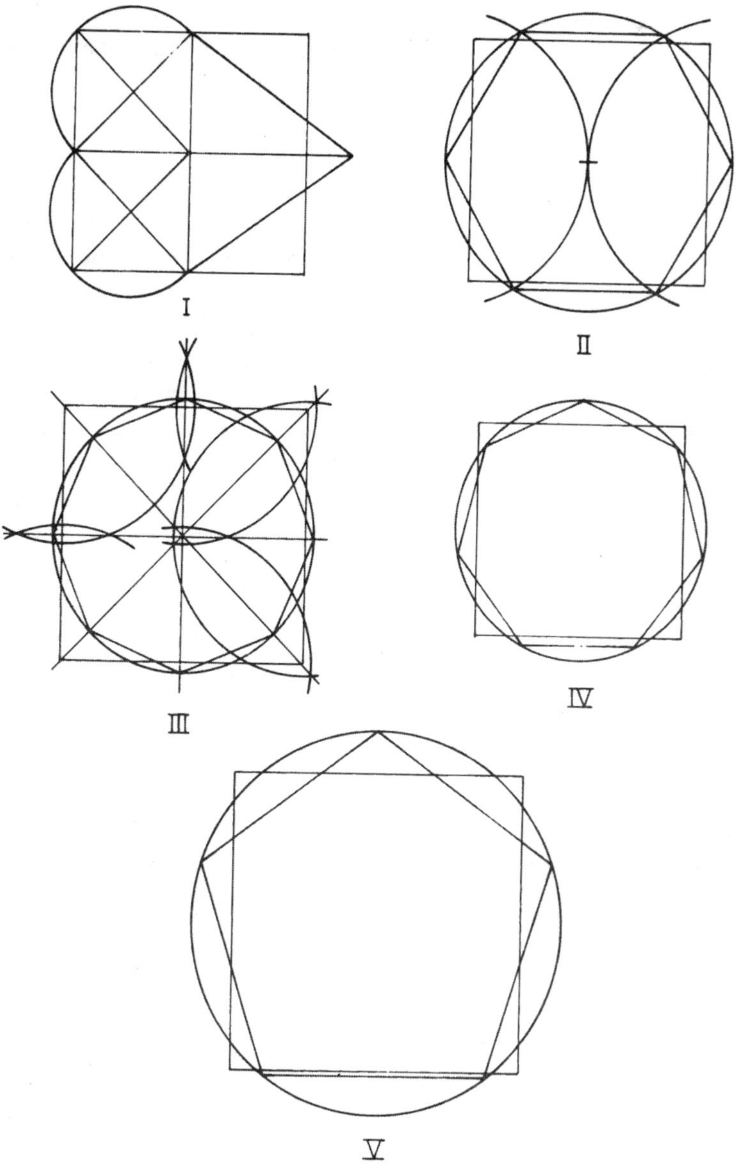

Fig. 17 Drawing the firepits

I. vulva form firepit (25.47); II. hexagonal firepit (25.50); III. octagonal firepit (25.52); IV. heptagonal firepit (25.53); V. pentagonal firepit (25.54).

25.46 In the centre of a firepit there is a lotus which is its navel; this lotus is round, its diameter being four, five or six digits and its height a quarter or a third that.

Vulva-form firepit

25.47 A point being marked in the east at a distance (from the east side of the basic square) equal to a fifth (of the width of this square), (straight lines) are drawn which connect this point with the middles (of the north and south sides of the square); then the (north-west) corner is surrounded by a circle and the same is done for the (south-west) corner which is symmetrical; the vulva shape is the result of the meeting of the two lines.

Semi-circular firepit

25.48 Two points having been drawn above and below, at a distance of one tenth (the width of the square) from the sides of the square, they are joined by a straight line and it is with this diameter that the semi-circular firepit is drawn, if the rule given by those well versed in the science of architecture is followed.

Triangular firepit

25.49a Three lines are to be drawn whose length is eight sixths the width of the (square) area; such is the triangular firepit.

Circular firepit

25.49b (The width of the square area) being divided into eighteen parts, the circular firepit should be drawn in such a way that it extends one part beyond (the sides of the square area).

Hexagonal firepit

25.50 The width (of the square area) being divided into five parts, a circle is drawn whose diameter is more than that width by a fifth (in a[1]l); then intersecting circles (*matsya*) are drawn on each side and the hexagon results from the six lines joining (the six points thus determined).

Lotiform firepit

25.51 To make a firepit in the shape of a lotus the sage first draws a circle as above, then he draws another one in the centre of the first; then, starting from the centre, he arranges the elements of a lotus beginning with the receptacle.

Octagonal firepit

25.52 The width of the (square) area being divided into twenty-four parts, a circle is drawn which extends one part (beyond the sides of the area); then mediating lines are drawn from opposite sides (and bissectrices from facing corners); the octagon results from the joining, by eight lines, (of the eight points thus determined).

Heptagonal firepit

25.53 The width of the square area having been divided into ten parts, a circle is drawn which extends one part (beyond each side of the square area); then a heptagon is drawn in that circle, the width of whose seven sides is thirty-three sixty-fourths the width of the square area.

Pentagonal firepit

25.54 The width of the square area having been divided into seven parts, a circle is drawn which extends one part (beyond each side of the square); then a pentagon is drawn the width of whose five sides is three quarters the width of the square.

25.55–56 [*This seems to give another method for drawing firepits.*]

Siddha type (cont.)

25.57–58 Otherwise, (if a pavilion of the *siddha* type) is placed in front of a temple, its base, pillars and entablature are like those of that temple; in this case there are one or two doors and the walls are decorated with *kumbalatā*.

25.59 In the middle of the facade is a porch (whose projection) is equal to the diameter of the pillars, if it is not double or triple; (this porch) has archways in front of it and all its decorative elements bear divine images.

25.60–61a The thickness of the walls (of this pavilion) is equal to that of the main shrine or may be three quarters or two thirds of it. (This pavilion), comprising porch and covered passage, may be found in front of all types of temple.

Padmaka type

25.61b–62 Square and four units wide, it has four doors. There is a porch in front, as behind, with a width of two units and a projection of only one. There are no pillars at the centre where there is (an inner court covered by) a lantern (*ūrdhvakūṭa*) two units wide.

25.63–64 It has thirty-six pillars and twenty-eight small false dormer windows. There is a stairway on each facade and ploughshare walls (*lāṅgalākārabhitti*) at the corners. There are eight big niches. Such is the pavilion called *padmaka* which is lovely as a lotus; it is most appropriate for gods' baths and should be placed in front of the temple.

25.65 It may however have but a single access; then it comprises an inner court open to the sky (*aṅgaṇa*). In this case it is suitable for rites such as sacrifice and its access may be in whatsoever direction desired.

Bhadraka type

25.66 The *bhadraka* type is square and five units wide; there is a central court three units wide, covered by a lantern and surrounded by a portico one unit wide.

25.67–68a It has thirty-two pillars and twenty-four false dormer windows; there are eight big niches and *kumbhalatā* decoration on the walls. There is a door on each facade and ploughshare walls at the corners.

25.68b It may however also comprise an inner court open to the sky, three units wide and bordered by pillars.

25.69 This pavilion is on the same level as the temple but may also be lower by a tenth or an eighth. It is appropriate for the dance and for the bathing (of images).

Śiva type

25.70–72a It is square and six units wide. In the centre is an inner court covered by a lantern which rests on eight pillars. There is a forepart on each facade, two units wide and jutting out one unit. This pavilion has sixty pillars but no central one and is decorated with twenty-four false dormer windows along with all necessary elements. It is named *śiva* and may be installed near any building whatsoever.

Veda type

25.72b–74a It is square and seven units wide. It has sixty pillars and, in the centre, an inner court three units wide, either covered by a lantern or open to the sky. Thirty-two false dormer windows adorn it. It has entrances on its four facades and a porch on its front facade, three units wide and projecting by one.

25.74b–75 There is a canopy (*raṅga*) in the middle and any one of the facades may be closed by a wall. This pavilion is fitting for the audiences of gods and of kings and may also serve for rites such as consecration. It is called *veda*.

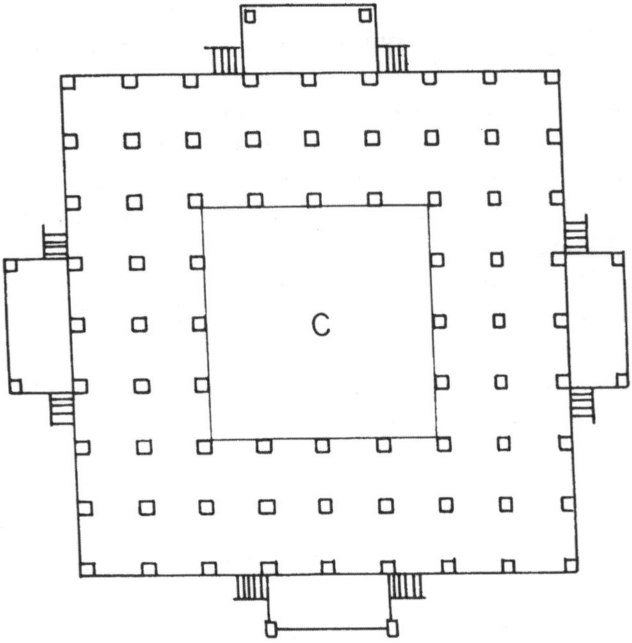

Fig. 18 Alaṅkṛta pavilion (25.76 *et sq.*) (C: inner court)

Alaṅkṛta type (fig. 18)

25.76–77 It is square and eight units wide and has eighty pillars. There is a lantern covered inner court in the centre, four units wide. There is a porch two units (wide) on each facade as well as a door with a side stairway. This pavilion, endowed with all possible decoration, is called *alaṅkṛta*.

25.78–79 There may be a basin in the centre of this pavilion, surrounded by a one unit walkway and a two unit wide gallery. The front porch is as given above and is placed on whichsoever facade desired. Such a pavilion is to be installed in the centre of a settlement such as a village.

Darbha type

25.80–81a It is (square), nine units wide and has one

hundred pillars. There are foreparts, three units wide and projecting by one, as well as four doors with stairways in front and ploughshare walls at the corners.

25.81b–82 There are nine canopies and the decoration is made up of forty-eight small false dormer windows. The nine (sons of) Brahmā are worshipped there and it should be situated in the middle of a palace or of a village. This pavilion, provided with all this decoration and of pleasing appearance, is called *darbha*.

Kauśika type

25.83 Square and ten units wide, it has a hundred and twelve pillars. It comprises nine inner courts covered by lanterns with intervals of one unit between them.

25.84–85a This *kauśika* pavilion is said to be *jātika* if (perfectly) square and *nanda* if it has a forepart on only one facade, *bhadrakauśika* if there is one on two of its facades, *jayakośa* if one on three facades and *prakośa* if one on all four.

25.85b–86a It has pillars and a base as well as ploughshare walls at the corners; it is endowed with all necessary elements and has forty-eight false dormer windows.

Kuladhāraṇa type (fig. 19)

25.86b–88a It is square, eleven units wide and surrounded on the outside by a one unit wide gallery. There are square inner courts covered by lanterns two units wide, in the four corners, and elongated ones, two units wide and three long, in the middle of the four facades.

25.88b–89 There is a canopy in the middle surmounted by a lantern, square and three units wide. There are walkways crossing at right angles between the inner courts covered by lanterns. Foreparts are in *jāti* or other modes; this pavilion is decorated with all necessary elements.

25.90–91a Above, the entablature is adorned with aediculae and niches and there are nine *bodhaka* (i.e. roofs corresponding to the nine lanterns?). This building may or may

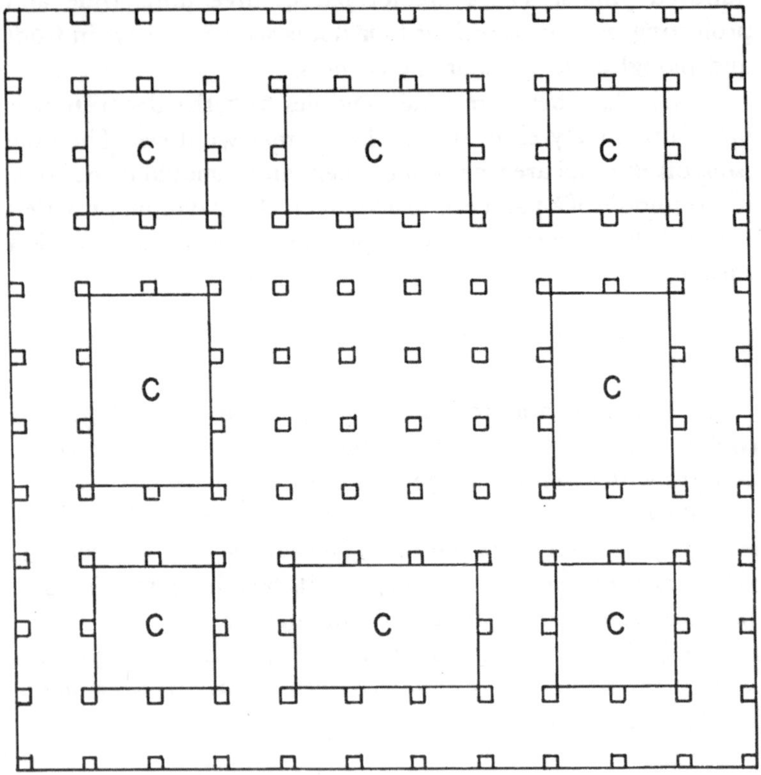

Fig. 19 Kuladhāraṇa pavilion (25.86 *et sq.*) (C: inner courts)

not be closed (by walls) depending upon whether it is intended to conceal anything. This square pavilion is called *kuladhāraṇa*.

Sukhāṅga type

25.91b–95a It is square and twelve units wide. There is an inner square court, two units wide and covered by a lantern, in each corner, in the middle of the four facades and in the centre. There is a gallery one unit wide all around the outside. Inner courts may be open to the sky or covered by lanterns. In the corners there are ploughshare walls and on each of the facades a forepart four units wide, projecting by two units and provided with a side stairway. This pavilion is endowed with eight large niches, its base supports a hundred and sixty pillars and the number of small dormer windows is according to specific circumstance. This pavilion is called *sukhāṅga*.

Saukhya type

25.95b–96a The *saukhya* pavilion is square and thirteen units wide. There is a two unit wide portico all around as well as a walkway, one unit wide and with right angled turns.

25.96b–97 The canopy in the centre is surmounted by a lantern which is three units wide and has a roof with a finial. There is an inner court without a central pillar and covered by a two units wide lantern in each corner and an elongated one, two units wide and three long in the middle of each facade.

25.98–99a Foreparts are in *nanda* mode . . . etc. The building may be closed by a wall on whichever side desired; it is provided with a hundred and eighty-four pillars. Endowed with all the necessary elements, it is fitting for gods, brahmins and kings.

Garbha type

25.99b–100 It is square and fourteen units wide. There is a two units wide central inner court covered by a lantern and surrounded by a gallery one unit wide; there is a one unit passage around it, open to the sky.

25.101–102a In the corners are two unit wide inner courts covered or not by lanterns; in the middle of the four sides there are elongated inner courts two units wide and four long, covered or not by lanterns. A one unit wide portico borders these courts all around.

25.102b–103 Whichsoever side desired may be closed by a wall, and a forepart may be arranged on the preferred facade. The base supports two hundred and eight pillars. This pavilion with its pleasant appearance is fitting for gods, brahmins and kings and is named *garbha*.

Mālya type

25.104–105a It is square· and fifteen units wide. At its centre is to be found either a canopy covered by a lantern or an inner court open to the sky; both are three units wide and surrounded by a one unit wide portico which is bordered by a corridor, also one unit wide.

25. 105b–106 Everything else is to be arranged as in the preceding case but the elongated covered inner courts are to be one more unit (long). There are two hundred and thirty-two pillars on the base. This pavilion, provided with all necessary elements, is called *mālya*.

Mālyādbhuta type

25.107–108 The *mālyādbhuta* pavilion is square and sixteen units wide. There is a two unit wide inner court at its centre covered by a lantern and surrounded by a one unit wide portico. (This portico) is preceded by a front porch, two units wide and projecting by one and there are ploughshare walls at the corners and stairways on the side; the entablature is decorated (?).

25.109–110 There is an open waterduct all around which is two units wide and bordered on its outside by a four unit wide portico; sixteen two unit wide inner courts are arranged in this portico; they are square and are divided by one unit intervals.

25.111–112a There are ploughshare walls at the (exterior) corners and a recessed decoration above. There is a forepart, two units wide, projecting by one and provided with a side stairway, on each of the four facades of this pavilion which is to be endowed with all necessary elements.

25.112b–114 These are the sixteen types of square pavilion fit for gods, brahmins and kings. The well advised man may build square pavilions up to thirty-two units wide, starting from the figures given above and adding a unit to each extremity each time. The sage gives the pavilion walls or porticoes according to whether it is open or closed and taking into consideration the specific circumstances and the appearance desired.

25.115a The rectangular plan pavilions are now presented.

Dhana type

25.115b–116 It is three units wide and its length is two units more than that. It comprises a one unit wide entrance (*vāra*) in front and has twenty-four pillars and twenty false dormer windows. It is called *dhana* and is wealth bestowing.

Subhūṣaṇa type

25.117–119a It is four units wide and two more than that in length. It comprises a one unit wide gallery on its periphery and the remaining space (in the centre) is occupied by an inner court. The front porch is two units wide and projects by one. There are thirty-two interior and exterior pillars on its bases (?). It is provided with all necessary elements and is called *subhūṣaṇa*.

Āhalya type

25.119b–120 It is five units wide and two more than that in length. It comprises a one unit wide gallery on its periphery and the remaining space (in the centre) is occupied by an inner court covered or not by a lantern. Its front porch is three units wide and projects by one.

25.121 Its profusely decorated base supports forty pillars. Provided with all necessary elements it is called *āhalya* and it is appropriate under all circumstances.

Sruga type

25.122–124a It is six units wide and two more than that in length. There is a lantern covered court in the centre, four units long and two wide; there is a two unit wide gallery all around and the front porch is arranged on the facade desired.

Its base supports sixty pillars and the number of false dormer windows is according to specific circumstance. This attractive building, provided with all necessary elements, is called *sruga*.

Koṇa type

25.124b–127a It is seven units wide and two more than that in length. There is a lantern covered court in the centre, five units long and three wide. There is a two unit gallery all around but any facade may, if so wished, be closed by a wall. The front porch is three units wide and projects by one. The number of false dormer windows varies according to specific circumstance but there should be seventy-two pillars. Provided with all necessary elements this pavilion is called *koṇa*.

Kharvaṭa type

25.127b–128a It is eight units wide and two more than that in length. In the centre there is a basin, two units wide and four long and surrounded by a one unit wide portico.

25.128b–130 On the periphery there is a gallery which is one unit wide and without median row of pillars. Any of the faces may be closed by a wall. There are sixty-eight pillars and a forepart as given above. The one unit wide entrance is on the front facade and is preceded by a stairway. This pavilion, called *kharvaṭa*, is provided with all necessary elements and is meant for gods, (brahmins and kings).

Śrīrūpa type

25.131–132 It is nine units wide and two more than that in length. In the centre is a two unit wide, three unit long basin surrounded by a one unit wide portico. All around there is a two unit wide gallery without a median row of pillars; it is bordered by a one unit wide walkway.

25.133–134a There are ninety-six pillars; walls and entrances are to be arranged according to circumstance. There may or may not be a walkway and the porch is as given above.

Provided with all the necessary elements, this pavilion is called *śrīrūpa*.

Maṅgala type

25.134b–136 It is ten units wide and two more than that in length. In the centre it comprises an inner court two units wide and four long, covered by a lantern and surrounded by a portico one unit wide; this portico is bordered by an open waterduct, one unit wide. There is a two unit wide gallery all around; pillars, walls and foreparts are to be arranged according to circumstance.

25.137–138 There may also be an inner court at the centre covered by a lantern and surrounded by a portico as above, but there is no duct. The rest of the plinth area is occupied by the gallery which is topped by six square two unit wide lanterns on the sides and by one, which is four units long and two wide, at both the front and the back.

25.139–140a There are ploughshare walls in the corners but this pavilion may be either closed and surrounded by walls or open and surrounded by pillars. It is provided with all necessary elements and is named *maṅgala*.

25.140b–142 Such are the eight rectangular pavilions intended for gods, brahmins and kings. Starting from the above mentioned plans and adding a unit each time to their length until it is double the width, the well advised man may build pavilions which he provides with columns, walls and all necessary elements, taking into consideration the specific circumstance and the appearance sought.

25.143a Now the eight types of rectangular pavilions suitable for vaiśya and śūdra are described.

Mārga type

25.143b–145a It is two units wide and twice as long. It has fifteen pillars and a front porch, two units wide with a projection of one and provided with a lateral stairway. It is decorated with false dormer windows. Its front facade is orientated in the desired direction. This pavilion is called *mārga*.

Saubhadra type

25.145b–147a It is three units wide and twice as long as wide. It has twenty-eight pillars and a one unit wide walkway on the front facade; its porch is two units wide and projects by one; pillars and false dormer windows are arranged in accordance with circumstance. This pleasing building is called *saubhadra*.

Sundara type

25.147b–149a It is four units wide and two more than that in length. It comprises a central court, two units wide and four long, which may or may not be covered by a lantern. It is endowed with thirty pillars and a porch (the projection of which) is one unit. This type of pavilion, its pillars and false dormer windows arranged according to circumstance, is called *sundara*.

Sādhāraṇa type

25.149b–152a It is five units wide and four units longer than that. It comprises two juxtaposed inner courts, open to the sky and two units wide and three long. Endowed with fifty-six pillars, it has a one unit wide walkway on the front facade. Its porch, three units wide and projecting by one, is preceded by a stairway. This pavilion, which is surrounded by walls and whose false dormer windows are arranged according to circumstance, is called *sādhāraṇa*.

Saukhya type

25.152b–153 It is six units wide and three more in length. There is a central court, two units wide and five long, covered by a lantern, and surrounded by a two unit wide portico. On the front is a one unit wide walkway.

25.154–155a The porch is as has been given above and is decorated with false dormer windows; there are sixty pillars. A pavilion provided with all these elements is called *saukhya* and is fitting for all.

Īśvarakānta type (fig. 20)

25.155b–157a It is seven units wide and four units more than that in length. There is a central square court three units wide which may or may not be covered by a lantern and is surrounded by a one unit wide gallery. On both sides of this, is a court open to the sky, two units wide and five long.

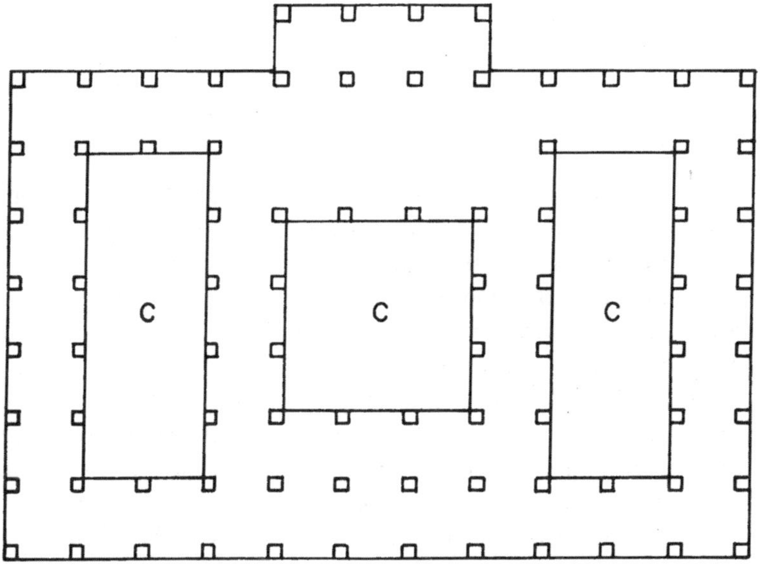

Fig. 20 Īśvarakānta pavilion (25.155b–159) (C: inner courts)

25.157b–159 The sage is to arrange a one unit wide portico all around. The front porch is three units wide and has one unit of projection. The base supports eighty-four pillars and there is a one unit wide walkway on the front facade. This pavilion which may be decorated in various ways and which comprises all necessary elements is named *īśvarakānta*.

Śrībhadra type

25.160–161 It is eight units wide and its length is calculated as above. In the centre there is a two unit wide square court, which may or may not be covered by a lantern and which is surrounded by a portico, one unit wide; on both sides of this, as above, are two courts covered by lanterns, their length being, however, two units more than in the above case.

25.162–163 A two unit wide gallery is arranged all around by the man of discernment. The porch is four units wide and projects by two. The base supports one hundred and ten pillars. This pavilion, provided with all these elements and suitable in all circumstances, is named *śrībhadra*.

Śarvatobhadra type

25.164–166a It is nine units wide and its length is calculated as above. There is a square court in the centre, three units wide, covered or not by a lantern and surrounded by a one unit wide portico; on either side of this, is a court open to the sky, two units wide and five long. The sage arranges a two unit wide gallery all around.

25.166b–168a There is a forepart in front and behind, five units wide and two deep; the foreparts on the sides are three units wide and one deep. There are ploughshare walls in the corners but elsewhere the pavilion is bordered by pillars and the base supports one hundred and twenty-eight of these in all.

25.168b–169a This pavilion, named *sarvatobhadra* and which is endowed with all necessary elements is arranged by the sage according to circumstance and to appearance sought.

25.169b This is the way in which the discriminating man is to construct pavilions suitable for gods etc. . .

Length of pavilions

25.170–171a The method for calculating the length of pavilions from their width is now indicated: the *jāti* mode is that which was used above; in *chanda* mode the length is one unit more than the width; in *vikalpa* mode it is two more and in *ābhāsa*, three.

25.171b–172 The quadrangular plans *daṇḍaka*, *svastibhadra*, *padma*, *krakarabhadra*, *ṣaṇmukhā*, *lāṅgala* and *mauli* are in *jāti* mode. Light buildings and pavilions built in *jāti* mode have pillars arranged to meet the specific case.

Other kinds of pavilions

25.173–175a A pavilion comprising elements peculiar to a house, having the plan of a house and provided with a canopy, is a "house-pavilion" (*gṛhamaṇḍapa*). A pavilion (the centre) of which is like a temple sanctum, which has a kind of aisle and which is provided with the (six) levels starting with the base, is a "pavilion in the form of a temple" (*prāsādākāra-maṇḍapa*). A pavilion which comprises elements peculiar to a house and those peculiar to a temple, is a "house-temple-pavilion" (*gṛhaprāsādamaṇḍapa*). A pavilion surmounted by a storey is a "gallery-pavilion" (*mālikāmaṇḍapa*).

25.175b A pavilion is built with bricks, stone, wood or metal pieces; there must always be a mixture of different materials.

Pavilion for water games

25.176 If the king so wishes, a rectangular pavilion may be built, provided with fountains and comprising one or several storeys.

25.177 This pavilion is a closed one, surrounded by a wall unless it is bordered by a colonnade; there is a porch on each of its four facades; there is a canopy in the middle or an open courtyard. Its upper storeys are closed by walls or bordered by pillars.

25.178 The stairway is behind a concealed door in front of which are installed all kinds of devices full of water: elephants, dwarves, *haṃsa*, tigers, monkeys and mechanical dolls.

25.179 The roof of this pavilion is *harmya* shaped or in the shape of pavilion or of *sabhā*; it is decorated with square aediculae, arcatures, latticed windows and false dormer windows of various types.

25.180 In front, or in the middle, of this pavilion is a brick or stone basin provided with fountains and supplied with ducts, whether concealed or not.

25.181 A pavilion like this, set up in a pleasant place, is intended for the king's water sports. If it is endowed with all prescribed elements and decorated in various ways it brings women, health, pleasure and happiness to the king.

Wood for making pillars

25.182–183 *Khadira*, *khādira*, *vahni*, *nimba*, *sāla*, *silindra*, *piśita*, *tinduka*, *rājādana*, *homa* and *madhūka* are the trees suitable for the making of pillars but they may be used in all construction intended for gods, brahmins and kings, for whom all the types of pillars described above may be used.

25.184-185a In buildings intended for vaiśya and for śūdra, on the other hand, the pillars are to be in *piśita*, *tinduka*, *nimba*, *rājādana*, *madhūka* or *silindra* and are circular, square or octagonal section or have sixteen sides.

25.185b–186a Bamboo is suitable for everyone however, as are the palm tree and the coconut tree, the *kramuka*, reeds and the *ketakī*.

25.186b–187 All buildings intended for gods and ascetics may be built in brick, stone or wood but stone is not to be used in those of vaiśya nor in those for śūdra.

Pavilions in front of the shrine

25.188–189 The most remarkable of pavilions are those installed in front of temples. Their base, pillars, architrave and entablature, are like those of the temple but have dimensions less by a seventh, eighth, ninth or tenth; the dimensions given above may also be used.

25.190a It is said that the orientation and overall proportions of pavilions are the same as those prescribed for the temples (they precede).

25.190b–191 The thickness of the (pavilion) walls is five, four, three times or twice the diameter of their pillars; if the pillars are in wood, however, the thickness of the walls will be three quarters, one third or half their diameter. Lastly, the width of a pilaster so calculated may be equal to the thickness of the walls.

Placing of the foundation deposit

25.192 The sages speak of three different places where the foundation deposit of a pavilion may be placed; (according to some) it may be at the bottom of the pillar which is in the south of the inner court whilst, according to others, it will be under the pillar to the right of the door or under the second lateral pillar (from the corner) (?).

The gallery

25.193 There may be a gallery in front, behind or all around, whose width should be one unit calculated from the width and the length of the pavilion. For gods, brahmins and kings, however, it is to be arranged all around and is to be one unit or one and a half wide.

Cloister-like gallery

25.194 The elements of the cloister-like gallery (*mālikā*) are arranged as those of a temple; the walls (of the upper floors) should be above those of the ground floor and pillars should be above pillars; there are one, two or three storeys according to circumstance.

25.195 According to some sages, the lengthwise and widthwise dimensions are to be taken on the exterior edge of the pillars (which border the building) whereas, according to others, they are to be taken on the axis of the walls.

25.196 On a dwelling pavilion there should be a wagon-roof (*śālākāra*) or a hipped roof (*sabhāśīrṣa*).

25.197 Pavilions have one, two, three or four facades with or without jutting porches; they comprise lanterns above and a canopy or an inner court in the centre; either rectangular or square, they are all suitable abodes for gods, brahmins and kings but only rectangular ones are suitable for vaiśya and śūdra.

HALLS[1]

Different types of halls

25.198–200 Now I give the characteristics of nine (types of) halls, the first of which is called *mallavasanta* and the second *pañcavasanta*; then there are *ekavasanta*, *sarvatobhadra*, *pārvata-kūrmaka*, *māhendra*, *somavṛtta*, *śukavimāna*, and *śrīpratiṣṭhita*. Five amongst these nine types are oblong plan, the others being square plan.

25.201–202 (The length of halls intended) for gods and men is greater than their width by one, two, three or four units. (The relationship between) the length and the width, the ornamentation and the proportions of walls and pillars are the same as given above (for pavilions) but all the elements which are above the consoles of the entablature are like the corresponding ones in temples. Everything regarding the arrangement of rafters conforms with what has been laid down in the chapter on roofs.

Characteristics of a kiosk

25.203 A square hall provided with corner rafters is called "kiosk" (*kūṭa*); either square (*kūṭa*) or elongated (*koṣṭha*) it has no *valakṣitasvasti* (?) at the corners.

1. The text of this description of *sabhā* is very corrupt and the meaning of several terms has eluded us.

Mallavasanta hall

25.204 *Mallavasanta* is the name for a hall, one unit wide with four pillars and with (four) corner rafters joined at a single newel (*kūṭa*); it has eight *pucchavalakṣa* (?).

Pañcavasanta hall

25.205–206a What is called *pañcavasantaka* is a square, two unit wide hall; it has eight pillars and eight "long rafters" (*dīrghalupā*) (?); it has eight *svastivalakṣa* and a central newel (?) (*mūlakūṭa*); at each corner is a *kūṭa* (?).

Ekavasantaka hall

25.206b–207 What is called *ekavasantaka* is a square hall three units wide and endowed with twelve pillars; it has sixteen *svastipuccha*, thirteen *kūṭa* (?) and eighteen *valakṣa*.

Sarvatobhadra hall

25.208–210a A square, four unit wide hall is endowed with sixteen peripheral pillars and with eight interior ones as well as with eight "long rafters" (*prāṃśuraśmi*). It has sixteen *kūṭa* (?), twenty-four *svastipuccha*, forty-eight *valakṣa* and only one median newel (*kūṭa*). It is called *sarvatobhadra*. These are the four square halls.

Pārvatakūrmaka hall

25.210b–212a The *pārvatakūrmaka* hall is rectangular and is four units wide and five long. It is endowed with eighteen peripheral pillars and ten interior ones as well as with eight rafters. It has sixteen and fourteen (?) *kūṭa* and six and fourteen (?) inside and outside (?). It comprises sixty-four *valakṣa* and sixteen (times?) four *koṣṭha* (?).

Māhendra hall

25.212b–213 (The *māhendra* hall) is four units wide and six long; it is endowed with twenty (peripheral) pillars and with twelve interior ones. It has eight interior *kūṭa* and sixteen exterior ones as well as sixteen long rafters.

25.214–215 It has twenty-four *svastika* and three median newels; it comprises eighty *valakṣa* and thirty-nine *kūṭa*. It may not have interior pillars and intercolumniations are then to be arranged accordingly. It is named *māhendra* and learned sages prescribe it for kings.

Somavṛtta hall

25.216–218 (The *somavṛtta* hall) is four units wide and seven long; it has fourteen interior pillars and twenty-two peripheral ones as well as twenty-four *svastipuccha*. It comprises sixteen long rafters and ninety-six *valakṣa*; it has four median *kūṭa*, ten interior ones and eighteen exterior ones. Endowed with four corner rafters and seven (?) *karṇadhārā* (?), this hall which is called *somavṛtta* may not have interior pillars.

Śukavimāna hall

25.219–221 (The *śukavimāna* hall) is five units wide and eight long; it is endowed with twenty-six (peripheral) pillars and with eighteen interior ones as well as with four corner rafters. It has thirty-two *svastika* and seventy-two *valakṣa*; it comprises four newels and sixteen long rafters in its roof. It has eighteen *kūṭa* inside and twenty-two outside; provided with eight *karṇadhārā* it is called *śukavimāna*.

Śrīpratiṣṭhita hall

25.222–224 (The *śrīpratiṣṭhita* hall) is five units wide and nine long; it has twenty-eight (peripheral) pillars, thirty-two *svastipuccha*, twenty interior pillars and as many median rafters (*madhyaraśmi*); it comprises five newels and four corner rafters in its roof. It is said that it should have one hundred and sixty *valakṣa* and that the number of *kūṭa* is a tenth (of that) (?). It is called *śrīpratiṣṭhita.*

25.225–227 Otherwise, if three units are added to the width and the length, (this hall) is like an elongated four main building house (?); it has twelve interior pillars and sixteen exterior ones, a verandah one unit wide and a *śālā* of two units (?). It is endowed with four times seventy-two pillars (?), inside and outside. It is arranged like a temple, it has four doors and two *cūlikā* (?). This hall which is the blessed support of the prince is called *śrīpratiṣṭhita.*

Common features to halls

25.228–229 Other varieties of hall are arrived at by adding one unit each time (to the above given dimensions) and are called accordingly *chanda*, *vikalpa* and *ābhāsa*. Pillars, rafters, *valakṣa* and *kūṭa* should be arranged according to circumstance; whatever the proportions of width and length calculated in units, they must accord with the harmony and appearance sought.

25.230a A kiosk (*kūṭa*) may be provided with long rafters or a kiosk may be square (?).

25.230b–235 The height of the architrave above the pillars is equal to the projection of the consoles (*daṇḍikā*) (?). The overhang of the *cūlikā* is in proportion with the entablature and the beams (?). The projection (?) of *valakṣa* is straight or *svastika* form (?) . . . ? . . . . A *varṇapaṭṭikā* is arranged between two *cūlīka* (?) . . . ? . . . .

25.236 The height of the base of the *pādabandha* type is half that of the pillars. All that is left unprescribed is to be adapted to circumstance.

25.237 A hall should be provided with ploughshare walls; its central part may or may not comprise a canopy. It is called "assembly hall" (*sabhā*) by those who are fit to be in the assembly (*sabhya*); in this world, the way followed by the men of the assembly always depends on the housing of the assembly.

Thus ends, in the *Mayamata*, treatise on dwelling, the twenty-fifth chapter: RULES FOR PAVILIONS AND HALLS.

Chapter 26
HOUSES

26.1 There are six types of house with one, two, three, four, seven or ten main buildings (*śālā*) for gods, brahmins and other classes.

26.2a (These main buildings) are not to be placed on the square of Aja (i.e. Brahmā); they have a front verandah and, (where houses comprising several of them are concerned), they are either separate from each other or they form a block.

26.2b–3a Their widths, lengths and heights, expressed in even and odd numbers of cubits, are now briefly presented, as well as their specific arrangements.

Width of main buildings

26.3b–4 When a house has only one main building, the possible widths of that building go from three to twenty-three cubits and four to twenty-four by successive increments of two cubits.

26.5–6a When there are two or three main buildings there are seven possible widths, from seven to nineteen cubits or from eight to twenty, by successive increments of two cubits.

Length of main buildings

26.6b–7 The length is one and a quarter, one and a half, one and three quarters or twice the width; (otherwise it is equal to double the width) increased by a quarter, half or three quarters; (or) it is equal to three times the width, this being the maximum. These are the eight ways (of calculating the length from the width).

26.8–9a All these widths are appropriate for gods but for (ordinary men the length must not be more than) double (the width); for the inhabitants of monasteries and hermitages, all lengths equal to, or more than, double (the width) are appropriate; lastly, in a house where (all such inhabitants) dwell together, the length must be at least equal to, or must be double, (the width).

Height of main buildings

26.9b–10 There are five ways to (calculate) the height from the width; by the *śāntika* mode, the height is equal to the width, by the *pauṣṭika* mode it is equal to the width increased by a quarter, by the *jayada* the increase is one half and by *dhana* three quarters; lastly, by the *adbhuta*, the height is double the width.

HOUSES WITH A SINGLE MAIN BUILDING

General characteristics

26.11–12a Houses with a single main building are appropriate for gods, brahmins and people of other classes, for the heterodox in hermitages, for those who fight from elephants, horses or chariots, as well as for officiants at sacrifices, oblations and other ceremonies of the kind; they are suitable too for women who live by their charms.

26.12b–13a *Daṇḍaka*, *maulika*, *svastika* and *caturmukha* are the four (types of houses of that sort) suitable for all the gods as well as for those who have been listed.

26.13b–16a (These houses) have one or several storeys; they have engaged structures etc. . . . They are in *arpita* or *anarpita* mode and are arranged in the same way as temples.[1] They may have a gallery all around: in front, behind and on the sides. For men, as for gods and for the heterodox inhabitants of hermitages, there should be a pavilion in front and a forepart behind and on the sides. For gods the chamber is in the middle (of the main building), for men it is at the side.

1. See above 21.64b–65.

26.16b–17 In a house with one single main building, this may be to the east, south, west or north and is appropriate for all classes; it may be to the south or the west, however, only when it is for men.

26.18 If the two main buildings of a *lāṅgala* house are to east and south or to east and north or to west and north, this will bring about the owner's death; if good fortune is desired they have to be placed to the south and to the west.

26.19 In a *śūrpa* (house, the three main buildings positioned) to the south, west and north bring luck; to east, south and west they bring victory; *śūrpa* houses without main buildings to the south and west are nothing but mistakes.

26.20–21 *Lāṅgala* houses are suitable for courtesans and people of that ilk and *śūrpa* houses for *ugropajīvin*.[1] In *lāṅgala* and *śūrpa* houses and in all those with only one main building, a wall with a door must be disposed so as to border them where there is no main building. Houses with two main buildings have one join and those with three, two.

26.22a I now present the arrangement of houses of the *daṇḍaka* type and of the other types listed above.

First type of *daṇḍaka* house

26.22b–24a The (total) width (of the house) makes up three parts and the length four. The width of the main building is two (thirds that of the house) and that of the verandah in front one third. The facade (?) is "broken-stick" (?) shaped. This dwelling, which is suitable for everyone, is called *daṇḍaka* and is the smallest of all houses.

Second type of *daṇḍaka* house

26.24b–25 The (total) width of the house makes up four parts and the length, which is greater, makes up six. The width of the main building is two (parts) as is the width of the verandah. This house which, in all other respects, is as given above, is called *daṇḍaka*.

1. "Those who live by violence"?

Arrangement of doors

26.26 In a single main building house, the length of the main building is to be divided into nine parts and then (a point is marked) at five parts from the right hand extremity and another at three parts from the left one. The access door is placed in between (them, in such a way that it is) farther from (the right end than from the left).

26.27 Some say, (more simply), that in a house intended for men the door must be to the left of the median line (of the building). In any case, in all these houses, the door must make up one part of the N parts by which is measured the length of the main building.

Third type of *daṇḍaka* house (fig. 21–I)

26.28–29a (The width and length of the house being as above), the width of the main building is three parts and its length six; the verandah makes up one part of the width (of the house). The main building is separated into two rooms by a median partition wall (*kabhitti*) which is broken up by a vaulted door (*kulyābhadvāra*) (?); all else should be arranged as has been given above.

26.29b–31a The chamber (*vāsa*) must be at the bottom of the axis (of the building) and the gynaeceum (*raṅga*) at its top. There are walls all around and the gynaeceum comprises pillars inside. There is a one part wide gallery in front, behind or at the sides. The disposition is that of a temple. This house is called *daṇḍaka*.

Fourth type of *daṇḍaka* house

26.31b–32 The gynaeceum may also be in the centre between two chambers placed at top and bottom of the axis; pillars are arranged inside according to circumstance but the door should not be placed on the axis (of the building). This house which, in other respects is as above, is called *daṇḍaka*.

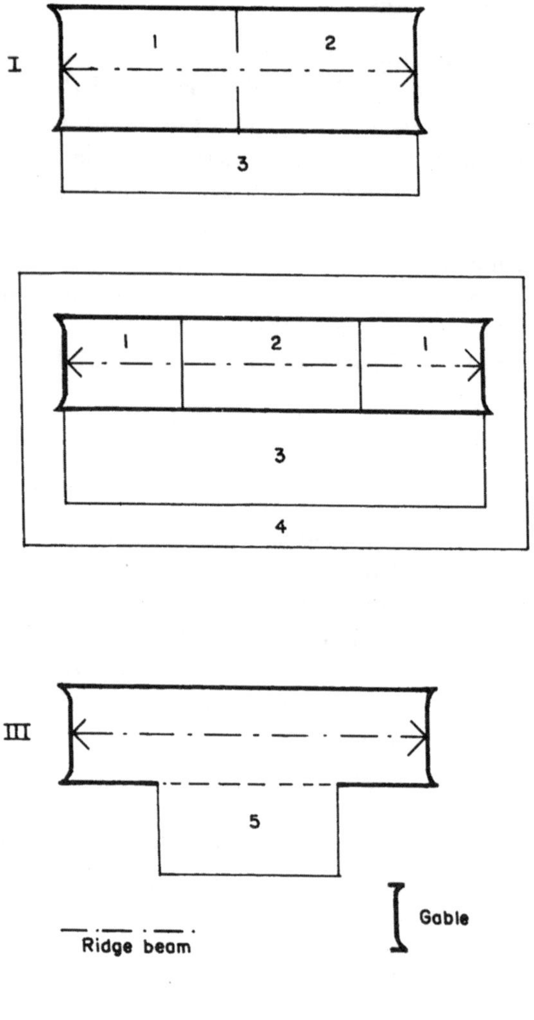

Fig. 21 Houses with a single main building

I. 3rd daṇḍaka type (26.28 *et sq.*); II. 5th daṇḍaka type (26.32-35); III. svastika type (26.39b–40).
(1. chamber; 2. gynaeceum; 3. front verandah; 4. surrounding gallery; 5. fore-part).

Fifth type of *daṇḍaka* house (fig.21–II)

26.33–34a (The total) width (of the house) makes up six parts and the length twelve; (the house) is surrounded by a one part wide gallery. The width of the main building is two parts as is that of the verandah in front of it; the interior pillars are arranged according to circumstance.

26.34b–35 There are two lateral chambers two parts wide, three parts long and arranged along the length of the main building; between them is the gynaeceum, two parts wide and four parts long. This house, which in other respects is as above, is called *daṇḍaka*.

Proportions of the verandah

26.36 In houses with one, two or three main buildings, the width of the verandah must be a third, two fifths, three sevenths or four ninths the width (of the building).

26.37 All *daṇḍaka* houses in *jāti* mode have been thus described, those such as are suitable for gods, brahmins, kings, heterodox, vaiśya, śūdra, soldiers and women who live by their charms.

Maulika type

26.38–39a (The main building of a house of the) *maulika* (type) has a hipped roof or it has only one gable. This *maulika* house is in *chanda* mode and is suitable for all those mentioned above, excluding women.

Svastika type (fig. 21–III)

26.39b–40 Or else, if the main building comprises a front forepart, two parts (wide) and with a two part projection, then there are three gables; that house is called *svastika*, which is in *vikalpa* mode and which is suitable for gods, brahmins and kings but not for lower classes.

Caturmukha type

26.41 Otherwise, there is a forepart at the back like the one in front; this makes four gables, including those at top and bottom of the main building's axis, which makes a right angle with that of the foreparts.

26.42–43 This house has six levels of elevation, the first being the base; it is disposed like a temple and has false dormer windows, arcatures and other similar elements as well as windows etc. . . . It is called *caturmukha* and is in *ābhāsa* mode. It is suitable for gods, brahmins and kings to whom it brings success.

Features common to *daṇḍaka* and other types

26.44 The four types of *daṇḍaka* and other houses have between one and five storeys; the interior disposition is to be in accordance with the wishes of the owner.

26.45 Buildings intended for elephants, horses, bulls etc. . . . will be separate, one from another, and will each have two or three *cūlī* (?) as well as a vestibule and a closing door (*talpa*).[1]

26.46 The height of [. . . ?][2] is equal to the width or to the width increased by a quarter or a half. The doors of *daṇḍaka* and *maulika* houses are on whichsoever facade desired.

HOUSES WITH TWO MAIN BUILDINGS

Caturmukha type (fig. 22)

26.47–48 This house with two main buildings, forms a square ten parts wide; from outside inwards there is, first, a one part wide gallery and then the two part wide main buildings; in front of the main buildings is a verandah one part wide; (in front of that) there is a (square) pillared court, three

1. For a description of stables see below 29.168 and following.
2. There seems to be a gap between verses 45 and 46.

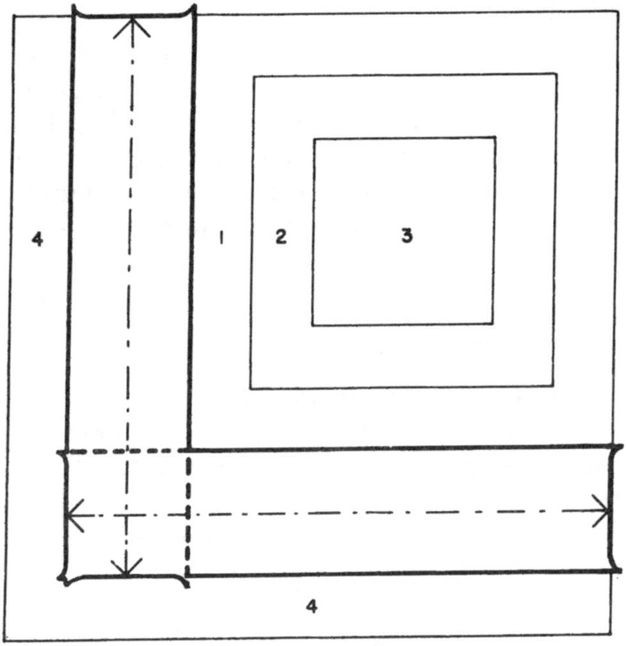

Fig. 22 Two main building house: caturmukha type (26.47 *et sq.*)
(1. verandah; 2. portico; 3. pillared court; 4. gallery)

parts wide: it is bordered by a portico and the remainder (in the centre) is for the court proper.

26.49 The facades of the two main buildings and the outside gallery are built according to *lāṅgala* plan (i.e. form a right angle) but, on the other hand, the arrangement of interior elements such as the front inner court is made on a square basis.

26.50–51a The principal main building comprises two chambers separated by the gynaeceum. There is a forepart with both a width and a projection of two parts beyond the outside gallery. This house which comprises two main buildings and which has four gables is called *caturmukha*.

Svastika type

26.51b–53 Otherwise, the length (of one of the two) main buildings is only five parts; the door is as has been given above and all the elements (previously mentioned) are to be found; the pillared court and the portico around it are however to be rectangular plan. This house has three gables and the forepart of the longest main building is elongated. This is a *svastika* house which, in other respects, is as above.

Daṇḍavaktra type (fig. 23)

26.54–55 Or else, if there are only two gables, the house is said to be of the *daṇḍavaktra* type; if it has no pillared court it will have a court open to the sky. Door and walls should be where there is no main building (on the border) of the house. This house with one or several storeys is to be built for women who live by their charms.

HOUSES WITH THREE MAIN BUILDINGS

Merukānta type (fig. 24)

26.56–57a The width of this three main building house is eight parts and its length ten. It has a central court, two parts wide and surrounded on three sides by a one part wide verandah and a two part wide main building. The foreparts of these main buildings have no central pillar and they are two parts (in width and projection).

26.57b–58 This house has six gables and its central court is covered; it has one or several storeys and its disposition is like that of a temple; it is as above as regards its door (and walls). This house fitting for *ugropajīvin* is called *merukānta*.

Maulibhadra type (fig.25)

26.59–61 The width of this house is ten parts and (its length) twelve. At the back, or on the sides, is an exterior gallery one

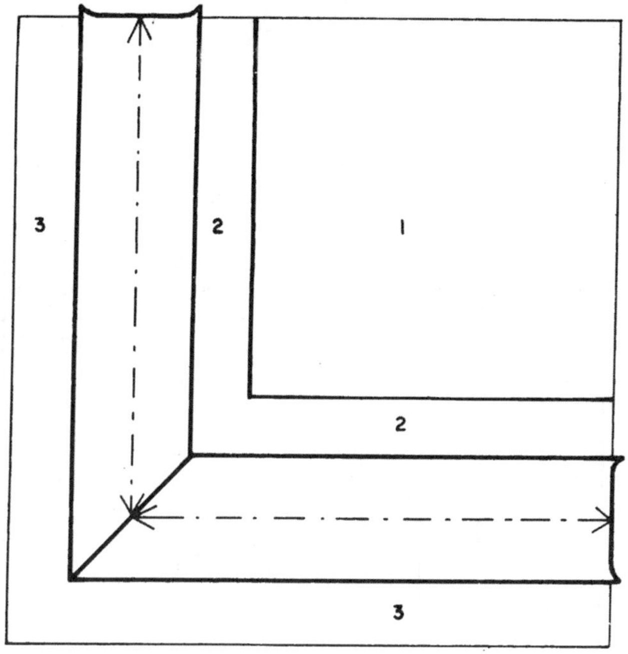

Fig. 23 Two main building house: daṇḍavaktra type (26.54–55)
(1. court; 2. verandah; 3. gallery)

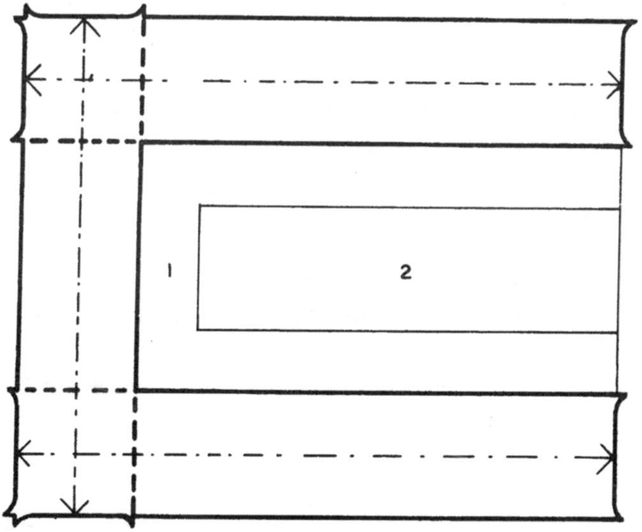

Fig. 24 Three main building house: merukānta type (26.56 *et sq.*)
(1. verandah; 2. court)

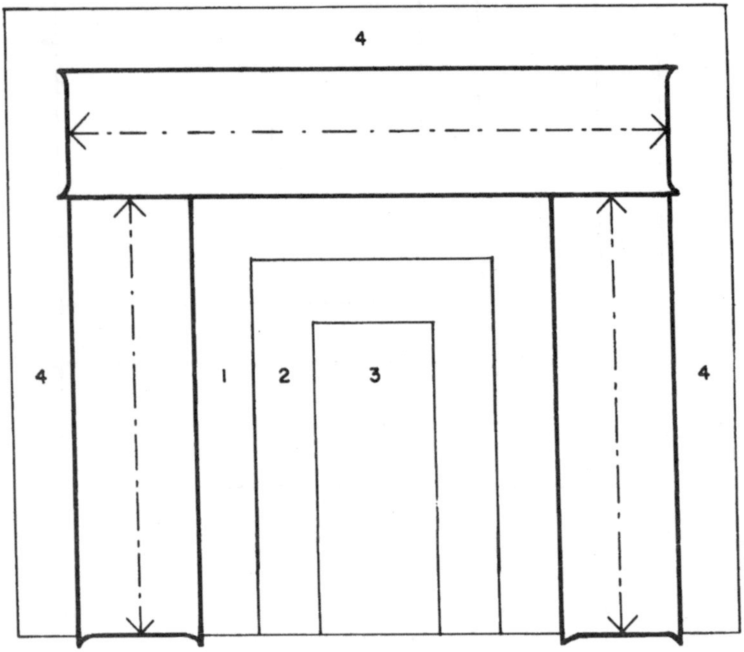

Fig. 25 Three main building house: maulibhadra type (26.59–62)
(1. verandah; 2. portico; 3. court; 4. gallery)

part wide. The (three) main buildings are two parts wide and their verandah one; the central court is two parts wide and surrounded by a one part wide portico, or it may be covered. (This house), whose length is more than its width by two parts, has four gables. On the front facade there is a porch four parts wide and projecting by two.

26.62 The principal main building, which is on the side or the back of the court, has two gables. This house which, in all other respects, is constructed as above is called *maulibhadra*.

Dimensions of houses with three main buildings

26.63 The five possible widths for the (main buildings of) houses with three of these main buildings, go from fifteen (to twenty-three) cubits or from sixteen to twenty-four by successive increments of two cubits.

HOUSES WITH FOUR MAIN BUILDINGS

Dimensions and types

26.64–66a There are twenty-nine possible widths for the (main buildings of) houses with four of them; these go from nine to sixty-five cubits or from ten to sixty-six by successive increments of two cubits. The first fourteen dimensions are for (houses whose) central court is covered and the others for those whose central court is not covered; the choice is to be made according to prescription.

26.66b–67 Here are the names of houses (with four main buildings) as must be known: the first is *sarvatobhadra*, the second *vardhamāna*, the third *svastika*, the fourth *nandyāvarta* and the fifth *rucaka*.

Calculating the length

26.68–69 The initial type is a square (house) whose side has the dimensions which have been given for the width. The length is in line with the *jāti* mode when it is two cubits more than the chosen width; if the difference is four cubits, it is then in *chanda* mode; if six, *vikalpa*; finally, if the length is eight cubits (more than the width), it is *ābhāsa*.

26.70–72 The length may be calculated differently, in terms of the number of units (making up the width). If the length is more than the chosen width by two units it is in *jāti* mode; if it is more than the standard width it is *chanda* mode; if it is six units more than the width, the mode is *vikalpa* and if longer by eight, *ābhāsa*.

First type of *sarvatobhadra* house (fig. 26)

26.73a Now a brief description of houses of the *sarvatobhadra* type is given.

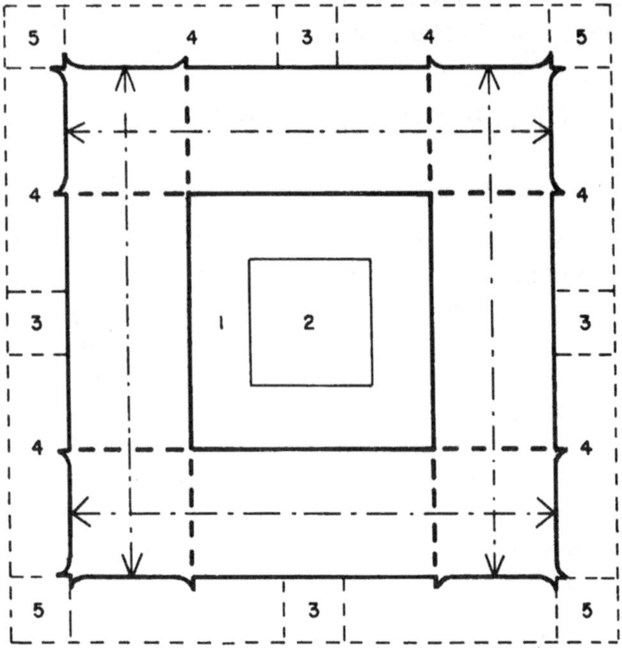

Fig. 26 Four main building house: 1st sarvatobhadra type (26.73 *et sq.*) (1. verandah; 2. court; 3. foreparts; 4. outward gallery; 5. outward corner rooms)

26.73b–74 The (total) width of the house is eight parts; the central courtyard makes up two parts of the width; the passage around it is half as wide and the main buildings make up two parts of the width. (Exterior) to the four corners (of the square formed by the four main buildings) there are square outward rooms (*sabhā*) and a gallery extends on each side between these rooms.

26.75–76a The master's chamber (*svāmyāvāsa*) is in either the east or the west main building; it is enclosed by walls and it has a vaulted door; the walls have latticed windows on the outside and there are pillars along their interior face.

26.76b–77a The main entrance (of the house) occupies one

part (along the length) of one of the lateral main buildings or of the eastern one; it has a door with plain shutters on the exterior and one with latticed shutters on the interior.

26. 77b–78a The ridge beams of the main buildings cross at right angles and thus there are eight gables, (each) of which has a porch roof. In the middle of the four faces of the house there is a forepart, in the shape of half a small hall.

26.78b–81a At the corners of the foreparts shaped like small halls (?) there is (a roofing whose) rafters are assembled to resemble a conch (?); there is a pediment (*mukhapaṭṭikā*) with *ardhakoṭi* (?). All around is a pent-roof supported by consoles and there are eaves on the roof (?). The entablature is provided with small false dormer windows and with a frieze (*antarapra-stara* ?). The rafters, doors and ridge beams (of the four main buildings) are all to be similar; any transgression of this rule will bring endless misfortune.

26.81b–82 In all empty spaces the appearance is that of a pavilion. There are one or several storeys and the arrangement is as for a temple. Such a house is always fit to be the dwelling of gods, brahmins and kings.

26.83 For increases and decreases nothing less than one complete cubit is ever to be used; this is common to all houses.

26.84–85 The gables which are at the ends of the four main buildings are at right angles; above these eight gables are a (second) storey (?) and an attic (?). There are finials on the ridge beams which are all at the same level. There are loggias (?) above the foreparts, accessible from inside and with a gable on the outside. This *sarvatobhadra* house is a dwelling fit for kings.

Second type of *sarvatobhadra* house

26.86–87 The total width of the house is twelve parts; the central court makes up two parts and the walkway around it one. Interior verandahs are one part wide, main buildings two and the outside gallery half of that. This house whose decoration and arrangement are as given above is called *sarvatobhadra*.

Third type of *sarvatobhadra* house

26.88–89a The total width is fourteen parts; the central court makes up two parts and the walkway around it one. The main buildings are two parts wide and the exterior gallery is half as wide. The big (surrounding) courtyard makes up two parts of the width.

26.89b–91 The four main buildings have hipped roofs with median false dormer windows. Foreparts and other elements are as above; no median pillar is to be placed in any of the four main buildings. This house has at least three storeys; it comprises engaged structures and others of the kind. It is called *sarvatobhadra* and is suitable for gods, brahmins and princes.

Fourth type of *sarvatobhadra* house

26.92 The total width is sixteen parts; the central court makes up four parts; everything else may be arranged as in the preceding case. The roof is almost flat (?).

26.93–95a This house is decorated with false dormer windows, arcatures and other elements of the kind, as well as with latticed windows; it has at least three storeys and is arranged as is a temple. A stairway leads from storey to storey. The middle of each storey is arranged like a pavilion, unless there is an uncovered inner court; everything not prescribed by name has to be adapted to the particular circumstance. This house, perfectly fit for kings, is called *sarvatobhadra*.

Fifth type of *sarvatobhadra* house

26.95b–97a The total width of the house is eighteen parts; the central court makes up two parts and the surrounding walkway one. Interior verandahs are one part wide, main buildings two and the outside gallery half that; the big (surrounding) courtyard is two parts wide and the portico bordering it towards the exterior is one part wide.

26.97b–98 There may be wagon-roofs or hipped roofs. There are at least three storeys and a decoration of engaged structures etc. . . . . What remains is to be arranged as given above and according to the particular circumstance and to the appearance sought.

26.99 The interior arrangement must conform to the wishes of the owner and the sensible man proceeds, in all else, as for a temple. This house, suitable for kings, is called *sarvatobhadra.*

Definitions

26.100 A *vimāna* is (a building) endowed with a wagon-roof. A *harmya* (is a building) whose roof is like a bald head. (A *mālikā* is) made up of different elements of various aspects on several storeys, all connected like the pieces of a garland (*mālā*).

26.101 When the width is six or eight parts, the length will be eight, twelve or fourteen (?) and the verandah of the main building will make up one or two parts of the width; when the length is eight parts, the verandah is one or one and a half (?).

First type of *vardhamāna* house (fig. 27)

26.102 I now give a brief description of (houses with four main buildings of) the *vardhamāna* type.

26.103 The (total) width (of the house) is six parts; the main buildings take up two parts of the width as does the central courtyard. There is a wall all around on the outside.

26.104 There is a one part wide passage to the east of the principal main building; (this principal main building) has a median partition wall and a vaulted door.

26.105–106a The western main building is elongated and has two gables; it is high(er) than (the others). The eastern main building is a little less elevated than (the western main building) and a little more than (the lateral main buildings) and it is elongated; the front facade (of the house) is to be found here. The lateral main buildings have no gables and their ridge beams are lower (than those of the other main buildings).

26.106b–107 There is a median porch with two part pro-

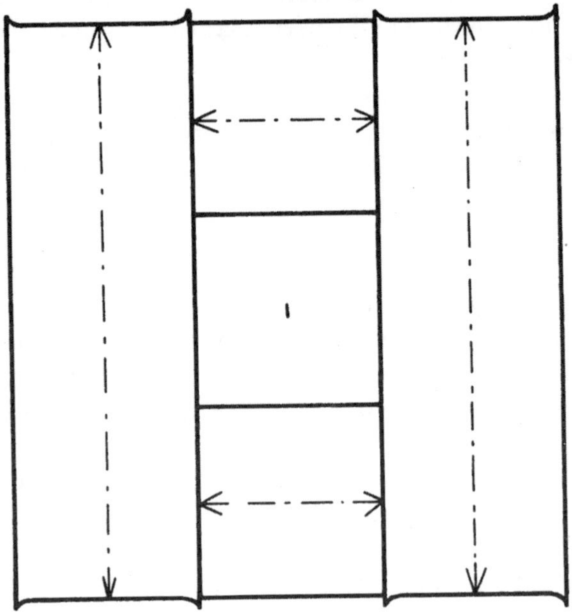

Fig. 27 Four main building house: 1st vardhamāna type (26.102 *et sq.*)
(1: court)

jection on each of the four facades of the house, the small pillars of which may be arranged as is convenient. Spiral stairways taking up two parts are to be arranged at the corners.

26.108–109a This house has false dormer windows, arcatures, pillars and latticed windows; the arrangement is as for a temple and everything not prescribed here must conform to what has been indicated above. This house has one, two or three storeys; if it is intended for kings, its door is not to be in the north.

Second type of *vardhamāna* house

26.109b–110 Otherwise, (the total width of the house being nine parts) there is an (outside) gallery one part wide and bordered by walls and pillars. The principal main building is in the south and its ridge beam is higher (than the others). The foreparts are in whichsoever direction desired and the same is true for the chamber.

26.111–112 This house has a pent-roof supported by consoles and its disposition is as for a temple; the well advised man arranges the doors, arcatures, false dormer windows, platforms (?) and latticed windows according to circumstance and to appearance desired. This house is called *vardhamāna* and is suitable for the four (classes).

Third type of *vardhamāna* house

26.113–114a (The total) width (of the house) is ten parts; the median courtyard takes up two parts of the width and the verandah around it one; the main buildings are two parts wide and the gallery along the outside is half as wide. The door is preceded by a porch.

26.114b–115a All elements, such as corner and elongated aediculae, are arranged according to circumstance and to the appearance required. This house is called *vardhamāna* and is suitable for the four (classes).

Fourth type of *vardhamāna* house

26.115b–116 Otherwise, two of the ten parts that make up (the total) width (of the house) are for the big surrounding courtyard. In the open places on each floor the appearance is that of a pavilion and it is according to this that the upper storeys are to be distributed as has been indicated.

26.117 There is no porch on the front facade but the rest is to be constructed as has been given above. A pavilion is positioned in front (of this house, its width being) the same (as that of the house) or three quarters or a half of it.

26.118 This pleasant *vardhamāna* house, possessed of three, four or five storeys and fitting for brahmins and for people of other classes is, in all other respects, to be built as previously indicated.

Fifth type of *vardhamāna* house

26.119–120a (The total) width (of the house) is twelve parts, two of which are for the central courtyard; the width of the main buildings is two parts and that of the gallery along the outside is (also) two parts; the portico beyond that (gallery) is one part wide and pillars and walls must be arranged as has been prescribed (?).

26.120b–122 On the two lateral facades (of the house), beyond the (gallery), there is an outward elongated annexe, two parts wide, projecting by one and comprising a verandah and a pediment (?). In front, on either side (of the center), are (similar) elongated annexes which are beyond the gallery as noted above. Between these two last there is: on the second storey, an eight part long gutter, on the third storey, a verandah and, on the fourth, there are outward elongated rooms in the same place as above.[1]

26.123–126a Two corner square outward rooms should be built at the back of the building on the fifth storey; between them, on the sixth, there is a loggia (?) shaped like a half of one of those square rooms, with a width of four parts and a projection of two. On the (same) sixth storey, but on the side facades of the buildings, there are square outward rooms and others on the corners of the front facade; between these last there should be a stairway. On the fourth storey there are corner constructions on the front facade; on the fifth there is an elongated room and, also, two loggias (*pañjara*) on the sides, placed lengthwise and two parts wide and long.

26.126b–127 There is a court (at ground floor level) and above that a pavilion-like space and, above that latter, a pillared space (?). There is a double door (?) and the stairway is on the left; this stairway leads from storey to storey and it is concealed in the front verandah (of the main buildings) (?).

26.128–131a At the back there should be a forepart which is four parts wide and projects by two; on the sides and in front there is a three storey verandah. On the fifth storey there is an

1. This description of a storeyed mansion is very confused.

(overhang ?) two parts wide and with a projection of one. At the rear is a construction with a verandah and a pediment. On the fourth storey there are two square rooms two units wide, on the sides. There is a portico all around whose width is the same as that of the house. Above the second storey there is an elongated construction which forms a forepart and which comprises a gable.

26.131b–132 Four lines are to be drawn to correspond to the middle of the four facades of the house. Doors are to be placed to the left of each of these lines in accordance with this rule; a median pillar is set up and the door is attached to the side of this pillar. Those with knowledge of the matter call a door installed according to this rule a "pillar-door" (*kampadvāra*).

26.133 This *vardhamāna* house provided as it is, on all storeys, with elements such as pillars, is the palace of the king of kings.

Sixth type of *vardhamāna* house

26.134–135a (The total) width (of the house) being fourteen parts, the central courtyard makes up two. The big courtyard (around the main building) is two parts wide and the portico beyond it is half as wide as that.

26.135b–137a There is a pent-roof all around, supported by consoles and decorated with fist-like mouldings and other elements. There are rooms at the top (?) (*cūlaharmya*) and other elements of that kind as well as walls, and above, a big gallery (?). All elements such as square and elongated constructions are to be arranged on this building according to the specific circumstance. This building, which does not have its door in the north when it is for kings, is called *vardhamāna*.

Seventh type of *vardhamāna* house

26.137b–139 (The total) width of the house being sixteen parts, the central courtyard is two parts wide as are the main buildings surrounded by walls. The big courtyard (beyond) is two parts wide and comprises interior pillars as has been said (?); beyond that, is a one part wide gallery and a two part wide court; pillars and walls are to be arranged according to circumstance and to appearance sought.

26.140–141a There are foreparts behind and on the sides, each with a porch roof supported by consoles; there are two lateral outward rooms connected in front by a long verandah (?) whose two pediments project by two parts each (?).

26.141b–142 The rear main building (?) is to be constructed so as to be in proportion (with the rest of the house) in order that the result is pleasant and decorative. Square and elongated outward rooms are arranged on each storey so that the result is attractive; on the second and third storeys the entablature is extended by a pent-roof.

26.143 In front there are spiral staircases in the corner constructions (?); the stairways (open) onto the front verandah on each storey.

26.144 A pillar is to rest on a pillar; a pillar is to be placed with a view to an attractive appearance and to solidity; when it rests only partially, or not at all, on a pillar, this gives rise to failure.

26.145–146 A gutter and a room at the top (?) (*cūlaharmya*) are to be arranged on each storey; the sensible man arranges there, where suitable, cornice, rafters, struts, dancer (-shaped supports), fist-like mouldings, ridge beams and *kacagraha* (?).

26.147–150 The sage is to give the appearance of a hall (*sabhā*), of a pavilion (*maṇḍapa*) or of a storeyed gallery (*mālikā*) to the (central) court of the houses that have been described; if that of a *maṇḍapa* is involved, then it has no central pillar. In front (of these houses) there may be a pavilion; its width is the same as that of the house or is three quarters or a half of it; it comprises interior pillars if necessary; it may have one, two or three storeys and may resemble a *mālikā*; it may not be bordered by pillars or may be surrounded by a portico; it comprises an interior stairway; anything not indicated here is to conform to what has been given above.

26.151 This *vardhamāna* house may have three to nine storeys or may have eleven; it is reserved for kings.

First type of *nandyāvarta* house

26.152a The arrangement and decoration of houses of the *nandyāvarta* type are now presented.

26.152b–153 (The total) width (of the house) being six parts, the median courtyard makes up two parts of that width; the width of a main building is two parts, which dimension is applicable to all four of them. The exterior gallery and (exterior ?) walls are to be arranged in *nandyāvarta* shape.

26.154 There is one main building without a door or else there are four (doors). Doors have latticed (shutters) inside and plain ones outside.

26.155–156 The principal main building is closed by a wall on each side; it comprises an internal partition wall with a vaulted door and has a front verandah bordered by a colonnade within and a wall without. On each of the four facades of the house there is a forepart, half-aedicula shaped; there is a pent-roof supported by consoles and the arrangement is that of a temple.

26.157a This house is fitting for the four (classes) but, for vaiśya and śūdra, the main facade must be in the east.

26.157b This house may also have a one part wide gallery all around it, the exterior door of which is ornamented.

26.158–159a Elements such as base and pillars are to be arranged by the sages in the manner previously indicated. (This house) has one, two or three storeys and looks like a temple (with) flat (roof). This is how the prudent man arranges this house which is appropriate for the four classes.

Second type of *nandyāvarta* house (fig.28)

26.159b–161a (The total) width of the house being ten parts, two are for the median courtyard; the passage around this (courtyard) takes up one part of the width and the main buildings, two each; the outside gallery is one part wide. The foreparts and other elements are as they are in the preceding case. (This house is to be built) in such a way that it is well adapted and beautiful; it partakes of the characteristics of a *harmya*.

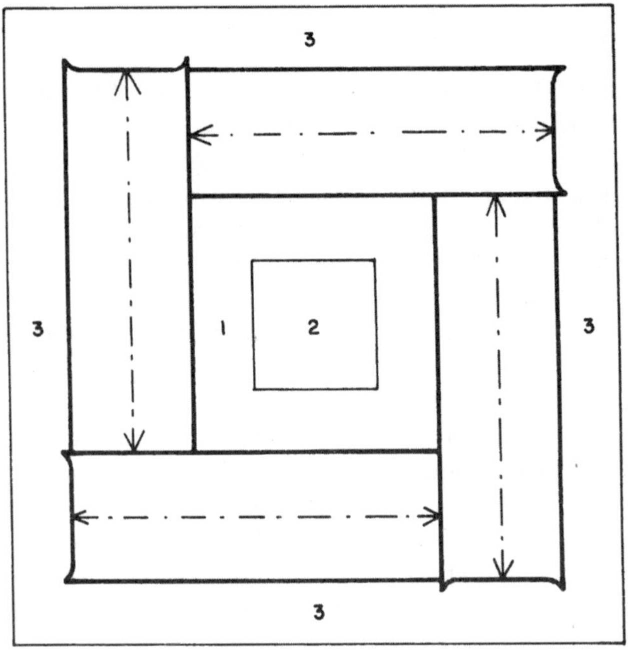

Fig. 28 Four main building house: 2nd nandyāvarta type (26.159 *et sq.*)
(1. walkway; 2. court; 3. gallery)

Third type of *nandyāvarta* house

26.161b–164a (The total) width (of the house) being twelve parts, that of the central courtyard makes up two; the main buildings are two parts wide and the principal one comprises an internal partition wall; there is a big courtyard around (the main buildings) and, beyond that, a one part wide gallery with wall or colonnade as desired. Should circumstance and required appearance call for it, there will be a *cūlyaharmyāṅga* (?) with a verandah. The door, the main porch and elements such as the base are as in the preceding case.

26.164b–165 The roof of each of the four main buildings has an axial ridge beam. There is a square outwork construction in front and behind and elongated ones with gables on the sides. This *nandyāvarta* house has four porches.

26.166 A court is to be built above a court and an outward room construction above an outward room. The central court looks like a hall, a pavilion or a storeyed gallery.

26.167 (This building) has three or more storeys with the corresponding elements; it is (like) a temple and is fitting for brahmins and kings.

Fourth type of *nandyāvarta* house

26.168–169 (The total) width (of the house) being fourteen parts, two are for the central courtyard which has a one part wide walkway around it; the main buildings are two parts wide; the big exterior courtyard is two parts wide and comprises interior pillars when necessary; beyond this (big courtyard) is a one part wide gallery with colonnades, walls . . . etc.

26.170 (This house), in the shape of a *nandyāvarta* figure, has a gable on each of its (ground floor) facades but the main buildings have eight (upper) gables arranged above the ground floor four; it may be said, in other words, that (this house) has twelve gables, counting those below and those above.

26.171–172a There is a forepart which allows for a porch, at each of the four cardinal points. In all that is not indicated, the sage should proceed as given above.

Fifth type of *nandyāvarta* house

26.172b–173 The total width of the house being sixteen parts, two are for the central court; the width of the main buildings is two parts as is that of the big courtyard (all around them); beyond is a one part wide gallery and beyond that a (second) one part wide gallery.

26.174 If specific circumstances and required appearance warrant it, there is a *cūlaharmyāṅga* with verandah (?). Above that, on each main building, is a wagon-roof.

26.175–177a (That house), which has three to nine storeys, is suitable for kings and brahmins. Doors, walls and all other elements should be in conformity with what has been given above. The house is to be arranged like a temple and the sensible man should arrange *nandyāvarta* type windows, with a view to circumstance and required appearance. The disposition of this house with all corresponding elements has now been given.

Svastika house

26.177b–178a (The total) width (of a) *svastika* (house) is six parts, of which two are for the central courtyard and the same number for the width of the main buildings. There is a vaulted door.

26.178b–179 There is an elongated outwork construction at the back and one in front too; on each side facade there is a square construction, perpendicular to the main building and provided with a pediment. The construction at the back has no pediment; it is blind.

26.180–181a (This house) has a pent-roof, supported by consoles, six gables and foreparts; as regards all else, the well advised man should arrange it like a temple. According to the sages, a *svastika* house facing east is fitting for vaiśya and śūdra.

26.181b–182a Otherwise, (the house) may be surrounded by a gallery, one part wide and decorated with engaged structures; there are foreparts as given above and the arrangement too is as previously given.

26.182b–183 (The total width of the house) may be divided into twelve, fourteen or eighteen parts; there is a central court as well as an exterior verandah, a big courtyard and a gallery; in any case the width of the main buildings should be two parts.

26.184–185 Doors, pillars, walls as well as foreparts are to be arranged according to the specific case; there is to be a (*cūla*)-*harmyāṅga* if specific circumstance and required appearance warrant it. There is a wagon-roof, a hipped roof or a flat roof. This is a *svastika* house; all that is not presented is to be as given above.

Rucaka house (fig. 29)

26.186–187a A house is called *rucaka* when the ridge beams (of its main buildings) do not intersect and when there are corner rafters; there are stairways at the corners, there are decorative elements (?) and it is specified that there is no door in the north. It is appropriate for the dwelling of the heterodox, brahmins and those of other classes as well as gods.

26.187b–187c According to the sages, all that is fitting for the four classes is fitting too for gods and brahmins whilst what is fitting for vaiśya is fitting for śūdra.

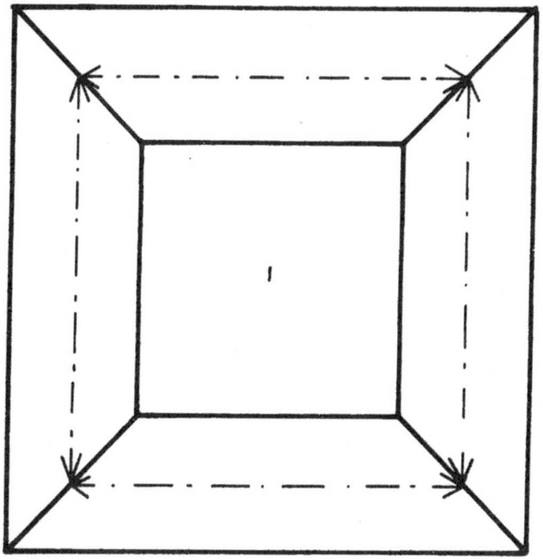

Fig. 29 Four main building house: rucaka type (26.186 *et sq.*)
(1: court)

General rules for houses with four main buildings

26.188 According to the learned, houses with four main buildings which are regular quadrilateral shaped but not elongated and which are of the prescribed width, are suitable for gods, brahmins, ceremonies such as those for donations, and for all heterodox sects.

26.189 Here is what the sages say: if the (total) width is nine, eight, seven or six parts, the width of the main buildings will be two parts but, if the total width is five parts, then the main buildings will only be one part wide.

HOUSES WITH SEVEN MAIN BUILDINGS OR MORE

26.190 A royal palace with seven main buildings is sixty-four cubits wide and twice as long as wide; it has two (main) entrances, ten gables, two (interior) courtyards as well as six joins between main buildings; it is decorated like a temple throughout (*fig. 30*).

26.191–192 The length is nine fifths the width or else it is eleven sixths, twelve sevenths, fourteen eighths or sixteen ninths; these are the seven (proportions possible) for the length of a house with seven main buildings. (The same figures) being used for the width of a house with ten main buildings, the length is thirteen (fifths of the width) or sixteen (sixths), seventeen (sevenths), twenty (eighths) or twenty-three (ninths).

26.193 An edifice with ten main buildings is prescribed for kings; eighty cubits wide and three times as long, it has twelve gables, three (main) doors, three (interior) courtyards and eight joins; it is to be arranged like a *harmya* (i.e. with a flat roof) (*fig. 31*).

26.194 The width (of the) verandah is a third or half that of the main building; the porch projects by a third or a sixth (of the width of the main building); inside, as outside, the projection of the gargoyles is half that of the porch. This is common to all houses dealt with here.

26.195 A house without a (central) courtyard which has courtyards in the corners and a large number of accesses and of facades and whose gables (are sometimes orientated) towards the interior and sometimes towards the exterior: such a house is called "limitless" and need not have a central courtyard in accordance with general rules.[1]

1. This seems to correspond to a house whose elements are separated (27.11).

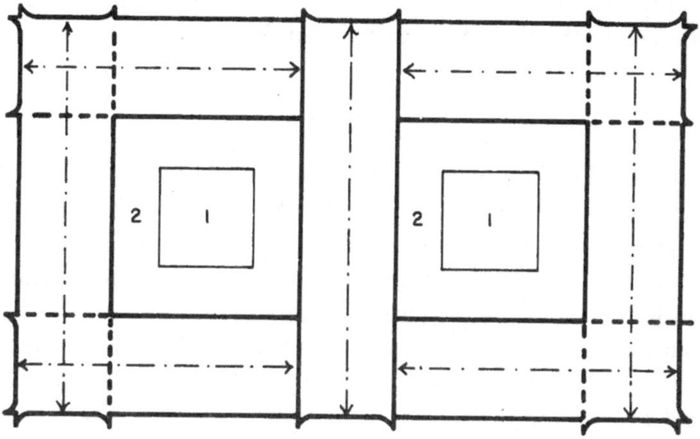

Fig. 30 Seven main building house (26.190)
(1: courts; 2: verandah)

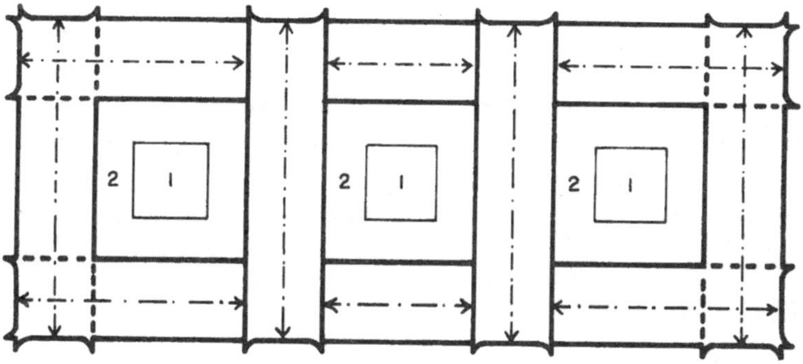

Fig. 31 Ten main building house (26.193)
(1: courts; 2: verandah)

26.196a In the houses of men, the number of cubits, pillars, beams (etc. . . .) should be odd; in houses of gods, even and uneven numbers of cubits (pillars, beams etc. . . .) may be used.

26.196b There is no harm in placing the door in the centre (of the front facade) of a building intended for gods, brahmins or kings but, for other categories of people, an auspicious door is placed to the side of the middle (of the facade).

Placing the foundation deposit

26.197 The foundation deposit is to be placed under that portion of the wall which is on the front facade, beneath the pit in which rests the bottom of a pillar. It is to be in the portion to the left of the middle of the house or of a main building and has to be in the principal building.

26.198 The thickness of the wall is to be divided into eight parts and (a point marked) at four parts from its external face (and another) at three parts from its internal one: (the foundation deposit is then to be installed between these two points). For gods, the foundation deposit is placed in the middle of the thickness of the wall; in the case of brahmins and people of other classes, however, this is forbidden.

The door

26.199 It is not proper to install an axial door in a house intended for brahmins or for people of the (other three) classes; there is no error though in installing such an axial door in a house intended for people such as heterodox sages.

Monasteries

26.200 The length of the principal (main building) is triple the dimension chosen for the width; other buildings are to be added to it, lengthwise, whose length is double the width (chosen initially) until the monastery's total length is twenty-two times (the chosen width); there are then eleven buildings in all.

26.201–202 (Each main building) has a porch on its front facade and is decorated with square and elongated outwork constructions and with false dormer windows. There is a verandah at the back; or else, (each main building) has two gables and resembles a *garbhakūṭa* (?). It has one, two, three or more storeys; there are various projecting elements in front and behind. A monastery is to be built like a temple.

Dimensions of house pillars

26.203–205 The heights appropriate for the pillars of all houses, (as have been dealt with) are now indicated, along with the corresponding diameters. The nine heights of the pillars go from two and a half cubits to three and a half or four (and a half) cubits according to whether the increments are of three or six digits; the corresponding diameters go from six to ten or fourteen digits by increments of a half or a whole digit. In response to specific necessities, the sage may equally use the dimensions previously indicated.

The *āyādi* formulae[1]

26.206–207a The width having been multiplied by three and (the product obtained) divided by eight, the remainder (corresponds to one of the eight elements of) the 'matrice' series, which are 'standard', 'cloud', 'lion', 'dog', 'bull', 'donkey', 'elephant' and 'crow'; amongst these, standard, lion, bull and elephant bring success, the others being inauspicious.

26.207b–208a The width having been multiplied by eight and (the product obtained) divided by twenty-seven, the remainder will correspond to one of the asterisms, the first of which is *aśvayuj*; it is by way of this remainder that zodiac signs (favourable to the building) are determined.

26.208b–209a The length having been multiplied by eight and then by nine and (the product obtained) having been divided by twelve and by ten, two different remainders are obtained, one called 'riches' and the other 'debt'; to be auspicious the gain must be greater than the debt.

26.209b–210 The perimeter having been multiplied by nine and (the product obtained) divided by thirty, the remainder (will correspond to one of the thirty lunar days);

1. See above 9.18b sq. (p. 26).

there is a conjunction of lunar and solar days - Sunday being the first - and the asterism and this conjunction must correspond to the conjunctions: *amṛta*, *vara* and *siddhi* and not to any other.

26.211 The house, whose asterism corresponds to that of the birth of its owner, is auspicious; this indication applies to constructions intended) for men. If the building is destined for the immortals then that which is auspicious for the builder is so for the building.

Annexes

26.212–213 The construction sheltering the annexes is exterior to the house; its width goes from thirty-one to sixty-one cubits by successive increments of two cubits and its length is (calculated) by whatsoever means are preferred. Walls and portico make for decoration within or without, as preferred; the roof is supported by rafters or is (similar to that of a) pavilion. This building containing annexes, surrounds a divine or a human dwelling. It has one or two storeys less than the building it surrounds.

26.214 In the eastern part (?) of the first or second enclosure is the women's apartment and the house for their confinements is on the square of Nirṛti as are the latrines, though the women's house may also extend from the square of Pavana to that of Indu.

26.215–216 The dining hall is situated where Yama is, the room where money is stored is where Soma is, Agni has the granary, and condiments for the cooking (are stored) on the square of Kha. The room for cult ceremonies is on the square of Īśa and the well is there too, though the baths are on the square of Uditi; as far as other (parts of the dwelling) are concerned, they should each be put in a suitable position.

26.217–218 Doors and walls are to be arranged as convenient according to the wishes of the owner and, for the rest, the well advised man follows tradition. Thus, the byre will be on the square of Śikhin, the sheds for goats and sheep on that of Nirṛti, that for buffaloes on the square of Pavana; in the corner consecrated to Īśa are the stables and the elephants' shed; all vehicles are to the left of the doors placed at the cardinal points.

26.219 What has been said goes for all four (classes); the procedure is, however, different for a house intended for kings which may have three enclosures, three rows of houses and three parts, even though the rule indicated is to be followed by the other three classes.

26.220 There are two or three enclosure walls for men whereas, for temples, there are five, three or one. That which has been indicated for setting the dimensions of houses is appropriate for men, according to specialists in the subject.

Thus ends, in the *Mayamata*, treatise on dwelling,
the twenty-sixth chapter: RULES FOR HOUSES.

Chapter 27

FEATURES OF HOUSES FOR THE FOUR CLASSES

27.1a Now the specific arrangements for houses (intended for each) of the (four) classes are given.

The wall of the enclosure

27.1b–4 Starting with four poles (that is, sixteen cubits) and continuing, by successive increments of two cubits, up to thirty cubits provides, one by one, the eight (possible widths) for (the enclosure) of small houses. For (the enclosure) of medium sized houses, it is said that the width goes from eight poles, (that is, thirty-two cubits) to thirty-two poles, by successive increments of two poles; for a large sized house (the width goes from thirty-two poles) to one hundred by successive increments of two poles. What has been indicated is the width of the walls within which is the house.

27.5–6a For brahmins and, (amongst the others), only for kings (the enclosure) is square; for kṣatriya, (vaiśya and śūdra) its length is greater than its width by an eighth, a sixth or a quarter, respectively. It is not appropriate to construct a house (the enclosure of which) measures less than sixteen cubits.

27.6b–7 (The wall of the enclosure) is nine, eight, seven or six cubits high and its thickness (at the bottom) is a third (or) a quarter of that; its thickness at the top is three quarters (of its thickness at the bottom). Its coping is plain (or) decorated with rounded false dormer windows.

27.8–9 There is a door at each of the four cardinal points, which can be closed; there are gateways too and various other decorative elements. There is a moat beyond the wall equipped with every kind of defence. This is the description of the wall of the enclosure surrounding the house.

Annexes

27.10 Annexes may however be built (around the house) in cobwork or wooden framework with thatch or covering of that kind; they have a base and pillars.

Houses with main buildings separated or in blocks

27.11 There are two ways to build a house: disjoined or joined fashions. More clearly, it is said that what is dealt with are houses (whose elements) are separated and those which form a block.

27.12 A house with separate elements has no join; a house whose elements are not separate has joins; in houses whose elements are separated, the four principal main buildings are at the cardinal points; there are pavilions and annexes at the intermediate points.

27.13 If there are three, two or just one main building within the wall of the enclosure this will lead to misfortune; that is why it is best to install, in the enclosure, a house which has four main buildings and whose dimensions are calculated from its width.

27.14–15a It is said that small dimensions are for lesser people and large ones for the great; whereas large dimensions are never to be used for people of little substance, everything that is fitting, with respect to dimensions which suit lesser people, is fitting as well for the great.

Layout

27.15b–16 (Whether the house) be small or large, a line delimiting it must first be drawn; whether it be rectangular or square (the area thus delimited) is to be divided into sixty-four parts and the six *rajju*, the four *vaṃśa* and the eight *sirā* are to be drawn as well as their intersections.[1]

27.17–18a Those knowledgeable in the subject of building

1. See above 7.49 sq. (description of the spirit of the site).

are to take care to avoid wounding the vulnerable points; a wound inflicted by the "limbs" of the house on the lines or other (vulnerable points), causes the complete destruction (of the house); care must also be taken to avoid (touching) the lines and other (vulnerable points).

27.18b–19 The (diagram's) median lines are called, respectively, and beginning with the one towards the east: *anna*, *dhānya*, *dhana* and *sukha*; the four principal main buildings are named accordingly: *annālaya*, *dhānyālaya*, *dhanālaya*, and *sukhālaya*.[1]

Dimensions of central pavilion

27.20–22a In the centre of the site (of the future house), the sages begin by constructing a pavilion with a width a quarter, a fifth, sixth, seventh, eighth or ninth that of the site (of the house). The six possible widths for small, medium and large pavilions go from seven to seventeen cubits by successive increments of two cubits.

27.22b–23 This pavilion may be one or two units wide and it comprises (accordingly) four or eight pillars. For brahmins, kings and vaiśya, the number of pillars is to be even whilst, for śūdra and other (lower castes) it is said to be uneven.

The central platform

27.24 Only for brahmins, kings and vaiśya is there a platform in the centre (of the house); offerings are made there three times a day and it is honoured with flowers, perfumes . . . etc.

27.25–26 Its height is three spans as is its width. In its centre is an altar to Brahmā with dimensions half those of the platform; these dimensions are decreased by six digits for princes and by six more digits for vaiśya. No platform (nor altar) to Brahmā should be set up for śūdra or other (low) castes.

1. For the laying out of these main buildings see above chap.6 (vv.24b–25).

Characteristics of the central pavilion

27.27a The pavilion's plan corresponds (to that of the house) whether the latter is rectangular or square.

27.27b–30 The nine heights possible for its pillars go from five to seven spans by successive increments of three digits; the nine corresponding diameters go from five to thirteen digits, the diameter of the top (of the pillars) being less by an eighth. The height of the base is half that of the pillars or is half, less a sixth or an eighth; or else, the height of the base is a third (or) a quarter that of the pillars. The pillar may be square, circular or octagonal section or of *citrakhaṇḍa* type; these are the shapes prescribed for pillars.

27.31–32 These pillars, when for brahmins and kings, are in *śamī*, *khadira* or *khādira* woods, for vaiśya in *silīndhra*, *piśita* or *madhūka* woods, for śūdra in *rājādana*, *nimba*, *silīndhra*, *piśita* or *tinduka*; bamboo however is appropriate for everyone.

27.33–34a This pavilion adorned with various ornaments, is built of bricks joined by mortar when for brahmins and kings; it is in unbaked bricks when for vaiśya and others. A light building may also be constructed with coconut palms, in the place of the pavilion.

27.34b–35 A passage must be left around the pavilion, between the pavilion and the main building; its width, which is uniform throughout, is to be three, four, five or six cubits or is, in the case of a small house, one or two cubits.

Positions of *annāgāra* etc. . .

27.36 The medians of the *annāgāra* (of the *dhānyālaya*, *dhanālaya* and *sukhālaya*) in relation to the site's medians, are displaced to the right by, respectively, twelve, nine, seven and five digits.

27.37–39a The position of the pillars is displaced by ten parts for the *annāgāra*, by nine (for the *dhānyālaya*), by eight (for the *dhanālaya*) and by seven (for the *sukhālaya*) (?). When the pillars are put into place each is to be installed in the following fashion (?): standing in the middle of the site, one turns successively towards the north, east, south and west of that site. The middle of the wall is to correspond to the point in the middle of the space between the middle of the main building and the middle of the pillars.

27.39b The main building is orientated towards the interior but, where the site is concerned, the orientation must be towards the exterior (?).

The *sukhālaya*

27.40–41 The *saukhya*, dwelling of brahmins, is to be built on the squares of Mahīdhara, Indu, Bhallāṭa, Mṛga and Aditi; its width and its length are, respectively, five and nine cubits or five and a half and ten or seven and eleven; these are its three possible sizes.

General proportions

27.42 The overall height of all main buildings is to be equal to their greatest width. The height of the walls is equal to that of the pillars and their thickness is triple the diameter of the corresponding pillars.

27.43–44 The interval between pillars is a third or a fifth the width of the main building; the diameter of the pillars is (calculated) as has been given or in relation to the number of cubits which make up the width of the main building; there are as many digits (in the diameter of the pillars) as cubits in the width of the main building; a diameter (so) calculated, is suitable for the pillars of all (types of) main building.

Sukhālaya (cont.)

27.45 The door is on the square of Mahendra and the drainpipe on that of Mukhya. A dwelling like this invariably brings success to brahmins.

Annālaya

27.46–47 For kings, a *mahānasa* (is to be built) on the squares of Mahendra, Arka, Āryaka, Satya and Bhṛśa, measuring three by five cubits or three and a half by six and a half, four by seven or four and a half by eight and a half or five by nine; these are the five dimensions of the *mahānasa*.

27.48 The door is on the square of Gṛhakṣata and the drainpipe on that of Jayanta. A dwelling like this, situated in the east, is fitting for the king, to whom it will bring an increase of treasure.

Dhānyālaya

27.49–51a There is a *dhānyālaya* (for vaiśya) on the squares of Gṛhakṣata, Ārkin, Gandharva, Bhṛṅgarāja and Vivasvant, for which the following widths and lengths are prescribed: five and nine cubits, six and a half and ten and a half, seven and eleven, nine and thirteen or eleven and fifteen cubits; these are the five possible dimensions.

27.51b–52a The door is on the square of Puṣpadanta and the drain course on that of Vitatha. This dwelling, situated in the south, brings wealth, rewards and good fortune to vaiśya.

Dhanālaya

27.52b–54a A *dhanālaya* is prescribed on the squares of Puṣpadanta, Asura, Śoṣa, Varuṇa and Mitra; similar to a *dhānya(-alaya)* but a little smaller, this dwelling, situated in the west, brings good fortune to śūdra. Its door is on the square of Bhallāṭa and its drain course on that of Sugrīva.

27.54b This is the rule for the order of habitation of the four classes.

Elements of the upper part of the house

27.55–57 Successively arranged above the pillars are: the

bracket capitals, the architrave and its fascia, the beams, the joists and the small joists as well as the planks which constitute the floor (of the upper storey); then comes the cornice and its frieze as well as projecting gargoyles; there are fist-like decorations, struts, consoles and the timber-work which is constituted by the main rafters; the covering (is supported) by rafters; there is a gable. The main door is big and is on the right side of the building.

Proportions for dwelling pavilions (?)

27.58–59 The unit measures two cubits; the dwelling pavilion's width (?) is from four to thirty-two units. Where a small (building) is concerned it will be a light construction; its width is from one to thirty-one units; it is covered with coconut palms and tal tree palms, supported by pillars and intersecting beams.

Position of the foundation deposit

27.60 I shall now indicate, in accordance with what has been given above, the position of the foundation deposit in the (different) houses, (corresponding to the different classes), and that in relation to the arrangement of the gods distributed (over the site).

27.61 In the four main buildings (corresponding to the four classes) and starting with the one in the north, the foundation deposit must be on the squares of, respectively, Puṣpadanta, Bhallāṭa, Mahendra and Gṛhakṣata, under the wall of the front facade and to the right (of the door).

27.62 The thickness of the wall is divided into eight or nine (?) parts; (a point is marked) at four parts of its external face (and another one) at three parts of its internal face; the foundation deposit is installed between (these two points).

27.63 The width (of the wall) of the master's chamber being divided into five, six or seven parts (a point) is marked at two (?) parts of its internal facade on the right side (?).

27.64–65 The deposit is placed at the base of a pillar and the better it is concealed the better it is; it may (also) be beneath the door's right upright, under the internal partition wall or under a concealed pillar, or else at the bottom of the pillar which is right of centre in the dwelling pavilion; these are the five places where the foundation deposit should be put in houses, whether those houses form blocks or are composed of separate elements.

The *muhūrtastambha*

27.66–69 A perfect *muhūrtastambha* is to be installed above (the foundation deposit); according to the knowledgeable it should be in *khadira*, *khādira*, *madhūka*, or *rājādana* wood; the values for its height and diameter are indicated here: its height is twelve, eleven, ten or nine spans and its diameter is as many digits (as there are spans in its height); its diameter at the top is less by an eighth. It is sunk to a point five, four and a half, four or three spans on its height; its top is circular or lotus bud shaped or "broken pointed" or bubble shaped. This is the pillar which is to be properly honoured by the four classes, the first of which is the brahmin class.

General rules

27.70–71a A house in one block must be built without a central pillar; the median wall of the main building should not coincide with the middle of a pillar and it is said that a double vaulted door is to be set in this wall.

27.71b–73a There, (i.e. in a *sukhālaya*) (?), the interior door is to the south-east of the main building (?); where a *mahānasa* is concerned, the side of the main building is to the south and it is on that side (that the interior door is to be (?); that interior door is in the north-west (of a *dhānyālaya*); in the case of a main building situated in the west, (a *dhanālaya*), the side of this main building is to the north and there, on this side, (is the interior door) (?).

27.73b–75a Assemblies are not to be made of the separate main buildings of houses (with separate elements). It is said that the gods (of the site) are to be installed in the joined main buildings (of houses in blocks); the installation of Padmaja and his surrounding divinities may be carried out as appropriate; the other (deities), those not in designated places, should be set up so that they guard (the house).

27.75b–80 It is sometimes said that there is no median pillar in a one block house. I am now going to indicate, once more, the number of pillars which are in front, behind and on the sides, in terms of dimensions expressed in cubits. When (the width) is three or three and a half cubits, there are eight pillars (in all); when the building is four, four and a half or five cubits (wide) it must have sixteen pillars (in all); when (the width) is six, six and a half or seven cubits it is to have twenty-four pillars; when it is ten and a half or eleven cubits there are forty pillars; when the width is twelve and a half or thirteen cubits there must be fifty-eight pillars. There should be the same number of pillars on the width as on the length.

The verandah

27.81–83a When the width (of a main building) is seven cubits, it must be divided into six parts, of which two, on the facade, are for the verandah; when the width is nine cubits, it is divided into eight parts, of which three are taken up by the part of the facade which is for the verandah; when it is eleven cubits, the division is into ten parts, of which four are (for the verandah); when it is thirteen cubits, there are eleven parts, of which six on the front make up the verandah. These are the proportions of the verandah.

The chamber of the master

27.83b–84 The width for the master's part is (at least) fifty-four digits and, in a big house, it is seventy-eight digits; (going from one to the next of these figures) by successive increments of six digits, yields five possible dimensions.

27.85 The height of (the house's) pillars having been divided into sixty parts, sixteen are allotted for the base of the master's chamber, twice that for its pillars and the remainder for its entablature.

27.86–87 The base is *pādabandha* type and the pillars are provided with all (requisite) elements; above the architrave is a frieze of dwarves and a cornice with its frieze decorated with *vyāla*, elephants, *makara* and lions as well as small false dormer windows and other motifs of the sort. There is an arcature in the guise of a door and the interior face of the walls is decorated.

27.88 This master's chamber is constructed inside the principal building and there is a *maṇḍapa* there (?). On no account should the bed, in the master's chamber, be positioned on the axis of (the main building).

27.89–90a The pillars erected in the master's chamber have double intercolumniations, unlike the exterior ones which are separated from each other (by simple intercolumniations); their diameter is half that of the pillars which were the basis (for the calculation of their height) and they are provided with decorative elements as desired.

27.90b–91 It is said that the master's part is found on each storey of the building. Its walls are of bricks, laid with mortar, or of planks and, when for the king, are covered with gold, copper or other metals.

Covering of the main buildings

27.92–93a *Pāñcāla* or other types of rafters are arranged two by two above an *annāgara* or (a principal main building) of another type; the arrangement and shape of the rafters is, in all respects, true to what has been previously prescribed. If there are not enough (rafters) the harvest is spoiled and, if too many, debts will lead to prison.

27.93b–94 For vaiśya and śūdra there are three finials, for kings six or seven, for brahmins nine, and eleven are required for a sanctuary; it is said that, where heterodox sects are concerned, there may be an even number of finials.

27.95a The foundation deposit's location, the verandah

and the median partition wall are in the principal main building.

27.95b–96a Neither the pillars nor the base nor the walls of houses for men should be made of stone. A cobwork building is to be covered with thatch whereas one otherwise constructed is to be covered with tiles.

27.96b–97a (The level of) the square of Brahmā is lower than the base and is said to be the interior floor of the house; if the floor of the house is low, the entrance is to be a covered shed providing shelter from the rain.

27.97b–98 It is said that, for people of all classes, the height (of the house's base) is half that of the pillars. There are those though who say that the base must be elevated to the height of the chest, thigh (?) or navel of the owner and this in accordance with the order of the four main buildings (corresponding to the four classes) (?) beginning with the one in the south.

27.99 The (secondary) main buildings of a designated house resemble its principal (main building); it is there that the appurtenances intended for the owner are to be installed.

Distribution of appurtenances

27.100 The vessel for the salted water from boiled rice is placed at the north-east, the hearth is to be on the square of Antarikṣa and the mortar on that of Satya; an oven on the square of Īśa is fitting for all.

The hearth

27.101 It is said that there are five types of hearth with dimensions from eight to sixteen digits by increments of two digits for the width, and from twelve digits to a cubit by increments of three digits for the height.

27.102 The width of the opening of the hearth goes from four to twelve digits as do the widths of the fireplace and the chimney, whose height is equal to the width; such are the dimensions appropriate for hearths, beginning with the smallest, suitable for the lowliest people.

27.103 For a king, the hearth is (round) like a human head (?), for gods and brahmins it is square, for vaiśya rectangular and the other forms are all fitting for the other classes.

Number of finials (?)

27.104 There are one, three, five, seven, nine or eleven finials (*cūli*) on the houses of men and on those of gods; there are odd or even numbers of them and all numbers are appropriate for gods, for gods on earth and for masters of the earth whereas, for other classes, say the sages, those numbers prescribed for each of them specifically should be used.

Distribution of appurtenances (cont.)

27.105–108 The *annaprāśana* takes place on the square of Ārya, on that of Mahendra (?) and on that of Savindra; the study (of the Veda) takes place on the square of Vivasvant and marriage on that of Mitra; it is to be known that 'haircutting' is done on the square of Indrajaya and on those of Vāyu and Soma, whilst accounts are done on the squares of Pitṛ, Dauvārika and Jala. It is said that the women's confinement room is on the squares of Sugala and Puṣpadanta, the cistern on that of Āpavatsa, the tank on that of Āpa, the millstone (*aṅkaṇa* ?) on that of Mahendra and the grindstone on that of Mahīdhara.

The four types of dwelling

27.109–110a I now present the different types of dwelling according to the order previously used in the description of houses. There are four sorts of dwelling: the first is called *diśābhadra*, the second *garuḍapakṣa*, third *kāyabhāra* and fourth *tulānīya*.

Diśābhadra dwelling

27.110b–111 The *diśābhadra* dwelling comprises a forepart

at each of the cardinal points which extends throughout the length of the corresponding main building; beyond, at the cardinal points, is a courtyard and there is a vacant space at each of the intermediate points (?). For the remainder, that previously indicated is to be adhered to in applying rules peculiar to brahmins and to kings.

Garuḍapakṣa dwelling

27.112a The rules relating to the *garuḍapakṣa* dwelling are the same as those for the royal palace.

Kāyabhāra dwelling (fig. 32)

27.112b–113a The (total) length (of the site) is double its width and that length is to be divided into five parts: two are left in the west and the rest (of the surface of the site) is divided according to the sixty-four square (diagram).

27.113b–114a All the elements (of this dwelling), beginning with the (median) pavilion, are to be arranged as has been given above; the principal main building is to the south, the rest of the house being the domain of the appurtenances.

27.114b–119a The women's quarters are on the squares of Bhṛṅgarāja, Dauvārika, Sugrīva and Pitṛ; there too, the housekeeping equipment is installed; the chariot is to the left of the door and the room where alms are given is on the square of Varuṇa; the granary is to be on the square of Asura and the armoury on that of Indrarāja, the guest chamber is on Mitra's square and the mortar on Roga's; the treasure is to be on the square of Bhūdhara, the clarified butter and the simples on that of Nāga; poison and antidote, the well and the shrine are on the squares of Jayanta, Āpavatsa, Parjanya and Śiva respectively; the kitchen and (storeroom for) condiments, together, occupy the squares of Savitṛ and Antariksa, the pavilion which serves as dining room is on the squares of Vitatha, Pūṣan and Sāvindra.

27.119b–120a This is what is prescribed for those powerful amongst vaiśya. A dwelling is called *kāyabhāra* when it com-

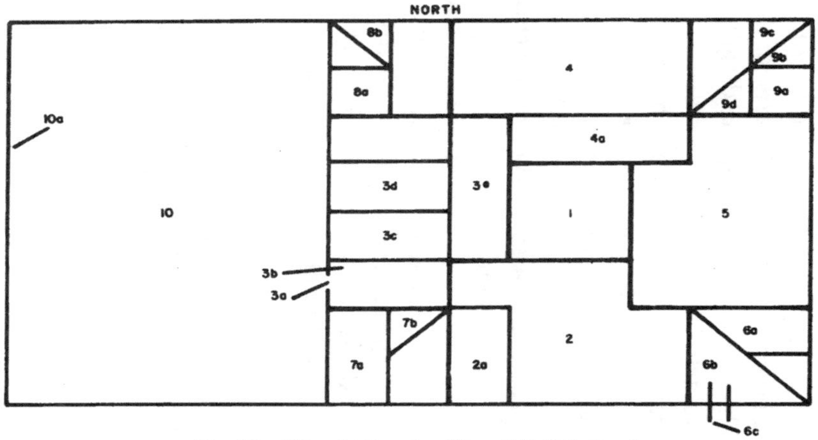

Fig. 32 Kāyabhāra dwelling (27.112 *et sq.*)

1. Central pavilion and altar of Brahmā.
2. Principal main building (dhānyālaya):
   2a: women's quarters (see also 7a).
3. Western main building:
   3a: entrance; 3b: chariot shed; 3c: alms room; 3d: granary; 3e: guest chamber.
4. Northern main building:
   4a: treasure room.
5. Eastern main building.
6. South-east outward building:
   6a: kitchen and store for condi- 6b: dining room; 6c: sewage outlet.

   South-west outward building:
   7a: women's quarters (see also 2a); 7b: armoury.
8. North-west outward building:
   8a: mortar; 8b: store for clarified butter and simples.
9. Nor'h-east outward building:
   9a: store for poisons; 9b: well; 9c: shrine; 9d: store for antidotes.
10. Garden (?):
    10a: enclosure wall.

prises all that is peculiar to vaiśya and when the western part is unoccupied.

Tulānīya dwelling

27.120b–121 Now the *tulānīya* residence is described. The (total) length of the site is double its width and that length is divided into seven parts; taking the three median parts (of the length of the dwelling) as the base, a sixty-four square diagram is drawn (on the space thus delineated).

27.122–123a All the elements (of this dwelling) beginning with the (median) pavilion, are to be arranged as has been given above, taking care to leave (two areas) unoccupied at east and west, each (corresponding) to two (sevenths of the total length). The sage must arrange the space (between them) according to the particular circumstance.

27.123b–125a The reception hall is to be on the squares of Vāyu, Bhallāṭa and Soma; the mortar is on Mukhya's square and the maids' apartments on Āpa's; the chariot is at the front and to the left (of the door). All else (is to be arranged) there as desired. It is said that this is appropriate for the rich amongst śūdra.

27.125b–126 If water falls on the wall around (the house) this brings ruin to the family and, consequently, the edge of the roof (of the house) is not to abut onto this (wall) for, if that should happen, then all chance of success is spoiled, no matter for what class the house is intended.

27.127 It is auspicious if the height of the house is (calculated) in relation to its width and length and to do otherwise is to cause death.

Door proportions

27.128 According to the learned this is the way to calculate (the proportions of) the door of a house intended for men: the height of the pillars (of that house) being divided into eight parts, the door takes up six and a half; half (the height of the door) being divided into nine parts, a half part is reserved and the remainder is the width (of the door).

27.129 The height of the pillars being divided into five parts, the height of the door makes up four; the (remaining part of the height of the pillars) is divided into six parts: three and a half are for the lintel and two and a half for the sill; on the door is a bolt (*bandha*) (?) whose thickness is calculated as above.

Time for construction

27.130–131 An *annaśāla* is to be built when the point of the gnomon indicates that the sun is rising and a *dhanagṛha* when, during the afternoon, the solar rays from the west are very low (on the horizon); for a principal main building to the south, (the sun), coming from the region of the Southern Cross, must be very high, very difficult to fix (or otherwise) very high indeed; lastly, a *sukhagṛha* should be built when the sun's rays appear in the region of the Great Bear or when the sun is very low on the horizon. This, according to the sages of old, is how (the moments favourable to the building) of houses, for brahmins, kings, merchants and śūdra, are chosen according to the rising and setting of the sun.

Door positions

27.132 To be auspicious, the main entrance of the house must be on the square of Rākṣasa, Puṣpadanta, Bhallāṭa or Mahendra. It is known that there is an increase in wealth, lineage and cattle for the owner, the entrance of whose house is of auspicious proportions and is placed between a pillar and a wall.

Apartment positions

27.133 The apartment on the right is that of the master of the house; the gynaeceum to the left is for his wife; confusion of these two positions brings bad thoughts to them and takes away their peace of mind.

27.134 For success, a house should be built in accordance with what has been given for the middle of the site, the middle of the house, of the pillars and of the wall. Any confusion between these prevents success. Thus work should begin only after a careful examination.

Period of beginning of construction

27.135–136a An *annagṛha* is to be built when the sun is in Aries or Taurus, a *dhānyālaya* when it is in Leo or Cancer, a *dhanālaya* when it is in Libra or Scorpio and a *sukhālaya* when it is in Capricorn or Aquarius. A man does not build a house at a cardinal point when the sun is in Pisces, Gemini, Virgo or Sagittarius.

27.136b If anyone, in disregard of this rule, insists on proceeding as his own wishes dictate, he goes to the city of Yama or brings about his servants' deaths.

Thus ends, in the *Mayamata*, treatise on dwelling, the twenty-seventh chapter: RULES FOR HOUSES FOR ALL FOUR CLASSES.

Chapter 28

FIRST ENTRY INTO A HOUSE

28.1 The entry into a house is made only when it is finished; there should be no hurry to enter an unfinished house; tardiness in entering a finished house means that none but the hosts of deities and spirits will establish themselves there.

28.2 Therefore, the work having been brought to completion, the house is to be entered in an auspicious way at the precisely suitable moment of an auspicious hour in a half day which accords with the horoscope, an auspicious day in an (auspicious) fortnight of an auspicious month.

Preparatory ceremonies

28.3 On the evening of the day before, a brahmin, some cattle and a bull are installed (in the house) and are propitiated with water (. . . etc.); recitations of the Veda are done as well as sacrifices and propitiatory ceremonies to delight the perfect brahmin (installed in the house); words of good omen are pronounced. The house should be cleaned and its walls coated with a mixture of orpiment, agalloche, mustard, *kuṣṭha* and *vāca*, then the floor should be sprinkled with sandalwood water.

28.4 The sage begins the preparatory ceremony in the evening, to the north-east of the house, in a pavilion adorned with multicoloured materials, surmounted by banners and comprising canopies and other essentials.

28.5 The architect wears, for the occasion, white garments, a gold sacrificial thread and white flowers; he is anointed with white and is in a good state of mind; he is adorned with gold jewellery or with all sorts of gems.

Putting in place of the vases

28.6 The sage first arranges twenty-five vases, full of water and (covered) with new cloth, containing gold and jewels, according to the *upapīṭha* diagram (of twenty-five squares) drawn with white rice on a heap of paddy.

28.7 To the north of these vases the food for the offering is arranged: (rice) - white, red, yellow and black - as well as cooked beans, milk rice, cooked barley, saffron rice, sesame rice, rice with molasses and white rice.

28.8. Next, the architect takes his place on a fine couch decorated with beautiful materials, with bed linen on its framework and with lamps and musical instruments (at the corners of the bed); he pronounces a formula.

28.9 Then, the food for the offering, for the oblation and for the god is to be put into a gold receptacle, mixed with gold and jewels, together with curds, molasses, honey, clarified butter, rice, grains of roasted rice and pure mixtures of orpiment, *tagaru* and *kuṣṭha*.

28.10–11a Next the architect installs the gods assigned to the house on their squares, in the form of flawless vases arranged in one cubit rows; according to the most learned sages, this builder[1] offers to these vases, perfectly white flowers, fumigations, lamps and perfumes and then, to each god, (his part of the offering) accompanied by his own (particular) formula which consists of his name preceded by OM and followed by *namas*.

Offerings

28.11b–12 Thus, after saluting Him whom the rule places in the first row, Aja, he presents Him with His share of the offering; then he satisfies, with offerings proper to them, the gods who are at the four orientations corresponding to the four faces of Svayambhu who is He.

28.13–14 (The offering) for Indra (is placed) in the east (for he holds that position) with those belonging to him, for Agni at the south-east, for Yama at the south, for Nirṛti at the south-west (for he holds that position) with the host of those

1. Takṣaka: see Introduction p. xi.

belonging to him; for Varuṇa the offering is to be placed in the west, for Anila in the north-west (because he holds that position) with those belonging to him; for Soma it is on the Soma square because the north is where (he rules) with those faithful to him; lastly, for Śiva, the offering is placed in the north-east (for he rules there) with the host of those belonging to him. This is how the offerings are to be arranged at the principal and intermediate orientations.

28.15 For Carakī (the offering is to be placed beyond) Īśa's square, for Vidārī (beyond) that of Jvalana and for Pūtanā, beyond Pitṛ's square; in the same way (that which) delights Pāparākṣasī is to be (arranged) beyond the square of Māruta.

28.16–17a (The offering) to the tree and the grass is made on the pillar; there too, towards the cardinal points, the offering is made to 'Those who go by day' and, at the intermediate points, to 'Those who go by night'. The offering to snakes and underworld deities is scattered on the ground whilst those for Dharma and Akhiladevatā are scattered into the air. The offering to Manu and others is made on the left doorpost and, lastly, the rule prescribes that the offering to Śrī be placed upon the bed.

28.17b–19 (Here is what is to be done next) on the inside of buildings; it may be in the central courtyard where houses, pavilions, halls or *mālikā* are concerned, or else in the pavilion in front of the shrine in the case of a temple: the gods of the interior (of the house) are invoked, all together on a sixty-four square diagram and then are worshipped with perfumes, flowers and other gifts; water is given to them and they are presented with a fine offering at the end. It is the architect who is to offer the water accompanied by fumigations; for a satisfactory fumigation it is always necessary to (use) *tulasī*, *sarja* juice, *arjuna*, *mañjarī*, compact (?) *vacāka*, *paṭola*, bdellium, *trapuṣa*, *hiṅgu*, *mahauṣadhi*, mustard and red amarant.

28.20 (Fumigation formula) "It bestows grain and wealth in abundance! Ah! It puts to flight spirits, demons and Rākṣasa! It burns against snakes, flies, mosquitoes, mice, spiders and ants."

28.21 Then the builder's implements are arranged on strewn grains contiguous to the vases in the west. Offerings should then be made to them and (these formulae) should be pronounced from the middle of them.

28.22 (Formula for tools): "Sustaining, happy, rich, renowned, glorious, full of marvels and great exploits, eternal place of rites that are not inauspicious, that Earth may live ever in the ways of Dharma."

28.23 "That this house be protected from collapse, from assaults by rain, from falling beneath the blows of elephants, from attacks by wind, from the flaring up of fire, from theft and the thief! That it may be propitious for me!"

Departure of the architect

28.24–25a That said, the architect, standing, salutes all the tools with head and both hands; then, assembling his tools without forgetting any, he takes them in his arms with the help of his family and servants; having taken them all up he returns to his house, his mind satisfied, accompanied by his family, his children and his assistants.

28.25b It is then that the remains of the food prepared for the offering are brought together and thrown into the water for the house deities.

28.26–27 Next, after the house has been thoroughly cleaned, the floor is lightly sprinkled with clear water, *kuṣṭha* water, agalloche water, sandalwood water and the water from the vases, with scented water and water of "gold and jewels". Then grains of paddy and roasted rice are scattered inside the building to ensure prosperity and, lastly, eight sorts of grain are arranged throughout the whole house along with seasonings and gems.

The entering in of the master and mistress of the house

28.28 It is in this way that the master and mistress of the house, holding amulets, and called upon by the names: "those with a beautiful family", "those with fine servants", "those with lovely children", enter into their dwelling which is full of household riches, meditating upon the Lord of the world.

28.29–30 Having entered the house with a joyful heart, having examined the domestic wealth in the house, the master and mistress must sit down on the bed. At that moment, the mistress is to take seasoned food, making thus the offering to the house; then, after giving the remains of the food to the maid servant who is attached to her and who is accompanied by her family, she is to satisfy the god, the brahmin, the builder and others, with sums of money, precious stones, betel and grains as well as clothing and other presents.

28.31 This is how the first meal is to be taken in the company of the family, the ancients of the family, the host of friends and servants and of all relations; after having saluted the Master, the master of the house is to feed the sons and grandsons of the family.

28.32 Rich in liquids (of all sorts), in full vases, in magnificent plantain trees laden with fruit, in areca trees, in lamps, in *aśvattha* leaves, in seedbeds, in flawless young girls, in perfect young women and in eminent brahmins: such is to be the perfect house whose entrance is framed by an arch (of greenery) and wherein the master of the house is installed.

28.33 The house is to be well furnished with lamps, liquids and white garments and (the master of that house) is to be adorned with flowers and pleasing white garments. At the moment of the entry into the house the ritual of 'the taking of the spouse's hand' is to be enacted before the master of the house just as at the moment of marriage.

28.34 Nothing but failure comes to he who enters a house where neither offering nor first meal has been given and where the roof has not been completed[1] or where there is no foundation deposit or where brahmin, architect and others have not appeased the (gods of the site) or one where there is no bed. For he (who enters into a house) with great ill-will in his heart, there can be nothing but misfortune (?).

28.35 It is with an utterly joyous heart that the master of the

1. *Anācchada* is to be read instead of *adacchada* (see *Pūrvakāmikāgama* 33.25).

house must enter the house in the company of his son, his wife, his family and his friends; once he has entered the house his ears hum with (their) cries of satisfaction.

28.36 In villages, *agrahāra*, towns, ports and other settlements, the offering to the Akhiladevatā is to be made on the square of Brahmā, at the major and intermediate directions and in the sixty-four squares (of the diagram) as well as in the god's temple and in the perfect shrine of Sarasvatī.

Thus ends, in the *Mayamata*, treatise on dwelling, the twenty-eighth chapter: ENTERING THE HOUSE.

Chapter 29

ROYAL PALACES

29.1a Herewith, a brief description of the royal palace which is surrounded by a town (or) by an entrenched camp.

Proportions of the royal palace

29.1b–3 The palace of a *narapati* is in the western part of the town, of which town it occupies a third or a quarter or it is at the prescribed (place) in the enclosure (?). For an *adhirāja*, it is to the south of the western part (of the town). The palace of *pārṣṇeya* kings and others of that category takes up a seventh or ninth (of the town) and is in the western part, and it is there too for princes (and other personages of the sort) including army commanders. An emperor's palace is in the centre (of a town) of which it occupies a third.

29.4–7 The dimensions (of a palace) have been given in relation to those of a town and are now given in poles: a palace is a hundred and forty-four poles wide and, this figure being reduced by, successively, four, eight, twelve and sixteen poles (?), thirty-two poles is the result; that is the width of palaces (of people) mentioned (above) (?). Taking each width as a starting point, the figure reaches five hundred and twenty-eight poles, which is the greatest width (for a palace) and there are, as well, up to thirty-two possible dimensions, starting from thirty-two poles (?). A width, whether great or not, is chosen according to specific circumstance.

29.8a The length is double the width or is double less a quarter or is (one) and a half (times) or (one) and a quarter (times) (the width).

29.8b–9a The enclosure may have one of these twelve plans: square, circular, rectangular, elliptical, "chariot-shaped", *nandyāvarta* shaped, "cock-shaped", "shaped like an elephant's temporal bone", *svastika* shaped or perfectly circular or (convex) like a *mṛdaṅga* or concave.

29.9b–11 Only one single (series of) dimensions is to be made use of and, once the width and length have been chosen, (the palace) is to be built in accordance with it. If, when the palace is finished, it is found to be smaller (than envisaged) for whatever reason, that will be inauspicious and will cause the king endless misfortune.

29.11b–12a If the enlargement of a palace built by the ancients is desired it is best to enlarge it to the north or east but it is not forbidden to extend it to all directions on the periphery.

Plan for a small palace (fig. 33)

29.12b–13 The main courtyard is in the east or may equally be in the south. There is an altar in the very centre of the palace with a height and a width of half a pole; the platform of Saha (i.e. Brahmā), upon which this altar rests, is larger than it by one pole all around.

29.1415 South of this platform, at a distance of thirty cubits, on a straight line, is the abode of the king, the median line of which is to the west of the platform; at an equal distance from this platform, towards the north, is the queen's dwelling with its median line to the east of the platform.

29.16–21 The big tank reserved for the king is placed at a distance of forty-eight, thirty-two, twenty-four or sixteen poles and the wall (of the first enclosure) is built beyond that; it is three cubits thick and eleven high. A seven cubit wide road runs along the outside of this wall and, beyond it, are three rows (of houses) nine cubits wide; beyond the last row of houses is the wall (of the second enclosure); it is one pole thick and its height is ten and a half cubits; a nine cubit wide road runs along the outside of this wall and, thirty-two poles beyond that, is the wall of the outer enclosure; it is one and a half poles thick and fifteen cubits high and has a three pole wide boulevard. running along the inside. Twelve guard posts are to be arranged outside the palace (?). The well advised man takes the measurements along the interior or exterior face of the wall.

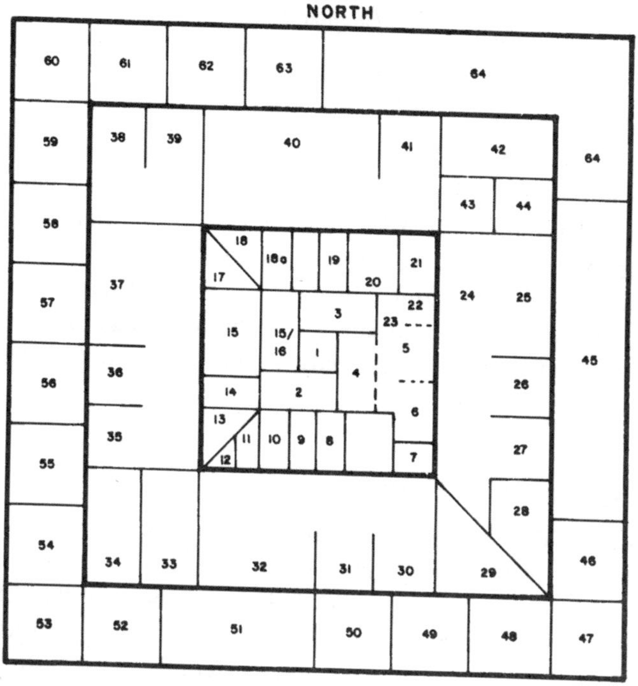

Fig. 33 Palace with three enclosures (29.12 *et sq.*)

1st enclosure:

1. Central pavilion and altar of Brahmā; 2. king's dwelling; 3. queen's dwelling; 4. entrance building; 5. courtyard; 6. vṛtta (?); 7. gold for honoraria; 8. entrance building and guard; 9. dance hall; 10. stable; 11. house for women's confinements; 12. reception pavilion; 13. ablutions room; 14. store room for salt and spices; 15. saṅkarālaya; 16. theatre; 17. residential quarters; 18. house for nurses and chambermaids; 19. masseuses' house; 20. baths and water reserve; 21. shrine; 22. dining room; 23. reception hall.

2nd enclosure:

24. courtyard; 25. storeroom for parasols and musical instruments; 26. alms giving room; 27. "water of charity"; 28. grinding stone and fuel; 29. stable; 30 armoury; gateway; 31. kitchen; 32. dwelling of the commander-in-chief; 33. house for fakirs and conjurors; 34. buffaloes' stable; 35. almsroom; 36. reception hall; 37. baths; 38. tank; 39. lodging for young girls and wetnurses; 40. lodging for artists; 41. lodging for hunchback, dwarf and barren women; 42. nurses quarters; 43. well, tank and flower garden; 43. buildings for the distribution of honoraria and alms.

3rd enclosure:

45. schools; 46. main kitchen; 47. stables for cows and calves; 48. storeroom for salt; 49. elephants' stable; 50. painting gallery; 51. store for condiments; 52. store for fuel; 53. store for alms; 54. wrestlers' house; 55. residential quarters; 56. dwellings for the crown prince and the purohit; houses' and elephants' stables; 57. indraśālā (?); 58. deer shed; 59. donkey and camel shed; 60. reservoir and lotus pool; 61. stable for elephants; 62. stable for horses; 63. buildings for initiation and confinements; 64. gardens, tanks, assembly hall. . . .

Gateways

29.22–24a The palace of a king of low status comprises three enclosures, three roads and three concentric sectors. It is not to have more than four gateways and the main one is to be the most elevated, the western gateway the least. The main gateway faces east or south since it is not auspicious to orientate it to the north or west. It is not suitable for kings to have five entrances, and access (to the palace) must conform to what has been given above.

Arrangement of buildings

29.24b–26 Some say that the queen's dwelling must be inside that of the king; however there is to be a court, or a covered area with a hundred pillars, in the middle (of the palace). The king's abode is in the south, the coronation (pavilion) in the west and the queen's abode, comprising one or several storeys, in the north. The main dwelling, intended for the king, extends westward but must face east.

The moat

29.27–29a There is a moat along the outside of the enclosure wall; its width is from six to nine poles; on the exterior and interior (berm) of the moat there must be a three pole wide road. The width of the moat at the bottom is a eighth what it is at the top but may also be calculated in terms of the depth and of specific exigencies (in such a way as to give to the moat) the profile of a bell-mouthed vessel.

Arrangement of buildings (cont.)

29.29b–30a There are buildings arranged, here and there, outside the queen's quarters, according to circumstance; I shall now indicate (their positions) on the divine diagram (of the site); a building outside the first enclosure is however to be placed in relation to the position of one of the gods (of the site) (?).

First enclosure

29.30b–33a A *dvāraharmya* gateway is situated on the square of Ārya and a large courtyard extends over those of Indra and Sūrya; there is a *vṛtta* (?)[1] on the squares of Bhṛśa and Vyoman and the gold for honoraria is kept at that of Pūṣan. It is known that in every enclosure the courtyard may extend from the square of Rākṣa(sa) to that of Vitatha. There is an entrance building on the square of Yama, greatly elevated and (occupied) by a guard, and there is (a building) in the shape of a niche on the square of Gandharva; it has a stage and is suitable for the dance and it may be a *vimānamandira*, a *śālā* or a *harmya*.[2]

29.33b–35a There is a stable on Bhṛṅgarāja's square, the house for the women's confinements on Mṛṣa's, a reception pavilion on Pitṛ's, a (room) for ablutions on those of Dauvārika and Sukanṭha and an annexe (*khalūrikā*) on Puṣpadanta's, where salt and spices such as pepper are to be stored as is prescribed.

29.35b–37a The *saṅkarālaya*[3] is on the squares of Varuṇa, Asura, Śoṣa and Mitra, with the queen's dwelling to the right of it and the room for confinements to its left. The room for the dance and for theatre is on the square of Mitra as well as the (building) where the properties necessary to (these two arts) are (stored). An entirely closed residential house is on the squares of Roga and Samīraṇa.

29.37b–40a There is a four main building house for nurses and chambermaids on the square of Nāga; it is of *vardhamāna* type or of any other type of dwelling house; the dwelling of young girls is on Mukhya's square. The infirmary is on

1. *Vṛtta*: it is said later on that there is, near the palace, a *vṛttaśālā* (round house?) for the bull.
2. This probably means that the theatre has a storeyed superstructure like a temple or a wagon-roof like a *śālā* or a flat roof life a *harmya*.
3. *Saṅkarālaya*: this building is always located near women's quarters (see also vv. 127a and 151a); it may be a "meeting house", that is to say a "pleasure house". It is however difficult to consider it as a "brothel" as may be the *śaṅkarārāma* mentioned in relation to the "house of a purveyor" (*bhujaṅganilaya*) in Chap. 3 (v. 15).

Bhallāṭa's square and the masseuses' house, an edifice with four main buildings of the *rucaka* type or another, on Mṛga's. Next to it are the baths on the square of Uditi and there is a building on the square of Āpa and (of Āpavatsa) with hot water (for baths) and cold (drinking) water and which, according to sages, is like a temple.

29.40b–41 (The king's) chosen deity is to be installed on the squares of Īśāna and Jayanta; the dining room is on the square of Mahendra as well as on those of Mahīdhara and Marīci where a reception room resembling a hall of the *pārvatakūrma* type may be set up.[1]

29.42 The door and the walls must conform in every respect to the desires of the lord. That which is in the first enclosure has been given, now follows that which is to be found in the second.

Second enclosure

29.43–45a Parasols and big drums are on Indra's square and on that of Āditya, where too are the other musical instruments, conches, *kāhala* drums . . . etc. The room reserved for alms giving is on Satya's square and the building for "the water of charity" is on Bhṛśa's square. The grinding stone and the storehouse for fuel are on the squares of Paṅktika (i.e. Antarikṣa) and Jvalana; there is a stable on the squares of Pūṣan, Sāvindra and Vitatha.

29.45b–46 Buildings situated in the east must have their doors to the west, those in the west face east and those in the north, south; they are each to be separated from the (main) house by a passage and, moreover, are to face that house.

29.47–49 The armoury is on Rākṣasa's square and there is a *dvāraśālā* type gateway to its left; the building where food and drink are prepared is on the square of Dharmarāja and is to have the plan of a four main building house with covered central courtyard. The square of Gandharva is meant for the commander-in-chief, which placing brings victory, but it is

1. *Pārvatakūrma* hall: see above 25.210–212 (p. 201).

also thought that (his) house will be invincible, situated on the square of Bhṛṅgarāja. The house for fakirs, conjurors and others of the kind is on the square of Mṛṣa.

29.50 Nirṛti's square as well as those of Dauvārika and Sukaṇṭha is where is found the buffaloes' stable; there is a room for alms, a reception hall and baths on Puṣpadanta's square and those beyond it.

29.51–53 There must be an elongated tank on the squares of Nāga and Rudra; the lodging for young girls and wet-nurses is on the square of Mukhya but, according to all the sages, there must be a different lodging for chambermaids and *madgu* (?); painters and artists of that kind have their dwelling on the square of Bhallāṭa, Soma and Mṛga whilst those of hunchbacked, dwarf and barren women are on the square of Aditi; the nurses' lodging is on the squares of Uditi, Īśa and Parjanya.

29.54–55a There is a reservoir, a well and a tank on the squares of Āpa and Āpavatsa and there, too, drinking water and the flower garden are to be installed. A building for the distribution of honoraria is on the square of Jayanta and another, for alms, on that of Surendra.

29.55b All these buildings, starting with those in the east (and going on to) those in the south, are to face the main building.

Third enclosure

29.56–58a The treatises (are taught) on Indra's square, mathematics on Ravi's and the Veda on those of Satya and Bhṛśa. The main kitchen is on the square of Vyoman and cows with their calves are installed on those of Pūṣan and Pāvaka. The salt, for (preserving) dried meat, gut and skins, is on Vitatha's square. There is an elephants' stable on the square of Rākṣasa. The building given over to painting and other entertainment arts is on the square of Dharma (-rāja) and is of *daṇḍaka*, *śūrpa* or *lāṅgala* plan.[1]

1. That is to say that it may be an edifice with one, two or three main buildings (see chap. 26).

29.58b–59 The store for condiments and such commodities is on the squares of Gandharva and Bhṛṅgarāja, fuel is on Mṛṣa's square and alms on those of Pitṛ and Dauvārika. The wrestlers' house is to be on the square of Sugrīva and there is a four main building house on that of Puṣpa(-danta).

29.60–62a A house or a *mālikā* for the crown prince (*yuvarāja*) is to be on the square of Varuṇa and a stable for horses and one for elephants are there too, as well as the residence of the *purohit*. The *indraśālā* is on Asura's square and, on Śoṣa's, there is a deer shed. The donkey and camel shed is on Roga's square and the infirmary should be there too. There is a reservoir on Vāyu's square and a lotus pool on that of Gotranāga.

29.62b–64a It is said that there must be a stable for horses and one for elephants on the squares of Bhallāṭa and Mukhya respectively. Confinements and initiations take place on the square of Soma. Tanks and amenities like that are to be on the squares of Mṛga, Aditi, Uditi, Īśāna and Jayanta, where too is the area for the orchard and the pleasure gardens and for a large assembly hall with a courtyard.

29.64b (The buildings of the third enclosure) have been enumerated; they all face towards the centre of the palace.

The town

29.65–66 The barracks for a portion of the royal army are in front and on the sides of the palace and the quarter of the merchants and such inhabitants is there as well. To the west of the palace is a large elongated tank and a well . . . etc., and a royal residence and barracks for hereditary (and) mercenary soldiers.

29.67–69 Tanks, orchards, reservoirs and wells are to be everywhere; people of all castes must cohabit (in this town), where there are courtesans of all kinds and artisans of all stamps; the six kinds of troops must be there in large numbers. In the north-east and south-east corners there are to be stables for horses and elephants. There must be people of every caste and those engaged in all sorts of commerce. Every class is to be designated by a name in accordance with the king's wishes.

The town's enclosure wall

29.70–72a A wall, two poles thick, must surround the town though it is also said that its thickness may be five, six or seven cubits; the height should be double or triple the thickness. There must be an earthen parapet outside or a moat with a glacis, of whatsoever width in poles, if desired. Outside there must be traps everywhere.

Palace gateways

29.72b–73 For all (rulers), the palace, be it large or small, must have a gateway. It is prescribed that the gateway of the exterior enclosure be similar (in dimensions ?) to the lodging of the lord except in the case of a small palace, the gateway of which has to have one storey less than the king's building.

29.74 When the main building has nine or eleven storeys the gateway of the outer enclosure has seven and, from exterior to interior, (the other gateways must have), each, one less than the preceding one.

29.75–76a It is the privilege of *narendra* kings to have the largest gate on the square of Mahendra but it may also be on that of Rākṣasa and have five or three storeys; the gates on the squares of Puṣpadanta and Bhallāṭa have less storeys.

29.76b–77 There are also to be one or two storeyed side gates on the squares of Sugrīva, Mukhya, Jayanta and Vitatha. The enclosure wall has loopholes and *cakra* (?) on its interior and exterior faces.

29.78 It is the *narendra*'s privilege to have their palace on Indra's square (?). A palace contiguous to Brahmā's square is a source of good fortune and of complete success.

Numbers of storeys for palaces

29.79–81 The palaces of universal monarchs are to have eleven storeys; for kings (belonging to the) brahmin (class) they are to have nine storeys and for (those who are) kṣatriya, seven; there are six storeys for the *maṇḍaleśa* and five for the crown prince, four (for those belonging to the) vaiśya (class) as well as for the commander of the troops and for the commander-in-chief. For those who are śūdra, one, two, or a maximum of three storeys are prescribed and, lastly, it is said that the palaces of vassal kings and other princes of the kind, must have five storeys.

29.82 The palace of a universal monarch may have an even or an odd number of storeys and the number of storeys may also be even or odd for kings and the queens, their wives.

29.83–84a (A house) with struts, a rafter framework, two gables and an entablature is suitable for all castes; it is built of earth and covered with thatch, has one or two storeys and no finial nor corner rafters.

29.84b–85a For the members of mixed castes (?) who delight in power and success, residences of the *rucaka*, or similar, type are to be installed, when necessary and according to circumstance.

29.85b–86a The man of sensible mind proceeds according to the specific circumstances in all cases where there is no prescription. The general rules, according to the learned, for a capital (*rājadhānī*) intended for a king have been given.

The palace of the *narendra*

29.86b The eternal palace fitting for a *narendra* king is now presented.

The enclosure walls

29.87–88 The (first) enclosure wall is a pole thick and the (corresponding) moat two or three poles wide; there is a four pole wide road and a row of buildings twenty poles wide around (this moat); then comes a four pole road bordered by houses where courtesans frolic and, beyond that again, is a three pole wide boulevard and the (second) enclosure wall, five cubits thick.

29.89–91 The moat corresponding to this (second wall) is four poles wide and surrounded (?) by roads eight cubits wide; beyond this, on an expanse forty-eight (poles) wide, is a row of various (buildings), beyond, and all around which, are roads, six or seven poles wide or more, as well as a boulevard four poles wide and a (third) wall seven cubits thick; there is a *bandhana* (?) full of snakes a pole farther on.

29.92–94 The moat is eight to twelve poles wide and there is a road, wide as the wall is thick, along its interior and along its exterior. Ten poles farther on is the boundary of residences for ordinary people or there is a (fourth) enclosure with residences as well as moats; the boulevard and the wall are to conform (to the rules laid down) by experts in town planning. When there are five enclosures the (fifth) one is to be eight (cubits thick); the elements within are to be arranged with a view to convenience.

Arrangement of the palace

29.95–97 Having divided the length and the width chosen (for the central part of the palace) into six and nine parts respectively, one part is reserved in front, one behind and one on (one of) the two sides; there are twenty-five squares on what remains, which are the position of Brahmā, and there is a hundred pillared pavilion there housing the platform and altar, or else, there is a temple there with a pillared area all around it. Beyond, there is a one part wide passage, with an annexe (*khalūrikā*) the same width around that; it has four doors and has to have square and elongated aediculae if it is to be auspicious (?).

29.98a This centre (of the palace) is described according to rule but (may also be arranged) with nine squares for the principal god (of the diagram? of the temple?).

29.98b–99a (The) royal (dwelling) is in a place selected, south of the temple, and that of the senior queen is to the north.

29.99b–100a There is a gateway at the square of Ārya, to the west of which is a canopy or a *śālā* or *sabhā*; these are for consecrations and are provided with all kinds of ornaments.

29.100b–102 There is to be a hall with sturdy interior pillars and with annexes connected to it (?) at each corner (of the central part of the palace); in the north-east corner there is water, baths and the shrine with, in front of it, the (place for) sacrifices; there is a terraced building or a rostrum, for review of the troops, in the south-east corner; a hall for music and dance recitals and other entertainments is in the south-west corner and the dwellings of singers and other performers is in the north-west corner.

29.103–107a There is a courtyard and the main gateway (*merugopura*) (consecrated) to Durgā, in the eastern section of the (exterior) enclosure; in the north-east there is water, a place for water sports and a hall; the hall for eating and drinking should be arranged there with all that is necessary; in the south-east corner of that there should be a hall with median courtyard; jewels, gold and rainment are kept there. There is a hall with a median courtyard in the south-west corner and the private apartments of the concubines are around this hall; there is a garden with residences and places for sport and for water; there is a lodging in the form of a hall occupied by women of all sorts.

29.107b–c Anything not ordained here, as regards the interior as much as the exterior of the palace, is to conform to what has previously been said. This dwelling, meant for kings, is called *padmaka* by the sages.

Saubala palace (*fig. 34*)

First enclosure

29.108–111a A *sthānīya* diagram (of one hundred and twenty squares) is drawn to the length and width chosen (for the palace). The altar of Brahmā (is placed on a single square) in the centre according to the *sakala* diagram; it rests on a platform in a pavilion. The queen's apartments are in the north and the south and the house for the emperor, with several storeys, is in the west. There is a courtyard in the east, embellished by a *dvāraśobhā* gateway. In the (same) eastern section there is the coronation pavilion just west of the gateway. (All) this is to be arranged according to the (nine square) *pīṭha*

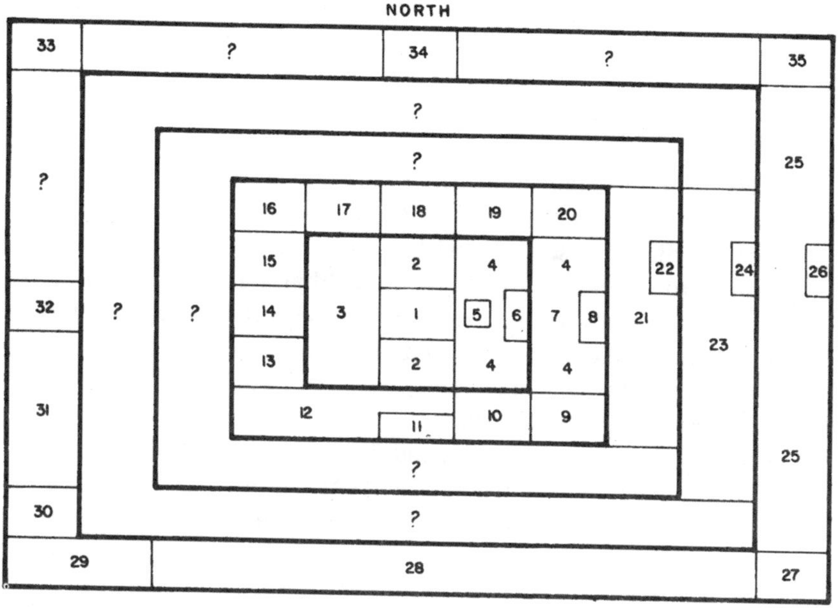

Fig. 34 Saubala palace (29.108 *et sq.*)

1st enclosure:

1. central pavilion and altar of Brahmā; 2. queen's apartments; 3. king's apartments; 4. courtyard; 5. coronation pavilion; 6. gateway.

2nd enclosure:

7. courtyard; 8. gateway; 9. kitchen; 10. treasury; 11. gateway; 12. women's lodgings; 13. theatre; 14. king's lodging; 15. purdah room; 16. tank for water sports; 17. queen's lodging; 18. places for tulābhara and hemagarbha ceremonies; 19. stores (gold, jewels, perfumes) and elephants' stable; 20. tank, latrines and hydraulic machine.

3rd enclosure:

21. courtyard; 22. gateway.

4th enclosure:

23. courtyard; 24. gateway (?).

5th enclosure:

25. courtyard; 26. main gateway and Durgā temple; 27. offices and main kitchen; 28. exercise place; 29. king's dwelling; 30. annexes; 31. women's house; 32. saṅkarālaya; 33. tank, garden and hermitage; 34. places for tulābhara and hemagarbha ceremonies; 35. Śiva temple.

diagram and the wall of this (first enclosure) is to conform to what has been given above.

Second enclosure

29.111b–113 The following elements are to be arranged beyond (the first enclosure) in the (twenty-five squares of the) *upapīṭha* diagram starting with those to the east: there is a courtyard on the squares of Jayanta, Bhānu and Bhṛśa with a *dvāraharmya* gateway of at least three storeys; the kitchen should be set up on Agni's square and the family treasure is on the square of Vitatha whilst the square contiguous to that is fit for a *dvāraprāsāda* gateway.

29.114–115 The women's lodgings are on the squares of Yama, Bhṛṅganṛpa and Pitṛ; the theatre is on Sugala's square and a lodging for the king on Varuṇa's; the purdah quarters are on Śoṣa's square and there is a tank for water sports on Vāyu's, and a house or a *mālikā* for the queen on Mukhya's.

29.116–118a Ritual weighing is carried out on Soma's square and, next to it, the ceremony of the gold embryo is performed. There are gold and jewels on the square of Diti and the perfume store is there, as well as an elephants' stable. There is a tank and a well on Īśa's square and it is said that the latrines and the hydraulic machine are there too. The wall (of this second enclosure) and the road along it are to be established as has been given above.

The third enclosure

29.118b–120 The (forty-nine square) *sthaṇḍila* diagram is to be followed exterior to (this second enclosure). The sage is to establish a courtyard on the squares of Parjanya, Mahendra, Bhānu, Satya and Antarikṣa, and the gateway is to be on the square of Mahendra and is to have four or five storeys; instruments are played there too, such as conches and *bherī* drums. Anything not indicated here is to be arranged all around in accordance with what has already been given.

Fourth enclosure

29.121–122a Outside (the third enclosure) an eighty-one square *paramaśāyin* diagram must be drawn; on its eastern part there is to be a courtyard occupying the most part of the squares between those of Jayanta and Antarikṣa. All else, beginning from that which is on the square (of the god Agni, with the appearance) of an eagle, is to be arranged as has previously been given.

Fifth enclosure

29.122b–124 A courtyard is to be placed on the squares of the eastern boundary of a (hundred and twenty-one square) *sthānīya* diagram; the width of this courtyard is two sevenths of its length and the exterior gateway is there, as well as the temple of Durgā. The main kitchen is to the south-east of this (courtyard) where are installed, as well, the scribes and those who work in the administration of the palace.

29.125–127 A huge closed courtyard occupies eight squares in the south of the diagram and is meant for exercising horses or elephants and there should be a rostrum there too. The king's dwelling is on the square of Nirṛti, there is an annexe in the neighbouring square and, in the next one, the women's house; in Varuṇa's square, to the left (of the) king's (house), there is a *saṅkarālaya* with a hall, or *mālikā*, for water sport and a residential building.

29.128–129a There is a tank and a place reserved for a garden and a hermitage on Vāyu's. The ritual weighing (is done) on the square of Soma and, next to that, the ritual of the gold embryo. Śiva's dwelling is installed, appropriately enough, on Īśa's square.

29.129b–c There is a town or a camp outside (this fifth enclosure) which is fortified as has been given above. This emperor's palace is called *saubala*.

The *adhirāja* palace

29.130–131a Now I shall give a brief description of the palace fit for *adhirāja*. A (sixty-nine square) diagram is drawn on an area whose width and length are those chosen for the palace; the seat of Brahmā is on its centre square, unless there is a hall there or a beautiful coronation pavilion.

29.131b–132 The king's house is to the west of that and comprises five, seven or nine storeys; behind and on both sides of (this house) is a one part wide row of annexes, comprising a courtyard (?). The dining room is to be arranged inside according to the king's pleasure.

29.133–136a The baths and the shrine are in the north-east corner of this (assembly) and a very wide, very long courtyard occupies nine squares at the east where a row of annexes should be installed, (as given above), with a (vacant) space in the centre; the gateway has two or three storeys and the drum is to be placed there. There is a building there (?) with a portico in front and a [. . . *gap* . . .] should be constructed on the side of the site (of this building) (?) and near to the door of the place where the king does his training. There is a place for ball games and other games (?) on two or three sides (of) the courtyard.

29.136b–137a A building in which the hereditary treasure is kept should be in the north-east corner and, to the west of that, should be built the edifice in which clothes and things like that are stored.

29.137b–139a A building with hot water in it (for baths) and (cold water), for drinking, should be built to the north of the gate, and the oven and the general storehouse should be there too; the dressing place is to the south and, to the south of that, is the store for perfumes and things of that kind.

29.139b–140a The building in the south-east corner is the family treasury; the dwelling of the lord of the earth is on Rākṣasa's square, that is, to the west (of that corner).

29.140b–141a The (place) dedicated to Śiva and the storeroom for gems and gold is in the south-west corner; a building for alms and for recitations of the Veda should be established in the north-west corner.

29.141b–142c There is a room where (the king) trains (?) and a small gate on the square of [. . . *gap* . . .]; at one side of this gate is a place where objects of value are kept and on the other side there is a tower; there is an elephants' stable there as well as the store for simples and the armoury. Everything else is arranged as the king wishes.

29.143 The dwelling of the emperor has a court in front of it (however) and should comprise a portico on the front; as far as fittings and defences [. . . *gap* . . .] are concerned, the house should follow the king's wishes.

29.144–148 There is a large elongated courtyard taking up twelve squares to the south of that; in the western part there is a pavilion or *mālikā* or a house which has baths and a pavilion (?) on either side. The main storehouse is in the southern part of the courtyard; in the east is a gate barred against elephants with a bretesse (*miṇṭhaka*) and a decoration of square and elongated aediculae. To the east and on both sides of the king's dwelling and of the courtyard, and in the west as well, is the women's residence; it comprises a central courtyard or else is a row of *mālikā*; the queen's residence is on the north side of the palace and is the same height as the palace; on three sides (of the queen's residence) is a row of *mālikā*, one part wide (?), for the king's wives, and the residences of the young girls are there too, along with those of hunchbacks and other servants of the king.

29.149–151a The garden stretches over one, two or three parts, from south to north, and should be surrounded by a wall. There should be a concealed place there, for water sports, and also the store of water and the tank reserved for the king. There is a residence for the king and a *saṅkaraśālā* for women in the west.

29.151b–152a The temple of the (king's) chosen deity takes up nine squares on the outside to the north-east; the house where the *āgrayaṇa* is performed, the flower gardens and the wells are there too.

29.152b–154a A large courtyard occupying thirty squares (of the diagram) is to be established in the east. There is a gateway on the square of Mahendra with three or four storeys.

The shrines of [Agajā?], Sarasvatī and [Śrī] are to the south of the gate[1]; they face inwards and have two, three or four storeys.

29.154b–157 The place where conches, drums and other musical instruments are stored is further to the east; the main kitchen is to the south and provided with all sorts of guards; there is a two or three storeyed gateway in the southern part of the courtyard with an office for a scribe on each side; a large hall should be built on the north side of the courtyard, facing south and decorated throughout; it is pleasant and elevated; there is a place to the west and east (of that?) where are the rooms meant for singers and other artists. All else is done according to the king's pleasure.

29.158 A stone and brick wall is to be built at the boundary of the palace; the width of its base and its height conform (to the rule) and there is a moat along its exterior. This perfect palace, built out of bricks and other materials is called *jayaṅga*.

29.159 The moat is filled with running water and in it are *kardama*, fish, leeches and numerous snakes as well as lotus, poisonous fish, tortoises, crabs and shell fish.

29.160 There is to be a wall with habitable overhanging turrets; it is covered with intermingled leaves and liana; irregular on its inner face, the wall comprises loopholes and numerous machines.

29.161 Royal palaces should be constructed thus, fortified without, within and in the middle. All the inhabitants must be protected by the king and there should be troops (of six sorts) outside the palace.

Different kinds of towns

29.162 According to specialists in the subject, there are four kinds of town suitable for kings: *sthānīya*, *āhuta* which is perfect, *yātrāmaṇi* and *vijaya*.

29.163 A town, installed in an elevated place in the middle of the country, by the ancient kings belonging to the family (of

1. Conjectural restoration: Agajā is a name of Pārvatī.

the reigning king), is called *sthānīya*[1]; it possesses the (three) basic elements: grass, water and earth.

29.164–165a This town, (*āhuta*) which enemies call 'the Inaccessible' has the three powers of the good ruler: power of the king, power of the counsel, power of action; it has too the basic elements: grass, earth, water; girdled by a river or some other protection, it must not be left empty.

29.165b–166 A town with earth and water, as well as grass, and which is founded at the moment of the departure of a warlike expedition is called *saṅgrāma*. A town provided with three fundamental elements, (founded) at the moment of a victory and whose essential function is the protection of the frontier, is called *vijaya* by the sages.

29.167 Even in a big palace it is dangerous if the building containing the bows is taken; a single building being thus captured, what remains will lose strength.

Elephant stable

29.168 (The dimensions of) the elephants' stable are determined with the aid of a unit whose five possible values go from three to five cubits by successive increments of half a cubit.

29.169–171a Three types of elephants' stable are distinguished according to their lengths and widths which are, respectively, nine and six units, seven and four or three and five. The choice is to be made according to what is suitable for a large or for a small (palace). The vestibule comprises a median (porch) with a width and projection of one unit; the place where (the animals) sleep is to the south and is one unit wide.

29.171b–172 Here are the woods suitable for the pillars (which support) the building and for (that to which) the elephant (is attached): *rājādana, madhūka, khadira, khādira, arjuna, tintriṇi, stambaka, piśita, śamī, kṣīriṇī, padmaka* . . . etc.

29.173–174a The height of the pillars of the building is seven, eight or nine cubits, not counting (their base) which is

1. Sthānīya: see above 10.31–32 (p. 40).

embedded in the ground; their diameter is related to their size and their sunken part is (calculated) in such a way as to give them solidity; these pillars are to have spikes similar to the branches of a tree.

29.174b–175 The pillar (for attaching) the elephant is to be perfectly circular and there are three possibilities for its diameter: one cubit, three quarters of a cubit and half a cubit; the diameter is to be reduced by an eighth at the top.

29.176–177a Having divided the width of the stable into sixteen parts, five are taken from the back and three from the pillar . . . ? . . . and the stakes for shackling are sunk there, their proportions being as has been given above.

29.177b–180 The walls rise to half the height of the pillar and there is a straw flap above, which can be opened and closed; a gargoyle (*gostana*?) projecting towards the exterior should be arranged on the rear. On the ground there should be a wooden floor which has the same dimensions as does the elephant; the ground should not be covered with flagstones or bricks; there is to be a drain for urine, so placed as to be in conformity with the position chosen for the door, and the floor is to have an appropriate slope. The sage arranges everything else according to the specific circumstances.

The horses' stable

29.181 The five values possible (for the unit of measurement) (pertaining to a stable) are nine, eight, seven, six and five cubits and the length (of the building) may be three to twenty-one units.

29.182–184 (A stable) has four main buildings and four facades and each main building has a vestibule. The height of the pillars is ten or twelve cubits; the joins between the walls (of the different main buildings) are to be made in a fitting manner, depending upon whether (these main buildings) are joined or not joined; there is a latticed window on the facade wall and on the rear wall of each building; the corner rafters . . . ? . . . at the ends of the main buildings, must be solid.

29.185–187 The ground is covered with a wooden floor which rests on an uneven number of joists, has a drain for urine and which is strong because made out of hard wood. Each individual, one unit wide stall has its own entrance. The hitching post, in hard wood, is fourteen digits long and its diameter is two (or) three digits; its (lower) extremity is pointed and is to be solidly driven in, once the shackle has been attached to the *agrabandha*.

Various buildings

29.188–189 There is a shelter for monkeys, peacocks and other animals as well as a cage for parrots; there are several buildings for pairs of bulls, for the cows and calves, as well as for drink, grain and goods; there are two closed buildings for raiment, jewels, sport and administration; there is a room for charity meals, one for sacrifices and one for (the distribution of) honoraria.

29.190a–c An aviary is to be installed in a convenient place to the south; it is ordained that the audience pavilion be in a garden in the proximity of a tank; there is a tower or a round (?) house (*vṛttaśālā*?) for the bull.

The council chamber, etc.

29.191 The king's council chamber has elevated walls; it is elongated from east to west and is pleasant. The hall, from which parades can be seen from far off, is surrounded by pillars and not by walls.

29.192–195a Otherwise there may be a tower. The royal throne-of-lions is to be installed in its western section in accordance with the rule and in such a way that it faces east; the minister's seat is to the south-east of this throne, that of the envoy to the north-east, that of the *praśāstṛ* to the north and that of the commander-in-chief to the south; all (these seats) are separated (from one another) by intervals which are both equal and narrow. The sceptre must be beautiful and must have six one digit wide knots; it is hollow, one digit thick and has a lotus bud at each end.

The bath house

29.195b–197a The length (of the building) is six parts and its width five and there is a courtyard in the middle, one part (wide) and two long; it is surrounded by a chest-high wall; in the middle of this courtyard is a round stone; to the north-east is a vessel with water and the divan for hair dressing extends from here towards the south.

29.197b–200a The door of this *maṇḍapamālikā*[1] is to the north-east; the seat of the woman attendant is on the square of Mitra and the women's reception pavilion is there too. Its width (expressed) in an odd number of cubits, goes from five to twenty-five cubits; the length conforms to the common rule for halls, pavilions and houses; when the width is fifteen cubits, the length is twenty-one; (the height of) this pavilion, up to and including the finial, is not more than thirteen cubits.

The coronation building

29.200b–202a The building for coronations is built to face east; there must be a hall with a canopy at the centre of this building; the royal pavilion is in the south and the room where the coronation takes place is in the north.

29.202b–205a There is a platform (in the centre) whose width is five, seven or nine cubits and its (length) is double its width and its height a third, a quarter or a fifth of that width. The pillars' height, that of the platform and their dimensions are as is convenient (?). Inside (the room where the canopy is) there are pillars, though there is not one in the middle; the diameter of these pillars is twelve, sixteen or eighteen digits and, so that the light may penetrate, there is a latticed wall at a distance of one unit (from the interior row of pillars).

Ritual weighing place

29.205b–207 A small square building or a pavilion is best

1. *Maṇḍapamālikā*: see above 25.175 (*mālikā-maṇḍapa*).

for the weighing ritual. The jambs of the frame (which supports the scales) are three cubits high and ten digits in diameter; at the top is a tenon of nine, eight or seven digits. This frame is to be installed in the middle of the building in such a way as to extend from south to north; its height is given as being equal to the distance between its two jambs.

29.208–210a The crossbeam resting (on these two pillars) has a (hook, the shape of a) curved beak, in the middle; the arm, which extends from east to west, should oscillate without shaking at the ends; there are chains (?) at the ends of (the arm) of the scales such as are suitable for a great king. A ring made of hard wood is (fixed) in the middle (of the arm) by a deeply embedded spike; this ring must be fastened to (the hook in the form of) a curved beak.

29.210b–211 The pans are to be made of planks but the use of male or neuter wood is to be avoided; they have strong chains of the same length and these are to be carefully attached, two by two, to both the (hooks, in the form of) a crow's beak, set at either end of the arm.

29.212–214 (The arches) at the cardinal points of the site, as well as at the eastern entrance (of the building) and the pillars, crossbeam and arm, are all to be made with hard and auspicious wood; there is a portico around the scales, its opening towards the centre of the site, and there is another similar one (?) around it. The arches (at the cardinal points) are to be in woods of, respectively, *udumbara*, *vaṭa*, *aśvattha* and *nyagrodha*, and the corresponding standards are yellow, red, white and blue-black.

29.215 When the lord of the earth has succeeded in bringing the scales into balance, he, whose face is turned towards the direction of the Indra of gods, attains happiness. Having contemplated the accumulated pile of his own gold he may consider himself as a sovereign equal to Dhanada on earth.

Place for gold embryo

29.216–218 The building for the gold embryo is surrounded by a wall nine or eleven (cubits) (?) long; it is square and its height, from ground level up, is equal to its width. The diameter of the pillars is ten or twelve digits; their sections are square or circular and they are to be firmly embedded (in the earth). When the wall which closes (the building) is three cubits high, the height of the corresponding base is one pole. (The building) is decorated inside with two series of sixteen crossbeams which are supported on the top of the pillars; they are to be of uniform height and the covering above is to be supported by rafters.

29.219–220 A platform is installed in the middle of this room; it is seven cubits wide and two cubits high or is five wide and two high; the vat is established in the centre of this platform,

29.221–223a The exterior wall is latticed and, beyond it, is a lean-to whose height is the same as that of the room and whose width is a pole. Twenty-three cubits farther on there is a fence; there is an arch and a door made of soft wood at each of the cardinal points. The installation of a stairway there, or where convenient, at the four cardinal points, is equally prescribed.

29.223b–225 The arch in front of (each of) the doors is the same height and width as the (corresponding) door. The eight propitious objects (are represented) on copper plates or those of other (metals) which cover the part of the arch which is above the pillars; a crest of *cakravartin* (?) is placed at each door. The series of eight propitious objects fitting for all is: parasol, flag, standard, drum, *śrī(-vatsa)*, vase, lamp and the *nandyāvarta*.

29.226 The lodging of the palace guard (?) is twice as high as the gateway and must be solid; outside the palace the guard is, so it is said, secured by patrols.

29.227 If the king so desires, an underground apartment (may be built) for the queen and princes, which is to be under the ground at the end of the *mālikā* (?) or where the imagination dictates.

29.228 As has been said, the palace, treasure and different appurtenances, as well as defences, ramparts, elephant sheds, horse stables and the queen's lodgings, are all to be arranged according to the king's best pleasure; a town should however be constructed taking the circumstances into account.

Thus ends, in the *Mayamata*, treatise on dwelling, the twenty-ninth chapter: RULES FOR KINGS' PALACES.

Chapter 30

DOORS

30.1 With success in mind, (I now give) the architectural precepts of the sages concerning the position, width and height of the front door of the houses of brahmins, kings, merchants and śūdra; (I give as well) each of the various types (of gateway) along with its decoration and name.

Dimensions of doors

30.2–3 A door is to be (at least) three spans wide and seven high; starting with this width and this height and proceeding by successive increments of six digits (for the width) and of twelve (for the height), up to fifteen spans (for the width) and thirty-one (for the height), twenty-five possible values are obtained for the width and the height of doors.

30.4–5a The first (of these dimensions) is appropriate for the door of a bedroom, the (following) twelve for that of a house and these are those prescribed too, by the sages, for annexes surrounding (a house); lastly, the twelve (larger) dimensions are suitable for towns, villages, forts and palaces.

30.5b–6a The height (of a door) is double its width, with the addition of six or nine digits; this is appropriate in all cases.

30.6b–8a Three possible widths are designated for a small door; two spans and six digits, two spans and three digits or two spans; the height is double the width, increased by six or two digits. Such an entrance is a good omen for a house meant for brahmins or for other people.

30.8b–9 (In a human dwelling) the height of the door is six and a half ninths the height of the pillars (of the corresponding storey); the width is eight and a half ninths of half the height. A small or medium door is prescribed for each storey; a door whose height is double its width is never appropriate for a human dwelling.

30.10–11a In a divine dwelling the height of the door is seven eighths, eight ninths or nine tenths that of the pillars (of the corresponding storey) and the width is half the height. It is prescribed that a door be placed on each storey whose dimensions are proportionate to those of the corresponding pillars.

Dimensions of door jambs

30.11b–12 The width of the door jambs is equal to that of the (corresponding) pillars or to that dimension less a quarter or increased by half; their thickness is half their width; the framework which goes above and below the lintel has a width three quarters that of the jambs.

Door-leaves

30.13–14 The width of the leaves is a third, a quarter or a fifth the width of the pillars (of the corresponding storey). (The doors) have only one leaf except when for gods, brahmins and kings in which case they have two; two leaves are also prescribed for people such as vassal princes.

30.15–17a (The heights possible for the leaves are) four and a half cubits, five, seven, nine and eleven cubits; (once one of) these heights has been taken from the interior height of the building, half of what remains is for the lintel and the other half for the elevated sill leaving, however, a small amount in excess (for one of those elements) if necessary for the solidity. The interior face of a leaf comprises a 'bar' (?) whose height is two thirds or four fifths that of (the leaf) as it has been determined above.

30.17b–19 When there are two leaves one is larger than the other; the height of the one on the right is divided into five parts and the width into three (which allows for the division of the surface of the leaf into fifteen equal squares); three (lengthwise) squares are reserved above and as many below; a vertical row of three squares is likewise reserved on each side; that which remains (in the middle is the emplacement for) a 'wicket-door'; it is to be strengthened and embellished with iron strap-hinges.

30.20–22a The socket's interior diameter is to be determined with proportions which are suitable according to whether (the door) is large, medium or small; it is three, four, five or six digits or is half, two thirds, three quarters or a third the exterior width (of the socket); otherwise the diameter is ten digits or is equal to the width of the hinge pin (?); the point (of the hinge pin) is placed inside the socket in such a way that the whole thing resembles the articulation of a hip.

30.22b–23 A leaf is to be composed of an odd number of planks and a join in the middle (of the leaf) is to be avoided. The *bheṣaṇī* (?) of the leaf (of a door that comprises only one) should be so placed as to avoid the middle of this leaf; when there are two leaves there is no *bheṣaṇī* (if it is not essential) to the solidity of the assemblage.

30.24–25 A leaf has three, five, seven, nine or eleven reinforcing pieces (?) whose thickness is half that of the leaf and whose width is double their thickness; their (profile is in the shape of) a horse's shoulder or hoof, of a peepul leaf, a *svastika* (?), a *ghaṭikā* (?) or *mirṇakā* (?).

30.26–28 A leaf is to be decorated with 'masks of Śrī', breast-like ornaments, stamens and small reinforcements; it is to be provided with bolts inside and out and with plaques (covering) the joins (of its planks); it is decorated with strap-hinges (in the shape of) bouquets, branches and bushes; it comprises interior handles (?), pendentives (?), a ring in the middle and protecting bars which are in horn, as are the small cross-beams. There is a vertical bolt, as well as all sorts of ornaments, and it is pleasant. It may, otherwise, be strengthened, conveniently, with pieces made of various metals.

30.29–30 As far as sill, lintel and joins are concerned, the assembly is to be made solidly, with care and grace, with the help of strips or horn plaques. Between the lotus buds, there are sharp and elongated *patratrinetra* (?). The sunken part of the jamb is to be a third its total height or (is to be calculated) so as to be solid.

30.31–32 The rabbet bar is a flat element whose thickness is the same as that of the leaf and which is twice as wide as thick; it is beautiful, being decorated with lotus leaves, and should be fixed on the leaf which is to the right as one enters. The right jamb bears the catch of the lock and the left the leaf.

Auspicious and inauspicious characteristics of doors

30.33–35 To open, the sage holds the leaf with his left hand and lifts the bar with the right; whether the door has two leaves or just one, attention should be paid to the noise it makes when it is opened or closed by hand; if it is like a drum beat, like trumpeting or like roaring or like a note on a *vīṇā* or flute, that is good; on the other hand, if it is like the clearing of a throat, a cry, an inarticulate sound or other noise of that kind, this is not appropriate.

30.36–38a The opening should be the same above as below. If the interior bolt is smaller than its clasp or if this bolt rubs against the jamb, this always brings about the ruin of the family and attracts the calamity of sorrow inflicted by enemies. The door which opens and closes of itself brings about the ruin of the family and is the cause of the destruction of happiness.

30.38b–40a Similarly, (when there is a door whose axis) interferes with a tree, a boundary, a corner, a pillar, a well, a temple, an anthill or a (heap of) ashes, a 'vein' or 'vulnerable point' or something else of that kind, such a door is a river of excrement or a nest of snakes.

30.40b A door meant to protect (a building) must be solid and massive; that is pleasing to the sages.

30.41 A door which causes the death of a brahmin as a result of his being struck by the vault when entering or leaving mounted on an elephant, such a door leads to the death of the king; if this occurs when one is on foot, the result will be the fall of (the king) (?).

30.42 The king who goes through a big door, undoubtedly goes towards a long life and towards supremacy over other realms and certainly not towards any decrease (in power).

Position of doors

30.43 A door (situated on) the median (axis of a building) is appropriate for gods, brahmins and kings; for all others it should be to the side of that (median axis).

30.44–47a Amongst the thirty-two squares (situated on the periphery of the diagram), those of Mahendra, Rākṣasa, Puṣpadanta and Bhallāṭa are the four where a door should be placed, if it is to be auspicious; it should previously have been put under (the protection of) the master of the corresponding direction. It is thus that the sage arranges a door, whether it be interior or exterior, for all other doors bring with them every sort of untoward consequence. It is forbidden (to place a door) opposite the square of Brahmā so that one's back is turned to Brahmā upon leaving. A door is not to be installed according to some fantasy unrelated to what has been said here.

30.47b–49 The dimension of the width of the door must be fixed and a difference, whether of more or less, brings illness. The door, when open and when closed, must stay in the position in which it has been put. It is auspicious if the dimension of the opening be the same, at the top and at the bottom of the door. If, from afar, (the door sounds) as noisy as a washerman this brings unfortunate consequences and brings misfortune to the master (of the building).

30.50 The positions of the drains, corresponding (to those indicated above for the doors), are the squares of Jayanta, Vitatha, Sugrīva and Mukhya; all others are to be avoided.

30.51–52 Secondary doors called 'underground passages' are to be established on the squares of Parjanya and Bhṛśa, Pūṣan and Bhṛṅganṛpa, Dauvārika and Śoṣa as well as Nāga and Aditi; these are buildings of one or two storeys provided with numerous defences.

GATEWAYS

Dimensions of the door

[. . . *gap*. . .]

30.53 . . . having reserved (out of this total) the height of the level of the pillars and the base, a remainder is obtained which corresponds to the height of the socle and from which the height of the door is taken, as given above.

30.54–55a In front is a visible or concealed stairway, fitted with a door. The master of the house (?) is to sink the jambs of the door to a depth equal to that (of the foundations) of the *dvāragopura*. It is said that the wall of the exterior enclosure is to mark the boundary of the palace and other buildings.

30.55b–56a Now the widths, lengths and heights are given, beginning with those of the *dvāraśobhā* and terminating with those of the (*dvāra*)-*gopura*.

30.56b–58 The five possible widths for the *dvāraśobhā*, which is on the first enclosure, are five, seven, nine, eleven and thirteen cubits; the width of the *dvāraśālā* goes from fifteen to twenty-three cubits; it is said that the four widths possible for the *dvāragopura* are from twenty-five to thirty-three cubits.

30.59–61a The corresponding lengths are, respectively, equal to the width, to that width increased by two thirds, by a quarter, a half or by three quarters. The height is as desired, or else the height of (the) above mentioned (gateways) is equal to their width, increased by five sevenths or seven tenths.

Single storeyed gateways

30.61b The appearance and arrangement of the five types of (gateway) are now given, the first being the *dvāraśobhā*.

30.62–63a The length (of a single storeyed gateway is divided) into two, four or six parts. The median passage (of the *śrīkara* gateway) occupies half the length, and the rest is for the thickness of the walls; the door is to be placed in the middle. (That building), with the shape of a pavilion and with three levels of elevation, is called *śrīkara*.

30.63b–66a Or else (the length is divided into four parts) and there is a large, one part wide aisle around; this aisle may be open or closed (on the outside) and has ploughshare walls; a stairway rises above this aisle . . . ? . . . There are two elongated aediculae (on the entablature) and an access, with gable, between them; the access has a median pillar and there is a false dormer window (above it) (?). There are eight niches on (the exterior wall of) the aisle. This building, suitable for a village, is called *śīta*.

30.66b–67 Otherwise, the facade has one single elongated aedicula with a median door and a gable; that building, appropriate in every case, is called *śrībhadra*. The three types of single storeyed gateway having been described, here are those with two storeys.

Two storeyed gateways

Ratikānta type

30.68–72 The (two storeyed) gateways are two parts wide and six long. For the *ratikānta* type the central room occupies one part of the width and three of the length; it is surrounded by a wall half a part (thick) and there is a one part wide aisle beyond. There is a pent-roof on the outside prolonging the entablature; it is three parts wide with a projection of one. (This building) has a socle under its base and has, as well, all the levels from that of the pillars; there are eight niches (on the exterior wall of) the aisle. The wagon-roof has a big niche both in front and behind; there may or may not be a forepart and, if there is one, it is a pillared structure; a dextrogyre stairway rises from the aisle. (This building) which increases the pleasure of all, is called *ratikānta*.

Kāntavijaya type

30.73 (Otherwise), if there are four niches, then this is *kāntavijaya* type which increases the beauty of everyone.

Sumaṅgala type

30.74–75a (Otherwise), if the roof is terraced (*harmya*) and not wagon shaped (?) and if there are projecting parts all around the (exterior wall of the) aisle, it is called *sumaṅgala*. Such are the two storeyed gateways and I now present those with three storeys.

THREE STOREYED GATEWAYS

Mardala type

30.75b–78 The dimensions of this gateway are four parts for the length and six for the width. A (square) room, one part wide and surrounded by a wall, half a part wide, must be arranged on both sides of the median passage. There is a one part wide aisle all around, with two niches (on its outside wall). There is a stairway in each of the side rooms and there are recesses upstairs; between the two side parts is a gutter (whose length) is equal to the width of the door proper. This *dvāra-harmya* is called *mardala* and is suitable for a royal palace.

Mātrakhaṇḍa type

30.79–84a The dimensions of this gateway are six parts for the width and ten for the length. On each side of the door there is a (square) room, one part wide; both these rooms are surrounded by a half part thick wall and by a one part wide aisle; in between these two rooms is a gutter with a width equal to that of the median passage. There is a one part wide gallery around the whole assembly; the (wall of the) aisle which surrounds the building has the commensurate number of niches in each case. The roof is not wagon shaped but terraced. Fourteen false dormer windows are to be placed on the aisle. The door, the stairway and the median passage are to be arranged as is suitable for this gateway called *mātrakhaṇḍa* which brings victory to the king.

Śrīniketana type

30.84b–88 The dimensions of this gateway are eight parts for the width and ten for the length. The median passage is two parts wide and the wall around it one; next there is a half part wide aisle with a one part wide gallery all around; outside, is (another) aisle, one part wide. One part wide recesses are to be set between the two part wide square aediculae and the elongated aediculae, which are six parts long (on the length of the building) and four on its width. The recesses should be one part wide and surmounted by structures with pointed roofs; it is also said that there should be a gutter between the square and the elongated aediculae. The ground floor proportions have been indicated; now here are those for the second storey.

30.89–91a The median passage and the wall which surrounds it are as above and there is a pent-roof all around which extends the entablature by half a part. There is to be a big aisle above with eight false dormer windows (on its outside wall). The length of the sloping wagon-roof is double its width and there is a big two part wide niche in front and behind.

30.91b–93a An entrance with a median pillar is to be arranged, as convenient, on each of the upper storeys; there is a dextrogyre stairway leading to each storey. The base is supported by a socle and (this building) comprises all levels from that of the pillars upwards. It is provided with principal and secondary elements and is called *śrīniketana*.

30.93b–94a The three types of three storeyed gateway have been described; they are to be built with one or several materials; they have various types of windows and are suitable for the inner enclosure.

30.94b Now the gateways with seven, (six, five or) four storeys are given.

Seven storeyed gateways

Bhadrakalyāṇa type

30.95–98a The dimensions of this gateway are fourteen parts for the width and sixteen for the length. The median passage is two parts wide and six long, including the wall which surrounds it. Four two parts wide aisles should be arranged around it with four half part wide walls (?); beyond that is (another) surrounding gallery one part wide and then a wall (?) of one part, and the exterior wall, which is half as wide and which borders the niche (?).

30.98b–100 At the bottom of each upper storey is a stereobate. On the third storey there is a decoration of engaged structures and other elements of the same kind, as well as gutters. There should be four big aisles on each (upper) storey as well as in the attic. A pillar is arranged befittingly in the middle of the door of each upper storey. There is a ridge at the summit of the roof with an odd number of finials.

30.101–104a The decoration is complete with arcatures, latticed windows and small false dormer windows. The false dormer windows on each storey are to be arranged as convenient in the aisle (?): there is one on each side of the door and between the square and elongated aediculae. It is fitting that a working stairway be set up for climbing the socle; the stairway, which goes from the gallery to the level of the aediculae, has three flights of stairs or is a spiral staircase going from storey to storey. This *dvāragopura* is called *bhadrakalyāṇa*

Subhadra type

30.104b–105a It may also have niches in the middle and on the sides of the roof and it is because there are niches in front and behind that this type is called *subhadra*.

Bhadrasundara type

30.105b–108a Above the central passage is a gutter with a square two part wide aedicula on each side and with four false dormer windows. This is said to be *bhadrasundara* type and it is added that, its width being sixteen parts and (its length) eighteen, (elements) arranged on the length are a quarter longer than those on the width. The rest is to be adapted to circumstance; one or several materials may be used.

SIX STOREYED GATEWAYS

30.108b–109 Thus, given the seven storeyed gateways of which three types exist, the six storeyed gateways called *subala*, *sukumāra* and *sundara* are the result of the omission of the lower storey.

Five storeyed gateways

30.110–114 The dimensions of the gateway are fourteen parts for the length, as for the width; the central room, the wall which surrounds it, the aisle and the external wall, should be arranged as in the previous case and their widths are, respectively, five, one half, one half and one part. The exterior aisle and its wall each make up one part of the width. Above that aisle are two part wide square aediculae and elongated six part ones; it is stated that there is a gutter between these two aediculae and that its width is two parts. There are three aisles and the remainder is as above for the five storeyed gateways called *śrīcchanda*, *śrīviśāla* and *vijaya*; all three types are decorated with various ornaments.

Four storeyed gateways

30.115–116 If two parts of the length are subtracted, however, and if there are only two aisles, square and elongated aediculae being as above, this gives three types of four storeyed gateway named *lalita*, *kalyāṇa* and *komala* which are suitable for settlements such as villages and for palaces too.

General rules

30.117–118 The first type of seven, (six, five or four) storey gateway has three aisles, the (second) two and the (third) one, the rest being for the walls. Thus there are three types of each and they are to be decorated so as to be beautiful and solid; the height and diameter of their pillars as well as their entablature are to conform to what has been given above.

30.119 What is called 'stereobate' is that which is at the dividing line between two storeys. The foundation deposit is beneath the wall, to the right of the entrance.

30.120 For houses intended for all four classes, the first of which is the brahmin class, a suitable gateway is to be chosen from amongst the twenty-one types of gateway with from one to seven storeys, as have been described by Maya.

30.121 The three first (types) are appropriate for the four classes, especially for those people who are rich amongst men; the second is for the *agrahāra*, *pura*, *pattana* and villages and all of them are suitable for royal palaces or for the gods.

Thus ends, in the Mayamata, treatise on dwelling,
the thirtieth chapter: RULES FOR DOORS.

Chapter 31
VEHICLES

31.1–2a I am now going to present the characteristics of vehicles and then those of couches. Palanquins and chariots are the vehicles, beds and other such furniture are the couches; thrones and other similar seats may also come under the heading of couches.

Different types of palanquin

31.2b–3 I consider there to be three types of palanquin, named *pīṭhā*, *śikharā* and *mauṇḍī*; similar in width and length, they are distinguished by the presence of sides (in the case of a *pīṭhā* type) or by that of a roof (similar to that of a *prāsāda*, in the case of a *śikharā* type) or by their three level structure (similar to that of a *maṇḍapa*, in the case of *mauṇḍī* type). Herewith, the height, width and length appropriate to each.

Pīṭhā palanquin

31.4–5 The width is three spans and the length five. The width of the small model being three spans, the medium model is obtained by adding one (?) digit to that and, by adding three more digits, the larger one; thus says the sage. The length is one and a half times or twice the width.

31.6–8a The height of the larger model's sides is half the width (of the palanquin); by subtracting three digits, the height suitable for the median model is arrived at and, by subtracting three more digits, that for the small model; these are the three (possible) heights. The three models of *paiṇḍikā*[1] palanquin have been thus determined, as regards their width,

1. *Paiṇḍikā* is an alternative name for the *pīṭhā* palanquin (both *pīṭha* and *piṇḍikā* designate a 'throne' or a 'pedestal').

length and height. It is said, as well, that their width may be thirty-one, thirty-five and thirty-seven digits, their height and length being calculated as above.

31.8b–10a Depending upon whether a large, medium or small model is involved, the width of the pieces of the frame (*īṣikā*) is five digits, (four digits) and a half or four digits, the thickness being equal, in each case, to half the width, and the length being as convenient; (otherwise) the width (of the pieces of the frame) is five, four or three digits and their thickness a digit and a half. The mouldings of the pieces of the frame are: a small band, a fillet, a groove and a doucine.

31.10b–11 The handrail is two and a half digits, two digits or one and a half digits wide and its thickness is three quarters, five eighths or half its width; it has a semi-circular profile or is 'parasol shaped' or is like a bamboo.

31.12–18 The height between frame and handrail is to be divided into six (equal) parts and four horizontal slats are to be placed (between frame and handrail); their width is two and a half, two, or one and a half digits. Planks are to be placed below and above, one digit (thick) with a height a sixth (of the space between frame and handrail). It being understood that no median slat is to be placed, the height of the side plank, determined with regard to circumstance, must correspond to the two median parts (out of the six previously dealt with); a plank is arranged, decorated with images of men and women, of *cakravāka*, liana and animals as well as of dancers and other subjects. *Vyāla*, and fist-like mouldings with a projection equal to twice their width, are to be placed in the upper part (of the space) between the handrail and the frame. The bannisters are below with a height corresponding to the space (remaining) below (the *vyāla*); their projection in relation to the slats is equal to their height or to half their width; these small metal or ivory pillars are ornamented with *makara* faces. There are five, seven or nine intercolumniations on the width (of the palanquin) and nine, ten or eleven on the length; the width and the thickness of these bannisters is equal to the width and the height of the slats.

31.19–20 A solid and suitable tenon is to be cut at top and

bottom of the big frame pieces so as to penetrate into the top and bottom of the smaller ones (whose length is equal) to the width chosen (for the palanquin); (at each end of the small pieces) is a projecting element five or four digits long and which is decorated with lotuses; its handle, ending in a lotus, is the same size or a quarter of it.

31.21--24a Above the short pieces there must be a broad slat or a plank one part in height. The decoration should be in accord with the circumstance; it is composed of small pillars and rounded elements (*gulikā*); there may also be a door in front occupying a fifth or a third (of the front part); it is three (or) four digits wide and its height is six, seven or eight digits. The bannisters are provided with a bell-capital, support and *hīra* (?) and their section is perfectly circular. Those whose minds are attached to life should fix a bolt with fastenings on the door sill.

31.24b This palanquin, whose elements are decorated, is called *paiṭhikā*.

Other types of palanquin

31.25 The palanquin called *śekharī*[1] is as high as it is wide; (the height of) its sides is a third or a half of its width; it is provided with pillars and has a roof (similar to that of a *prāsāda*).

31.26 The *mauṇḍī* palanquin is in the shape of a bald head; it has sides similar to those of the *śekharī* type; its height is equal to its width; it resembles a pavilion and is to be so regarded.

31.27a The dimensions of each of these (palanquins) are determined (by passing the reference line) through the middle of the pillars (placed on their periphery).

31.27b-c The following trees are suitable according to the ancients (for the making) of a vehicle or a couch: *śāka*, *kāla*, *tiniśa*, *panasa*, *nimba*, *arjuna* and *madhūka*.

1 *Śekharī* – *śikharā*.

31.28 When a happy man climbs into a vehicle, the essence of his happiness becomes manifest: success and fortune result from this vehicle being provided with the characteristics of palanquins.

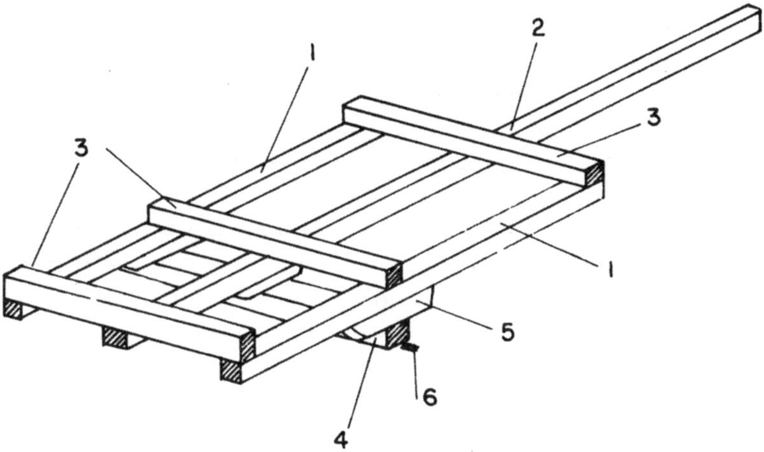

Fig. 35 Simplified drawing of a chariot frame.

1. long beams; 2. pole and main long beam; 3. crosspieces; 4. crossbeam holding the axle; 5. long beam support; 6. axle.

Chariots (fig. 35)

31.29–30a The width of (the chariot) taken from the outside of the wheels is six, seven or eight spans; this dimension may also be the value of the distance between the ends of the two naves or that of the length of the beam which is above the axle, or that of the exterior width of the body of the vehicle; the length (of the chariot) is one and a half times its width.

31.30b–31 There are five long beams (*bhāra*) whose thickness and width are four, three or two digits; or else there are three, seven or nine of them with the same widths and thickness as given above. They are placed lengthwise and their matching crosspieces should be solidly fixed.

31.32–33 Above the median long beam, and beginning from the assembly (of this beam) and the median crosspiece, there is a pole whose length, taken from the front (of the chariot), is at least three cubits and whose extremity is bent round; it is also called 'median long beam' and it supports the yoke. Above the beams is a broad plank floor one digit thick.

31.34a The following elements are now described: the axle, the crossbeam above the axle, the felly of the wheel and the long beams' support.

31.34b–35 The long beams' support is five, six or seven digits high, two or three thick and eighteen digits long; these supports are on the sides and are in the shape of bracket capitals and are reinforced by iron bands.

31.36–38 The crossbeam above the axle has a hole in the middle whose width is equal to its depth; there is a fastening on each side of its lower face for holding the axle in position. Its thickness is half its width, which is the same as that of the (long beams') supports; its length is the same as that of the axle; if this crossbeam is in wood it is to be square section and it should be reinforced with iron bands, nails and pins in the same wood. The crossbeam is to be firmly fixed on the top of the axle with wooden pins.

31.39–42a The diameter of the wheels is equal to the length of the crossbeam surmounting the axle; the nave has a diameter of ten digits and a width of one span. There are thirty-two, twenty-four or sixteen (spokes) between the felly and the nave or there is an otherwise convenient number of them; they are three digits wide at their extremities in accordance with their shape (?) or else, they are narrow at the bottom, only a digit and a half or, lastly, they (bulge) like barley seeds; there is a tenon at each of their ends. When the wheel is massive, the spindle of the axle-pole resembles an eye.

31.42b–43 The long beams are (to be reinforced) with iron bands, nails and cords and what is suitable is fixed there with iron bands, twice as long as wide (?); the base (*upapīṭha*) of the superstructure and the concealed (parts of its framework) are to be properly placed there.

31.44–46a The height of the pillars which, midway up, support the handrail (*kara*?) is as high as half the diameter of the wheel, and the height of the architrave is half their height.

Rounded elements (*gulikā*?) are to be arranged in the intervals between the (upper and lower) bands, in front, on the sides or on the base; behind, there is a lintel (?) five digits high. There are lotus buds on the architrave, between the corner pillars (?).

31.46b–48a Long beams, axle, crossbeam, shaft and shaft's extremity (are to be assembled) with ironbands and nails and this is to be done with the joins proper in each (of these instances specifically), at the suitable place and with regard to the assembly envisaged; a wooden pin is disposed in the middle for (assembly of) the axle and the crossbeam surmounting it.

31.48b–49 The time for mounting into a chariot is when universal kingship is attained, when war is being waged by the king, at the time of the annual festival, at the time of worship of the god and at the time of sacrifice to the Moon and, lastly, when ritual so demands.

31.50–53 The diameter of the wheel is twice or thrice the width of the sanctum (of the temple chariot). This diameter may also be seven spans and the thickness (of the wheel) is then three or four digits; in this case, the rest of the chariot, starting from the axle crossbeam, is to be constructed according to the (dimensions of the) pillars (calculated from that of the wheel). Above the frame there is an interval occupied by sixty-four bannisters resembling pillars. There are one, two or three storeys and one or four entrances. The appearance is that of a pavilion except for the wagon-roof.

31.54–56a Otherwise, the diameter of the wheels is three, four, five, six or seven cubits and their thickness is a quarter, a fifth, a sixth, seventh or eighth that. The axle, as well as its crossbeam and the long beam supports, are to be of the widths and thicknesses suitable in each case and are to be reinforced with wooden pins. There are one, two or three storeys and the general appearance resembles that of a temple (with six level elevation).

31.56b–57 (Otherwise) there are sixteen pillars and a fore-part and an entrance on each of the faces; this is a canopy (shaped chariot) which is to be solidly assembled. It is thus that the sages make (a chariot), taking the wishes of the specialists into account.

31.58 On the initial drawing there must be the plinth and then, as second element, a doucine (with amorous couples); the pillars are the third element (and images of deities are there); the frieze forms the fourth element (and is decorated with horses ?), the *bodhi* (which is the roof) (?) is the fifth whilst the sixth is the lotus bud (of the finial).

31.59–60 The distribution may be made with [two], three, two (?) or nine elements and should be calculated accordingly. There is the doucine, the dado with string course and the entablature decorated with *vyāla* and crocodiles (?). The doucine makes up two parts, the plinth, which is (like) a base for an entrance (?), and the torus make up one part (each).

31.61 When (the distribution) is made with sixteen parts there are three for a string course, one for a stereobate, one for the base, five for the doucine, two for the frieze, two (?) for the stereobate and two for the attic (?). The entablature element . . . ? . . . is to be like a support (?).

Thus ends, in the *Mayamata*, treatise on dwelling, the thirty-first chapter: RULES FOR VEHICLES.

Chapter 32

BEDS AND SEATS

Beds

32.1–3a The width of a bed is three spans and its length five and the dimensions of a big bed (are arrived at) by adding three and five digits to the width and length respectively. The width of the pieces of the bedstead is four or five digits and their thickness is half their width, whilst the median band (which decorates them) takes up a third of their width; it is also stated that the thickness of the pieces is a third or a quarter of their width.

32.3b–4 The two long pieces at the head and foot (of the bed) either continue to the end of the frame or stop at the corner or, otherwise, the (small) sides (of the frame) reach to the head and to the bottom of the long pieces; a pin should be placed at the centre (of their assembly) so as to make it secure; the big pieces being more or less elongated in this way, they should be solidly put together with the legs.

32.5–6 The leg of a bed should not have a height of more than a span and a half or of less than one. When a bed is supplied with legs, these legs are to be straight, tiger-foot or deer-foot. The pin driven into the big timbers must penetrate into the small ones. The names given to the beds correspond to the shapes (of their legs).

Divans

32.7 A divan may be of planks or of straps in various materials, strung on a frame: a divan provided with legs and straps to be of the same width, length and height as a bed.

32.8 A "divan-litter" is suspended from (a pole in the shape of) an arch with rings and nails and with hooks in the shape of a crow's beak: this is considered to be suitable as well for queens as for brahmins and other classes.

32.9 If the head of a divan is to the east its occupant should lie facing south, and west if the head is to the south; the other directions are not appropriate.

32.10a A tiger-foot or gazelle-foot bed is reserved for brahmins and kings and the third type (with straight feet) is perfect for the other two classes.

Seats

32.10b–13a A seat with straight legs is to be made in the same way as a bed; depending upon whether it is large, medium or small, its width is twenty-nine, twenty-seven or twenty-five digits and its height is equal to its width. If square, it is called *pīṭha*, if rectangular it is called *āsana* and its length should be more than its width by one eighth (at least, without being more) than double. It is provided (with legs in the shape of) lions, elephants, dwarves or bulls, when it is for gods as well as when for brahmins and for kings; according to whether it is provided with (legs of) lions or of elephants it is designated by the corresponding name: (lion throne or elephant throne).

Lion throne[1]

32.13b–15a Now the (lion throne) is described, which is decorated in various colours and meant for gods and for kings. It has a *padmabandha* (base)[2] and, if necessary, a socle. (Its mouldings are) an upper string course and lotiform cornice as well as listels and grooves; there are decorative lions forming colonettes at the corners, in the centre and between the corners and the centre.

32.15b–17a The lion throne proper is above this; it comprises an arcature as well as a (back) with a decoration of waves; it is covered with gold and precious stones. The plank, which is in the position of the seat, is as wide (as the body of the throne) and twice as long; the height of the legs will not be

1. See below 34.54b–56a.
2. *Padmabandha* base: see above 14.34 (p. 67)

more than five digits and the upper crosspiece is one half less high.

32.17b–18 The back (occupies) the rear half (of the throne) and its 'hollow' is equal to its width; a cushion occupying a fifth of the width and length (?) should be placed in the middle. A seat is to have a suitable back and it is inauspicious for the back not to be so.

32.19 Where a bed or a seat are concerned, the dimensions of length and width are to be the best amongst the category (thought) desirable; heights and widths are to be increased or decreased, according to the proportions appropriate for them.

The stand for worship

32.20–21 There are ten possible widths (for the stand for worship) going from six digits to a cubit by successive increments of two digits; some say that this width may be four digits. It is square, rectangular or circular and its height is half, a sixth or an eighth its width; there are lion foot legs with crosspieces and a frame.

32.22–23 There are lotus petals on its upper face which is embellished in the centre by the receptacle. It is called *śobhana* for it is to be honoured amongst the gods. With multicoloured decoration, it is what is called a stand, intended for domestic worship; it is in hard wood: *nyagrodha*, *udumbara*, *vaṭa*, *pippala*, *bilva* or *amala*; all these woods are suitable for the stand which should be made for all rituals.

Āyādi formulae[1]

32.24 The 'gain' is obtained by multiplying by eight (*aṣṭa*) and dividing by twelve (*bhānu*); the 'loss' is the result of multiplying by nine (*dhana*) and dividing by ten (*diś*); the ('matrice'), which is hidden, results from multiplying by three (*raśmi*) and dividing by eight (*sarpa*); the asterism and the 'age' result from multiplying by eight (*ibha*) and dividing by twenty-seven

1. See above 9.18 sq (p. 26).

(*bha*); the 'part' from multiplying by four (*turya*) and dividing by nine (*nanda*), the day from multiplying by nine (*graha*) and dividing by seven (*ṛṣi*). A chariot and a seat, in accordance with the general rule regarding vehicles and couches, are to be determined on the basis of these elements.

Thus ends, in the *Mayamata*, treatise on dwelling, the thirty-second chapter: RULES FOR SEATS.

Chapter 33
THE LINGA

Different kinds of divine representations

33.1-2a It is said that there are three sorts of representation of the god, symbolic, iconic and mixed. Those which are symbolic (*niṣkala*) are called Liṅga; the iconic (*sakala*) are called 'image'; the Mukhaliṅga is a combination of these two and is similar to the Liṅga as to shape and height.

33.2b–3 The manifestation in the form of an image is analogous to a body and is provided with one of the specific aspects of the universal form of the god. Images incorporate the characteristic signs (of each of the forms of the god) and the god is designated by the names which correspond to these images. It is of the symbolic representation (of Śiva) that we are now going to speak.

Characteristics of stones

33.4–5a A white stone should be taken (to represent the god), this being suitable for brahmins; (for kṣatriya) it is red, (for vaiśya) yellow and (for śūdra) black. The stone should be of uniform colour and should be dense, smooth and deeply embedded in the earth; it must be of appropriate length and width and it must be 'mature' and of pleasing appearance.

33.5b–7 The sages reject a stone licked by the wind, by blazing sun or by fire; they reject a (too) soft stone or one that has been in alkaline water; they reject one which is shaky or which has been displaced; they reject one which is rough or which has already been used; they reject a stone with 'streaks', 'spots' or 'flaws' and one that is 'aged' and cross grained; they reject a stone which contains grit or which is of indefinite colour; they reject one with 'cracks' and one found inside a building; they reject one which gives off no sound and one which is alveolar, fissured or 'pregnant'.

33.8–9 A stone is said to be 'male' when it is of uniform colour, dense, smooth and perfectly cylindrical and when it gives off the sound of an elephant bell. A 'female' stone has a wide bottom and a narrow head and gives off the sound of a cymbal. A 'neuter' stone has a narrow top and bottom, a wide median part and gives off no sound.

33.10–12a The sage makes an iconic, symbolic or mixed representation with a 'male' stone but commits no error if he makes the image of a female deity or a pedestal with a 'female' stone. A 'neuter' stone is used to make 'Brahmā's stone' and 'Kūrma's stone' as well as the '*nandyāvarta* stone'.[1] The sensible man will build the base, the walls and other parts of the temple, in the same way.

33.12b These (male, female and neuter) stones may be of three sorts, 'young', 'mature' or 'aged'.

33.13 A 'young' stone is soft when struck by an implement such as a hatchet and it gives off a sound similar to that of a partly baked brick. Connoisseurs proscribe the use of these stones for anything at all.

33.14–15a A 'mature' stone is smooth and round and gives off a deep sound; it is 'cold' and sweet, is not fragmented and it glows; this stone 'in the prime of life' is suitable for every sort of use and contributes to the success of all work (for which it is used).

33.15b–16a An 'aged' stone, rough as a toad's or a fish's skin is not auspicious; it has 'streaks', 'spots' and 'flaws' and great care is to be taken that it be set aside.

33.16b–17a A stone in which circumvolutions are to be seen when it is cut or worked, is a 'pregnant' stone and is one which the knowledgeable will be careful to discard.

33.17b–19a When a stone is quarried out, its face is on the underneath; its upper part is its head and, when the bottom is to the south (or the) west, the head is to the north or (east).

1. These stones are the liners on which rest the pedestal and the bottom of the Liṅga (see 34.44 sq).

When the rock lies vertical in the ground, the head is above and the bottom below. (A stone lying) south-west (to north-east) has its head in the north-east whereas, when north-west to south-east, its head is in the south-east.

Searching for stones

33.19b–21 (A stone intended for making) a representation of a god should be sought in a month when the solar path is to the north, in the course of the bright fortnight, on a day when the sunrise is beautiful, in the prescribed half of the *nakṣatra* and at an appropriate moment during the auspicious half of the day. The search takes place in a forest or a wood, on a mountain or in a pure region rich in concealed stones, which region may be to the north-east, north or east.

33.22 The donor goes there in the company of the *sthāpaka* and the architect, having performed the solemn rites; premonitions and portents are to be favourable; sounds of good omen are (to accompany the search).

33.23–24a The *sthāpaka* and the architect are to be clothed in white and anointed with white perfumed ointment; they each wear a white undergarment and a scarf; their heads should be crowned with white flowers and the five parts of their bodies decorated.

33.24b–25 The forest deities, along with the chosen trees and stones must be appeased first of all, with perfumes, flowers and fumigations as well as offerings of meat and blood, boiled (sesame) rice, rice cooked in water, fish and various foods.

33.26 The offering to the spirits and to the bloodthirsty deities once having been made, an appropriate stone is chosen. Then the perfect architect, clothed in white and facing east, pronounces the formula given here:

33.27–28a 'OM! That spirits, deities and demons depart! This offering is for you, bloodthirsty (deities), forest deities! I am going to perform this act, you must change your dwelling place!'

33.28b–30a That said and homage paid, the splitting of the stone is embarked upon. At that very moment the *sthāpaka* is to make an oblation, in conformity with the ritual and to the north of the stone; he then makes a cut with a gold point and with a pebble (in the guise of mallet), then the stone is struck with a sharp edged chisel and a big pebble.

33.30b–31a (A block of stone), greater in length and in width than (the dimensions) chosen (for the finished object), having been carefully taken, it should be shaped into a regular parallelepiped and the making of a mark on its 'face' should not be overlooked.

33.31b–33 (This block) is to be cleaned next and honoured with perfumes and other commodities according to the ritual indicated above; whenever a Liṅga, a pedestal or an image is to be made, the material being wood or stone, the (rough hewn shape) is to be covered with cloth and very carefully placed on a chariot; then, amidst great ceremony, it is taken to the workshop where it is properly fashioned according to rule, and hidden from outside eyes.

33.34–36 If the sage has not found (a block of stone) which accords with the rule given, (here is what he should do): after having taken a rock from an un-(-suitable) place, he is to (perform) the prescribed ritual to the north (of the suitable place) and then he should take the block there and, at an auspicious time under a favourable planet, hollow out (a hole as if to extract the block). The block is then taken out and an oblation made according to the rule. He then washes the block with water and pays homage to it with perfumes and other commodities and with cries of good omen; it is then taken to (the workshop) as above. The (stone) is thus freed from faults (resulting) from an irregular origin.

Dimensions of Liṅga

33.37a The dimensions of a temple (may be calculated) from those of the Liṅga or (those of) the Liṅga from those of the temple.

Position of Liṅga

33.37b–38a The sage places the Liṅga, or the image, in the centre of the shrine to the left of that line (which passes through its exact centre), so that it is slightly displaced towards the north-east.

33.38b–40a (For that purpose) the width of the door is divided into twenty-one parts and the median part must be taken on the axis of Brahmā's square; (that median part) is next divided into six parts, two of which, starting from the left boundary (in relation to the god), are taken for the placing of a point, from which a line is drawn towards the east, with a displacement towards the north (?). (The line which passes through the exact centre) is the line of Brahmā; the line, (displaced towards the left) passes through the centre of (the representation) of Śiva.

Dimensions of *nāgara* Liṅga

33.40b–43a Herewith the dimensions of a *nāgara* Liṅga installed in a *nāgara* temple: the least height for (this symbol of) Śiva is equal to half the (width of the sanctum); the greatest is equal to three fifths (of that width); (a total of) nine (possible heights) for the Liṅga result from dividing the distance between these two limits into eight. There are large, medium and small ones and, thus, three of each category. The width (of these Liṅga) is respectively five, four or three sixteenths of their height (proportions which correspond) to the *jayada*, *pauṣṭika* and *sārvakāmika* types in the *nāgara* class.

Dimensions of *drāviḍa* Liṅga

33.43b–45a The least height for a *drāviḍa* Liṅga installed in a *drāviḍa* temple is equal to ten twenty-firsts (of the width of the sanctum) and the greatest to thirteen twenty-firsts. The difference between these two is divided as above. For the *drāviḍa* class, the widths corresponding to the *jayada* and other types are, respectively, six, five and four twenty-firsts of the chosen height.

Dimensions of *vesara* Liṅga

33.45b–47 The least height possible for the Liṅga of a *vesara* temple is equal to thirteen twenty-fifths the width of the shrine and the greatest is sixteen twenty-fifths; as previously, a total of nine (possible widths for the Liṅga) results from dividing the difference between these two (extremes) by eight. For the *vesara* class the widths corresponding to the types listed above, *jayada* and others are, respectively, eight, seven and six twenty-fifths of the chosen height.

33.48a In all cases the width is equal to five sixteenths the circumference (of the rounded element).

Dimensions expressed in cubits

33.48b Following the dimensions calculated from those of the shrine are the dimensions determined in cubits.

33.49–51a It is said that there are thirty-three heights possible for the Liṅga, going from one to nine cubits by successive increments of six digits. It is said, however, that for temples of twelve or more storeys, these thirty-three (heights) start at five cubits whilst the increments are (the same as those given above). Some say too that the increments should be three digits when the starting point is one cubit.

33.51b–52a It is not a fault if a height is chosen which is more or less, by one digit, than the heights given above, if this is done in accordance with the *āya* and other formulae.

33.52b–53 The Liṅga suitable for small, medium and large temples have nine possible heights, starting from twenty-five digits with increments of eight (or) sixteen digits.

Dimensions calculated from those of the door and from other elements of the temple

33.54–55 The greatest (height possible for the Liṅga) is

equal to the height of the door and the least to a quarter of that. (Otherwise the greatest) is equal to seven ninths that of the pillars and (the smallest) to five ninths. In either case, nine possible heights for the Liṅga result from dividing the difference (between the extreme of the proportions indicated above in relation to door or to pillars) by eight; the (corresponding) widths are determined as given above, depending upon whether a *nāgara* temple is in question or one of another class.

33.56 Some excellent sages, such as Kumbhayoni, say (that the height of the Liṅga can be calculated) from the dimensions of the base of the temple or from those of its finial, attic or roof.

33.57 Once a dimension has been chosen for the height, it is to be divided (with a view to subsequent operations) into (a whole number) of digits; the sage is to avoid increasing or decreasing (that height) by fractions of a digit.

Āyādi formulae

33.58a-b The height having been multiplied by eight and (the product) divided by twenty-seven, a remainder is obtained which corresponds to one of the twenty-seven asterisms, the first being Aśvayuj.

33.58b–60 The height having been multiplied by four, (the product) should be divided by nine, so that a remainder is obtained which corresponds to one of the 'parts', of which the first is 'thief' and the others, 'enjoyment', 'power', 'wealth', 'king', 'eunuch', 'absence of fear', 'adversity' and 'success'; these are the names of the nine 'parts', according to connoisseurs; 'thief', 'eunuch' and 'adversity' are to be rejected.

33.61–62 Remainders, corresponding to 'wealth', 'debt' and 'matrices', are arrived at by multiplying the height by eight, nine and three and then by dividing (the products) obtained by twelve, ten and eight. If 'wealth' is large and 'debt' reduced, the chosen dimension will bring success. Amongst the (eight) 'matrices', the 'standard', 'lion', 'bull', and 'elephant' are beneficient.

33.63 The height having been multiplied by nine and the resulting product having been divided by seven, the remainder obtained corresponds to one of the days of the week, the first of which is Sunday; the 'bloody' days are to be avoided.

33.64 A Liṅga which is not in opposition to the asterism of the village or the town nor to that of the sculptor, brings good fortune to the country, to its sovereign and to its inhabitants.

Fashioning of the Liṅga

33.65–66 *Jāti* mode is the one adopted (if the block), in which the representation of the god is to be sculpted, is first shaped into a regular parallelepiped with the dimensions, in length and width, chosen (for the finished Liṅga); if it is in the shape of an octagonal prism, *chanda* mode is adopted, if the prism has sixteen sides, *vikalpa* mode and, if cylindrical, *ābhāsa* mode. That is the rough shape that should be sculpted in a triple natured Liṅga.

33.67 The height of the Liṅga being divided into three parts, the Brahmā element is at the bottom and is square section, that of Viṣṇu, which is octagonal, is in the centre and Īśa's element is the circular summit.

33.68–69 There are three ways (to draw an octagon) in a square whose width is that prescribed (for the Liṅga); the sought-after octagon may be drawn by taking the bisectrices from opposite angles (and the mediatrixes from opposite sides); (an octagon may, as well, be drawn) with a side equal to the mean between a quarter and a third (of the width of the initial square); the side of the octagon may be equal to three sevenths the width (of the initial square).

33.70–71 (That octagon once obtained), a circle is drawn which is tangential to the sides (of that octagon) and the diagonals (of that octagon) are drawn; then by marking the middle of the arc (between the middle of two sides of the octagon) a regular sixteen-sided polygon is obtained. The wise man must proceed like this to obtain (polygons with more) sides; then, cutting off the corners, he obtains a perfectly regular circle.

Proportions of the *sarvatobhadra* type of Liṅga and others.

33.72 The first type of Liṅga is the *sarvatobhadra* type, the

second the *vardhamāna*, the third that "where-Śiva's-element-is-the-largest" and the fourth is the *svastika*.

33.73 The *sarvatobhadra* type is fitting for brahmins to whom it brings good fortune; the *vardhamāna* type allows for the increase of kings, that "where-Śambhu's-element-is-the-largest" brings wealth to vaiśya; lastly, the *svastika* brings luck to those belonging to the fourth class.

33.74 The height of the *sarvatobhadra* Liṅga is divided into thirty parts, ten of which are for the lower part; there are as many for the median part and as many again for the top; Śambhu's element is perfectly circular and this Liṅga is invariably suitable for brahmins.

33.74b–76 Herewith, that appropriate for princes: these are the four varieties of *vardhamāna* Liṅga determined by the heights of the elements of Brahmā, Viṣṇu and Śiva; the proportions, starting from the bottom (of the Liṅga), may be four parts (for Brahmā's element), five (for Viṣṇu's) and six for Śiva's, or there may be five parts, six parts and seven parts, or six, seven and eight, or lastly seven, eight and nine. To princes, this Liṅga brings escalating success, victory and an increase in the number of their sons.

33.77–78 I now present the four varieties of the Liṅga "where-the-element-of-Śiva-is-the-largest"; the three elements, beginning with that of Aja (i.e. Brahmā) make, respectively, seven parts, seven parts and eight parts or five, five and six, or four, four and five or, lastly, three, three and four. It is said that this Liṅga brings all sorts of riches to vaiśya who have mastered their senses.

33.79 Where the *svastika* Liṅga is concerned, the chosen height is to be divided into nine parts, of which two are for the bottom, three for the median element and four for the worshipped element. It is prescribed for śūdra whose desires it fulfils.

Varieties: *surārcita* and others

33.80 Liṅgas of the following varieties bring the satisfaction of all desires to everybody: *surārcita*, *dhārāliṅga*, *sāhasraliṅga*, *trairāśika*.

33.81 That Liṅga, to which is given a width equal to a quarter of its height and the rest of which is as above, is called 'honoured by the host of gods' (i.e. *surārcita*).

33.82 A faceted Liṅga may be made on the same basis as a regular one; there are eight, sixteen or four faces on the bottom part and twice as many above that. This faceted *dhārāliṅga* is suitable for all classes.

33.83 If twenty-five facets are cut, side by side, on the worshipped element of a *sarvatobhadra* Liṅga and if forty superposed (Liṅga) are drawn on each of these, a thousand Liṅga result from this design and this is said to be a (*sāhasra*)-Liṅga.

33.84 This is how a *trairāśika* Liṅga is to be: the circumference of its circular element is six ninths of its total height and the perimeter of the octagonal element is seven ninths (of that height) whilst that of the (square) base is eight ninths. Three ninths (of that total height) are for that of the Aja element, three others for that of Hari and the three (last for that of Hara).

Liṅga installed by *Ṛṣi*

33.85 There are four varieties of Liṅga fitting for Ṛṣi, depending upon whether the bottom is wider (than the other two elements) or whether the median element is (convex, like the middle of) a barley grain or (concave, like the middle of) an ant or, lastly, whether the upper element is the widest (of all).

33.86 Depending on the circumstance, the width of bottom, middle or top is to be decreased by an eighth of the chosen width. In the case of a Liṅga fitting for Ṛṣi, both the Aja and Viṣṇu elements are square section.

Self-generated Liṅga

33.87–90a A self-generated Liṅga (*svayambhuliṅga*) is shaped like a plank or it has two or five sides or is triangular or has eleven, nine, six, seven or twelve sides, or the number of its sides is different from those indicated above. It may also be pointed at the top or in the shape of a horn; it may be of one specific type and its rounded top drawn according to another type or it may not be in conformity with the prescribed dimensions; such a Liṅga may also have protuberances and hollows like a *jharjhara* cymbal or be of an indefinite colour, or its worshipped element may have protuberances and hollows or crooked and not crooked parts; it may also be made from a stone containing gravel and may have streaks, spots and flaws or may have one single engraved line on it (instead of three).

33.90b–91a In no case does the sensible man rectify the original form of one of these Liṅga; it is a mistake to amend this original form, whether in ignorance or because of infatuation.

33.91b–92a When the Liṅga is installed (on a pedestal) (the lower limit of) its honoured element must be at a lower level (than that of the upper face of the pedestal). If the honoured element is circular or faceted, it brings liberation to those who have mastered their senses.

The cutting of a rounded shape at the top of the Liṅga

33.92b–93 The manner in which the top of the Liṅga is to be rounded is now given. The sages say that this rounded part may have one of five profiles: parasol, cucumber, hen's egg, hemisphere and bubble.

33.94–96b The rule gives four (possible heights, for) the rounded part shaped like a parasol, which are equal to a sixteenth the width of the Liṅga or to two, three or four (sixteenths of it). (Starting at the top) a regular and perfectly symmetrical contour is to go downwards. The first two dimensions are appropriate for a regular Liṅga, the third to that 'where-the-element-of-Śiva-is-the-largest'; lastly, the heights suitable for the *vardhamāna* Liṅga (are those equal) to four (sixteenths the width of the Liṅga). It is inauspicious if confusions enter into the choice of the type of rounded top.

33.96c–97 (The height of the rounded part) in the shape of a cucumber is equal to two and a half sixths (the width of the Liṅga). When it is like a hen's egg its height is half (the width of the Liṅga); the height of the hemispheric rounded part is a third, and that of the bubble shaped one, three and a half eighths.

33.98–99 (The proportions) now indicated are common to all types of Liṅga; the rounded part of the head (of the Liṅga) occupies a third of the height of the upper element of the Liṅga (?); (or the height of the rounded part) is equal, in all types of Liṅga, to once, twice or thrice one thirty-sixth the height of the Liṅga, proportions fitting for, respectively, small, medium and large heads of Liṅga.

33.100 [*This gives another method for drawing the rounded top of the Liṅga*].

Bringing out the characteristic signs

33.101–102 The manner in which the characteristic signs of all these Liṅga are brought out is now given. (The Liṅga) must have been polished in a single operation using stones, cow-hair cords impregnated with fine sands and other utensils; (in doing this) great care must be taken to respect the characteristics (of the Liṅga); next, having checked to see that the representation (of the god) is very beautiful, the bringing out of its characteristics is undertaken.

33.103–104a A pavilion, situated near the temple and decorated with coloured hangings, is where the Liṅga should be installed, on a couch covered with a white cloth and arranged on a stand, which is (itself) placed upon a beautiful spread of white rice, paddy and other grains.

33.104b–105 The Priest and the architect, wearing new garments, gold (jewellery) and flowers and with the five parts of the body decorated, should adorn themselves with pastes and white garlands, using nothing but beautiful ornaments.

33.106 Bearing the formula NETRA in mind, the Master roughs out the lines, the line of Aja and the lateral ones, using a gold point to do so.

33.107–108a Next, once the work has been outlined with a gold chisel, the architect, in his turn, (sculpts) the frenum which is outlined (on the Liṅga), which is sprinkled with clarified butter, milk and honey; he does this lightly with a light grooving tool and for a favourable result, giving it the shape of a waterfall.

33.108b–109a It is then covered with (heaps) of pure grain and with a white cloth and to it are offered a cow, a brahmin, a calf and a young girl; the sage draws what remains to be drawn.

Bringing out the characteristics of *nāgara* Liṅga

33.109b–114a The height of (the element of) Śiva is divided into sixteen parts for a Liṅga of the first category, *nāgara*: if a small Liṅga is involved, six parts are to be subtracted at the top, five (for a medium Liṅga) and four (for a big one) and three are subtracted below, no matter what the size of the Liṅga; the three possible heights for the frenum are arrived at in this way. Next, the two lateral lines are drawn, towards Viṣṇu's element; their join is made on the 'back' with (a contour of four, three and two parts, in the case of a small Liṅga; in the case of a medium Liṅga, this join is made 'at the back' with (a contour of) five, four, three and two parts. The width of the frenum is equal to two thirds (of a sixteenth of the height of Śiva's element); or else the frenum may be of even width throughout its height: a *kṛṣṇala* (i.e. three barley grains), less a 'barley grain'. This is how Maya prescribes that a frenum be drawn on a *nāgara* Liṅga.

Bringing out the characteristics of *drāviḍa* Liṅga

33.114b–117a The height of Śiva's (element) of a *drāviḍa* Liṅga is divided into fifteen parts, the height (of the frenum) making up nine, ten or eleven depending upon whether (the Liṅga) is small, (medium or large). The two (lateral) lines are to be drawn from (a point situated at) eight (ninths), nine (tenths) or ten (elevenths) on the height of the frenum; their join is made at the 'back' with a (contour of four, three and two parts, for a small (Liṅga) or five, four, three and two for a medium one and six, five, four, three and two for a large. The width of the frenum of a *drāviḍa* Liṅga is to be equal to half a (fifteenth of the height of the Śiva element).

Bringing out of the characteristics of a *vesara* Liṅga

33.117b–119a The height of the venerated element of a *vesara* Liṅga is divided into fifteen parts; the height of the frenum takes up ten and (the lateral lines are to be drawn) starting from a point at eight (tenths the height of the frenum); their join is made with a contour of five, four and three parts. The width (of the frenum) is equal to a sixteenth of the diameter (of the Liṅga). This is appropriate for the largest sized *vesara* Liṅga.

33.119b–122a (The height of the Śiva element) of a medium sized Liṅga is to be divided into eight parts, (the frenum) making up four of the height. (The lateral lines are to be drawn) from a point situated at three (fourths on the height of the frenum) and their join is made (with) two or one parts. The width (of the frenum) is equal to two thirds (of an eighth of the height of the Śiva element). For a small sized *vesara* Liṅga it is said that the height (of the Śiva) element is to be divided into twelve and the procedure is to be as above for what remains; the width of the frenum is equal to two (twelfths the height of the Śiva element).

Width and depth of lines

33.122b–123a The lines (delimiting the frenum) on all types of Liṅga must be regular; their depth and their width are to be equal to a ninth the fraction (of the Śiva element) chosen as unit.

33.123b–125a (Otherwise), the man of firm intelligence is to calculate exactly a ninth (of a length) of eight 'barley grains'; (the width and the depth of the lines) of a one cubit Liṅga are then equal to that ninth; a nine cubit Liṅga, whose lines are eight barley grains long and deep, is arrived at by adding a ninth (per supplementary cubit).

33.125b–126a (Otherwise, a depth and width) of half a barley grain are given to the lines (of a one cubit Liṅga), and a depth and width of four and a half barley grains for the largest Liṅga are arrived at as above, by adding half a barley grain (per supplementary cubit) for each.

33.126b–127a The width of the lateral lines is half that of the median lines. All the lines are to have the same depth and width.

General rules

33.127b Now I indicate the way of bringing out the characteristics according to the rule common to *nāgara* and other Liṅga.

33.128–129 The height of the venerated part is divided into sixteen parts and two are subtracted below and four above; the frenum and its bud thus take up ten, (in all, of the height). The lateral lines are to be drawn, subtracting two parts, starting from the bottom (of the venerated element) and one (part is subtracted) starting from the bud; they meet at the 'back' (of the Liṅga). The width of the bud is equal to (a sixteenth of the venerated element).

33.130 Or else, the height (of the Śiva element) is divided into sixteen parts, two being subtracted below, ten are taken for (the height of) the urethra and, in all else, the procedure is as above. This is fitting for all Liṅga.

33.131 (Otherwise) the Rudra element is divided into twelve parts, two are subtracted at the top and bottom and nine taken for (the frenum and) its bud; the rest is as given above.

33.132 (Or else), the Śiva element is divided into eighteen parts, two are subtracted from the lower part and five above, and eleven are taken for the Aja line of which one is for its bud whilst, in all else, the procedure is as above.

33.133–134 (Otherwise) the Śiva element is divided into sixteen parts, two are subtracted below and four above and ten are taken for the height of the frenum. The two lateral lines start from a point situated at eight (tenths on the height of the frenum) and they follow a contour for five, seven and eight (parts) (?), meeting at the 'back', at one part (below the bottom of the Śiva element). Everything else is as indicated above.

33.135 The frenum is first to be drawn with ash-coated twine and its summit is then rounded with a stiletto and the characteristic lateral (lines) are drawn with twine.

Shapes of top of frenum

33.136–138a A rounded contour must always be drawn at the top of the frenum. It may (be drawn) according to the shape of the summit of the Liṅga or in accordance with the general rule. (Rounded) shapes, common to all Liṅga, are those of the *aśvattha* leaf, *kadalī* bud and *ambuja* bud. The width and height of the frenum are equal to the fraction (of the Śiva element) chosen (as unit of calculation for the lines).

33.138b–140 (The shapes of) the top of the frenum are now indicated according to the rule for (the specific shapes) of Liṅga. On a Liṅga with a parasol top, the top of the frenum is to be shaped like an elephant's eye; on a Liṅga (with a top) shaped like a half-moon or bubble, (it) is like the point of a spear; on a Liṅga with a top like a cucumber, the top is like a hen's egg and a Liṅga with a summit like a hen's egg has a frenum like a parasol.

33.141 The width of the median frenum is equal to two thirds of a seventeenth of the diameter (of the Liṅga) and the two lateral lines are half as wide.

33.142 Whatever is suitable for a (given) Liṅga height is applicable, by and large, (for all Liṅga of that height) (?).

33.143 I have indicated that which is suitable for *nāgara* Liṅga and for others of the same series: height, width, particularities and corresponding names, dimensions (and shapes) of their tops, parasol or other, and the lines.

Crystal Liṅga

33.144–147a Now I describe the small, medium and large

crystal Liṅga, one after the other. The height of the venerated element of a small-sized Liṅga goes from one to six digits by successive increments of one digit. That height, in a medium-sized Liṅga, is from seven to twelve digits. The six possible heights for the venerated part of a large-sized Liṅga go from thirteen to eighteen digits by successive increments of one digit.

33.147b–148a (Otherwise), the increment from the smallest height may be half a digit, in which case there are eleven possibilities (for each category of Liṅga), small, medium and large, making thirty-three possible heights in all.

33.148b–151a The height of (that portion) of the crystal Liṅga which is sunk into the socle is equal to half or one third the height of the venerated element. The width of the venerated element is equal to its height or is three quarters or half of it. Crystal Liṅga are circular or faceted; their top is to be rounded in the manner (indicated above), for *nāgara* Liṅga and others. On a small or large sized (crystal) Liṅga, the frenum is to be drawn as previously, but, even if a crystal Liṅga has no frenum, it still grants wishes.

33.151b–152 The width of the socle is equal to twice, two and a half times, or three times that of the Liṅga; a tank with suitable spout is to be arranged upon this socle, the height of which is equal to that of the venerated element or is three (quarters) of it.

Liṅga in various materials such as earth

33.153–155 Liṅga made of earth, wood, precious stones or metal, should conform precisely to what has already been given for the crystal ones. The Liṅga of earth may be in baked or unbaked earth, depending on the circumstances and preference. The wooden Liṅga (is to be made with) flawless wood. It is said that the metal Liṅga is to be massive; an iconic representation in massive metal may be in one or several pieces; the rewards for making a representation in metal are enjoyment and liberation. Any Liṅga which is not in stone is called ***maṇiliṅga***.

33.156–158a The pedestals for the crystal Liṅga and others may be of the same material as the Liṅga or may be in metal; the metals (of the Liṅga and pedestal) are to correspond to one another, where the pedestals of Liṅga in materials other than crystal are concerned. A Liṅga in precious stones must be firmly installed on a metal pedestal. (The elements of) Maheśvara, Viṣṇu and Brahmā appear due to the wish of the faithful alone. A Liṅga arranged by the sages in fitting fashion brings enjoyment and deliverance.

33.158b–159 A *bāṇaliṅga*[1] is to be set (into its pedestal) in a manner fitting to the circumstance; its venerated element (is visible) on three fifths, half or two thirds of its height, the rest of which may provide the link with the socle; (this is what is done) in the case of a *bāṇaliṅga*.

33.160 (In order to make a Liṅga of precious stones) it is necessary to reject, conclusively, gems which have streaks, spots and flaws as well as those of ill-defined colour or which have 'flies', '(crow's) feet', cracks or gravel.

Installation of Liṅga

33.161 The wise man installs a small Liṅga in a finished temple; it is when a temple is half built that a medium Liṅga is to be installed and a large one is installed when the base has been constructed.

Fruits of installing a Liṅga

33.162 A Liṅga of prescribed shape is to be installed; it brings good fortune, well being, health and enjoyment. If not made according to the norm, it will be to the founder a failure and a source of illlness and of distress without end.

Thus ends, in the *Mayamata*, treatise on dwelling, the thirty-third chapter: FEATURES OF LIṄGA.

1. *Bāṇaliṅga*: generally a pebble.

Chapter 34
PEDESTALS

34.1 I now give the characteristics of pedestals according to the rule common to the pedestals of symbolic and iconic representations.

Materials used for pedestals

34.2–3 One kind (of material) only is to be used (for representation and socle) and different materials should not be used together. It is however said by some, that a stone or a wooden (representation) may have a baked brick pedestal. The pedestals of idols in precious stones, and of metal ones, are to be in metal. It is the choice of a 'female' stone which is crucial to the making of the pedestal of a Liṅga.

Pedestal dimensions

34.4–5a The smallest size for a pedestal is double the (height of) the venerated element (of the Liṅga) and the biggest is equal to the height of the Liṅga; nine widths for the pedestal result from dividing the difference between these two (extremes) by eight; there are three large, three medium and three small.

34.5b–6a Otherwise, the smallest width is equal to half the height of the Liṅga and the greatest to three quarters of that height; as above, (nine) pedestal widths are arrived at by dividing the difference between these (extremes) by eight.

34.6b–7 Otherwise (the width of the pedestal is equal) to triple the diameter (of the Liṅga) or to the Liṅga's circumference, or to a third of it, or it is a quarter the width of the sanctum or is equal to twice, two and a half times or thrice the width (of the Liṅga).

34.8–9 The width chosen for the pedestal must be decreased

by an eighth at (its) summit and, by way of decoration, that width may be either increased or decreased by an eighth. The width at the bottom of all pedestals corresponds to the borders of the plinth whilst the width at the top corresponds to that of the big (upper) string-course.

34.10a The height of the pedestal corresponds to that (of the top) of the Viṣṇu element or is more by a quarter or by a half.

Pedestal shapes

34.10b–11 (A pedestal may be in the shape of a regular polygon) with four, eight, six, twelve or sixteen sides or it may be a perfect circle or may have these same shapes elongated; otherwise it may be triangular or semi-circular; these are the fourteen possible shapes.

34.12–13a Those amongst these pedestals whose shapes are regular are fitting for Liṅga, whereas those which are elongated are the 'thrones' for images; the triangular and semi-circular pedestals are appropriate for symbolic and iconic idols respectively.

Pedestal names

34.13b–15a Herewith the names of nine types of pedestal: *bhadrapīṭha*, *padma*, *vajrapīṭha*, *mahāmbuja*, *śrīkara*, *pīṭhapadma*, *mahāvajra*, *saumyaka* and *śrīkāmya*. The triangular and half-moon pedestals are designated in relation to their particular forms.

34.15b–15c The ornaments for each of these pedestals are now given, along with the proportions of the pedestals, calculated according to the height indicated (above), and their specifications.

Bhadra pedestal

34.16–17 (The height of the pedestal) is divided into fifteen parts: the plinth takes up two parts, the lower string-course (*vapra*) four, an (inverted) doucine one and a half, the fillet which tops it half a part, the torus two and the fillet which tops it half; the dado, above, takes up one and a half parts and the fillet which tops it (half a one) as previously; next, the upper string-course takes up two parts and the rim half a one. Such are the characteristics of a *bhadra* pedestal, which is pleasing to the eye and which brings happiness, riches, health and enjoyment to brahmins, lords of the Earth, vaiśya and others.

Padma pedestal

34.18 The height of the *padma* pedestal is divided into sixteen parts: the plinth takes up two parts, the (inverted) doucine five, the torus two, the (upright) doucine four, the upper string-course two and the rim one.

Vajrapadma pedestal

34.19–20 (The height of the pedestal) is divided into fourteen parts: the plinth takes up one and a half parts, a groove half, the (inverted) doucine three and a half; next, a fillet takes up half a part, a groove half a part, a *vajra* (?) one and, as previously, a groove and a fillet (half a one each); then, the (upright) doucine takes up three parts, a groove half a one, the upper string-course one and a half and that used to (hold) libations half a one. This *vajrapadma* pedestal is suitable for all Liṅga.

Mahābja pedestal

34.21–22 (The height of the pedestal) is divided into eighteen parts: the plinth takes up two and a half parts, the (inverted) doucine four, a fillet half a one, a dado one and a half, an upright doucine two and a half, a reed half a one, a small doucine half a one, a groove half, a string-course three, a small doucine half a one, the *śrī* (?) upper string-course one and a half and the receptacle for liquids half a one. This pedestal is called *mahābja* and is suitable for man-(made) Liṅga and for the Liṅga of Ṛṣi.

Śrīkara pedestal

34.23–24 The selected height is divided into sixteen parts: the plinth takes up one part, the lower string-course three and the (inverted) doucine four; next, a fillet takes up half a part, a torus two parts, a fillet half a part, the (upright) doucine three parts and the upper string-course one and a half; the height of the rim takes up half a part and so does its thickness. The spout is three or four parts long and wide (at its beginning) and its width at the end is a third (what it is at the start); this end has an auspicious shape. The *śrīkara* pedestal is like this.

Pīṭhapadma pedestal

34.25 The height of the *pīṭhapadma* pedestal is divided into ten parts: the plinth takes up one and a half parts, a groove half a one, the (inverted) doucine two and a half, a fillet half, a groove half, another fillet half, the (upright) doucine two and a half; a groove, a fillet and the (recessed) rim take up (half a part each).

Mahāvajra and *saumya* pedestals

34.26–28a The chosen height is divided into fifteen parts; at the bottom there may be a plinth taking up one and a half parts, a groove of one part and a lower string-course of four parts; (otherwise) there is a plinth taking up one and a half parts, a groove one part and an (inverted) doucine four parts; next, a *vajra* shaped (?) string-course takes up two and a half parts, a torus one and a half, an (upright) doucine two and a half, the upper string-course one and a half and the recessed (top) half a one. This *saumya* pedestal is called *mahāvajra* and brings all success. If it is the torus which is *vajra* shaped (?)

however, this *saumya* pedestal is called *tuṅga* and brings success and health.

Śrīkāmya pedestal

34.28b–29 The chosen height is divided into twelve parts: the plinth takes up one part, the lower string-course two, a groove half a part, an (inverted) doucine one and a half, a fillet half, a small doucine half, a torus one and a half, an (upright) doucine one and a half, a fillet half, a small doucine half, the upper string-course one and a half and the recessed top half. This is the *śrīkāmya* pedestal which I have thus described.

Features common to all pedestals

34.30–31 The bases of a shrine must be such that their decoration corresponds to that within. The recess and the projection of the mouldings of all pedestals must be such that (the pedestal) will be solid, good looking and well adapted.

34.32–33 The spout of a pedestal is to be so made that its width, at the start, and its length are, respectively, a third and a quarter the width of the pedestal itself; the width of the spout at the end is half, two thirds or a third the width at the start; its thickness is equal to its width or is three quarters of it.

34.34–35 (This spout) is the shape of an elephant's lower lip or of the muzzle of a cow. Its gutter is inclined, with a width equal to a third the (total) width (of the spout) at its starting point and at its end. Once the Liṅga is orientated in the desired direction, the spout is placed in the middle of the pedestal's left side and (the spout) may be embellished with a support.

34.36–37 The width of the upper rim (of the pedestal) must be equal to its height or to that height augmented by a quarter, a half or three quarters according to the resistance required. The sage is to dig out (the tank) at the base of (that rim) to a depth equal to the rim's thickness; (that tank) is to be made in such a way that its bottom rises progressively towards the meeting with the Liṅga.

34.38 (The bottom of) the Śiva element is to be slightly lower than the top face of the pedestal; if it is above that, endless misfortune will fall upon everyone.

34.39–40a In the case of a semi-circular pedestal, its rectilinear side is to face the door; where a triangular pedestal is concerned, it is one of its sides that should face the door. The sages ascertain that (the line of) a side of a (triangular) pedestal does not intersect the line of the door.

34.40b–41 It is best to make a pedestal monolithic and without assemblage; however, if it is not possible to procure a block (suitable for the making of it) then (at least) the upper element of the pedestal is to be monolithic. Where a large or small (socle) is concerned, the join should not coincide with the middle of its elements.

34.42 On the elevation, the assemblage (of the different parts) of pedestals is to correspond to the limits of the mouldings. The join is not to be made in the middle of the spout nor at the centre point of half (the height of the pedestal), nor at the corners.

34.43 The long and the short are to be assembled to the right and left according to the rule. The lower part (of the pedestal) may be in three pieces or in whatever number is suitable in the specific instance.

The 'Brahmā stone'

34.44–45 The greatest (possible) width for the Brahmā stone is equal to the height of the Liṅga and the least to double (the height) of the venerated element (of the Liṅga); the difference between these two (extremes) is to be divided into eight which yields (as previously) a series of nine widths. Its greatest thickness is equal to half the corresponding width and the least to a quarter of that width; the difference between these two (extremes) is to be divided as above.

34.46–47a Or else, the width (of the Brahmā stone) is equal to double the diameter of the Liṅga, at most, and to one and a half times this diameter, at least; the thickness is then, at most, three quarters of the corresponding width and, at least, half that width. For widths and thicknesses, the procedure by which nine possible dimensions are arrived at is as above.

34.47b–49a Towards the placing of the Brahmā element (of the Liṅga), a mortice is hollowed out, at the centre (of the 'stone of Brahmā'), in the form of the Brahmā element and with a width equal to that of the Liṅga. The depth (of that mortice) is equal to half its width or to an eighth (the height) of the lower part of the Liṅga. It is to be set with precious stones and (its sides) must adhere firmly to the lower part of the Liṅga.

34.49b The 'stone of Brahmā' is to be made with a 'neuter' stone.

Nandyāvarta stones

34.50 Four stones, making up a dextrogyre *nandyāvarta* figure, are to be disposed in the interval between the pedestal and the stone of Brahmā.

Statue pedestals

34.51–52 Amongst pedestals intended for images, there are some that are suitable for seated figures and others for standing ones. The (width of the pedestals of) seated images is greater (than the width of those images) by one, two, three, four, five or six digits and the pedestals' length is greater than their width by (at least) an eighth; the width of the pedestal itself however is not to be more than double (its width). (The proportions) of the mouldings are to vary in the same way as (those of the) pedestal.

34.53–54a The height of the pedestal is a third that of the image if the image is reclining, a quarter if it is sitting and a fifth if standing. The length and width (of the pedestal) of a reclining image is to be calculated as above.

34.54b–56a The seat intended for gods, such as Brahmā, and for goddesses is called 'lion's throne' when it is placed on a socle and when it has (images of) lions for its legs. It is decorated with 'waves' on three sides; its decoration is varied; it is to be constructed with reference to the rules given above for the lion's throne (of kings).

Dimensions of temples as calculated from those of pedestals

34.56b–60 The sage may, if he so wishes (?) give the shape of the shrine to the pedestals intended for *bāṇaliṅga* and other Liṅga of the kind, as well as for Ṛṣi Liṅga and self-generated ones. The width and other dimensions of these pedestals are to be calculated as has been given above apropos the (man-made) Liṅga. The width of the temple is calculated from the dimensions of this pedestal; the width of the sanctum is double, quadruple or quintuple that of the pedestal if it is not calculated as above; the thickness of the wall (which surrounds the sanctum) is a third or a half (that of the sanctum) or else (merely in such a way that the wall is) solid; it may or may not have an aisle, and corner and elongated aediculae . . . etc. (are to be arranged) as previously indicated. These are the prescriptions for a temple (whose dimensions are calculated) from those of the Liṅga and whose height is determined as has previously been ordained.

Dimensions of temples calculated from those of the images

34.61–64a A temple may be constructed with reference to the dimensions chosen for the building's pillars and doors as well as with those for the image. Here is how a temple, for housing an iconic representation, is to be constructed: the (width of the) sanctum may be equal to the height of the image to that height augmented by a half or to double that height, or to five thirds the height of the image; but it may be said, as well, that the height of the image is equal to a quarter, a third or half (the width of the sanctum and that its width is equal to half (its height).

Making of eight-(ingredient) mortar

34.64b–66 Equal parts of wax, molasses, beeswax and

bdellium are taken and a quantity of *sarja* resin is added, equal to or double (the total of the first four commodities), as well as pounded brick; all this is put into a metal receptacle with a quantity of oil equal to that of all (the other ingredients put together). Everything is mixed together with a metal spoon and cooked slowly. This is how 'eight ingredient mortar' (*aṣṭabandha*) is obtained such as makes joins rock-hard.

Position of representation of gods in the shrine

34.67 According to the wishes of the donor, one or several representations may be installed in a (temple); they may be installed in the centre, on the sides or against the wall, according to preference.

34.68 Whether the shrines are one or several, the biggest must be that which houses the Liṅga and the trident. The rest must be deduced by right minded craftsmen.

34.69 The sanctum is to be divided according to the forty-nine square diagram; in the middle is Brahmā's square and the eight surrounding ones are those of the gods, whilst the sixteen beyond are those of men and the twenty-four on the periphery those of Piśāca.

34.70 The representation of Śiva is to be on the square of Brahmā and that of Viṣṇu in the zone of the gods, whilst all the other deities are to be installed in the zone of men and, lastly, in Piśāca's zone, the others: Mothers, Asura and deities of that kind, as well as Yakṣa, Gandharva, Rakṣas and others.

34.71 The line of Brahmā is in the middle with that of Śiva to its right and, between them, is that of Viṣṇu. The gods are installed in order on the Viṣṇu line when these lines have been drawn towards the cardinal points.

34.72 The architect, knowing the rules and endowed with steadfast intelligence, gives all his attention to the installation of the representation, whether it is iconic, symbolic or mixed; (to do this he is to be) girdled with a beautiful gold thread, covered with fine ornaments and is to be gifted with preeminence in all fields; the *sthāpaka* accompanies him.

34.73 The universal Liṅga is (formless like) Ether; thus the Liṅga which is to be installed is a man-made one. According to circumstance the sages install it in a sufficiently large temple and they do not fix the crowning bricks until they (have installed) (the Liṅga).

34.74 This is how the socle for symbols or the throne of images are to be, with their tank and their spout. The installation of the (man-made) Liṅga is to be accomplished according to rule and in a fitting shrine.

Thus ends, in the *Mayamata*, treatise on dwelling, the thirty-fourth chapter: FEATURES OF PEDESTALS.

Chapter 35

RENOVATION WORK

35.1–2a Now come the rules, compiled from other works, relating to the renovation of temples, Liṅga, pedestals, images and other constructions; they are laid out in a brief and systematic way.

Temple renovation

35.2b–3a A temple (may be) ruined, broken down, fallen down, aged as to its materials or decrepit, or it may not conform to *jāti*, *chanda*, *vikalpa* or *ābhāsa* modes.

35.3b–4 Those (temples) whose characteristics are no longer (perceptible) are (to be renovated) with regard to the specific type of Liṅga (found there). In this case different, or better, materials (than those employed during the initial construction) should be used, as well as new pitchers, and the heights, widths and other dimensions which conform to the *āyādi* formulae, and, as well, (suitable) ornaments.

35.5–7 Those (temples) whose characteristics are still (perceptible) in their principal and secondary elements (are to be renovated) with their own materials. If they are lacking in anything or have some similar type of flaw, the sage wishing to restore them, (must proceed in such a way that) they regain their integrality and that they are pleasantly arranged (anew); this (is to be done) with the dimensions — height and width — which were theirs and with decoration consisting of corner, elongated and other aediculae, without anything being added (to what originally existed) and always in conformity with the initial appearance (of the building) and with the advice of the knowledgeable.

35.8–9a In the case of a *nāgara* temple, a *nāgara* temple is to be rebuilt and in that of a *drāviḍa* temple, a *drāviḍa* (temple), in that of a *vesara* one it is auspicious (that the temple be) *vesara*; in the case of a temple with no aisle, the temple (should be) without aisle and, in the case of a temple which is not lacking in such an aisle, the temple should not lack one either.

35.9b–12a The sage must always dispose an assembly of dwellings according to the order suitable (for that assembly). (Thus) in a temple with an enclosure, (the edifices) prescribed for within and without the enclosure wall (are to be placed on the inside and outside, respectively, of that wall). In a temple the (buildings of the) courtyard are to be arranged according to the rule which I lay down with precision here: (these edifices) may be the same (height) as the original shrine or may be bigger, either being acceptable; (those which are arranged) at the cardinal points should, however, be the same height (as the original shrine); on the other hand, those at the corners or elsewhere, (may be higher but) should not be more than an eighth or a quarter, according to circumstances, of the height of the original shrine.

35.12b–14 The extension of the enclosure may be made according to rule, towards the north or the east, or towards all points on the periphery. When it is desired that a ruined (building) be (re)constructed in an (existing) sanctuary in another place, he who has knowledge of architecture avoids making it at the cardinal points or outside the sanctuary; a transgression of this rule brings bad luck and the procedure should thus be carried out according to the appropriate mode. A building should be re-erected without the foundation rituals, (already accomplished) for the destroyed monument.

Renovation of Liṅga

35.15–18a A Liṅga (may have) fallen, may be split or may be hard to walk round, may be imperfectly circular or twisted; (it may be) a Liṅga 'gone down' from a Liṅga or it may be a 'gone up' Liṅga[1]; (it may have been) installed according to the fantasies of quibblers or by the ignorant; it may have been bruised, scorched by fire or may be decrepit, split or broken;

1. See below vv.21–22.

(it may have been) lifted out by thieves; it may have been lost or put in a place sullied by impure people or it may have been knocked over; such Liṅga are improper and if found in this world are declared to be pernicious by those who, amongst the universe of creatures, know this.

35.18b–20 If a fallen Liṅga is, nevertheless, installed by some ignorant person, another Liṅga is to be installed in its place, one which has not yet been touched by the fierce rays of the sun. A Liṅga is called 'mean' if it is placed in the very midst of impure things or if it touches the bottom of the mortice (of its pedestal) or if it is not visible above the top of the pedestal; it is the same if its 'face' is not orientated in the appropriate direction; yet one who knows may improve (such Liṅga) and that goes for a twisted Liṅga or one found to be imperfectly rounded, when it is measured (to the end of seeing if it is of the prescribed dimensions).

35.21–22 A Liṅga, buried for a known period of time, is a 'gone down' Liṅga; it is to be reinstalled after it has been measured (to see if it has the prescribed dimensions). A Liṅga, buried for an unknown period of time, is a 'gone up' Liṅga and there is no error in reinstalling it in the same place.

35.23 A Liṅga which has fallen into a water course must be installed afresh and according to the rule pertaining to 'divine' Liṅga, in a place (situated) at one hundred poles (from its old position); its face is to be orientated in the manner already given.

35.24–26 A Liṅga that has been installed, by mistake, according to erroneous rituals and formulae, should be installed (anew). A Liṅga which is incomplete, scorched by fire or which is decrepit, split or broken, even though still in worship, is to be rejected and replaced. A Liṅga which, due to the folly of the ignorant, has been installed upside down or has had its face located elsewhere, (than in the place where it actually is), or has been knocked down: such a Liṅga is to be rejected immediately; a new Liṅga should be installed in its place, according to the rule.

35.27–28 A Liṅga with the prescribed characteristics but without 'oil' or 'eyes' is not to be reclaimed; equally, a Liṅga which is in a field is not suitable; it should invariably be rejected and a new Liṅga installed in its place according to rule. When a Liṅga has been lifted up by thieves and has fallen back again inside the assembly of the five (liner-stones), there is no error in reinstalling it, in the same place and according to rule.

35.29–31 A Liṅga that has been touched by caṇḍāla, śūdra or others of that ilk, is known to be no longer suitable; if it has been touched near a river (?), however, it is a Liṅga deprived of abode; after it has been taken to another place, a pure one this time, towards the north or east, it is a well installed Liṅga, once it has been transported according to rule. When an image is concerned, once it has been taken to a new place chosen according to circumstance, there is no error in installing it, and everything that has not been prescribed for here is to conform to what has been prescribed for the Liṅga.

35.32 Some say that a Liṅga, abandoned for more than twelve years, should not be reclaimed even if flawless.

35.33a The sage must make haste to throw into the water a stone (Liṅga or image) that has been rejected.

Renovation of pedestals

35.33b–34a A pedestal of stone or of some other material may be reclaimed if it is flawless and fitting; the Brahmā stone, other stones, the elements (of the foundation deposit?) and the pedestal are to be reinstalled as has been previously given.

35.34b–36 The pedestal must however be rejected instantly if its characteristics are no longer (perceptible), if it is incomplete and if it has cracks or other flaws of that kind; a (new) pedestal then has to be made, according to rule, similar to the old one, in that stone is used if the old was in stone and brick if it was in brick. When a pedestal has fallen (?) as has been mentioned above, it is to be remade in brick, if it was in brick and, too, if it was in a stone that is no longer available.

Renovation of images

35.37–38 A stone or wood image which is incomplete is to

be rejected instantly and a new image installed in its place. An image of the required height and thickness, but which is split or which has any flaw of that kind, must be rejected and another image installed in its place according to rule.

35.39–40a A metal or earth image lacking hands, nose, adornment, ears or teeth is to be restored to its original condition but if it is a principal limb which is missing it must be thrown out and a new one put in its place.

General rule

35.40b–42 When a temple, a Liṅga, a pedestal or images are to be renovated, the work is always to be done with materials similar (to those used initially) or better ones and never with less good ones. In the case of a decrepit (object), the knowledgeable one wishing to restore it, will proceed as indicated above in order to return it to its original condition according to rule; (but), if the object was small it is desirable that it be restored to at least equal size or even to a larger one for that is always auspicious.

35.43 That which is made smaller has to be of better materials or may be made identical, with the same materials as previously, and with its dimensions in accordance with those calculated from the sanctum, the pillars and the doors of the sanctum.

35.44 To be rid of a clay image, one throws it into water, a wooden one is put into the fire and a metal one melted by fire and the purified metal recovered.

Renovation of villages etc. . .

35.45–47a Where settlements, such as villages, and dwellings, such as houses, are concerned, the specific rule pronounced by the sages is that the length and the width (chosen for the renovation) should not be less than the original dimensions and that they should be the same or greater. Subject to the particular circumstances, the possible extensions may be to all points on the periphery or may be in the directions prescribed above, for an extension to the south or the east is the ruin of a building.

35.47b–47c In the case of a house or a *mālikā*, these should be so constructed that the number of storeys is never less (than what it was) and the rule appropriate (to the building) is to be applied.

Provisional installation

35.48 A provisional installation is to be made at the very beginning of the work of construction of a new building or at the time of the repairing of a decrepit or ruined building or when there has been the collapse of a Liṅga or of an image or when these are cracked or when parts of them are missing or, lastly, at the time of the fixing (of the Liṅga or image) in the socle.

35.49 The (provisional) shrine (is to be installed) at nine poles to the north of the (main) shrine; the dimensions of the provisional shrine are a third, a quarter, a fifth or a sixth (those of the main shrine) or the provisional shrine measures three, four, five, six or seven cubits (depending upon whether the main shrine) is small or large.

35.50 The thickness of the walls (of the provisional shrine) is double or triple that of the pillars of the bottom storey of the main (shrine); the rest (of the surface of the provisional shrine) is occupied by a low room; this provisional shrine may be a pavilion or a hall.

35.51 (The height of the provisional Liṅga) is from a quarter to a half of that of the cella; nine possible heights (for the Liṅga) result from dividing the difference between these two dimensions by eight. The circumference of the Liṅga is equal to its height; it is well rounded and its summit is parasol shaped but without marked characteristics.

35.52 Nine dimensions for a provisional Liṅga, determined from (the size of the digit) of the founder, are obtained by starting with fifteen digits and adding a digit each time. (The provisional Liṅga) is embedded in its socle to a depth equal to a third or a quarter its height.

35.53 The greatest height possible for a provisional Liṅga

is equal to that of the base of the main (shrine) and the least to half that same height; a total of nine heights results from dividing the difference (between these two dimensions) by eight.

35.54 There are (potentially) nine heights for a provisional Liṅga, starting with seven digits and adding two each time. The procedure for a manifest representation is as for an unmanifest one.

35.55 When the Liṅga is to be used in ceremonies, the greatest dimension for the provisional image is half the height of the original mobile image and the least is a quarter; to arrive at nine (potential) heights, the difference between these two dimensions has to be divided by eight.

35.56 The greatest height and width (for a provisional pedestal) are equal to those of the original fixed socle and the least are three quarters of that: nine potential widths and heights are arrived at by dividing the difference between these dimensions by eight.

35.57 There are stone, metal or wood (images or Liṅga) in provisional shrines. [These are the trees suitable for provisional Liṅga: *sarala*, *kālaja*, *candana*. *sālaka*, *khadira*, *māruda*, *pippala* and *tinduka*].

35.58a There is to be a perfect manifest image installed in the provisional shrine throughout the period of the erection of the main shrine until it is accomplished (and it is to stay there) until the desired goal has been achieved.

35.58b The ancients say that it is not proper for a provisional shrine to last more than twelve years; that is the limit for all the other works too and all sorts of mistakes are engendered if it is exceeded.

35.59 The work of renovation has thus been presented where it relates to temples, Liṅga, pedestals, images and dwelling sites such as villages; (they are to be renovated when they are) seriously flawed and it is certain that procedures other than those prescribed will bring about mistakes of all kinds.

Thus ends, in the *Mayamata*, treatise on dwelling, the thirty-fifth chapter: RULES FOR RENOVATION.

Chapter 36

ICONOGRAPHY

36.1 Now, successively presented, are the arrangements, colours, attributes, mounts, decoration, emblems and emplacements (?) of the gods, of whom the first is Brahmā, and of the goddesses.

Brahmā

36.2–4a Brahmā has four faces and four arms; he is the colour of pure gold; his braided hair is shaped like a diadem and like a crown (from which emanates) reddish rays like a garland of lightning. He wears ear-pendants, armlets and a necklace; his scarf, a gazelle skin, must cover him up to the base of the neck according to the *upavīta* mode. His tawny thighs are encircled by *muñja*; he wears white clothing and white garlands and is immaculate.

36.4b–6a He holds the *akṣa* rosary and a bundle of *kuśa* in his two right hands and the water-pot and *kuśa* grass in his left ones; or he holds the spoon and the ladle in his right hands and the pot of clarified butter and the *kuśa* grass in his left ones; or else his two lower hands make the gesture of bestowing and that of absence of fear. His braided hair, shaped like a crown, adorns him.

36.6b–7 Sāvitrī is to his right and Bhāratī to his left; the Sages make up his retinue. His mount is the goose and his emblem the *kuśa* grass. Whether standing or seated Brahmā is on a lotiform pedestal.

Viṣṇu

36.8–10a Viṣṇu is provided with a tiara, armlets and bracelets; he is adorned with a hip girdle and other ornaments and his clothing is yellow. He has four arms and (his anterior hands make) the gesture of bestowing and that of absence of fear whilst, (in the other two), he holds the conch and the discus. He is immaculate. Whether he is standing or seated, Avanī is on his left and Ramā on his right. He is on a throne or is on a lotus; dark in colour he is immovable and shining.

36.10b It is prescribed that, in villages and other settlements, he be installed in the centre of the site and at the eight directions.

36.11–12a It is said that the radiance of Śrīlakṣmī and Bhūmi makes him shine and that his eyes are like lotuses. This is the one image that is to be installed by the sages for those who seek liberation. Garuḍa is said to be his emblem and his mount.

Varāha

36.12b–14a (Varāha's) two hands make the bestowing gesture and that of absence of fear; he carries Vasundharā on his arm and his foot is set upon the head of the king of the snakes. He is the colour of pure gold and he wears a sacrificial thread and is provided with all ornaments. The Varāha manifestation (of Viṣṇu) is thus described.

Trivikrama

36.14b–15a Trivikrama is standing, his back to the sanctum wall, the colour of a storm cloud and glittering with the brilliancy of five weapons; such also is Vāmana.

Nārasiṃha

36.15b–20a Nārasiṃha is the form of Viṣṇu with a lion's visage. Markedly fearsome and provided with terrifying fangs, he is exceedingly strong; his two crooked thighs are well fleshed and his mane is like a crown. He wears ear-pendants, has a big tongue and wears a resplendent tiara on his head. He is white and has a large body. Beneficent is he, yet impetuous as a torrent. He has eight or ten arms; his teeth and his nails are sharply pointed. Wearing a yellow sacrificial thread, adorned with garlands of flowers, he is provided with necklets, armlets, hip girdle and other adornments. The god is dressed in red; his two (principal) hands hold no weapons for the fight (against Hiraṇyakaśipu): with his bare hands he lacerates Hiraṇyakaśipu's gaping chest. Seated, in the manner indicated (?), he is honoured by all the gods.

36.20b–21a According to the knowledgeable, Nārasiṃha must be installed at the top of a mountain, in a cave, or in a forest in the depths of an enemy realm, so as to bring about the death of the adversary.

36.21b–24 In villages and other settlements though, he is to have four arms, hold the conch and the discus (in his upper hands) and is to be of glittering appearance. Nārasiṃha, provided with all decorations, wearing yellow clothing, immaculate, is to be installed in the north-west, standing or seated. (If he is seated) his legs are held in place by a band and his two (lower) hands (make) the *daṇḍa* gesture and that of the absence of fear, or other gestures; he must wear the belt of an ascetic. When he is standing on a lotiform pedestal, his two (lower) hands make the gesture of bestowing and that of absence of fear. He gives serenity, prosperity, victory, health, enjoyment, power and wealth.

Anantaśāyin

36.25–28a Anantaśāyin is to be represented on a couch which is in the shape of Ananta, which latter is to be in three coils and to have five or seven hoods. The head (of the god) is to be to the east or south; he has two arms and he glitters; his right hand holds the mace or supports his head and his left holds a flower. Thus is the Splendour of cosmic sleep; for the four *yuga*, beginning with Kṛtayuga, his colour is, respectively, white, yellow, black as khôl and dark; he is to be decorated as previously.

36.28b–30a On a lotus issuing from the navel of (Viṣṇu), is Dhātṛ, in meditation. Śrī and Bhūmi, each with a flower in hand, are to be placed near the head and near the feet (of

Viṣṇu); in both cases it is the hand nearest the god which holds a flower whilst the other hangs down to the knee. The left leg (of the god) is stretched out to the right of Śrī and Bhūmi (?).

36.30b–34a The conch, the discus, the mace, the bow and the sword are to be represented in their manifest forms; the Master of the conch is a dwarf who is white, the discus is a red man, the mace a gold-coloured woman, the bow a black man and the sword a dark woman adorned with all decorations; they are standing to the left (?) and they point the left hand in a menacing way whilst the right arm is raised; all of them wear multi-coloured raiment and each has his (eponymous) weapon on his head. Madhu and Kaiṭabha are to be represented as angry and standing beside (Viṣṇu). Surendra faces east and is accompanied by the other gods and by the great seers.

36.34b–35a Those who seek the happiness of all should install Hari, according to rule, in a settlement such as a village, at the centre of the site or outside of it, to the cardinal and intermediate directions.

Maheśvara

36.35b–38 With his shaggy hair, shining like pure gold, with well fleshed thighs, (Maheśvara) has hair which is stamped with the crescent moon with its intense rays; he has four arms and three eyes; he wears an amiable look and is in the prime of life; his chest is big and he is mounted on a bull. He carries a chain (?) and an elephant hook and a noose. Muscled and with an arm raised, his hand like an elephant's trunk (?), he has a necklace and anklets as well as bracelets, hip girdle and ear-pendants in serpent form; his garment is a tiger skin and his waist is clasped by a belt.

36.39–41 When he has eight or ten arms (Śiva) is provided with all adornments; his right hands hold the goad, trident, sword, mace and the fire and therefore, to the left, are the snake, the *khaṭvāṅga*, the shield, the skull and the noose in serpent form. Śiva is immaculate and dressed in a tiger skin. When Maheśvara has only eight arms, the mace and sword are omitted (from the list given above). Whether seated or standing, he has the bull for mount and for emblem.

36.42–43a (He is accompanied) by Bhṛṅgin, who dances, rejoicing in music and dance (?) and (who is represented) as above. The god is accompanied too by the Gaṇa with Nandin leading them, and he is honoured by the host of gods. He is to be installed in villages or towns by those who seek happiness for others.

The sixteen manifestations of Śiva.

36.43b–46a I now reveal the sixteen images (of the manifestations of Śiva), according to rule and in the following order: Sukhāsana, Vivāha, Umāskanda, Vṛṣārūḍha, Purāri, Nṛtta, Candraśekhara, Ardhanārī, Viṣṇvardha, Caṇḍeśānugraha, Kāmāri, Kālanāśa, Dakṣiṇāmūrti, Bhikṣāṭana, Mukhaliṅga and Liṅgasambhūta.

36.46b–48 These are the features common to the sixteen manifestations: (Śiva) has three eyes and four arms; he has the crescent moon for his crest and a tiger skin for his clothing; he is adorned with necklaces and armlets, provided with a sacrificial thread and adorned with two ear-pendants. Now, one by one, I present the images.

Sukhāsana

36.49–51a The god is comfortably seated on a seat and, of his (anterior) hands, one makes the gesture of bestowing and (the other) that of absence of fear; the axe is to be placed in his (posterior) right hand and the antelope in his left. His left leg is stretched along the seat whilst his right one hangs down in front of it. Anything not specified here is to be as given above. By paying homage to such an (image) of Sukhāsana, liberation can certainly be attained.

Kalyāṇa

36.51b–53a His body, slightly sway-hipped, in accordance

with one of the three modes and his left leg bent, the god is to hold, in his (anterior) right hand, the hand of the goddess whilst the left one makes the gesture of bestowing and the other two hold the antelope and the axe. Hara is provided with all sorts of adornment and wears a linen garment.

36.53b–56a The goddess should be so fashioned as to come up to the god's arm. She has two arms and two eyes; her countenance is pleasing, she is dark in colour and her appearance is delightful. She leans slightly forward and she wears armlets, bracelets and rings; there is a tiara on her head; Gaurī is adorned with all ornaments and wears a linen garment. She holds an *utpala* and her lotus feet are made to shine by her anklets. She is to be to the right of Śiva.

36.56b–58a Lakṣmī's colour is gold; she has two arms and two eyes and is provided with all ornaments and she is to be placed beside Umā. It is by Śilā (i.e. Himavat) or by a form of Viṣṇu, that the water is poured. Brahmā, on a lotus with sixteen petals, is turned towards the nuptial oblation.

36.58b–58c It is thus that Kalyāṇa is to be represented; he is accompanied by the host of all the gods; the deities, from the greatest down, are rendering him reverent homage. He bestows success upon all undertakings.

Umāskanda

36.59–60 Seated on a semi-circular throne with Gaurī on his left knee, (Śiva, in the form of) Umāsahita, holds the goddess in his arms. The sage must give Umā and Maheśvara the appearance which has previously been given for each of them and should place the goddess to the left of the god.

36.61–62a Skanda, with the appearance of a child, is to be placed between Umā and Śiva. When he is accompanied by Umā and Skanda, the god is to be represented sitting comfortably, according to rule. In the form of Umāskanda the god fulfils all wishes and desires.

Vṛṣārūḍha

36.62b–64 The couple composed of Umā and Maheśvara

is on a pedestal, behind which stands the bull. Śiva's (anterior) right arm lies along his body and his (anterior) left hand holds the trident; (his two posterior hands) hold the antelope and axe. Such is Vṛṣārūḍha; he is honoured for doing away with poverty and he gives success to all beings.

Tripurāntaka

36.65–67a (The god) is balanced on one leg, the other being bent; equipped with bow and arrow, antelope and axe, he is installed in a chariot drawn by a bull; the host of gods surrounds him and Umā accompanies him. It is thus that (Śiva), destroyer of Tripura, is to be depicted; homage is to be paid to Tripurasundara in order to bring about the death of an enemy.

Dancing forms

36.67b Now the dance of Śiva playing-with-the-serpent is described, which is also called "twilight dance".

36.68–69a (Śiva) holds the *ḍamaru* drum in his right hand and the fire is in the (corresponding) left one. In his (other) right hands he is to have the trident, axe, sword and arrow; in the left he holds the shield and the bow, makes the *daṇḍa* gesture and carries the noose.

36.69b–71 His feet are made radiantly beautiful by the delicate movement of the steps of the dance. His right leg is bent and his left foot lifted to the height of his (right) knee; the space between the (left) heel and the (right) knee may be three times the value of the height of the face; the displacement of the right leg (in relation to the axis of the image) is nine eighths of the distance indicated above and the displacement of the left leg is to be determined according to circumstance.

36.72–74a The face is upright but the body is slightly sway-hipped, according to one of the three modes. The thumb of the right hand which makes the absence of fear gesture (?) points towards the nipples; the (right) hand which holds the *ḍamaru* is raised to the ear lobe; the left arm, like an elephant's trunk, goes down to the level of the left foot and the sage is to arrange the left hand holding the fire in such a way that it comes up to the shoulders.

36.74b–75a It is the same for the distance between armpit and arm (?)[1]. (Śiva) carries a tiger skin (arranged) (?) in regular fashion; he makes the serpent gesture with one left hand and with a right one, or with a left, makes that of absence of fear (?).

36.75b–76 His flying, knotted locks are ornamented with cranes' feathers; his knotted coil of hair, which is encircled by a garland of skulls, has the moon in it and his flying locks are five, seven or nine.

36.77–80a On his left is Gaurī (whose height is) a third (that of Śiva) and, to his left, Nandikeśvara; both are rejoiced by the dance and the music, and Bhṛṅgin, who dances, is represented as above. Accompanied by gods, demons, Gandharva, Siddha and by Vidyādhara, (Śiva) is surrounded by the Sages and honoured by the multitude of the gods. He is on a pedestal or a lotus. (The dancing form) called "(dance) of dread caused by the serpent", is to be installed in the same manner but (with the additional) Apasmāra as support for the (right) foot (of Śiva). The worship of dancing forms (of Śiva) brings in return the immediate death of an enemy.

Candraśekhara

36.80b–81a The god who-has-the-moon-as-crest is represented standing perfectly upright; (of his anterior hands) (one) makes the gesture of absence of fear and (the other) that of bestowing whilst the (other two) hold the antelope and the axe.

Ardhanārīśvara

36.81b–83a The left half corresponds to Umā and the right to Īśa. (The right half) has hair in a matted coil of bright

1. This half-verse seems to pertain to an iconometric description of Śiva.

yellow with vivid decorations; the left half, that of Umā, has a *dhammilla* hair arrangement with curls and a parting and has a mark on the forehead. A pendant in the form of Vāsuki is arranged in the right ear and, in the left, a *tālika* pendant or a *pālika* one.

36.83b–85a The two right hands hold the skull, or the trident, and the axe. The single left hand holds an *utpala* and (the corresponding arm) is adorned with armlet and bracelet. The sacrificial thread is arranged (on the) right (of the bust) and a rosary on the left. The left half of the neck wears a necklace and the right half is the colour of fire (?).

36.85b–86 The half corresponding to Umā has a breast and the right half pectoral muscles. The right half of the waist wears a garment made of a tiger skin and the Umā half a hip girdle and a long garment in several colours.

36.87–88a The two feet, that of the god and that of the goddess, rest on the same lotus but the left leg, decorated with an anklet, is slightly bent; the left foot, that of the goddess, is decorated and wears rings.

36.88b–89 The half corresponding to Īśa is red and that to Umā dark coloured. The sage makes the statue of Ardhanārīśvara, giving him the characteristics (indicated for both the deities of whom he is composed).

Harihara

36.90–91 The half corresponding to Viṣṇu and that corresponding to Īśvara are to be made in accordance with what has previously been said (concerning each of these two gods). The half corresponding to Kṛṣṇa has the conch and the mace and that to Śiva the trident and the axe. Each part is covered with the decoration befitting (the one represented) and the god is to stand on a single lotus. The Viṣṇu half is to the left and that of Śaṅkara to the right.

Caṇḍeśānugraha

36.92–93a Śiva is in the posture of the "drawer of the bow"

and Caṇḍeśa, hands folded on breast, has an axe between his forearms; he carries the garland of flowers (offered by Śiva) and shines with an extraordinary light. Thus is the image of He-who-bestows-the-boon-upon-Caṇḍeśvara.

Kāmāri

36.93b–95a Now comes the description of (Śiva)-adversary-of-Kāma. Kāma is placed next to the god and his appearance is described thus: he is approaching (Śiva's) bed of rest (?) and, bowing, holds his hands up in front of him. (Śiva, in the form of) Kāmāri is represented in terrifying aspect and with the characteristics (previously indicated).

Kālanāśa

36.95b–97 (The god) has his right leg forward and the left bent; in his (anterior) right hand he holds the trident and in the left the axe; his (other) right hand holds the noose in the form of a serpent and his (other) left one is pointed (in menacing fashion). His (right) foot presses upon the heart of Kāla and his trident points downwards. Thus is Śiva, in the guise of the Slayer of Kāla; his appearance is terrifying and his eyes ferocious.

Dakṣiṇāmūrti

36.98 One of Śiva's right hands makes the teaching gesture and the other holds the *akṣa* rosary whilst his left hands hold book and fire. He is represented in white and with three eyes.

36.99–101 His hair hangs in tawny ringlets, has the (crescent) moon in it and is decorated with skulls and with *arka* and *dhurdhūra* flowers. He is seated and his left leg rests on his right thigh. He should be represented on a throne with the Apasmāra as his foot rest. The god, encircled by the Sages, and in the aspect of Dakṣiṇāmūrti, is on the top of a hill; he is master of wild beasts, of birds and of sages.

Bhikṣāṭanamūrti

36.102–103 The Mendicant is to be represented naked, with three eyes and four arms; in his left hands are the peacock's tail and the skull; one of his right hands stretches out towards the mouth of an antelope and the other holds high the *ḍamaru*; the god wears sandals on his feet; he is represented about to begin walking.

Kaṅkālamūrti

36.104–105 Otherwise Maheśvara may have eight, four or six arms; adorned with precious stones, pearls and snakes, he wears an ear-pendant in serpent form (on the right) and a *pālika* or *patra* pendant on the left. The god is white and has three eyes; there is a dagger at his belt and he is dressed in a tiger skin.

36.106–107a He has sandals on his feet and his hands hold a (bowl) made of half a tortoise shell. (Śiva, in the form of) Kaṅkāla, wears a fine garment; he is adorned with all ornaments, accompanied by the host of Bhūta and surrounded by women distracted by passion.

Mukhaliṅga

36.107b–110a Now I present (Śiva in the form of) Liṅga with faces; (it is to be installed) so that all desires may be fulfilled. The width (of the element-of-)-Śiva makes up three tenths of the height of the Liṅga; two tenths of its height are for the shoulders, one for the neck, three for the visage, one for the top of the head, two for the hair arrangement and one for the (top of) the Liṅga (which is showing above). The thickness of the face is a (tenth of the height of the element of Śiva) and its width is that of the upper (element) of the Liṅga. The Viṣṇu and Pitāmaha elements are to be treated as for a Ṛṣi Liṅga.

36.110b–111 The forehead, the (crescent) moon, the mouth, the lips, the nostrils, as well as eyes, ears, cheeks and head: these are all represented, by the perfectly knowledgeable one, in the manner which has been prescribed for a manifest image and with the heights, widths and thicknesses prescribed.

36.112–113 Now the particular features of the four faces are presented. The face to the east is that of Tatpuruṣa; it has three eyes and is smiling; the knotted hair bears the crescent moon and is red like *kuṅkuma*; it has earrings in the form of *makara* and the eyes are (wide) as lotus leaves.

36.114–115 The south face is that of Aghora; it has lion's eyes, a lion's mouth and its colour is that of lapis lazuli; it is adorned with snake earrings and the mouth is obstructed by snakes; the loose locks are stamped with the crescent moon. It has fangs, a thick tongue, a reddish beard and three eyes.

36.116–118 The west face is pure and pleasant, it is adorned with ear-pendants and precious stones; its knotted, coiled locks are mingled with snakes and bear the crescent moon; the face is like the full moon and is called Sadyojāta. (The face) which is on the north, (that of Vāmadeva), has the lustre of *bandhu* flowers; the knotted coiled hair bears the crescent moon; it has ear-pendants and the mark is on the forehead; with decoration appropriate to a young girl, this face sparkles due to its *dhammilla* hair arrangement. It is said that the Liṅga may have one, two, three or four faces. [. . . *gap* . . .][1]

Ṣaṇmukha

36.119–120a Ṣaṇmukha, who is provided with all ornamentation is the colour of *kuṅkuma*; the two goddesses Gajā and Vallī are, respectively, on his right and left; the first is yellow, the second dark in colour, and they are provided with all ornaments.

36.120b–121 Ṣaṇmukha is to be installed in villages and other settlements, either in the centre or at the four cardinal points. Installed at the beginning of, or midway along, a street he increases power; if enjoyment is sought he is to be placed in the west, if liberation, in the centre.

1. The missing portion of the text contained the description of the Liṅgasambhūtamūrti (see the list given above vv. 43–46).

Gaṇādhipa

36.122–124a He has an elephant's face and only one tusk; he is upright and holds himself to the right; he has three eyes; he is red; he has four arms and looks like a dwarf with a huge belly; a snake is his sacrificial thread. His thighs and knees are fat and heavy; he is seated on a lotiform throne with left leg stretched out and right bent. His trunk uncoils to the left.

36.124b–125 In one of his right hands he holds his broken tusk and, in the other, an elephant hook; the *akṣa* rosary should be in one of his left hands and a sweetmeat in the other. His hair is coiled into a tiara; he is adorned with necklaces and other jewels.

36.126 This is Gaṇādhipa who may also be standing on a lotiform pedestal. When he is dancing he has six or four arms. The rat is his mount [and his emblem].

Sūrya

36.127–129a The big chariot (of Sūrya), with only one wheel, is drawn by seven horses and Aruṇa drives it. (Sūrya) has two hands, each holding a lotus; his chest is covered by a breast-plate. His beautiful hair is uncurled and he is adorned by a nimbus. He may also wear a cloak. He wears gold jewellery and precious stones; he may also be given a tiara and any kind of beautiful ornamentation.

36.129b–131 (Sūrya) is to be installed in his human form, with a single face and two arms and with a lotus in each hand whose extremity touches the shoulder. He is to be represented on a horse (?) or on a lotus, as appropriate for private worship. On the vermillion nimbus of Sūrya is the dark coloured Uṣā and the golden Pratyuṣā.

36.132 When Sūrya has four arms, his two (posterior) hands hold a red lotus whilst the front two make the gesture of absence of fear and that of bestowing.

36.133a Aruṇa, the charioteer, has two arms and stands up in the chariot.

36.133b–136a This god is the unique soul of all the worlds

and his body is always to be incomplete. The (image of) the Lord of day must be installed because He is Brahmā, Viṣṇu, Śiva and the other gods. The two goddesses, Prabhā and Sandhyā are to be to his left and right, respectively. The planets and his other attendants are to be arranged around him in fifteen rows. Both for festivals and for regular worship, the rule is that given in the Āgama. It is said that Sūrya may have the lion for standard and for mount.

LORDS OF THE DIRECTIONS

Indra

36.136b–138 He who has the thunderbolt in his hand has huge arms, the shoulders of a lion and big eyes; he wears a tiara, ear-pendants, necklaces and armlets; his mount is an elephant. He has two arms, is black and wears a red garment; he is benevolent (?). His forehead, breast and legs are adorned with all ornaments; he has big eyes and a thick neck: the king of the gods, the spouse of Śacī.

Agni

36.139–140 Agni has the appearance of an old man; he stands upon a semi-circular pedestal and shines like pure gold; his eyebrows and eyes are russet. He has a golden beard and hair of the same tone and wears a garment the colour of the rising sun and a sacrificial thread in the same shade.

36.141–142a In his right hand is a *karaka* pitcher and, in his left, an *akṣa* rosary. He has seven weapons and a form rendered brilliant by his curls and braids which are seven rays of light (?); glowing from his garland of fire and dazzling, he is surrounded by a nimbus of fire.

36.142b–143 He is mounted on a ram and is near a firepit and he must wear the ascetic's belt. Svāhā is on his right, adorned with jewelled earrings. Agni, whose adornments are russet and who is favourable towards all sacrifices, is pure.

Yama

36.144 He who holds the mace in one hand and the noose in the other has eyes like dazzling fires. Mounted on a big buffalo, he is the colour of khôl and he shines.

36.145–147a He is surrounded by his enchmen who resemble him; they have muscled chests and they are divine; these are the "catchers" (?) who are extremely strong; they stand at the door and are cruel, since they spread fear throughout the worlds. Citragupta and Kali are in the south and north respectively, the one black and the other dark; dressed in red they are attentive.

36.147b–149a Next to the throne (of Yama) are Mṛtyu and Saṃhita, in terrible aspect; on each side is a woman holding a fan one dark and the other red: on the right, Dharmā, Adharmā on the left. Yama must be seated and he has the buffalo as emblem and mount.

Nirṛtti

36.149b–150 Nirṛtti has big eyes; he holds a sword in his hand; he has big arms. His clothing is yellow; he is mounted (on a corpse), is dark and enormously strong. He is adorned with all ornaments but the Lord of the world [has no companion].

Varuṇa

36.151–152 He who holds the noose in his hand, is white as the moon, as jasmine, as shells, and he is very strong. Adorned with two sorts of gold earrings as well as with necklaces and armlets, he wears yellow raiment, is incomparable, is golden is colour and nothing but joy. Whether seated or standing, Varuṇa must be on a *makara*.

Vāyu

36.153–154a He with the flag in his hand is very strong, his eyes are red and he is a smoky colour; Vāyu has arched eyebrows and he is clothed in motley colours. He rides a gazelle and is to be installed with all adornments.

Kubera

36.154b–156 Kubera, chief of all Yakṣa, must be adorned with a crown and other ornaments. He has the glow of pure gold and one of his hands makes the gesture of bestowing, the other, absence of fear. Mounted on a ram, he has a sword in his hand and has two legs and two hands (?). Riding a man, he is surrounded by (?) Śaṅkhanidhi and Padmanidhi. The sage represents him provided with all ornaments and accompanied by his wife.

Candra

36.157–159a Candra sits on a lion throne; he is (white) as a conch and as jasmine. Encircled by a nimbus he has two arms and his face is white. Whether he is standing or seated his hands shine with the lotuses he holds. The strands of his sacrificial thread are gold. Soma is pleasant; he increases and decreases. He wears garlands and white clothing, is the colour of gold and has red eyes.

36.159b–161a Revatī and Rohiṇī hold ears of wheat; their eyes are like shining lotuses, their raiment is black and they are immaculate. Niśā and Jyotsnā are in the west, each holding a fan; it is said that Niśā is the wife of Śaśin and that Jyotsnā is the light of mankind.

Īśāna

36.161b–162a He who rides a bull is very powerful; he is white with white eyes; Lord of the world, he holds a trident, has three eyes and is the world's benefactor.

Kāma

36.162b–163 Kāma is gold coloured and adorned with all jewels; he has two arms; his appearance is charming and pleasant and he is all yellow. Whether on a throne or in a chariot, he illumines all the worlds.

36.164–167a Haima, Mada, Rāga and Vasanta are his companions; Tāpanī, Dāhinī, Sarvamohinī, Viśvamardinī and Māraṇī, the teeth of lovers, are his five arrows. His sugarcane bow and his five arrows are to be placed in the west (?). Rati is on his right; she is dark coloured . . . (?) and adorned with all ornaments; her mass of hair is loose and scintillating. Such is Smara to be, whose emblem is said to be the *makara*.

The two Aśvin

36.167b–170 The two Aśvin are seated on a lion throne and look like horses; they have the brilliance of *dāḍimī* flowers and they both wear sacrificial threads on each shoulder. Thus are to be represented these two healers. There are, too, a pair of female fan bearers; the one who is Mṛtasañjīvanī is shown in yellow and Viśālyakaraṇī is red and is to the rear. There are two (other) (?) women, one yellow, the other reddish. Dhanvantari and Atreya are on the left; the one is yellow, the other red and both are dressed in black.

The Vasu

36.171–173a They hold sword and shield, are adorned with all jewels, have two arms and are red, wear white raiment and are immaculate; whether seated or standing, they are terrible. Such are the eight Vasu: Dhara, Dhruva, Soma, Āpa, Anala, Anila, Pratyūṣa and Prabhāva.

The Marut

36.173b–174 (The eight Marut) have coiled knotted hair that beautiful women love to caress with their breasts; all carry divine flowers and are garbed in white linen; these are the eight Marut whose images are appropriate in all sacrifices.

The Rudra and the Vidyeśvara

36.175 The (eleven) Rudra resemble a furious fire (?). The (Vidyeśvara) are blue-black and red like blood, as to the first amongst them and, then, dark like a cloud (?), (red) like *kuṅkuma* and (dark) like crushed khôl.

36.176 The (Vidyeśvara) have four arms and three eyes; they carry axe and trident (in their posterior hands) and make the gesture of bestowing and that of absence of fear (with their two other hands). They are dressed in linen and are immaculate.

36.177 Ananta, Sūkṣma, Śivotkṛṣṭa, and Ekanetraka, as well as Ekarudra, Trimūrti, Śrīkhaṇḍa and Śikhaṇḍin: these are the eight Vidyeśvara who attend all sacrifices.

Kṣetrapāla

[. . . *gap* . . .][1]

36.178–179a . . . in his *tāmasa* form he is black like a storm cloud. In *sāttvika* form he has two or four arms; when he is *rājasa* he has six and, when *tāmasa*, eight. Locations (appropriate to him) are in the countryside.

36.179b–180a When he has two arms he holds the skull and the trident or the *khaṭvāṅga* and the axe; when he has four arms (his posterior hands hold the attributes just given) and his (anterior) ones make the gesture of bestowing and that of absence of fear.

36.180b–181a (When he has six arms) he has the trident, sword and bell in his right hands and, in his left, the shield, skull and serpent noose.

36.181b–182 When he has eight arms he holds the arrow and the bow in addition to the attributes just mentioned. He is then as he is in *rājasa* form and has hair that stands up and that floats, arched eyebrows, three eyes and two terrifying fangs.

1. The missing portion probably indicated that the *sāttvika* form is white and the *rājasa* red.

36.183–185 Protector of the hosts who are at the ends of roads, he looks like a child and a dog is his mount. He is to be placed outside settlements, such as villages, whether at the gates, in a wood or on a mountain. He is to be to the east or north-east, at the position of Parjanya or of Diti. When he is seated on a lotiform throne he fulfils all desires; when he has four or six arms . . . (?) he is honoured by dogs, cocks and other creatures, and is encircled by Yoginī and Siddha.

Caṇḍeśvara

36.186–187a Caṇḍeśvara is a beautiful red mixed with white. He has two arms; his hair is wreathed by leaves and he has *śaṅkha* and *patra* (types of ear-pendants); he wears a sacrificial thread, his clothing is white and he is immaculate.

36.187b–188 His hands are joined over his heart, an axe is between his arms, he sits on a semi-circular seat and is adorned with a garland of flowers. He is adorned with all ornaments and has his hair braided or knotted in a coil.

The Āditya

36.189–190a The twelve Bhāskara all have [two arms and hold a lotus]; each is set on a lotiform pedestal; they have jewelled ear-pendants, are adorned with all ornaments and wear red clothes.

36.190b–191 Aryaman is the first, then come Mitra, Varuṇa, Bhaga, Indra, Vivasvant, Pūṣan, Parjanya as well as Tvaṣṭṛ, Viṣṇu, Ajaghanya and Jaghanyaja.

The seven Sages

36.192–194a The seven Sages make the gesture of teaching, stretching out (their hands); they have coiled hair, are dressed in various colours, have two arms and reddish eyes; they are yellow and very old; they wear red clothes, have knotted hair and are adorned with various jewels (?).

The seven Rohiṇī

36.194b–195a The seven Rohiṇī are beautiful; they are the colour of gold, serpents are their adornment and they may be seated or standing.

Garuḍa

36.195b–198a Tārkṣya is a [man?] with rounded eyes; he is yellow and very strong. He has two arms and his hands are joined, or rest lightly on his thighs (?). He wears a breast-plate, is of five colours and has red wings. He has fangs; the tip of his nose is dark and his hair is coiled into a glowing crown. Serpents are his adornment; his ears are full of yellow feathers and his clothing is red. He is the enemy of snakes and is the mount of Viṣṇu.

Śāstā

36.198b–200 Śāstā, the offspring of Mohinī, has two arms and is dark in colour. He is on a seat with his (left) leg folded and the right hanging. His left arm resembles an elephant's trunk and rests on the seat beyond his left knee and thigh. He (holds a stick, whose extremity) is rounded, or a twisted one. His curling hair is coated with crushed and shining unguent.

36.201–202a He has an elephant as emblem and mount; he wears ornaments, including necklaces. He may also have a blue-black horse or a bull for mount. When he has four arms and three eyes, that is when his emblem will invariably be the cock.

36.202b–204a Knower, Perpetual seeker (in texts) or Saint, he sits in the ascetic's posture. He is young and he wears a sacrificial thread on each shoulder and is sitting in *vīrāsana*. Essence of music and games, Essence of gods, sitting comfortably, his right leg resting on his left thigh, He is resplendent.

36.204b–206a He is accompanied by nine Śakti and surrounded by sixty-four Yoginī. Of his two wives, Pūrṇā is on his left and Puṣkalā on his right, (Pūrṇā) being black and (Puṣkalā) the colour of gold. Both hold a *saugandhya* flower and both are adorned with jewels; (Pūrṇā) is clothed in yellow and (Puṣkalā) in white.

36.206b–208a His maker-of-*madhu* is to be placed on his left; he is the shade of honey and has two arms; he is fat, his face is open and his plumpness pronounced; in his left hand is a bowl of fermented cane juice alcohol and, in his right, a mace. Daṇḍin and Lāṅgalin are the doorkeepers of his shrine and are armed with spears.

36.208b–210 Śāstā, beloved of the gods, is to be installed in the haunts of lower castes, in the houses of courtesans and in forts as well as in *nigama*, *kharvaṭa* and *kheṭa*. He is Essence of gods, Essence of knowledge; those who seek what is good must install him in villages and other settlements, whether in the centre or outside the site or to the right of the gates. When he is Essence of music, he may be installed in a town or a port.

The Mothers

36.211–212 I now present the characteristics of the Mothers as well as (the rules relating) to their installation and (to the choice) of their position. They are: Brāhmī, Māheśvarī, Kaumārī, Vaiṣṇavī, Vārāhī, Indrāṇī, and Kālī. Vīrabhadra Vināyaka are to the right and left (respectively) of the Mothers.

Vīrabhadra

36.213–214a Vīrabhadra is mounted on a bull and holds the trident (in one of his upper hands) and the mace (in the other); his two (lower hands) hold the *vīṇā* or else make the gestures of absence of fear and bestowing, respectively. He has four arms and three eyes; his coiled hair is adorned with the crescent moon.

36.214b–215 He is provided with all jewels and is white and he has the bull for emblem. The god, seated on a lotiform seat, rests his back against a banyan. He is the Lord of the world, Śaṅkara, Śambhu, who is at the head of the Mothers.

Brahmāṇī

36.216–217 She has four arms and large eyes; she is the colour of pure gold. One of her four arms makes the bestowing gesture, one the gesture of absence of fear and the other two hold the trident and *akṣa* rosary. She is seated on a red lotus and has the goose for mount and emblem. Brahmāṇī is to be in the image of Brahmā; she is dressed in a tiger skin (?)[1].

Māheśvarī

36.218–219 (Māheśvarī) has three eyes; she is red, holds the trident and has the bull for emblem; she makes the gestures of bestowing and absence of fear and she holds the *akṣa* rosary. Māheśvarī's hair is coiled into a crown and she is adorned after the fashion of Śambhu. She is represented beside a *candana* tree and mounted on the bull.

Kaumārī

36.220–222a (Kaumārī) has her hair tied in a cloth (?), she holds the spear and the cock; she is red, she is powerful and is adorned with necklaces and armlets. She makes the gesture of bestowing and that of absence of fear and is the colour of *kuṅkuma*. She is provided with all jewellery and has the peacock for emblem and for mount. The well advised man represents Kaumārī with her back to an *udumbara*.

Vaiṣṇavī

36.222b–224a The goddess holds the conch and the discus and makes the gesture of bestowing and that of absence of fear. She stands straight and her colour is black, her garments are yellow and she has beautiful eyes. Her tree is the peepul; Garuḍa is her emblem and her mount. The sage represents Vaiṣṇavī adorned with Viṣṇu's ornaments.

1. The text is corrupt and the name of the tree specific to Brahmāṇī is missing.

Vārāhī

36.224b–227a Vārāhī makes the gestures of bestowing and absence of fear; she holds the mace and the plough; she is dressed in leather (or else) she is (white) as a conch (?); she makes the gestures of bestowing and absence of fear and holds a mace. She has fangs, a big body and her crown sparkles. This goddess, who is dressed in black, is provided with all ornaments and has the *karañja* for her tree and the buffalo as mount and emblem.

Indrāṇī

36.227b–228 The goddess wears a tiara and is adorned with all jewels; she makes the gestures of bestowing and absence of fear and holds the noose and the lotus; her colour is that of the moon. Indrāṇī is to be represented by the sages with *kalpa-druma* for her tree.

Cāmuṇḍī

36.229–231a Cāmuṇḍī holds the skull and the trident and makes the gestures of bestowing and absence of fear. (Otherwise) she is represented with eight arms; she holds, in addition to the trident and the skull: the mace, the bow, the sword, the shield, the noose and the arrow, on the left (?). Such are (the attributes) (held) in her eight hands. When she has ten arms however, the *ḍamaru* and the trident (?) are to be added to what has already been given.

36.231b–233a She has red eyes; she is seated aslant (?) and has a cobra in place of a breast band; she wears a garland of heads as sacrificial thread and her mount is a corpse. She has a thin stomach and she is skeletal; her mouth is wide open, her tongue is thick and she has three eyes. She is clothed in a tiger skin and has a hair arrangement of bristling snakes. She grants wishes.

36.233b–234a Kālī's limbs are emaciated and she is black

and has her back to a banyan. Her face is marked by terrifying fangs; Cāmuṇḍī's emblem is a vulture.

Vināyaka

36.234b The sage is to represent Vināyaka, giving him the appearance already indicated.

Installation of the Mothers

36.235–236a (The Mothers are to be installed) at a great distance from a village and to the north and north-east, in the form of tridents, after they have been invoked with (the formula) ŚŪLA and incense has been offered them (?); they must face east or north and they are to be near to the main door (of the place).

36.236b–237 After they have been installed (in the centre of the site), starting from the right, an increase in serenity, prosperity, success, health, pleasure, power and longevity may be observed; should they be installed starting from the left however, this will certainly bring about the insanity of the enemy.

36.238–239a If the rule indicated above is followed, but with Brahmāṇī placed in the centre (each time), this installation which mystifies all people, brings the satisfaction of all desires; when Cāmuṇḍī is in the centre it is the obtaining of children which is sought through the installation.

36.239b–240a (For he who seeks) the mastery of self (the Mothers must be) in *kāmāsana*; for serenity, *vīrāsana*, and the *sukhāsana* posture shows that (the installation) brings the satisfaction of all desires (?).

New description of Cāmuṇḍī

36.240b–242 The sage may also represent Cāmuṇḍī with eight or ten arms or with twelve or sixteen, using wood, earth or stucco. He may also make her with eight arms and in conformity (with what has been given for Śiva) dancing; or (he may represent her) beside (Śiva) dancing the twilight dance or as (Śiva) dancing that same dance. When the image has six or four arms it brings perfect serenity to the world.

The Mothers' Attendants

36.243 The guardians placed outside the door are dwarves armed with tridents and other weapons; they are fearsome, and are accompanied by a band of dwarves and surrounded by Piśāca.

36.244–246a Inside the pavilion (which is in front of the shrine) two beautiful young women of pleasing appearance are to be installed; one is red, the other dark and it is said that these two women are Yoginī; they each have a skull and bones in their hands and they have *vyāla* for mounts; they have the *dhammilla* hair arrangement, and their hair, which is parted, glitters; they are provided with all jewels, have comely faces and three eyes.

36.246b–247a Dwarves are to be installed there too and vampires, Ḍākinī and other monsters of the kind. (In the worship of the Mothers) the regular rituals prescribed in the Mantrasāśtra, and in the Yāmala(-tantra),[1] must be performed.

Lakṣmī

36.247b–252a Lakṣmī is seated on a lotus; she has two arms; she is golden and shines with gold and jewels; one of her earpendants is in *makara* form whilst the other is in the form of a conch. She is a beautiful, accomplished young woman whose limbs are harmonious and who plays with her arched eyebrows. Her figure is rounded; she has *karṇapūra* and her eyes are like lotuses; her lips are red, her cheeks plump and her breast covered with a bodice. Lotus, parting, conch and discus are her head ornaments. It is prescribed that a lotus be placed in

1. The *Yāmalatantra* is a collection of *śākta* texts dealing with the worship of the Goddess.

her right hand and the *śrīphala* in her left. Her beautiful breasts and large hips are covered with a fine garment; she wears a waist girdle and a hip girdle. Her hair is arranged in a tiara (?) and she is sitting in lotus posture.

36.252b–253a Female fan bearers should be represented at her sides, along with two elephants which sprinkle her from vases which they hold with their trunks.

36.253b–255 For domestic worship, Lakṣmī is represented with four arms; (her two anterior hands) make the gestures of bestowing and absence of fear and she is illustrious with the brilliance of the red lotuses (which she holds in her posterior hands). She is provided with all ornamentation and is brilliant or pure gold in shade; she is seated in *paryaṅkabandhāsana* on a lotus. Lakṣmī who fulfils all desires is represented thus.

Yakṣinī

36.256–257 Yakṣinī [Hemamālā] is shown with the characteristics (of Lakṣmī) but has no elephant. Siddha and Apsaras worship her; she sings with the Kinnara and is venerated by Yakṣa and Gandharva. She should be installed, it is said, inside and outside villages and other such places.

Kātyāyanī

36.258–260a Kātyāyanī stands, in the act of chopping off the buffalo's head; she wears a tiara; she is covered with ornaments and has ten arms. (In her right hands) she holds: the spear, arrow, mace, trident and sword and, in the left, a buffalo skin (?), shield (?), bow, elephant hook and the noose in the form of a snake. All her lotus hands bear these weapons.

36.260b–262 She has a fine garment and blue-black hair; her eyes are like the leaves of a blue-black lotus; she may also have three eyes. Her limbs are harmonious, her breasts swelling and upstanding and her chest is beautiful. She is dark and is clasped by serpents in lieu of a breast band. She is mounted on a lion and has the lion for emblem and she is dressed in a lion skin. Kātyāyanī has ten arms and stands on a buffalo's head.

Durgā

36.263–264 The goddess has four arms and stands on a lotiform pedestal. It is said that her (anterior) hands make the gestures of bestowing and absence of fear and that (her posterior hands) hold, one the conch and the other the discus. When she has eight arms her shield and spear are omitted (from the list previously given) and she then holds a parrot. This is Durgā (who may be installed) in a fortified place or in a settlement such as a village.

Sarasvatī

36.265–266a Sarasvatī whose hair is braided (?) has four arms; she is seated on a white lotus and wears ear-pendants of precious stones as well as a sacrificial thread and beautiful pearl necklaces; she has lovely eyes.

36.266b–268a With her (anterior) right hand she makes the gesture of teaching (and her posterior hand) holds an *akṣa* rosary; in her left hands are a hook and a *kuṇḍika* pitcher. She has three eyes and her appearance is pleasing; her face is upright. She is worshipped by sages and is perfect. People in quest of the god should install her in the centre of the site (of a settlement), or at one of the four cardinal points.

Jyeṣṭhā

36.268b–271a Jyeṣṭhā has pendulous lips, prominent nose and fallen breasts and stomach. She is the elder sister of Mahālakṣmī and holds red lotuses in her hand. The spouse of Kali is seated on a throne, legs hanging. She is dressed in red and is dark in colour. She is born in the same instant as ambrosia. She is adorned with all ornaments and her hair is held in place by a band of cloth; she has a crow for her emblem and she wears the convex mark upon her forehead.

36.271b–273 Her son has a bull's face and is seated comfortably, a mace in his hand. He has large arms and is white; he should be installed to the south (of Jyeṣṭhā) whilst her daughter is to the north; she has beautiful breasts, fine clothes and a pleasing appearance; she is black and wears all ornaments. In every (Jyeṣṭhā?) temple, at each door, there must be a young girl or . . . ?

Bhūmi

36.274–275 Bhūmi is dark like an ear of wheat and her eyes are big like lotuses; she has big eyes, wears the mark on her forehead and her hair is curly. She is adorned with all jewels and has a flower in her hand and she is beautiful; her tiara shines. She, who supports all beings, is dressed in yellow and is seated on a throne.

Pārvatī

36.276–277a (Pārvatī) has a comely face, a sweet look and she is marvellously beautiful; she is provided with all jewels, is dark in colour and has two arms. She is dressed in linen, has a lotus in her hand and is extremely pleasant.

36.277b–278 This accomplished woman who is Pārvatī is to be installed, surrounded by all her attendants, at one of the cardinal points or in the centre (of the settlement) or at the place of Bhallāṭa. Worshipped by Siddha and Vidyādhara, she grants all wishes.

Saptamātā

36.279–280 Saptamātā is to be installed on the outside of villages and towns. She has a heavy body and fat stomach and is flanked by two young women. She is black, has big eyes, red clothing and two arms. She is especially worshipped by Bhūta, Preta and Piśāca.

Buddha

36.281–283 Buddha is represented sitting with his legs crossed. He has red clothing, two arms, a red mantle and a russet (under)-garment; he has no head ornaments. He is seated on a lion throne and venerated by Indra and the other gods, as well as by Yakṣa, Vidyādhara, Siddha, Gandharva etc. . . . ; he is to be represented thus, with the appearance proper to him and with *aśvattha* next to him.

The Jina

36.284–287a The Jina, who is blue-black like khôl, is installed beneath as *aśoka*. He stands on a lotus throne or on a lion throne. His arms lie along his body, his regard is fixed on the points of his nipples; his proportions are those of a god and the height of the fan bearer is thirty digits, (taking as starting point the image) of the god. The rest is as has been given above but his body must be [naked]. He must be worshipped by the gods and other deities and must have a triple parasol. His hanging arms, the liana which surrounds him and the jewels (?) are each the appropriate colour (?). He has two arms.

36.287b–288a [Next to him], Yakṣendra [and Aparājitā, both of whose heads come up to his belt] are to be represented as has been given above (?) by the knowers of treatises and by those who have crossed the ocean of technique.

General rule

36.288b–291 When it is any other god who is to be represented, then the characteristic signs peculiar to him are to be shown. Serpents with seven or three coils, Rākṣasa, Piśāca, beings resembling Rudra (?), Preta and all the sorts of dwarves, vampires and others of that ilk are to be designed with the appearance proper to them. All are to be placed according to circumstances and in all the desired places. I have thus described in full the characteristics of images.

Proportions of images

36.292–294a It is said that the height of an image is equal to that of its founder or to that height, less one or two eighths, according to whether the image is large, medium or small. It may or may not be made in the likeness (of the founder), according to preference. It is said as well that the (statue) is as high as the shoulders, nipples or navel of the founder, according to whether it is large, medium or small, but (this system of calculation) is to be avoided when (the founder) is a hunchback or a dwarf.

36.294b–296a The height of the vertical reference line once determined, from the height of the temple, of the cella, of the pillars, of the door or of the architect, the sage is to divide it into equal digits. The practised man, avoiding fractions of digits and playing with addition and subtraction, puts these dimensions into harmony with (the formulae) of plus and of minus, of the asterisms, days, eight matrices and fractions.

36.296b–298 The Sages say that the plus and minus correspond respectively to the gain and loss.[1] The height of the image having been multiplied by eight, nine and three, (the products obtained) are divided by, respectively, twelve, eight and eight, which correspond, respectively, to plus, minus and the matrices. If the plus is higher and the minus lower, this is a source of success. Amongst the eight matrices [. . . *gap* . . .].

36.299 It is said that the best height for an image is equal to one and a half times that of the pillars; or, it is said that (the height of the image) is eight ninths or seven eighths that of the pillars which gives two possible dimensions.

36.300–301 There are other (different ways) of obtaining the height of an image. Depending upon whether the image is large, medium or small, the three possible heights will be fifteen, ten or five cubits. The dimensions calculated from those of the temple are to be used for small buildings, and those calculated in cubits when the buildings are not small.

36.302–303 Starting from thirty-one digits and going up to nine cubits and seven digits by successive increments of six digits, thirty-three heights are obtained, which are those prescribed by those knowledgeable in measurements for (images of) temples which are five to twelve cubits (wide).

1. See above 9.18 (p. 26).

Dimensions of portable images

36.304–305a According to the greatest sages, the specific heights of portable images are a seventh, a sixth, a fifth, a quarter, a third or half that of the principal image.

36.305b–307a The height of a portable image, calculated from the dimensions of the Liṅga, is equal to the venerated part (of that Liṅga) if the image in question is small, to that height increased by a half if it is medium and to double that height if it is a big image. According to the second method, the calculation of the height of a portable image, from the height of a Liṅga, gives a height half or three quarters of the venerated part, or equal to it, depending on the circumstance.

36.307b–309a Starting from thirteen digits and going up to thirty-one by successive increments of two digits, is how ten possible heights are obtained for a portable image. If this image is intended for a private house however, (its height) goes from three to fifteen digits (by successive increments) of half a digit. [. . . *gap* . . .]

36.309b–309c If so desired, the digit of the founder may also be used (as unit) whilst, in the case of small images, a grain of barley will be employed as unit.

Guardians of the doors

36.310 Nandin and Kāla are in the east, Daṇḍin and Muṇḍin in the south, Vaijaya and Bhṛṅgirīṭi in the west, Gopa and Anantaka in the north. The first named is always to be installed to the right of the door.

36.311 These are the colours appropriate for the guardians of the doors: (Nandin) is dark, (Kāla, red) like *kuṅkuma*, (Daṇḍin) sapphire blue (?), (Muṇḍin red) like cochineal, (Vaijaya) white, (Bhṛṅgirīṭi blue-green) like a peacock's throat, (Gopa) dark like a lotus and (Anantaka) black.

36.312a They bear the following weapons: (Nandin) a mace, (Kāla) an axe, (Daṇḍin) a sword, with well honed point, (Muṇḍin) a combat mace, (Vaijaya) an arrow, (Bhṛṅgirīṭi) a trident, (Gopa) a thunderbolt and (Anantaka) a spear with a sharp point.

36.312b–313a They have four arms, three or two eyes and terrifying fangs. Their bodies are decorated with snakes and they bear a gleaming trident on the side of their headgear. Each has one hand pointed (in a menacing fashion) whilst another is (like) a half-moon and another like a blossoming lotus. Their bodies are provided with flesh as is desirable for a body (?) or they have limbs . . . (?).

36.313b Their faces constantly provoke fear and absence of fear, even amongst the gods; they are terrifying due to their appearance alone. They have various aspects, their hair is coiled and they have trident in hand, those who are in the temple of He who bears the moon.

36.314 For all (the guardians of the doors) it is the nine *tāla* system which is prescribed, and the learned craftsman must determine the proportions appropriate to this system in accordance with the treatises given by Hara (i.e. the Āgama). They all have one leg bent; in temples they are established as the guardians of the doors; they all have a tawny light, are adorned with a multitude of serpents and wear whatsoever garments may be desired.

36.315 For those who follow the perfect Āgama, the descriptions have here been given in comprehensive fashion, of the appearance, colour, remarkable decorations, the mounts and the emplacements, the emblems, attributes, particulars and postures of the immortals, at whose head are Brahmā, Hari, Īśvara and Kumāra.

Thus ends, in the *Mayamata*, treatise on dwelling,
the thirty-sixth chapter: ICONOGRAPHY.

APPENDIX

Where and when a well is to be established[1]

1–2 It is said that a well, established in the south-west corner of a village or other settlement, will bring torment and sickness; in the west it brings about an increase in cattle and, in the north-west, death at the hands of enemies; in the north it brings nothing but happiness and in the north-east it leads to prosperity.

Candragupta says:

3 "In fields and in gardens, it is best if the well is in the north-east or west".

[Varāhamihira says]:

4–5 "A well in the south-east corner of a town or a village brings endless fear and certain death to men; in the south-west corner it leads to the loss of riches and in the north-west one, to the loss of the wife. A well brings success when it is established in any direction other than these three".

Rules, according to Nṛsiṃha, for the (choice of) lunar days:

6–7 All lunar days bring success, leaving aside those where the new moon is in the asterism Citrā and those which are 'empty' (i.e. the 4th, 9th and 14th of the fortnight). Those which birds and other presages indicate (as being inauspicious) are also to be avoided. All sunrises in the *varga* of Venus, Mercury, Jupiter and the Moon are equally auspicious.

Rule for (the choice of) asterisms:

8 It is auspicious to dig a well or works of that kind when in the asterisms which 'face downwards': Mūla, Kṛttikā, Maghā, Āśleṣā,

1. These verses are scattered throughout the 36th Chapter of the *Mayamata* as it is given in two manuscripts.

Viśākhā, Bharaṇī and the three 'Anteriors' (i.e. Pūrvaphalgunī, Pūrvāṣādhā and Pūrvabhādrapadā).

9–11a Rohiṇī, Ārdrā, Śraviṣṭhā, Puṣya, Śatabhiṣaj, Śravaṇa and the three 'Ulteriors' (i.e. Uttaraphalgunī, Uttarāṣādhā and Uttarabhādrapadā) are the asterisms which 'face upwards' and which are recommended, with the (six zodiacal signs) of which the first is Libra, for extension work and for other works. The five asterisms which begin with Aśvinī, (the five) which begin with Citrā and the (five) whose first is Mūla bring increase and some say that they are appropriate for the work involved in dykes, canals and other works.

11b–12 It is auspicious to dig a reservoir, a well, a pond or other works of that type during the descending phase of one of these four asterisms: Pūrvāṣādhā, Svāti, Kṛttikā and Śatabhiṣaj.

Candragupta (says):

13 "Hastā, the three 'Ulteriors', Dhaniṣṭhā, Maghā, Śatabhiṣaj, Jyeṣṭhā, Rohiṇī, Śravaṇa, Mūla, Āśleṣā, Citrā and Tiṣya are recommended when digging is involved."

Here is the rule for the undertaking (of the digging) of a well:

14 Starting in the north-east, a well in each of the directions, respectively, will bring: prosperity, wealth, loss of a son, death of the wife, death, success, a wound from weapons and a certain amount of happiness; in the middle of the house it brings ruin.

This is what Devarāta says:

15 "(A well) in the centre brings ruin, in the east, happiness, in the south-east, the death of the son and in the south, nothing but destruction".

(End of the Appendix)

Glossary of Architectural Terms

— abbreviation 'g.' (for 'god') is applied to all divine, semi-divine and other non-human beings.
— identification of trees and other botanical items are tentative.

A

aṃśa: 1. part (in calculation of proportion). 2. square (of a diagram). 3. part (one of the *āyādi* series).

akala: = *niṣkala.*

akṣa: 1. two. 2. axle (ref. vehicle). 3. urethra. 4. myrobolan (beleric-; wood not to be used in buildings for mortals, sap used for preparing coating, *Terminalia belerica*).

akṣamālā: rosary of *akṣa* beads (attribute). See *akṣasūtra.*

akṣasūtra: = *akṣamālā.*

akṣāntara: = spindle, end of the axle (ref. vehicle).

akṣi: two.

akṣottara: crossbeam holding chariot axle.

akhiladevatā: g. (= Viśvadevatā).

aga: inaccessible (ref. vaulted parts of a building).

Agajā: g. (Pārvatī).

agama: type of royal city (= *āhuta*).

agaru: eagle-wood tree (used for temples only, *aquilaria agallocha*).

Agastya: g. See Kumbhayoni.

Agni: 1. g. 2. g. (a vāstudevatā). 3. fire (attribute). 4. three. See Anala, Jvalana, Pāvaka, Prajvalana, Vahni, Śikhin, Śyena.

agra: head (ref. stone or timber).

agrapaṭṭa: = *snehavāri.*

agrabandhana: an element of hitching post (in stable).

agrahāra: type of village. See *maṅgala.*

Aghora: g.

aṅkaṇa: = *aṅgaṇa* (1).

aṅkurārpaṇa: ceremony of the growing of seeds.

aṅkuśa: elephant goad (attribute).

aṅga: architectural element, moulding (etc.).

aṅgaka: 1. street. 2. one.

aṅgaṇa: 1. inner court (whether or not covered by lantern); see *aṅkaṇa.* 2. courtyard. 3. training ground (for horse or elephant).

aṅgaṇaka: place (in a town).

aṅgada: = *keyūra.*

aṅgula: 1. digit (absolute linear measure unit) (*passim,* see). 2. digit (ref. iconometry). See *mātra.*

aṅghri: 1. pillar, pilaster. 2. level of pillars 3. newel (ref. stairway). 4. upright (ref. window). 5. upright (ref. partition wall).

acyuta: g. (= Viṣṇu).

Aja: 1. g. (= Brahmā). 2. g. (a vāstudevatā, = Brahmā).

ajakarṇin: a tree (used for pillars, *Terminalia alata*).

ajaghanya: g. (an Āditya).

ajabhāga: = *brahmabhāga.*

ajasūtra: line of the urethra of the liṅga.

ajākṣa: three.

aṭṭāla: fortified tower.

adarbha: ? (ref. roofing of stable?).

Aditi: g. (a vāstudevatā). See Devamātṛ.

adbhuta: category of building (according to height/width ratio).

Adharmā: g.

adhika: = *īṣikā.*

adhiṣṭhāna: base, level of base. See *ādyaṅga, kuṭṭima, tala, dharātala, pāduka, masūra, vastvādhāra.*

adhogataliṅga: = 'found again' Liṅga.

adhogṛha: = *garbhagṛha* (1).

Ananta: 1. g. (a nāgarāja). 2. g. (a Vidyeśvara). 3. g. (a dvārapāla).

anarpita: with an aisle (ref. building).

Anala: 1. g. (a vāstudevatā, = Agni). 2. g. (a Vasu). 3. three.

anācchāda: with an incomplete roof (ref. house).

Anila: 1. g. (= Vāyu). 2. g. (a Vasu).

anu: small false dormer-window (?) (for *anunāsī?*).

anukarma: restoration work, renovation work.

anukoṭi: an intermediate rafter.
anumārga: small joist.
anuvaṃśa: common rafter (= *lupā*) or purlins or small joist (= *anumārga*).
anūpa: moist (ref. ground).
antaraprapā: inner light building (placed in the middle of a house = *vāstumaṇḍapa*).
antaraprastara: stereobate (placed upon entablature below aediculae). See *madhyamamañca*.
antarāpaṇa: bazaar.
antarāla: 1. covered passage between sanctum and pavilion. 2. corridor, inner passage.
Antarikṣa: g. (a vāstudevatā). See Kha, Gagana, Paṅktika, Vyoman.
antarita: groove (moulding).
antarmaṇḍala: first enclosure (of a temple or palace).
antarhāra: second enclosure (of a temple).
antaḥpura: inner royal residence; more specially queen's dwelling, women's quarters inside the palace.
antaḥpuravāsa: = *antaḥpura*.
andhārā: aisle. See *andhārikā, andhārī*.
andhārikā: 1. outside wall of aisle. 2. = *andhāra*.
andhārī: = *andhāra*.
annagṛha: = *annālaya*.
annaśālā: = annālaya.
annasūtra: layout line for *annālaya*. See *trisūtra*.
annāgāra: = *annālaya*.
annālaya: principal main building in *catūśśāla* meant for *kṣatriya*. See *annagṛha, annaśālā, annāgāra, mahānasa*.
apakveṣṭakā: unbaked brick.
apacchāyā: noon shadow of the gnomon.
Aparājitā: g. (?).
Apasmāra: g.
apāmarga: a medicinal plant (*Achyrantes aspera*).
abja: 1. lotus (attribute). 2. doucine (moulding, see *padma*).
abjakapota: cornice with lotus profile.
abjakṣepaṇa: lotiform band (on door frame).
abdhi: four.
abhaya: 1. absence of fear (a 'part' in the *āyādi* system). 2. chebulic myrobolan (wood for temples only, sap for coatings and mortars, *Terminalia chebula*).
abhaya (-hasta): absence of fear (a gesture).

abhinna: with joint main buildings (ref. house). See *piṇḍa*.

abhiṣekamaṇḍapa: coronation pavilion.

Amara: g. (group of divinities).

amṛta (-yoga): an astrological conjunction.

ambuja: 1. lotus (attribute). 2. doucine (moulding, see *padma*). 3. lotiform base of the finial (*stūpi*).

ambujapīṭha: = *padmapīṭha*.

amburuha: lotus (attribute).

ara: spoke (ref. wheel).

aratni: regular cubit (= *hasta*).

arimeda: a tree (used for temples only, *Acacia farnesiana*.)

ariṣṭāgara: women apartment.

Aruṇa: g.

Arka (= Sūrya): 1. g. (a vāstudevatā). 2. twelve.

argala: 1. bolt. 2. bolt catch. 3. small street, alley, cul-de-sac.

arcanapīṭha: stand for worship.

arcā: image, manifest representation of a god.

arjuna: a tree (used for pillars, vehicles, furniture, *Terminalia arjuna*).

ardhakūṭa: half-aedicula shaped (ref. forepart) (?). See *ardhasabhā*.

ardhakoṭi: a piece of timber work.

ardhakoṣṭha: elongated aedicula set in the roof.

ardhagomūtra (-sopāna): dog-leg stairway.

ardhacandra (-pīṭha): semicircular pedestal.

ardhacandra (-hasta): a gesture.

Ardhanārīśvara (-mūrti): g.

ardhapāṇi: scarf-joint (ref. joinery).

ardhasabhā: = *ardhakūṭa* (?).

ardhendu: a decorative element of wall coping (semicircular merlon?).

arpita: without an aisle (ref. building).

Aryaman: g. (an Āditya).

alakamala: a gesture (= *harapallava*).

alaṅkṛta: type of pavilion.

alindra: 1. aisle. 2. gallery, portico, verandah.

avakāśa: entrance, porch.

Avanī: 1. g. (a vāstudevatā = Bhūmi). 2. storey (= *tala*).

avaya: architectural element (espec. moulding).

avalagna: = *valagna*.

avalamba: overhang.

aśoka: aśoka-tree (used for making the finial axis, *Saraca indica*).

aśmari: a tree (perhaps = *aśmarighna, Crataeva roxburgii*).

aśvattha: peepal-tree (*Ficus religiosa*).

aśvapāda: starting step (of stairway).

aśvamāra: a shrub (wood used for temples only, *Nerium odorum*).

aśvaśālā: stable. See *turagaśālā, vājiśālā, hayasadana.*

Aśvin: 1. g. 2. two.

aṣṭabandha: mortar made up of eight ingredients (used for fixing Liṅga or images).

aṣṭamaṅgala: eight auspicious items.

aṣṭāśra: type of pillar.

aṣṭhīla: pebble (used as a mallet).

asakala: = *niṣkala.*

asañcita: category of building (built with brick or wood and partly hollow).

asana: a tree (used for pillars, *Terminalia tomentosa*).

asi: sword (attribute). See *khaḍga, nandaka.*

asīmaka: without limit (ref. *bhinna* type house).

Asura: 1. g. (a vāstudevatā). 2. g.

asthi: bone (attribute).

ahikuṇḍala: type of ear-pendant (= *nakrakuṇḍala*).

Ā

ākarṇalupā: an intermediate rafter (= *anukoṭi*).

āgāra: building, edifice.

ājusūtra: reference line (= *mānasūtra*).

ājyasthāli: pot of clarified butter (attribute).

ājyārthabhāga: = *snehavāri.*

āṇi: peg (ref. joinery).

Ātreya: g.

Āditya: 1. g. (the twelve). See Bhāskara. 2. g. (a vāstudevatā, = Sūrya). 3. twelve.

ādyaṅga: = *adhiṣṭhāna.*

ādhāra: 1. supporting piece (ref. joinery). 2. socle (= *upapītha*). 3. lower part of pillar.

ādheya: supported piece (ref. joinery).

ānana: facade or gable.

ānīka: a kind of palanquin(?).

Āpa: 1. g. (a Vasu). 2. g. (a vāstudevatā).

Āpavatsa: g. (a vāstudevatā).

ābhāsa: 1. category of temple (according to arrangement of aediculae). 2. category of pavilion (according to width/length ratio). 3. category of house (according to width /length ratio). 4. mode of cutting a stone to make a Liṅga. 5. type of hall.

āmalaka: 1. emblic myrobolan (used only for temple building, *Emblica officinalis*). 2. type of temple-roof.

āmra: mango-tree (sap used for making bricks, coatings..., *Mangifera indica*).

āya: gain (in the *āyādi* system). See also *dhana* and 26.206 sq., 33.58 sq.

āyatana: seat.

āyādi: cf. See *aṃśa, āya, āyus, uḍu, ṛkṣa, guhya, tithi, dhana, yoni, vāra, vyaya.*

āyus: age (in the *āyādi* system). See *vayas.*

Āyudhapuruṣa: g.

āyudhamaṇḍapa: 1. pavilion for ritual utensils. 2. armoury.

ārādhanagṛha: private chapel (in a house).

ārāma: hermitage.

Ārkin: g. (a vāstudevatā = Yama).

ārtavasūtika: confinement room.

Ārya: 1. g. (= Śāstā). 2. g. (avāstudevatā). See Marīci.

Ārṣaliṅga: Liṅga installed by Ṛṣi or fitting for them.

ālambana: overhang.

ālaya: building, edifice.

ālāna: shackling post (ref. elephant stable).

āliṅga: fillet (moulding).

āvantika: 1. type of roof. 2. type of four-storeyed temple.

āvaraṇa: enclosure (ref. temple, palace, house).

āvara: wicket-door.

āvasatha: lodging, apartment.

āvāsa: 1. house, lodging. 2. main building (ref. house = *śālā*). 3. building, edifice.

āvāsana: lodging.

āvṛttamaṇḍapa: surrounding portico, cloister like gallery.

āveśa: recess (ref. architectural elements, as opposed to *nirgama*).

āśrama: hermitage.

āsana: 1. seat. 2. rectangular throne or pedestal (as opposed to square *pīṭha*). 3. diagram with 100 squares. 4. line used to draw rafters.

āsanaphalaka: plank where one seats (ref. throne).

āsthānamaṇḍapa: audience pavilion, reception pavilion.

āspada: building, edifice.

āsya: 1. string-course, frieze (moulding). 2. facade or gable. 3. mouth (ref. oven).

āhatya (-bali): individual offering (to vāstudevatā).

āhalya: type of pavilion.

āhuta: type of royal city (= *agama*).

I

inā: a fragrant plant.

Indu (= Candra): 1. g. (a vāstudevatā). 2. one.

Indra: 1. g. 2. g. (an Āditya). 3. g. (a vāstudevatā). 4. g. (a vāstudevatā, = Mahendra). See Vajrapāṇi, Vajrin.

indrakānta: 1. diagram with 1024 squares. 2. type of pillar.

indrakīla: 1. vertical bolt. 2. stake. 3. nail (or peg).

Indrajaya: g. (a vāstudevatā). See Indrarāja.

Indrarāja: g. (a vāstudevatā, = Indrajaya).

indraśālā: council chamber (?) (ref. palace).

Indrāṇī: g. (a Mātṛkā).

indriya: 1. five. 2. eleven.

ibha: 1. elephant (a 'matrice' in the *āyādi* system). 2. eight.

ibhakumbha: type of walls arrangement (ref. town).

ibhasadana: = *hastiśālā.*

Ibhānana: g. (= Gaṇeśa).

iriṇa (-durga): fort surrounded by desert.

irvāru: cuncumber (*Cucumis utilssimus*).

iṣikā: see *īṣikā.*

iṣu: five (*passim*).

iṣṭakā: brick. See *apakveṣṭakā, prathameṣṭakā, mūrdhneṣṭakā, pakveṣṭakā.*

Ī

īkṣaṇaśālā: reception house (ref. palace).

Īśa (Īśāna): 1. g. 2. g. (a vāstudevatā). 3. one. 4. eleven (= rudra).

īśakānta: see *īśvarakānta.*

īśadṛk: three.

īśākṣa: three.

Īśvara (= Śiva): g.

īśvarakānta (īśakānta): 1. diagram with 961 squares. 2. type of two-storeyed temple. 3. type of pavilion.

īṣikā (iṣikā): piece of frame (ref. palanquin or bed). See *adhika, edhita.*

U

Ukṣa: g. (= Vṛṣa).

ugrapīṭha: diagram with 36 squares.

uḍu: asterism (one of the *āyādi* series = *nakṣatra*).

uttara: 1. architrave. 2. lintel (= *vimalā*). 3. an element of enclosure wall coping. 4. top-fillet (Moulding, = *uttarakampa*). 5. *akṣottara*. 6. back (ref. seat).

uttaramaṇḍa: architrave.

uttarīyaka: scarf.

utpala: lotus (*Nymphea stellata*).

utsandhi: upper joint (moulding of *maṇḍī*).

udara: hollow part of a niche.

udarabandha: waist-belt.

udavasita: building, edifice.

Uditi: 1. g. 2. g. (a vāstudevatā). See *Diti*.

udumbara: a tree (used for temple and cart building, *Ficus glomerata*).

upadvāra: small (or secondary) door. See *tiryagdvāra*, *suruṅga*.

upadhāna: long beam support (ref. chariot, = *bharopadhāna*) (?).

upanītika: place for initiation ceremony.

upapīṭha: 1. socle (ref. building). 2. socle (ref. altar, throne, pedestal).

upavīta: 1. = *yajñopavīta*. 2. mode of wearing the scarf (*uttarīyaka*).

upasañcita: category of buildings (partly hollow and partly massive).

upāna: 1. plinth (moulding). 2. regulating course, adjustment layer.

upopāna: regulating course.

ubhayacaṇḍita: diagram with 169 squares.

Umā: g. See Gaurī.

Umāmaheśvaramūrti (Umāsahitamūrti): g.

Umāskandamūrti: g.

uragabandha: type of base.

urvī: floor (of room).

Ullāsin: g. (= Śāstā).

Uṣā: g.

uṣṇiṣa: 1. line used to draw rafters. 2. top of the Liṅga.

Ū

ūrdhvakūṭa: square lantern and court it covers(?).

ūrdhvakoṣṭha: elongated lantern and inner court it covers.

ūrdhvagataliṅga: 'discovered' Liṅga.

ūrdhvavaṃśa: purlin.

Ṛ

ṛkṣa: asterism (one of the *āyādi* series, = *nakṣatra*).

ṛjukriyā: type of latticed window.

ṛjupāda: straight leg (ref. furniture).

ṛjusūtra: = *mānasūtra.*

ṛṇa: loss (in the *āyādi* system, = *vyaya*).

ṛtu: six.

Ṛṣabha: g. (= Vṛṣa).

Ṛṣi: 1. g. (the seven Sages). 2. seven.

E

eka: a tree (used for pillars).

ekatala (ekabhū, ekabhūmi): single storeyed building.

Ekanetra: g. (an Āditya).

ekapatrābja: a medicinal plant.

ekabhoga: village inhabited by one brahmin family only.

Ekarudra: g. (a Vidyeśvara).

ekavasanta: type of hall (*sabhā*).

ekaśāla: house with a single main building.

edhita: = *īṣikā.*

elā: cardamom (*Elettaria cardamomun*).

AI-AU

Aindra: g. (a vāstudevatā, = Jayanta).

aiśaka: = *śivabhāga.*

aiṣṭakakuḍya: brick partition-wall.

auṣadha (°dhi): simple, medicinal plant.

K

Ka: 1. g. (a vāstudevatā, = Brahmā). 2. one. 3. roof (*śikbara*). 4. line used to draw rafters.

kakara: type of stereobate (*prati*) (?).

Kaṅkālamūrti: g.

kaṅku: Italian millet (*Panicum italicum*).

kacagraha: a decorative element (of halls and houses).

Kajāyā: g. (= Sarasvatī).

kañcuka: breast-plate, bodice.

kañja: doucine (moulding, see *padma*).

kaṭaka: bracelet.

kaṭisūtra: hip girdle.

kaṭphala: a tree (used for pillars, *Myrica nagi*).

kaṇṭaka: a tree (not to be used in mortal dwellings).

kaṇṭaki: a tree.

kaṇṭha: 1. recessed moulding (dado, groove...). 2. dado (ref. pedestal, altar, socle). See *kandhara, gala, grīvā.*

kathā: historiated panel.

kadamba: a tree (wood to be used for temples only, sap for bricks and mortars, *Antocephalus cadamba*).

kadara: a hardwood tree (variety of *khadira*).

kadalī: banana-tree (banana is used for making coatings, *Musa sapientum*).

kandhara: 1. recessed moulding (dado, groove... see *kaṇṭha*). 2. dado (ref. pedestal, alter, socle, see *kaṇṭha*). 3. attic (fourth level of elevation). 4. element of arcature (its gable?).

kapāla: skull (attribute).

kapittha: wood-apple tree (used for temples only, *Feronia elephantum*).

kapota: 1. cornice, dripstone. 2. entablature (= *prastara*).

kapotabandha: type of base.

kapola: an element of roof (?, or w.r. for *kapota?*).

kabhitti: partition wall separating *svāmivāsa* and *raṅga* in a house.

kamaṇḍalu: water-pot (attribute).

kamala: 1. lotus (attribute). 2. doucine (moulding, see *padma*).

Kamalaja: 1. g. (= Brahmā). 2. g. (a vāstudevatā, = Brahmā).

kamalāsana: lotiform pedestal (= *padmāsana*).

kampa: 1. fillet (moulding). 2. transom, crosspiece (ref. latticed window, partition wall). 3. small rafter (of a lean-to shaped dripstone). 4. pillar, pilaster (= *stambha*).

kampadvāra: door whose hinges are set in a pillar.

kara: 1. regular cubit (= *hasta*). 2. handrail (ref. chariot).

karaka: water-pot (attribute).

karañja: a tree (used for temples only, *Pongamia glabra*).

karaṇḍamakuṭa: type of tiara.

karaṇḍikāmauli: = *karaṇḍamakuṭa.*

karāgraja: digit (= *aṅgula*).

karāla: type of mortar or of coating.

karoṭimālā: = *śiromālā.*

karkaṭa: type of stereobate (*prati*).

karṇa: 1. projecting part (ref. joinery). 2. probably w.r. for *kaṇṭha.*

karṇakūṭa: 1. corner square aedicula. 2. corner square outward construction (ref. houses). See *karṇaprāsāda, karṇasabhā, kūṭa, sabhā, sauṣṭhika.*

karṇadhāra: a piece of timber work (ref. halls and stables).

karṇapāda: corner pillar.

karṇapālikā: foliage set at corner of cornice or dripstone (decorative element).

karṇapūra: ear ornament.

karṇaprāsāda: = *karṇakūṭa.*

karṇaraśmi: corner rafter (= *koṭilupā*).

karṇalupā: corner rafter (= *koṭilupā*).

karṇasabhā: square outward construction (ref. houses, = *karṇakūṭa*).

karṇasirā: diagonal (ref. diagram). See *sirā.*

karṇāṣṭaka: diagram with 324 squares.

karṇikā: 1. element at top of altar (fashioned like a lotus receptacle). 2. an ornament of entablature (?).

kartarīdaṇḍaka: type of town.

karpūra: camphor (wood used for temples only, *Cinnamomum camphora*).

karmamaṇḍapa: workshop.

kalaṅka: stain (ref. stone).

kalaśa: 1. bell of bell capital. 2. vase (used in the consecration ceremony). 3. type of base.

kalā: sixteen.

Kali: g.

kaliṅga: type of rafter.

kalka: chalk paste(?).

kalyāṇa: 1. type of two-storeyed temple. 2. type of four-storeyed gateway.

kalyāṇamaṇḍapa: wedding pavilion.

Kalyāṇa (-mūrti): g.

kavāṭa: leaf (ref. door or window). See *talpa.*

kāka: crow (a 'matrice' in the *āyādi* system).

kākaṇi: square measure (= 8 square *daṇḍa*).

kākaloha: an aquatic plant.

Kātyāyanī: g.

kānana: gable.

kāntavijaya: 1. type of *dvāraśobhā* gateway. 2. type of two-storeyed gateway.

Kāma: g. See Madana, Smara.

Kāmārimūrti: g.

kāmāsana: a posture (= *sukhāsana*?).

kāya: rafter (= *lupā*).

kāyapāda: strut.

kāyabhāra: type of dwelling for *vaiśya.*

kāraskara: a tree (used for temples only, *Strychnos nux-vomica*).

kārtamāla: a hardwood tree.

kārmuka: 1. bow (attribute). 2. pole (= *daṇḍa*).

Kāla: 1. g. 2. g. (a dvārapāla). See Mahākāla. 3. a tree (used for pillars and vehicles).

kālaja: a tree (= *kāla*?).

Kālanāśamurti: g.

Kālī: g.

Kālīsuta: g.

kāṣṭha: chair.

kiṃśuka: a tree (used for temples only, *Butea frondosa*).

Kinnara: g.

kirīṭa: tiara.

kiṣku: regular cubit (= *hasta*).

kīla: 1. peg, nail. 2. = *stūpikākīla.* 3. bolt (= *indrakīla*). 4. hitching post.

kukkuṭa: cock (attribute).

kukṣi: hollow part of a niche (?).

kuñjarākṣa: type of latticed window.

kuṭaja: a tree (used for temples only, *Holarrhena antidysenterica*).

kuṭika: type of village (= *ekabhoga*).

kuṭikāmukha: apse (ref. theatre building?).

kuṭikāmukhadaṇḍaka: type of town.

kuṭikāsana: a posture (aslant?).

kuṭīra: hut.

kuṭumbāvani: family plot (in a village).

kuṭumbāvalika: quarter (in settlement).

kuṭṭima: 1. base (= *abhiṣṭhāna*). 2. small street.

kuṭhārikā: roof of a porch(?).

kuḍmala: bud (tip of finial).

kuḍya: wall.

kuḍyastambha: pilaster.

kuṇḍa: 1. ritual firepit. 2. tank.

kuṇḍala: 1. door-ring. 2. ear pendant. (See *ahikuṇḍala, nakrakuṇḍala, patrakuṇḍala, makarakuṇḍala, ratnakuṇḍala, vāsuki-kuṇḍala, śaṅkhakuṇḍala*).

kuṇḍikā: water-pot (attribute).

Kubera: g. See Dhanada, Naravāha, Dhanādhipa.

kuberakānta: type of two-storeyed temple.

Kumāra: g. (= Skanda).

kumuda: 1. lotus (*Nymphea esculenta*). 2. torus (moulding).

kumbha: 1. bell capital. 2. bell of bell capital. 3. vase (element of the finial). 4. = *stūpikā*. 5. torus (moulding). 6. element of *kumbhalatā*.

Kumbhayoni: g. (= Agastya).

kumbhalatā: creeper rising from a vase (a wall ornament).

kulattha: horse-gram (*Dolichos biflorus*).

kuladhārana: (kuladhāriṇa) type of pavilion.

kulyābhadvāra: door pierced through *kabhitti*, vaulted door.

kulyāvimāna: underground room.

kuśa: 1. a king of grass (*Desmotachya bipinnata*). = *darbha*. 2. idem (used as an attribute).

kūṭa: 1. square aedicula (on entablature; most often placed at corners, see *karṇakūṭa*). 2. square outwork structure (loggia?, ref. houses, gateways). 3. square lantern and inner court it covers (see *ūrdha-vakūṭa*). 4. newel (ref. roof). 5. an element of timber work of roof (ref. halls). 6. small square four pillared hall, kiosk. 7. rostrum (?) etc... See *karṇaprāsāda, karṇakūṭa, sabhā, sauṣṭhika.*

kūṭagṛha: rostrum.

kūṭāgāra: rostrum (?).

kūpa: well.

kūpara (kūbara): pole (ref. chariot).

kūrca: bundle of *kuśa* grass (attribute).

kūrmaśilā: type of liner (for *Liṅga*).

Kṛṣṇa: g.

kṛṣṇala: linear measure (= 3 *yava*).

ketaka: a shrub (*Pandanus odoratissimus*).

ketakī: a tree (used for pillars).

ketu: emblem.

keyūra: armlet. See *angada.*

kevala: type of town.

kevalāmbhas: pure water (used for coatings and mortars).

keśabandha: type of hair arrangement (hair twisted into a chignon).

keśabhāra: type of hair arrangement (hair twisted into a chignon).

Keśava: g. (= Viṣṇu).

keśaviśālaka: type of *dvāraprāsāda* gateway.

kesara: type of single-storeyed temple.

Kaiṭabha: g.
kairava: doucine (moulding).
kailāsa: type of two-storeyed temple.
koṭi, koṭilupā: corner rafter. See *karṇaraśmi, karṇalupā.*
koṇa: type of pavilion.
kotmakolaka: type of settlement.
kodrava: a kind of grain (*Paspalum scrobiculatium*).
komala: type of four-storeyed gateway.
kolaka: a unit for iconometry (= 2 digits).
kollaka: type of rafter.
kovidāra: a tree (used for temples only, *Bauhigania variegata*).
kośagṛha: treasury room.
koṣṭha: 1. elongated aedicula (on entablature); see *śālā.* 2. elongated outwork structure (ref. houses). 3. elongated lantern and inner court it covers (see *ūrdhavakoṣṭha*). 4. elongated small four pillared hall. 5. main building (ref. house, = *śālā*). 6. wagon roof. 7. square (of a diagram).
kaukkuṭa: type of walls arrangement (ref. town or palace).
Kaumārī: g.
kaurava: type of roof.
kauśika: 1. type of rafter. 2. type of pavilion.
kausala: type of roof.
krakarakoṣṭha: cross wagon-roof.
krakarabhadra: type of plan for pavilions.
krakarīvaṃśa: with ridge-beams arranged crosswise (ref. house).
kramuka: areca-tree (used for pavilion pillars, *Areca cathechu*).
krośa: linear measure ('kos', = 500 *daṇḍa*).
Kṣatagṛha: g. (a vāstudevatā, = Gṛhakṣata).
kṣaya: building, edifice.
kṣīradruma: peepal-tree (sap used for bricks and coatings = *aśvattha*).
kṣīriṇī: a hardwood tree (used for pillars etc..., *Mimusops indica?*).
kṣudra: 1. small street. 2. fillet (moulding). 3. eave of cornice (?).
kṣudrapaṭṭikā: fillet (moulding).
kṣurikā: dagger (attribute).
kṣetra: building, edifice.
Kṣetrapāla: g.
kṣepaṇa: 1. projecting fillet

(moulding). 2. coping (of wall). 3. bolt (placed outside the doorleaf).

kṣepaṇastambha: type of pillar.

kṣauramaṇḍapa: pavilion for hair cutting.

kṣmā: storey (= *tala*).

Kh

Kha: 1. g. (a vāstudevatā, = Antarikṣa).

khaḍga: sword (attribute). See *asi*.

khadgin: g.

khaṇḍa: 1. mortice (ref. joinery). 2. = *vīrakānta* (?).

khaṇḍabhavana: engaged structure.

khaṇḍaharmya: = *khaṇḍabhavana*.

khaṇḍottara: type of architrave.

khadira: a hardwood tree (used for pillars etc., *Acacia catechu*).

khara: donkey (a 'matrice' in the *āyādi* system).

kharvaṭa: 1. type of settlement. 2. type of pavilion.

khalūrikā: annexe surrounding a house.

khātapāda: pillar with sunken bottom (= *nikhātastambha*).

khātavāri: well water (used for coatings and mortars).

khātaśaṅkhu: stake sunk into ground at time of layout.

khādira: a tree (variety of *khadira*, same uses).

khura: plinth (moulding).

kheṭa: type of settlement.

kheṭaka: shield (attribute).

G

ga: three.

Gagana: g. (a vāstudevatā = Antarikṣa).

gagra: an element of timber work of roof.

gaṅgā: four.

gaja: elephant (a 'matrice' in *āyādi* system).

gajapṛṣṭha: apsidal (ref. building).

Gajamukha: g. (= Gaṇeśa).

Gajavadana: g. (= Gaṇeśa).

gajahastopama (-hasta): a gesture (see *daṇḍahasta*).

Gajā: g.

Gajānana: g. (= Gaṇeśa).

Gaṇamukhya: g. (a vāstudevatā, = Mukhya).

Gaṇādhipa: g. (= Gaṇeśa).

Gaṇādhyakṣa: g. (= Gaṇeśa).

gaṇita: diagram with 360 squares.

Gaṇeśa: g. and g. (a vāstudevatā); see Ibhānana,

Gajamukha, Gajavadana, Gajānana, Gaṇamukhya, Gaṇādhipa, Gaṇādhyakṣa, Mukhya, Vighneśa, Vināyaka.

gati: courtyard (ref. temple).

gadā: mace (attribute).

Gandharva: 1. g. 2. g. (a vāstudevatā).

Garuḍa: g. See Tārkṣya, Pakṣirāja, Vainateya.

garuḍapakṣa: type of dwelling for *kṣatriya.*

garbha: 1. foundation deposit. 2. sanctum (= *garbhagṛha*). 3. type of pavilion.

garbhakūṭa: central lantern (of pavilion) (?).

garbhagṛha. 1. sanctum. 2. central passage of gateway. See *adhogṛha, garbhanālī, garbhāgāra, gṛha, nālīgṛha, vāsa.*

garbhanālī: sanctum.

garbhabhitti: wall separating sanctum and aisle. See *gṛhapiṇḍi.*

garbhasūtra: line drawn for layout of sanctum.

garbhāgāra: 1. sanctum. 2. central passage of gateway. 3. confinement house (= *sūtigṛha*).

garbhiṇī: pregnant (ref. stone marked with circonvolutions).

gala: 1. recessed moulding (groove, dado...). 2. attic (4th level of elevation).

gavākṣa: type of window.

gavyūta: linear measure (= 2000 *daṇḍa*).

gātra: pillar (= *stambha*).

gāndhāra: 1. type of two-storeyed temple. 2. type of three-storeyed temple. 3. type of roof.

gillikā: palanquin.

Gītabhāvin: g. (= Śāstā).

guṇa: three.

gulikā: 1. circular window. 2. rounded bannister (ref. palanquin).

gulpha: elevated sill.

gulmāṣa: a kind of mortar or coating.

Guha: g. (= Skanda).

guhā: niche.

guhya: 1. matrice (one of the *āyādi* series, = *yoni*). 2. concealed part of chariot body(?).

guhyasopāna: concealed stairway.

gṛha: 1. building, edifice. 2. house. 3. main building (ref. house, = *śālā*). 4. room. 5. sanctum.

Gṛhakṣata: g. (a vāstudevatā). See Kṣatagṛha, Rākṣasa.

gṛhapiṇḍi: = *garbhabhitti.*

gṛhaprāsādamaṇḍapa: type of pavilion.

gṛhamaṇḍapa: type of pavilion.

gṛhaśreṇi: quarter in a town.

gṛhāvali: quarter in a town.

geha, geha°: see *gṛha, gṛha°*.

Gotranāga: g. (vāstudevatā, = Nāga).

gopāna: 1. dripstone (= *kapota*). 2. cornice *or* lean-to, pentroof.

gopānaprastara: lean-to, pentroof.

gopānamañca: = *gopā-naprastara.*

gopānārudhamañca: = *gopā-naprastara.*

gopura: 1. gateway (of temple, town, palace). 2. gateway of 5th enclosure (see *dvā-ragopura*). 3. fortified gateway (ref. town).

gośālā: cow stable.

goṣṭha: cow stable.

gostana: spout, gargoyle.

Gaurī: g. (= Umā).

grāma: settlement (espec. village).

grīva: 1. recessed moulding. 2. attic (4th level of elevation). See *kaṇṭha, kan-dhara, gala.*

Gh

gha: four.

ghaṭa: 1. vase (part of the finial). 2. = *stūpikā.*

ghaṭikā: 1. a piece of roof timber-work. 2. closing bar (of door). 3. an element of doorleaf(?). 4. drawing instrument.

ghaṇṭā: bell (attribute).

ghana: massive (ref. building).

ghāṭana: opening of door.

ghṛtavāri: = *snehavāri.*

C

cakra: 1. discus (attribute, may appear under a manifest form; see Rathanemi). 2. wheel (ref. vehicle). 3. a war machine (?).

cakrapaṭṭa: felly. See *paṭṭa.*

cakṣurmokṣaṇa: ceremony of the opening of the eyes.

caṅkramaṇa: court, inner court.

Caṇḍa: g. (= Caṇḍeśa, Caṇḍe-śvara).

caṇḍita: 1. diagram. 2. diagram with 64 squares (= *maṇḍūka*).

Caṇḍeśa, Caṇḍeśvara: g. See Caṇḍa.

Caṇḍeśānugrahamūrti (Caṇ-ḍeśvaraprāsādamūrti): g.

caturgṛha: house with four main buildings (= *catuśśāla*).

caturmukha: 1. type of *dvāragopura* gateway. 2. types of house with one and two main buildings.

caturmukhaharmya: type of house (= *caturmukha*).

catuśśāla: house with four main buildings. See *caturgṛha, pādaśālā, yugakoṣṭha.*

candana: sandal-wood tree (white-, used for pillars, *Santalum album*).

Candra 1. g. 2. one... See Indu, Śaśin, Soma.

candrakānta: type of bell capital.

candranāsī: rounded false dormer window.

Candraśekharamūrti: g.

Carakī: g. (a vāstudevatā).

caraṇa: 1. pillar, pilaster (= *stambha*). 2. level of pillars.

cāpa: bow (attribute).

Cāmuṇḍi: g.

cāra: door.

cārubandha: type of base.

cikkaṇa: a kind of mortar or coating.

citrakhaṇḍa: 1. type of pillar. 2. type of frieze (*prati*).

Citragupta: g.

citratoraṇa: type of arcature.

citrapotikā: type of bracket capital.

cihna: characteristic sign (ref. images).

culli: hearth.

cūta: mango-tree (sap used for bricks, coatings..., *Mangifera indica*).

cūrṇa: chalk, quick lime.

cūlaharmya: a feature placed on upper storeys (ref. houses, gateways).

cūli, cūlika: 1. tenon (ref. joinery). 2. a piece of roof timber-work. 3. top of a pillar (?). 4. finial.

cūlyaṅga: an element of the roof.

cerikā: type of settlement.

Ch

chatra: umbrella (attribute).

chatraśīrṣa: coping (of wall).

chada: roofing.

chanda: 1. category of temple (according to arrangement of aediculae). 2. category of pavilion (according to width/length ratio). 3. category of house (according to width/length ratio). 4. type of hall. 5. mode of cutting a stone to make a Liṅga.

chādana: roofing.

chāyamāna: overhang.

chīdra: 1. duct. 2. loophole.

J-Jh

jagatī: plinth (moulding). See *upāna, janman, paṭṭa, pāduka, mohāmara, vapra, hṛt, homa.*

Jaghanyaja: g. (an Āditya).

jaṅgama (-pratimā): portable image.

jaṅghā: 1. pillar, pilaster. 2. level of pillars (= jaṅghā-varga).

jaṅghāvarga: level of pillars.

janavīthi: circular street (ref. towns).

janman: plinth (moulding, = *jagatī*).

jayakośa: category of pavilion (according to arrangement of foreparts).

jayaṅga: 1. type of town. 2. type of king's palace.

jayada: 1. category of building (according to height/width ratio). 2. mode of cutting a stone to make a Liṅga.

Jayanta: 1. g. 2. g. (a vāstudevatā). See Aindra.

jayantī: joist.

jayāvaha: type of four-storeyed temple.

Jala: g. (a vāstudevatā = Varuṇa).

jalakośa: storage for water.

jalaka: gargoyle, spout.

Jalada: g. (a vāstudevatā, = Parjanya).

jaladurga: fort surrounded by water, island fort.

jaladvāra: drain, sluice.

Jalapati: g. (= Varuṇa).

jalapātana: open duct.

jalapāda: = *jalapātana.*

jalamārga: drain, sluice (= *jaladvāra*).

jalayantra: hydraulic machine.

jalasthala: 1. basin. 2. gutter.

Jalādhipa (= Varuṇa): 1. g. 2. g. (a vāstudevatā).

jalāśaya: tank, basin.

Jaleśa (= Varuṇa): 1. g. 2. g. (a vāstudevatā).

jāṅgala: dry (ref. ground).

jāti: 1. category of temple (according to arrangement of aediculae. 2. category of pavilion (according to width/length ratio). 3. category of house (according to width/length ratio). 4. category of pavilion (without forepart). 5. mode of cutting a stone to make a Liṅga.

jātigarbha: foundation deposit proper to a caste.

jātihiṅgulya: cinnabar.

jānu: a piece of roof timber-work.

jālaka: 1. latticed window. 2. latticed doorleaf.

jālakakuḍya: latticed wall.

Jina: g.

Jīva: g.

Jñānabhāvin, Jñānin (= Śāstā): g.

Jyeṣṭhā: g.

Jyotsnā: g.

Jvalana (= Agni): 1. g. 2. g. (a vāstudevatā). 3. fire (attribute).

jhaṣakhaṇḍa: arched piece (decorated with *makara*) of arcature.

jhaṣadanta: type of assembly (ref. joinery).

jhaṣāṃśa: = *jhaṣakhaṇḍa.*

jhaṣālastambha: pillar rising from top of base.

Ṭ-Ḍ

ṭaṅka: axe (attribute).

ḍamaru: drum (attribute).

ḍuṇḍuka: a tree (used for temples only).

T

takkola: a fragrant plant (*Pimenter acris,* Wight.).

takṣaka: 1. carpenter, mason. 2. architect (= *sthapati*).

tagara: a plant (*Tabernaemontana coronaria*).

Tatpuruṣa: g.

taraṅga: wave (decorative motif).

taraṅginī: type of bracket capital.

taruṇapratimā: provisional image.

taruṇabimba: = *taruṇa-pratimā.*

taruṇaliṅga: provisional Liṅga.

taruṇālaya: provisional temple (= *bālālaya*).

tala: 1. storey (*passim*; also see *kṣmā, bhū, bhūmi, sthala*). 2. floor (of room). 3. base, level of base (= *adhiṣṭhāna*).

talipa: 1. pillar, pilaster (= *stambha*). 2. level of pillars.

talpa: 1. doorleaf (= *kavāṭa*). 2. bench, couch.

talpabandhana: bed linen.

taskara: thief (a 'part' in *āyādi* system).

tāḍikā: see *tālikā.*

Tāpanī: a Kāma's arrow.

tāpasavāsa: hermitage.

Tārāpati: g. (= Candra).

Tārkṣya: g. (= Garuḍa).

tāla: 1. span (= 12 *aṅgula*). 2. an iconometric measure. 3. palmyra tree (*Borassus flabellifer*).

tālavṛnta: flywisk (= *cāmara*).
tālikā: type of ear pendant.
tiṇḍuka (tinduka): a tree (used for pavilion pillars, *Diospyros Embryopteris*).
tithi: 1. fifteen. 2. lunar day (one of the *āyādi* series).
tinduka: see *tiṇḍuka.*
tintriṇī: a tree (to be used for temples only, *Tamarindus indica*).
timiśa: a tree (used for pillars).
tiryagdvāra: secondary gate (ref. town, = *upadvāra*).
tila: sesamum (*Sesamum indicum*).
tilaka: 1. mark of the forehead (ref. goddesses). 2. a tree (used for temple pillars only, perhaps mistake for *tilvaka*: *Symplocos racemosa*).
tīvra: 1. height, thickness etc...). 2. projection (= *nirgama*) etc...).
tīvrapaṭṭikā: eave plank.
tuṅgakūṭa: rostrum.
turagaśālā: stable (ref. horses).
turagasthāna: stall (ref. stable).
tulā: 1. scales. 2. beam (supporting joists, ref. ceiling). 3. crossbeam holding chariot axle (= *akṣottara?*).
tulāṇīya: type of dwelling for *Śūdra.*
tulābhāra: ritual weighing (ceremony of-).
Toya: g. (a vāstudevatā, = Varuṇa).
toraṇa: 1. arch, arcature. 2. frame (supporting scales). 3. arched pole (ref. palanquin).
trāsa: crack (ref. defective gems).
trikhaṇḍa: 1. type of assembly (ref. joinery). 2. with three flights of steps (ref. stairway).
tritala (tribhū, tribhūmi...): three storeyed building.
tripaṭṭa: champfered string-course.
tripaṭṭakṣepaṇa: moulding (n. of a — of entablature).
Tripurasundaramūrti (Tripurāntakamūrti): g.
triphala: sap of the three myrobolans (used for bricks, coatings...).
Trimūrti: g. (a vidyeśvara).
triyaśraka: champfered string-course or fillet (= *tripaṭṭa?*).
triyuta: diagram with 256 squares.
trivargamaṇḍapa: pavilion with three level elevation.
Trivikrama: g.

triśāla: house with three main buildings. See *śūrpa.*

triśikhā: trident (attribute, = *triśūla*).

triśūla: 1. trident (attribute, also see *triśikhā, śikhā, śūla*). 2. a medicinal plant.

trisūtra: = *annasūtra.*

trairāśika: type of Liṅga.

tryaṃśa: with three level elevation (= *trivarga*).

tvaksāra: bamboo (for pillars and roofing of pavilions).

Tvaṣṭṛ: g. (an Āditya).

D

Dakṣa: g.

dakṣiṇāgāra: = *dhānyālaya.*

Dakṣiṇāmūrti: g.

daṇḍa: 1. pole (linear measure, = 4 cubits). 2. module. 3. reinforcing lath of doorleaf (?). 4. mace (attribute). 5. a gesture (see *daṇḍahasta*).

daṇḍaka: 1. type of village. 2. type of settlement. 3. type of plan for pavilions. 4. type of house with a single main building.

Daṇḍapāṇi: g. (= Yama).

daṇḍavaktra: type of house with two main buildings.

daṇḍaśālā: elongated building *or* = *daṇḍaka* (4).

daṇḍahasta: a gesture (= *gajopamahasta*).

daṇḍikā: 1. console (ref. entablature or roof). 2. type of assembly (ref. joinery).

daṇḍikāvara: pent-roof or lean-to (resting on consoles).

Daṇḍin: g. (a dvārapāla).

danta: tenon (ref. joinery).

darbha: 1. a grass (*Desmotachya bipinnata*). = *kuśa.* 2. type of pavilion.

dala: leaf row (moulding).

daśatala (daśabhū, daśabhūmi): ten storeyed building.

daśaśālā: house with ten main buildings. See *dvipañcaśālā, paṅktiśālā.*

dānaśālā: alms-giving room.

Dāhinī: a Kāma's arrow.

Diti: 1. g. 2. g. (a vāstudevatā, = Uditi).

Dinakara: g. (= Sūrya).

Dineśa (Dineśvara) (= Sūrya): 1. g. 2. twelve.

diś: ten.

diśābhadra (diśibhadra): type of dwelling for brahmins and kings.

diśāsvastika: type of *dvāraharmya* gateway.

dīrghalupā: long(?) rafter

(ref. roofing of halls). See *prāṃśuraśmi, lupā.*

dīrghikā: tank.

durga: fort, fortified town.

Durgā: g.

dūrva: a grass (*Cynodon dactylon*).

dṛk: 1. two. 2. a moulding of the base (= *dhṛk?*).

devagṛha: shrine and especially chapel in a house or a palace.

Devamātṛ: g. (a vāstudevatā, = Aditi).

Devabhāvin: g. (= Śāstā).

devabhāvin: type of assembly (ref. joinery).

devāṅgula: digit (ref. iconometry, = *aṅgula*).

devālaya: shrine, chapel.

deśīya: diagram with 144 squares.

dehalabdhāṅgula: digit (ref. iconometry, = *aṅgula*).

daiva: a zone of plan (ref. town, sanctum).

daivadurga: fort with natural defences.

Dauvārika: g. (a vāstudevatā).

dravya: 1. building material. 2. timber piece (ref. joinery).

drāviḍa: 1. category of temple. 2. category of Liṅga. 3. type of rafter.

dvāra: 1. door; chapter 30 *passim.* 2. gate, fortified gate. 3. gateway. 4. nine. See *upadvāra, kampa, kulyābha, tiryag, pakṣa, vaṃśa*; also *āvāra, cāra, gopura, surunga.*

dvāragopura: gateway of 5th (or last) enclosure. See *gopura.*

dvārapāla: g.

dvāraprāsāda: 1. gateway of 3rd enclosure (of temple). 2. gateway of interior enclosure (of palace).

dvāraśālā: 1. gateway of 2nd enclosure. 2. entrance of house.

dvāraśobhā: gateway of 1st enclosure.

dvāraharmya: 1. gateway of 4th enclosure (of temple). 2. gateway of interior enclosure (of palace).

dvārāyatana: gateway (of temple or town).

Dvijarāja: g.

dvitala: two storeyed building.

dvipañcaśāla: = *daśaśāḷa.*

dviśāla: house with two main buildings. See *lāṅgala.*

dvyaśravṛtta: apsidal. See *gajapṛṣṭha, hastipṛṣṭha.*

Dh

dhana: 1. type of pavilion. 2. category of main building (according to height/ width ratio). 3. = *dhanālaya.* 4. gain. 5. wealth (a 'part' in *āyādi* system). 6. nine.

dhanagṛha: = *dhanālaya.*

Dhanada: g. (= Kubera).

dhanadhānyagṛha: treasure room (in temple).

dhanasañcayāvāsa: treasure room (in house).

dhanasadman: = *dhanālaya.*

dhanasūtra: layout line for *dhanālaya.*

Dhanādhipa: g. (= Kubera).

dhanālaya: principal main building in *catuśśāla* meant for *śūdra.* See *dhana, dhanagṛha, dhanasadnam.*

dhanur: 1. pole (= *daṇḍa*). 2. bow (attribute). See *cāpa, kārmuka, pināka.*

dhanurgraha: cubit of 27 *aṅgula.*

dhanurdaṇḍa : pole (= *daṇḍa*).

dhanurmuṣṭi: cubit of 26 *aṅgula.*

dhanvana: a tree (used for pillars).

Dhanvantari: g.

dhammilla: type of hair arrangement.

Dhara: g. (a Vasu).

dharā: site.

dharātala: base (= *adhiṣṭhāna*).

Dharma: 1. g. 2. g. (a vāstudevatā, = Dharma-rāja). 3. ten.

Dharmarāja: g. (= Yama).

Dharmā: g.

dhātu: 1. coloring substance (used for foundation deposit). 2. five. 3. seven.

Dhātṛ: g. (= Brahmā).

dhānyavāsa: granary.

dhānyasūtra: layout line for *dhānyālaya.*

dhānyāgāra: 1. = *dhānyālaya.* 2. granary.

dhānyālaya: principal main building in *catuśśāla* meant for *vaiśya.* See *dakṣināgāra, dhānyāgāra.*

dhāman: 1. building, edifice. 2. main building (ref. house, = *śālā*).

dhārā: 1. side (of roof) (?). 2. facette (ref. Liṅga).

dhārāliṅga: type of Liṅga.

dhiṣṇya: 1. building, edifice. 2. subshrine, chapel (= *parivārālaya*).

dhūma: cloud (a 'matrice' in *āyādi* system).

dhṛk: 1. a moulding of pedestal (= *ḍrk?*). 2. recessed moulding of finial.

dhṛkkaṇṭha: a moulding of the abacus (*maṇḍi*).

Dhruva: g. (a Vasu).

dhvaja: 1. emblem, banner; 2. standard (a 'matrice' in the *āyādi* system). 3. mast (= *dhvajadaṇḍa*).

N

nakrakuṇḍala: type of ear pendant. See *ahikuṇḍala, phaṇī, vāsuki.*

nakṣatra: asterism (one of the *āyādi* series). See *uḍu, ṛkṣa.*

nagara: town, city.

nanda: 1. nine. 2. category of pavilion (according to number of foreparts).

nandaka: sword (attribute). See *asi.*

Nandikeśvara: g.

Nandin: g. (a dvārapāla).

nandyāvarta: 1. type of house with four main buildings. 2. type of village. 3. type of walls arrangement (ref. town, fort). 4. type of entablature. 5. type of window. 6. type of assembly (ref. joinery).

nandyāvartaśilā: type of liner (for Liṅga).

napuṃsaka: neutral (ref. buildings or building material). See *ṣaṇḍa.*

nayana: two.

Naravāha: g. (= Kubera).

Narahari: g. (= Nārasiṃha).

nalinaka: type of building (?).

Navabrahma: g.

Nāga: 1. g. (a vāstudevatā, = Gotranāga). 2. snake (attribute). 3. eight.

nāgapāśa: snake-like noose (attribute).

nāgara: 1. category of building. 2. category of Liṅga.

nāgavaktra: type of frieze (*prati*).

nāgavāsa: = *hastiśālā.*

nāgavṛtta: type of walls arrangement (ref. town).

nāgaśālā: = *hastiśālā.*

nāṭaka: dancing figure (decorated brace or strut).

nāṭyasabhā: dance hall, theatre.

nābhi: 1. street surrounding central part of a settlement (= *brahmavīthi*). 2. nave (ref. wheel).

Nārasiṃha: g. See Narahari.

nārācapatha: small street, alley.

nāla, nālikā: 1. gargoyle, spout. 2. urethra (ref. Liṅga).

nāli, nālikera: coconut tree (*Cocos nucifera*).

nālīgṛha: 1. sanctum. 2. cen-

tral passage of gateway. See *garbhagṛha*.
nāsa, nāsī, nāsikā: false dormer window (or similar projecting element), niche.
nāsyaṅga: projecting element (forepart, etc...).
nāsyaṅghri: pilaster.
niketana: building, edifice.
nikṣepa: recess (of moulding).
nikhātastambha: pillar whose bottom is sunk into base.
nikhātāṅghri: = *nikhātastambha*.
nigama: type of town.
nidrā: an element of entablature (w.r. for *nīvra*?).
nidhi: nine.
nimna: groove (moulding).
nimba: neem-tree (used for pillars, *Azadirachta indica*).
Nirṛti: 1. g. 2. g. (a vāstudevatā, = Mṛṣa).
nirgama: 1. projection (of moulding or any other element). 2. projecting element, forepart.
nirguṇḍin: a tree (*Vitex negundo*).
nirhyūhavalabhī: lean-to, pentroof.
nilaya: building, edifice.
nivāsa: house.
Niśā: g.
Niśācara: g. (category of-).
niṣkala: symbolic, unmanifest (ref. divine representations). See *akala, asakala.*
niṣkrānta: projection (= *nirgama*).
nīḍa: = *nāsī*.
nīpra: 1. projection. 2. see *nīvra*.
nīvra: eave (of roof or cornice).
nṛtta: dancing (posture).
nṛttamaṇḍapa: dance pavilion, theatre.
Nṛttamūrti: g.
netra: 1. two. 2. facade or gable. 3. a *mantra*.
netrabhitti: facade wall.
netraśālā: elongated forepart(?).
nyagrodha: banyan (*Ficus bengalensis*).

P

pakveṣṭakā: baked brick.
pakṣa: 1. fifteen. 2. two. 3. lateral (ref. buildings).
pakṣadvāra: side door, small door.
pakṣaśālā: elongated outward construction(?).
Pakṣirāja: g. (= Garuḍa).
paṅkaja: doucine (moulding, = *padma*).
paṅkajāsana: = *padmāsana*.

paṅkadurga: fort with earthen wall.

paṅkti: 1. ten. 2. row of houses.

Paṅktika: g. (a vāstudevatā, = Antarikṣa).

paṅktiśāla: = *daśaśāla.*

pacanageha: pavilion for oblations.

pacanasthāna: kitchen.

pañcatala: five-storeyed building.

Pañcavaktra: g. (= Śiva).

pañcavasanta: type of hall.

pañjara: 1. aviary. 2. intermediate aedicula (on entablature), niche. 3. loggia (ref. houses).

paṭṭa: 1. string-course. 2. plinth (= *jagatī*). 3. stren-gthening band (in metal). 4. strap (ref. divan). 5. felly (= *cakrapaṭṭa*).

paṭṭāmbuja: string-course decorated with lotuses.

paṭṭikā: 1. string-course. 2. stereobate (= *prati*). 3. gable, pediment (= *mukhapaṭṭika?*). 4. entablature (?). 5. ridge (ref. roof). 6. = *yogapaṭṭa.*

paṭṭikākṣepaṇāmbuja: = *paṭṭā-mbuja?*

paṭṭī: string-course.

pattana: type of town (harbour).

patra: a piece of timber work (ref. roof).

patrapotikā: type of bracket capital.

patrabandha: type of architrave.

patha: 1. street, road, way. 2. corridor.

pada: 1. diagram. 2. square (of a diagram). 3. building, edifice. 4. pillar, pilaster (= *stambha*), doorjamb. 5. crow-foot (ref. defective gems, = *bākapāda*).

padma: 1. lotus (*Nelumbium speciosum*). 2. a tree (used for temples only, perhaps *Juniper communis*). 3. doucine (moulding); see *abja, ambuja, kañja, kamala, kairava, paṅkaja.* 4. slab at bottom of finial. 5. lotus like top of altar. 6. type of palace (= *padmaka*). 7. type of village. 8. type of plan for pavilion. 9. type of firepit.

padmaka: 1. type of pavilion. 2. type of palace (=*padma* 6).

padmakumbhalatā: a wall ornament (see *kumbhalatā*).

padmakesara: type of base.

padmagarbha: diagram with 225 squares.

Padmaja: g. (a vāstudevatā, = Brahmā).

Padmanidhi: g.

padmapaṭṭikā: lotiform string course.

padmapīṭha: type of socle or pedestal. See *padmāsana.*

padmabandha: type of base.

padmasaṅghapaṭṭikā: a decorative band (?) (ref. assembly of plank-wall).

Padmā: g. (= Śrī).

padmāsana: 1. lotiform pillar base. 2. lotiform pedestal; see *ambujapīṭha, kamalāsana, paṅkajāsana, padmapīṭha.*

panasa: jacktree (used for pillars and chariots, *Artocar-pus integrifolia*).

pa'raga: type of village.

paramaśāyin: diagram with 81 squares.

paramāṇu: atom.

paralekhā: line used to draw roof(?).

paraśu: axe (attribute). See *ṭaṅka.*

parikhā: moat.

parighā: protective bar (on door).

paridhi: enclosure wall (ref. town).

parivāra: 1. attendant deity, shrine of an (= *parivārālaya*). 2. temple servant.

Parjanya: 1. g. (an Āditya). 2. g. (a vāstudevatā, = Jalada).

paryaṅka: bed, divan.

paryaṅkabandha: 1. = *paryaṅka.* 2. a posture.

paryaṅkaśibikā: type of litter.

paryantasūtra: outermost reference line (ref. layout).

parvata: type of two-storeyed temple.

palāśa: a tree (used for temples only, *Butea frondosa*).

Pavana: g. (a vāstudevatā, = Vāyu).

pavitra: = *yajñopavīta.*

pāṃsucaya: earthen parapet (around wall, between wall and moat?).

Pāñcajanya: g. (= Śaṅkha).

pāñcāla: 1. type of roof. 2. type of rafter. 3. type of two-storeyed temple.

pāṭala: a tree (used for temples only, *Bignonia suaveolens*).

pātala: seven.

pātra: casket (= *phelā*).

pād: pillar, pilaster (= *stambha*).

pāda: 1. pillar, pilaster (= *stambha*). 2. level of pillars. 3. door jamb (= *yoga*). 4. leg (of seat). 5. four.

pādabandha: type of base.

pādavarga: level of pillars.

pādaśāla: = *catuśśāla*.

pādukā: 1. plinth (= *jagatī*). 2. base (= *adhiṣṭhāna*). 3. sandals.

Pāparākṣasī: g. (a vāstudevatā).

pārijātaka: coral tree (used for temples only, *Erythrina indica*).

pārvatadurga: mountain fort.

Pārvatī: g.

pāli: flat slab (element of finial).

pālikā: 1. a decorative element (of cornice, see *karṇa*). 2. type of ear pendant.

pālyābha: overhanging.

Pāvaka: g. (a vāstudevatā, = Agni).

pāśa: 1. three. 2. noose (attribute).

piccha: peacock tail feather (attribute).

piṇḍa: 1. with joined main building (ref. house, = *abhinna*). 2. pedestal (= *piṇḍikā*).

piṇḍikā: pedestal.

piṇḍin: a tree (used for temple pillars only, *Vangueria spinosa*).

Pitāmaha: g. (a vāstudevatā, = Brahmā).

pitāmahābhāga: = *brahmabhāga.*

Pitṛ: 1. g. 2. g. (a vāstudevatā).

pippala: peepul-tree (= *aśvattha*).

Piśāca: g.

piśita: a tree (used for pillars).

pīṭha: 1. pedestal. 2. elongated seat (as opposed to square *āsana*). 3. altar for offerings. 4. = *brahmapīṭha.* 5. diagram with 9 squares. 6. nine.

pīṭhapadma: type of pedestal.

pīṭhā: box-like palanquin. See *paiṭhikā, paiṇḍikā.*

pīlu: a tree (used for temples only, *Careya arborea*).

puṃs: male (ref. stone, timber, buildings).

puṃnāga: laurel (*Calophyllum inophyllum*).

pucchavalakṣa: an element of roofing of *sabhā*.

puṭa: fire place.

putrajīva: a tree (used for temples only, *Putranjiva roxburgii*).

pura: type of town.

Purandara: g. (= Indra).

Purārimūrti: g. (= Tripurasundaramūrti).

puruṣa: 1. see *vāstupuruṣa*. 2. a tree (used for pillars, *Grewia elastica*).

puṣkara: an element of timber work of roof.

puṣkala: g.

Puṣpa: g. (vāstudevatā, = Puṣpadanta).

puṣpakhaṇḍa: type of window.

Puṣpadanta: g. (a vāstudevatā). See Puṣpa.

puṣpapuṣkala: type of base.

puṣpamaṇḍapa: pavilion for storing flowers.

pustaka: book (attribute).

pūkaparva: type of assembly (ref. joinery).

pūjābhāga: = *śivabhāga*.

Pūtaṇa: 1. g. 2. g. (a vāstudevatā).

Pūrin: g. (= Śiva).

pūrṇakośa: category of pavilion (according to number of foreparts).

Pūrṇā: g.

pūrvāśra: type of pillar.

Pūṣan: 1. g. (an Āditya). 2. g. (a vāstudevatā).

Pṛthivī: g. (= Bhū).

Pṛthivīdhara: g. (a vāstudevatā). See Bhūdhara, Mahīdhara.

pṛṣṭhakūṭa: chimney(?).

pṛṣṭhavaṃśa: ridge beam.

pṛṣṭhaśālā: rear outward construction(?).

pecaka: diagram with four squares.

paiṭhikā: = *pīṭhā*.

paiṇḍikā: = *piṭhā*.

Paiśāca: 1. g. 2. a zone of plan (ref. town, sanctum).

paiśācapīṭha: altar for offerings (located outside temple enclosure).

pota: foundation work of a house (?).

potikā: bracket capital.

pauruṣaliṅga: type of Liṅga.

pauṣṭika: 1. category of building (according to height/width ratio). 2. mode of cutting a stone to make a Liṅga.

prakīrṇaka: type of village.

pragrīva: vestibule (ref. stables). See *mukhaśālā.*

Pracaṇḍa: g.

pracchādana: roofing.

Prajāpati: g.

prajvalana: fire (attribute = Agni).

praṇāla: gargoyle, spout. See *nāla.*

prati (pratī): 1. stereobate (between two levels of elevation, see *antaraprastara, paṭṭikā, madhyamamañca, vitardi, vṛti, vedikā, vedī*). 2. frieze (part of entablature). 4. upper string-course. 4. elevated sill (= *gulpha*).

pratikrama: type of base.

pratibandha: type of base.

pratibhadra: type of socle.

pratimā: image, manifest representation of a god. See *bimba, bera, sakala.*

pratimukha: frieze, string-course.

prativaktra: frieze, string-course.

prativāṭabhū: vacant spot (? = *vāṭadhara*).

pratistambha: type of pillar.

pratyālīḍha: a posture (alike that of a bowman in action).

Pratyuṣā: g.

Pratyūṣa: g. (a Vasu).

prathameṣṭakā: first brick (ref. foundation ceremony).

prapā: light building (often a mere synonym with *maṇḍapa*).

Prabhā: g.

prabhāmaṇḍala: nimbus.

Prabhāva: g. (a Vasu).

pramāṇa: reference dimension (ref. building, site).

pramāṇasūtra: reference line.

pramālikā: brace. See *mṛṇālikā, vakrastambha.*

prayogaśālā: training hall (?).

pralambana: overhang.

pralīnaka: type of house.

praveśa: 1. recess (of moulding or any other element). 2. entrance, porch.

prasūtigṛha: confinement room. See *sūtigṛha.*

prastara: 1. entablature (and the ceiling which is at the same level). See *kapota, paṭṭikā, mañca.* 2. plank floor. 3. type of village.

prastala: ? (perhaps w.r. for *prastara*).

prahīnaśikhara: flat (or almost flat) roof (= *harmyākara?*).

prāṃśuraśmi: long(?) rafter

(ref. roofing of halls, = *dīrghalupā*).
prākāra: enclosure (of town, palace, temple...).
prāgvaṃśa: purlin.
Prājāpatya: cubit of 25 aṅgulā.
prāsāda: building (especially temple with a six level elevation).
prāsādavant: temple-like (ref. buildings with six-level elevation).
prāsādabījamantra: formula for consecration.
prokṣaṇa: consecration ceremony.
proṣṭanā: bed, seat.
plakṣa: a tree (used for temples only, *Ficus infectoria*).

Ph

phaṇikuṇḍala: type of ear pendant (= *nakrakuṇḍala*).
phaṇihasta: a gesture.
phalakā: 1. plank. 2. plank or stone slab set above foundation deposit. 3. abacus (= *maṇḍi*). 4. an element of finial (= *pāli*).
phalakāsana: bench.
phalika: roof (= *śikhara*).
phālakakuḍya: plank partition wall.
phelā: casket (ref. foundation deposit). See *pātra, bhājana, mañjuṣā*.

B

badara: a tree (used for temples only, = *Zizyphus Jujuba*).
bandha: 1. assembly (ref. joinery). 2. mortar. 3. bolt, closing device. 4. three. 5. type of stereobate.
bandhana: 1. assembly (ref. joinery). 2. diadem. 3. moat (?).
bandhodaka: binding water (used in coatings).
barbara: type of rafter.
balālokamaṇḍapa: rostrum for military reviews.
baliviṣṭara: altar (placed within temple enclosure).
bāṇa: 1. arrow (attribute). 2. five.
bāṇaliṅga: type of Liṅga.
bāla: young (ref. stone).
bāhudaṇḍaka: type of town.
bindu: drop (ref. defective gems).
bimba: image (manifest representation of a god = *pratimā*).
bilva: a tree (*Aegle marmelos*).
bījamantra: formula for consecration.

Buddha: g. See Sugata.
buddhi: five.
Bṛhaspati: g.
bera: image, manifest representation of a god (= *pratimā*).
bodhaka: a decorative element (of roof of *maṇḍapa:* perhaps a lantern, = *raṅga*?)
Bodhana: g. (a vāstudevatā = Dauvārika or Sugrīva).
brahmakānta: type of pillar.
brahmapīṭha: altar for domestic ritual (in centre of house or palace). See *pīṭha.*
brahmabhāga: square part of a three-section Liṅga. See *ajabhāga, pitāmahabhāga, brahmāṃśa.*
brahmarāja: type of assembly (ref. joinery).
brahmavastu: = *brahmasthāna.*
brahmavīthi: street surrounding central part of settlement. See *nābhi, brahmāvṛtapatha.*
brahmavedikā: socle of the *brahmapīṭha.*
brahmaśilā: type of liner (for Liṅga).
brahmasūtra: 1. median line of the plan of sanctum. 2. urethra (ref. Liṅga, = *nāla, ajasūtra*).
brahmasthāna: centre (of building or settlement) (*passim*).
Brahmā: 1. g. 2. g. (a vāstudevatā). See Aja, Ka, Kamalaja, Pitāmaha, Śambhu, Saha.
brahmāṃśa: = *brahmabhāga.*
Brahmāṇī: g. See Brāhmī.
brahmāvṛtapatha: = *brahmavīthi.*
brahmāsana: = *brahmasthāna.*
brāhma: a zone of plan (ref. town, sanctum).
Brāhmī: g. (= Brahmāṇī).

Bh

bha: twenty-seven (for there are 27 asterisms).
bhakti: intercolumniation (relative unit for *maṇḍapa, prapā, sabhā*).
Bhaga: g. (an Āditya).
bhadra: 1. projecting moulding. 2. forepart, projecting element.
bhadraka: 1. type of town. 2. type of pillar. 3. type of pavilion.
bhadrakalyāṇa: 1. type of town. 2. type of seven-storeyed gateway.
bhadrakūṭa: type of four-storeyed temple.
bhadrakoṣṭha: 1. type of

three-storeyed temple. 2. type of four-storeyed temple.

bhadrakauśika: category of pavilion (according to number of foreparts).

bhadrapīṭha: type of pedestal.

bhadramahāsana: diagram with 96 squares.

bhadramukha: type of town.

bhadrasundara: type of seven-storeyed gateway.

Bhallāṭa: g. (a vāstudevatā).

bhavana: 1. building edifice. 2. palace.

bhājana: 1. = *phelā*. 2. socket (ref. door hinge).

Bhanū: 1. g. (a vāstudevatā). 2. twelve (*passim*). See Sūrya.

bhāra: long beam (part of chariot frame).

Bhārati: g. (Sarasvatī).

bhāropadhāna: long beam support (part of chariot frame).

Bhāskara: 1. = Āditya (the twelve-). 2. g. (a vāstudevatā, = Sūrya).

Bhikṣāṭanamūrti: g.

bhiṇḍipāla: combat-mace (attribute).

bhitti: wall. See *kabhitti, kuḍya, garbhabhitti, gṛhapiṇḍi, madhyabhitti.*

bhinna: whose main buildings are separated from each other (ref. houses).

bhukti: enjoyment (a 'part' in *āyādi* system).

bhuktigeha: dining room.

bhuja: regular cubit (= *hasta*).

Bhujaṅgatrāsa: g. (a form of Śiva's Nṛttamūrti).

Bhujaṅgalalita: g. (a form of Śiva's Nṛttamūrti).

bhū, bhūmi: 1. g. See Avanī, Pṛthivī, Vasundharā. 2. site; 3. storey (= *tala*). 4. floor (of room).

bhūta: five.

Bhūdhara: g. (a vāstudevatā, = Pṛthivīdhara).

bhūmideśa: floor level.

Bhṛgu: g.

bhṛṅgaka: a herb (*Eclipta erecta*).

Bhṛṅganṛpa, Bhṛṅgarāja: g. (a vāstudevatā).

Bhṛṅgiriti: g.

Bhṛśa: g. (a vāstudevatā).

bheṣaṇī: an element of door (?).

bhoga: 1. appurtenances (ref. house or palace). 2. vaulted (ref. room).

bhojanaśālā, bhojanasthāna: dining room.

bhauma: a tree (used for pillars).

M

makaratoraṇa: type of arch.

makṣikā: fly (ref. defective gems).

maṅgala: 1. type of village inhabited by brahmins only (= *agrahāra*). 2. type of pavilion. 3. see *aṣṭa-maṅgala.*

maṅgalavīthi: peripheral road (ref. town, village, etc.).

majjanāgāra: baths.

mañca: 1. throne, bench. 2. entablature (= *prastara*).

mañcabandha: type of base.

mañcilikā: divan.

mañjuṣā: = *phelā.*

maṭha: 1. hermitage, monastery. 2. village inhabited by ascetics.

maṇirekhā: lateral line (ref. Liṅga).

maṇiliṅga: a Liṅga (any - which is not in stone).

maṇḍa: see *uttaramaṇḍa.*

maṇḍana: 1. decoration. 2. top part of pedestal (rim, cavity and spout).

maṇḍapa: 1. pavilion (espec. with a three level elevation). 2. covered gallery, portico. 3. flat roof. 4. = *mukhamaṇḍapa.* 5. = *vāstumaṇḍapa.* 6. = *yāgamaṇḍapa.*

maṇḍapamālikā: pillared gallery-like building.

maṇḍala: 1. diagram. 2. circumvolution (ref. stone). 3. nimbus; see *prabhāmaṇḍala.*

maṇḍi: abacus. See *phalakā.*

maṇḍitastambha: decorated pillar (?), pillar with an abacus(?).

maṇḍūka: diagram with 64 squares. See *caṇḍita.*

Mada: g.

Madana: g. (= Kāma).

Madirā: g.

Madhu: g.

Madhukara: g.

madhūka: a hardwood tree (used for pillars, etc., *Bassia latifolia*).

madhyakaraṇalupā: an intermediate rafter.

madhyabhāra: median long beam and pole (ref. chariot).

madhyabhitti: = *kabhitti.*

madhyamamañca: = *antara-prastara.*

madhyamaśilā: = *yauvanaśilā.*

madhyamasūtra: urethra (ref. Liṅga). See *nāla, brahmāsūtra.*

madhyaraśmi: median rafter.

madhyalupā: median rafter.

madhyavaṃśa: ridge beam.

madhyavedikā: = *brahmavedikā.*

madhyahāra: third enclosure (ref. temple).

manas: one.

Manu: 1. g. 2. fourteen.

manohara: 1. pavilion (= *maṇḍapa*). 2. type of two-storeyed temple. 3. type of four storeyed temple.

mantra: see.

mantranālikā: sceptre.

mantraśālā: council chamber.

mandira: 1. building, edifice. 2. palace.

Marici (Marīci): g. (a vāstudevatā, = Ārya).

Marut: g. (the eight-).

mardala: type of *dvāraharmya* gateway.

marma: vulnerable point (ref. Vāstupuruṣa).

maryādi: fifth (or exterior) enclosure (of temple or palace).

malla: an element of timber work of roof.

mallalīla: type of assembly.

mallavasanta: type of hall.

masūra: base (= *adhiṣṭhāna*).

mastaka: roof (= *śikhara*).

Mahākāla: g. (a dvārapāla, = Kāla).

mahādruma: a tree (used for temples only).

mahānasa: 1. kitchen. 2. = *annālaya.*

mahāpīṭha: diagram with 16 squares.

mahābja (mahāmbuja): type of pedestal.

mahāvajra: type of pedestal.

mahāvṛtta: type of tenon-and-mortice assembly.

Mahīdhara: g. (a vāstudevatā, = Pṛthivīdhara).

Mahendra: g. (a vāstudevatā).

Maheśvara: g. (= Śiva).

maheśvarabhāga: = *śivabhāga.*

māgadha: type of roof.

Mātṛ.: g. (the seven-).

mātra: 1. absolute unit (= *aṅgula*). 2. a relative unit (used in iconometry, = *aṅgula*).

mātrakhaṇḍa: 1. type of *dvāragopura* gateway. 2. type of three-storeyed gateway.

mātrāṅgula: a relative unit (used for sacrifices).

mānasūtra: reference line. See *ṛjusūtra, pramāṇasūtra.*

mānāṅgula: absolute unit (= *aṅgula*).

mānuṣa: a zone of plan (ref. town, sanctum).

Māraṇī: a Kāma's arrow.

Māruta: g. (a vāstudevatā, = Vāyu).

māruda: a tree (= *kaṭphala?*).

mārga: 1. street. 2. corridor, walkway. 3. type of pavilion.

mārtaṇḍa: twelve.

mālāsthāna: frieze decorated with garlands (element of pillar).

mālikā: gallery-like building.

mālikāmaṇḍpa: type of storeyed pavilion.

mālya: type of pavilion.

mālyādbhuta: type of pavilion.

māṣa: 1. gram (used for offerings and for making coatings, *Phaseolus radiatus*). 2. square measure (= 4 kākaṇi).

māhendra: type of hall.

Māheśvarī: g.

miṇṭhaka: bretesse (?).

Mitra: 1. g. (an Āditya). 2. g. (a vāstudevatā).

mitravāsa: guest room.

mithuna: 1. two. 2. amorous pairs (decorative motive), element decorated with amorous pairs.

mirṇakā: an element of doorleaf(?).

miśra: 1. mixed (ref. building made up of two materials). 2. mixed representation (at the same time manifest and non-manifest = *Mukhaliṅga*).

miśradurga: fort with natural and manmade defences.

mukula: 1. bud (tip of finial, = *kuḍmala*). 2. bud (tip of urethra of Liṅga).

mukha: 1. facade or gable. 2. face (ref. stone).

mukhapaṭṭikā: gable, pediment.

mukhamaṇḍapa: pavilion built in front of the sanctum. See *maṇḍapa.*

Mukhaliṅga: See *miśra.*

mukhaśālā: vestibule (ref. stables, = *pragrīva*).

Mukhya: g. (a vāstudevatā, = Gaṇamukhya).

muṇḍa: an element of timber work of roof.

muṇḍatulā: ridge beam(?).

muṇḍākāra: flat (ref. roof).

Muṇḍin: g. (a dvārapāla).

mudga: green gram (*Phaseolus mungo*).

mudgin: a kind of mortar or coating (?).

Muni: 1. g. (the seven-). 2. seven. See Ṛṣi.

muṣṭibandha: moulding (?) with fist-like decoration.

musala: mace (attribute).

muhūrtastambha: pillar set up above foundation deposit.

mūtracchidra, mūtradvārga: drain for urine (ref. stables).
mūrti: 1. incarnation, manifestation (see). 2. three.
mūrtipa: guardian of image (attendant of *sthāpaka*).
mūrdhan: roof (= *śikhara*).
mūrdhaneṣṭakā: crowning brick (ref. completion ceremony).
mūla: bottom (ref. stone, timber).
mūlakośa: hereditary treasure.
mūlatala: first storey, first floor, ground floor.
Mṛga: 1. g. (a vāstudevatā). 2. lion (a 'matrice' in *āyādi* system).
mṛgapāda: deer-foot (ref. furniture).
mṛṇālikā: brace (= *pramālikā*).
Mṛtasañjīvanī: g.
Mṛtyu: g.
mṛdaṅga: type of walls arrangement (ref. town).
Mṛṣa: g. (a vāstudevatā, = Nirṛti).
mekhalā: 1. step (ref. firepit). 2. belt.
meruka: type of pavilion.
merukānta: type of house with three main buildings.
merugopura: type of outermost gateway (ref. palace).
meṣāyuddha: type of tenon-and-mortice assembly.
mokṣa: three.
mohāmara: plinth (= *jagatī*).
Mohinī: g.
mauñjika: belt of *muñja* grass.
mauṇḍī: type of palanquin.
mauli: type of pavilion.
maulika: type of house with a single main building.
maulibhadra: type of house with three main buildings.

Y

Yakṣa: 1. g. 2. g. (a vāstudevatā, = Roga or Śoṣa).
Yakṣiṇī: g.
Yakṣendra: g.
yajñasūtra: = *yajñopavīta.*
yajñopavīta: sacrificial thread.
yantra: 1. war machine; see *cakraka.* 2. = *jalayantra.*
Yama: 1. g. 2. g. (a vāstudevatā). See Ārkin, Daṇḍapāṇi.
yamin (or yamī): seven.
yaṁīśa: seven.
yava: barley grain (linear measure, = an eighth of *aṅgula*).
yaṣṭi: pole (= *daṇḍa*).
yāgamaṇḍapa: sacrificial pa-

vilion. See *maṇḍapa* and *vimāna*(?).

yātrāmaṇi: type of royal city (= *saṅgrāma*).

yāna: vehicle.

Yāmalatantra: n. of a śākta collection of texts.

yukta: crossroad.

yuga: four.

yugakoṣṭha: = *catuśśāla*.

yugala: two.

yugma: two.

yugaśāla: = *catuśśāla*.

yūkā: louse (formless unit of linear measurement).

yoga: door jamb.

Yoganidrāsubhadraka: g. (= Anantaśāyin).

yogapaṭṭa: ascetic's belt. See *paṭṭikā*.

yogāsana: a posture.

Yoginī: g.

yojana: linear measure (= 8000 poles).

yoni: 1. matrice (one of the *āyādi* series, see *guhya*). 2. type of firepit (*kuṇḍa*). 3. vulva (element of a firepit).

yauvana: adult (ref. stone). See *madhyamaśilā*.

R

Rakṣaka, Rakṣas: g.

raṅga: 1. canopy. 2. chamber of house-mistress (in principal main building of *catuśśāla*). 3. type of cart. 4. theatre(?).

rajju: 1. rope. 2. rope (linear measure = 4 poles). 3. line of diagram.

Rati: g.

ratikānta: type of *dvāraśobhā* gateway.

ratnakuṇḍala: type of ear pendant.

ratni: 1. regular cubit *hasta*. 2. fourteen.

ratha: cart, chariot.

Rathanemi: g. See Cakra.

rathamārga: chariot-road (ref. villages or towns).

rathareṇu: speck of dust (formless unit of linear measurement).

randhra: bay, opening of window.

Ramā: g. (= Lakṣmī).

raśmi: 1. rafter (ref. *sabhā*). 2. three.

rasa: six.

Rākṣasa: g. (a vāstudevatā, = Gṛhakṣata).

rāja: king (a 'part' in the *āyādi* system).

rājagṛha: King's palace.

rājadvāra: royal gate (at end of *rājavīthi*?).

rājadhānin: capital city.

rājavīthi: street leading to centre of city.

rājādana: a tree (used for pillars, *Mimusops indica*).

rāma: three.

rucaka: type of house with four main buildings.

Rudra: 1. g. (the eleven-) (?). 2. g. (a vāstudevatā). 3. eleven.

Rudraja, Rudrarāja: g. (a vāstudevatā).

rudrākṣa: three.

rūpottara: type of architrave.

rekhā: 1. streak (ref. defective stones or gems). 2. characteristic line (ref. Liṅga).

Revatī: g.

Roga: g. (a vāstudevatā).

Rohiṇi: 1. g. 2. (the seven-).

rohāroha: wheel.

L

lakṣaṇoddhāraṇa: drawing the characteristic lines of Liṅga.

Lakṣmī: g. See Ramā, Śrī.

latāphala: a fragrant plant (*Trichosanthes dioicea*).

lambanīḍa: overhanging niche.

lambapañjara: = *lambanīḍa*.

laya: building, edifice.

lalāṭa: 1. gable or facade. 2. front of a chariot.

lalita: type of four-storeyed gateway.

lāṅgala: 1. house with two main buildings (= *dviśāla*). 2. type of plan for pavilions.

lāṅgalākārakuḍya, lāṅgalākārabhitti: corner wall.

lāṅgalākāraśikhā: ploughshare-shaped tenon (ref. joinery).

Lāṅgalin: g. (a dvārapāla).

likuca: a tree (used for pillars, *Artocarpus lacucha*).

likṣā: nit (formless unit of linear measurement).

Liṅga: see 33.1.

Liṅgasaṃbhūtamūrti: g.

lupā: rafter. See *anukoṭi, anuvaṃśa, karṇaraśmi, karṇalupā, koṭi, prāṃśuraśmi, raśmi.*

lupākoṭi: = *koṭilupā.*

lodhra: a tree (used for temples only, *Symplocos racemosa*).

loṣṭa: tile.

lohaloṣṭa: element of metallic roofing.

V

vaṃśa: 1. beam. 2. ridge beam. 3. floor beam (between ground and plank floor). 4. bone of Vāstupuruṣa and/or line of diagram. 5. axis of a main building (ref. houses).

vaṃśadvāra: axial door (ref. houses).

vaṃśanāsī: false dormer window set in gable.

vakula: a tree (used for temples only, *Mimusops Elengi*).

vaktra: 1. frieze. 2. porch, entrance. 3. facade gable.

vakradaṇḍa: crooked stick (attribute).

vakrastambha: brace or strut (= *pramālikā?*).

vajra: 1. an attribute. 2. a moulding.

vajrapadma: = *vajrapiṭha.*

Vajrapāṇi: g. (= Indra).

vajrapīṭha: type of pedestal. See *vajrapadma.*

vajrābha: dovetail assembly (ref. joinery).

Vajrin: g. (= Indra).

vaṭa: *banyan.*

vadana: gable.

vana: four.

vanadurga: forest fort.

vapra: 1. parapet, city wall. 2. plinth (= *jagatī*). 3. fillet (a moulding).

vaprabandha: type of base.

vapramārga: road along rampart.

vayas: age (in the *āyādi* system).

varayoga: an astrological conjunction.

varaṇa; a tree (used for temple only).

varada: gift (a gesture).

varāṭa: type of rafter.

Varāha: g.

Varuṇa: 1. g. 2. g. (a vāstudevatā). See Jala, Jalādhipa, Jaleśa, Toya.

varga: 1. level of elevation. 2. moulding.

varcas, varcogeha: latrines.

varṇapaṭṭikā: a moulding (?).

vartanaka: square measure (= 16 *kākaṇi*).

vardhaki: fitter (assistant to *sthapati*).

vardhamāna: 1. type of house with four main buildings. 2. type of window. 3. type of entablature. 4. type of Liṅga.

varṣasthala: gutter.

valakṣa: an element of roofing of *sabhā.* See *puccha-valakṣa, svasti-valakṣa.*

valagna: a recessed element of finial. See *skandha.*

valabhī: see *niryūhavalabhī.*

valaya: lierne (ref. roof or pent-roof).

valīka: = *valaya?*

Vallī: g.
vallīmaṇḍala: spiral staircase (with newel).
Vasanta: g.
vasantaka: frieze (?, moulding of entablature).
Vasu: 1. g. (the eight=). 2. eight.
Vasundharā: g. (= Bhū).
vastu: 1. dwelling site. 2. building, edifice. 3. dwelling (house with its annexes).
vastusubhadra: type of town.
vastvādhāra: base (= *adhiṣṭhāna*).
Vahni: 1. g. (= Agni). 2. g. (a vāstudevatā, = Agni). 3. fire (attribute, = Agni). 4. three (= Agni). 5. a tree (for pavilion pillars).
vāḥsthala: gutter.
vāḥsthāna: tank.
Vāgvadhu: g. (= Sarasvatī).
vājana: 1. fillet, string course (mouldings). 2. upper fascia (of architrave). 3. architrave (= *uttara*). 4. door frame. 5. an element of seat.
vājiśālā: = *aśvaśālā*.
vāṭadhara: undeveloped area (in settlement).
vāṭabhitti: enclosure wall (of house).
vāṭikā: square measure (= 80 *kākani*).
vātāyana: window.
vādyasthāna: store for musical instruments.
vāpī: tank, basin.
Vāmana: 1. g. 2. small street, alley.
vāyasa: crow (a 'matrice' in the *āyādi* system).
Vāyu: 1. g. 2. g. (a vāstudevatā). See Anila, Pavana, Māruta, Samīraṇa.
vāra: 1. solar day (one of the *āyādi* series). 2. inner court (covered or not covered), verandah, portico.
varaṇa: 1. inner court. 2. entrance, porch.
Vārāhī: g.
vāritala: gutter.
vāriniḥsrava: drain, sewage outlet (= *jaladvāra*).
vālāgra: tip of hair (formless unit of measurement).
vāsa: 1. temple. 2. = *garbhagṛha*. 3. dwelling house. 4. main building (= *śālā*). 5. room. 6. quarter (in town).
vāsaguhā: niche.
vāsapaṅkti: quarter (in town).
vāsikabaddhamakuṭa (*śekhara*): type of headdress.

vāsukikuṇḍala: type of ear pendant (= *nakrakuṇḍala*).

vāstala: gutter.

vāstu: 1. dwelling (see chapter 2). 2. site. 3. building, edifice.

vāstudeva: god protecting the site (and the building).

vāstupuruṣa: g. ('Spirit of the building').

vāstumaṇḍapa: central pavilion (of house or palace). See *maṇḍapa*.

vikalpa: 1. category of building (according to arrangement of aediculae). 2. type of plan for pavilions. 3. category of house (according to length/width ratio). 4. type of hall. 5. mode of cutting a stone to make a Liṅga.

vikāra: sixteen.

vikṣepa: projection (= *nirgama*).

Vighneśa: g. (= Gaṇeśa).

vici: see *vīcī*.

vijaya: 1. type of four-storeyed temple (= *jayāvaha*). 2. type of pavilion. 3. type of town. 4. type of five-storeyed gateway.

vijayadvāra: a gate of the city (= *vijayaviśāla* or *vijaya* 4).

vijayaviśāla: type of *dvāraśālā* gateway.

viṭa: an element of roof timber work.

viḍamba: type of town.

Vitatha: g. (a vāstudevatā).

vitardi: stereobate (= *prati*).

vitasti: 1. span (= *aṅgulas*); see *tāla*. 2. a projecting element(?).

vitāna: canopy.

Vidarī: g. (a vāstudevatā).

viddha: tenon (ref. joinery).

Vidyādhara, Vidyeśvara: g. (the eight-).

Vidhātṛ: g.

Vināyaka: g. (= Gaṇeśa).

viniṣkrānta: forepart.

vinyāsasūtra: layour line.

vipat: adversity (a 'part' in the *āyādi* system).

vipulabhoga: diagram with 676 squares.

vipulasundara: type of two-storeyed temple.

vipragarbha: diagram with 576 squares.

vipratīkānta: 1. diagram with 729 squares. 2. type of *dvāraśālā* gateway.

viprabhaktika: diagram with 841 squares.

vimalā: lintel. See *uttara*.

vimalākṛti: type of three-storeyed temple.

vimāna: 1. building, edifice (often temple as opposed to human dwelling). 2. building with wagon roof(?). 3. (?) (= *yāga-maṇḍapa?*).
Vivasvant: 1. g. (an Āditya). 2. g. (a vāstudevatā).
Vivāhamūrti: g. See Kalyāṇa-mūrti.
Viśalyakaranī: g.
viśāla: 1. width. 2. diagram with 529 squares.
viśālākṣa: diagram with 784 squares.
viśālāya: type of *dvāraśālā*.
Viśvakarman: g.
viśvakoṣṭha: = (*havyakoṣṭha* or *annālaya*).
Viśvamardinī: one of the Kāma's arrows.
viśveṣa: diagram with 625 squares.
viśveṣasāra: diagram with 900 squares.
Viṣagraha: g.
viṣṭha: crossbeam or ridge-beam.
viṣṭara: 1. cushion. 2. pedestal.
Viṣṇu: 1. g. 2. g. (an Āditya).
viṣṇukānta: 1. type of pillar. 2. type of two-storeyed temple.
viṣṇukrānta: a medicinal plant (*Clitoria ternatia*).
viṣṇubhāga: element of Viṣṇu (ref. Liṅga). See *haribhāga*.
Viṣṇvardha: g. (= Harihara).
vihāra: monastery.
vihāraśālaka: monastery (made up of several main buildings joined together).
vīcī: back of seat.
vīṇā: an attribute.
vīthi: street.
vīrakāṇḍa (°kānta): dye with human figure (part of pillar) (?).
Vītrabhadra: g.
virāsana: a posture.
vṛti: frieze (= *prati*).
vṛtta: 1. a rounded moulding. 2. = *vṛttaśālā* (?).
vṛttakūṭa: type of three-storeyed temple.
vṛttaśālā: a building in the palace (in connection with the bull?).
vṛttasphuṭita: a wall ornament.
vṛttaharmya: type of two-storeyed temple.
vṛddha: aged (ref. stone).
Vṛṣa: 1. g. 2. bull (a 'matrice' in the *āyādi* system).
Vṛṣārudhamūrti: g.
veṇuparva: type of assembly (ref. joinery).

vetra: 1. reed (moulding) see *vṛtta*. 2. tip of hinge pin. (ref. door).

Veda: 1. g. (a vāstudevatā). 2. four. 3. type of pavilion.

vedikā, vedī: 1. stereobate (= *prati*) (?). 2. low base (of *prapā*). 3. platform, altar. 4. = *brahmavedikā*.

vedibhadra: 1. type of town. 2. type of socle.

vela: spear (attribute).

veśa: 1. porch. 2. gateway (= *gopura*).

veśana: 1. entrance, porch. 2. recess (ref. moulding).

veśāyatana: gateway.

veśman: 1. building, edifice. 2. palace.

vesara: 1. category of temple. 2. category of Liṅga.

Vaijaya: g. (a dvārapāla).

vaijayanta: type of single-storeyed temple.

vaideha: type of roof.

Vainateya: g. (= Garuḍa).

Vaivasvata: g.

vaivāhikamaṇḍapa: = *kalyāṇamaṇḍapa*.

Vaiśravaṇa: g.

Vaiṣṇavī: g.

vyañjana: a half.

vyaya: loss (in the *āyādi* system). See *ṛṇa*.

vyākhyānahasta: teaching gesture. See *saṃdaṃśahasta*.

vyamiśra: types of rafter and of *puṣkara* (?).

Vyoman: g. (a vāstudevatā, = Antarikṣa).

vratabhoga: diagram with 289 squares.

Ś

śakata: 1. gnomon. 2. stake. 3. peg. (ref. joinery).

śakti: 1. spear (attribute). 2. power (a 'part' in the *āyādi* system).

śaktidhvaja: pole, mast.

Śaṅkara: g.

śaṅkhu: 1. gnomon. 2. stake. 3. peg. (ref. joinery) (?).

śaṅkha: shank (attribute; may appear under a manifest form). See Pāñcajanya.

śaṅkhakuṇḍala: type of ear pendant.

Śaṅkhanidhi: g.

śaṅkhamaṇḍala: spiral staircase. See *śaṅkhāvarta sopāna, śṛṅgamaṇḍala*.

śaṅkhasaṅgalupā: arrangement of rafters for a pyramid roof(?).

śaṅkhāvartasopāna: = *śaṅkhamaṇḍala*.

Śacīpati: g. (= Indra).

śami: a tree (used for stakes and pillars, *Mimosa suma*).

Śambhu: 1. g. (= Brahmā). 2. g. (= Śiva).

śambhubhāga: = *śivabhāga.*

śambhubhāgādhika: type of Liṅga (= *śivādhika*).

śayana: 1. couch (any piece of furniture where one can lie or sit).

śayanasthāna: 1. dormitory (for images in temple). 2. box, stall (ref. *hastiśālā*).

śayanīyagṛha: bedroom.

śayita: horizontal (ref. timber).

śara: five.

śalmalī: cotton-tree. (used for temples only, *Bombax ceiba*).

śalya: peg (ref. joinery).

śavāvāsa: cremation ground.

Śaśin: 1. g. 2. g. (a vāstu devatā). 3. one. See Candra.

śastraśālā: armoury.

śāka: teak tree (*Tectona grandis*).

śāntika: category of building. (according to height/ width ratio).

śārṅga: bow (attribute). See *dhanur.*

śālā: 1. house. 2. main building (of house). see *ekaśāla, dviśāla,* etc. 3. elongated aedicula (= *koṣṭha*). 4. = *ūrdhvakoṣṭha.* 5. elongated outward building (of house). 6. wagonroof. 7. enclosure (= *sāla*).

Śāstā: g. See Ārya, Gītabhāvin, Jñānabhāvin, Devabhāvin, Surapriya, Surabhāvin.

śiṃśapā: a tree (used for pillars, *Dalberghia sissoo*).

Śikhaṇḍin: g. (a vidyeśvara).

śikhara: roof. See *ka, phalika, mastaka, mūrdhan, śiras, śīrṣa.*

śikharā: = *śekharī.*

śikhā: 1. tenon (ref. joinery). 2. peg (ref. joinery). 3. = *stūpikā.* 4. trident (attribute, = *triśūla*).

Śikhin: 1. g. (a vāstudevatā). 2. three. See Agni.

śikhipāda: peacock foot (support of finial).

śibikā: palanquin.

śibira: camp (ref. army).

śiras: 1. roof (= *śikhara*). 2. head, top (of Liṅga).

śirīṣa: a tree (used for temple pillars only, *Albizzia lebbeck*).

śiromālā: garland of skulls (= *karoṭimāla*).

Śilā: g. (= Himavant?).

śilīndhra: banana-tree, plantain.

śilpika: war machine(?), trap(?).

śilpin: 1. builder, technician. 2. an assistant to *sthāpaka*.

Śiva: 1. g. 2. g. (a vāstudevatā = Īśa). 3. one. 4. three (= *śivākṣa*). 5. eleven (= Rudra). 6. type of pavilion. 7. = *śivabhāga*.

śivabhāga: top element of three section Liṅga. See *aiśaka, pūjābhāga, raudra, śambhubhāga, śiva, śaiva, harābhaga*.

śivādhika: type of Liṅga. See *śambhubhāgādhika, śaivādhika*.

Śivotkṛṣṭa: g. (a vidyeśvara).

śīta: type of single-storey gateway.

śīrṣa (śīrṣaka): 1. roof. 2. coping of wall.

śukanāsī: a decorative element.

śukavimāna: type of hall.

Śukra: g.

śuṇḍupāda: type of pillar.

śuddha: pure. (ref. building made up of only one material).

śūrpa: house with three main buildings (= *triśāla*).

śūla: 1. stake. 2. trident. (attribute, = *triśūla*). 3. a mantra.

śṛṅkhalā: chain (attribute) (?).

śṛṅgamaṇḍala: = *śaṅkhamaṇḍala*.

śaiva: 1. image of Śiva. 2. = *śaivabhāga*. 3. one.

śaivala: a plant (*Blyxa octandra?*).

śaivādhika: = *śivādhika*.

śobhana: type of stand for worship.

śobhā: see *dvāraśobhā*.

Śoṣa: g. (a vāstudevatā).

śauṇḍika: type of rafter.

śaurasena: type of roof.

śmaśāna: cemetery.

Śyena: g. (a vāstudevatā, = Agni).

Śrī: g. See Lakṣmī.

śrīkara: 1. type of bell capital. 2. type of single storeyed temple. 3. type of *dvāraśobhā* gateway. 4. type of pedestal.

śrīkānta: type of *dvāraprāsāda* gateway.

śrīkāmya: type of pedestal.

śrīkeśa: type of *dvāraprāsāda* gateway.

Śrīkhaṇḍa: 1. g. (a vidyeśvara). 2. type of pillar.

śrīcchanda: type of five-storeyed gateway.

śrīniketana: type of three-storeyed gateway.

śrīpaṭṭa: a moulding of pedestal (perhaps w.r. for *tripaṭṭa*).

śrīpratiṣṭha: type of village.
śrīpratiṣṭhita: type of hall.
śrībandha: type of base.
śrībhadra: 1. type of pavilion. 2. type of single-storey gateway.
śrībhoga: 1. type of temple with one storey. 2. type of temple with three storeys.
śrīmukha: a decorative motive (of door leaf).
śrīrūpa: type of pavilion.
śrīvajra: type of pillar.
śrīvatsa: type of village.
śrīviśāla: 1. type of temple with one-storey. 2. type of temple with four-storeys. 3. type of *dvāragopura* gateway.
śreṇibandha: type of base.
ślesmātakin: a tree (used for temples only, *Cordia lati-folia*).
śvan: dog (a 'matrice' in *āyādi* system).
śvabhra: foundation pit.

Ṣ

ṣaṭśikha: type of assembly.
ṣaṇḍa: 1. neutral (ref. buildings, materials) (= *upasañcita*); see *napuṃsaka*. 2. eunuch (a 'part' of in *āyādi* system).
Ṣaṇmukha: 1. g. (= Skanda). 2. type of plan for pavilions.

S

sakarṇa: type of latticed window.
sakala: 1. image, manifest representation of a god. 2. diagram with one square. 3. one(?).
sagarbhaśilā: = *garbhiṇi.*
saṇkaraśālā: = *saṅkarālaya.*
saṅkarārāma: = *saṅkarālaya.*
saṅkarālaya: brothel (?).
saṅkīrṇa: mingled (ref. building made up of three materials).
saṅkīrṇakīla: type of assembly (ref. joinery).
saṅgrāma: type of royal city (= *yātrāmaṇi*).
saṅgha: assembly. (ref. joinery).
Saciva: g.
sañcita: category of building (built with stone or brick and massive from entablature to top).
Satya: g. (a vāstudevatā).
sadana: building, edifice.
Sadādyāyin: g. (=Śāstā).
sadman: building, edifice.
saṃdaṃśahasta: teaching gesture. See *vyākhyānahasta.*

sandhāna: assembly. (ref. joinery).

sandhi: 1. assembly. (ref. joinery); 2. join (between two main buildings). 3. crossing-point (ref. lines of diagram).

sandhikāryamaṇḍapa: pavilion for alliance.

sandhipatra: flat piece covering joins of door leaf(?).

Sandhyā: g.

Sandhyānṛttamūrti: g. (a dancing form of Śiva).

saptaparṇaka: a tree (used for temple pillars only, *Alsthonia scholaris*).

Saptamātṛ: g.

saptaśāla: house with seven main buildings.

sabhā: 1. hall. 2. square aedicula (= *kūṭa*). 3. lantern (= *ūrdhvakūṭa*). 4. hipped roof. 5. square outward room. (ref. houses, see *kūṭa*).

samakara: type of frieze (*prati*).

samaliṅga: type of Liṅga (= *sarvatobhadra*).

Samīraṇa: g (= Vāyu).

samaliṅga: g. type of Liṅga (= *sarvatobhadra*).

sambādha: reception hall(?).

sarapa: protection bar (of door) (?).

sarala: a tree (used for temples only, *Pinus longifolia*).

Sarasvatī: g. See Bhāratī, Vāgvadhu.

sarpa: eight.

sarpamāra: a tree (= *arimeda*).

sarvatobhadra: 1. type of house with four main buildings. 2. type of assembly. (ref. joinery). 3. type of town. 4. type of window. 5. type of pavilion. 6. type of hall. 7. type of entablature. 8. type of Liṅga; see *samaliṅga, sarvaliṅga.*

Sarvamohinī: one of the Kāma's arrows.

sarvaliṅga: type of Liṅga (= *sarvatobhadra*).

Savitṛ: 1. g. 2. g. (a vāstudevatā, = Savindra).

Savindra: g. (a vāstudevatā).

sahakāra: a tree (variety of mango-tree).

sahavedī: = *brahmavedikā.*

sahā: a medicinal plant. (*Aloe perfoliata?*).

Sahita: g.

sādhāraṇa: type of pavilion.

sārvakāmika: 1. a category of building 2. mode of cutting a stone to make a Liṅga.

sāla: 1. rampart, wall, city wall.

2. a tree (*Vatica robusta*).

Sāvitṛ: g. (a vāstudevatā, = Sāvindra).

Sāvitrī: g.

Savindra: g. (a vāstudevatā). See Sāvitṛ.

sāhasraliṅga: type of Liṅga.

siṃha: 1. lion (a 'matrice' in *āyādi* system). 2. a tree (used for pillars *siṃhakesara?, Mimusops elengi*).

Siṃhaketu: g.

siṃhāsana: lion throne.

Siddha: 1. g. (group of-). 2. type of pavilion.

siddhiyoga: an astrological conjunction.

sirā: vein, diagonal line of diagram.

silīndhra: = *śilīndhra.*

sīmāsūtra: = *paryantasūtra.*

Sukaṇṭha, Sukandhara: g. (a vāstudevatā, = Sugrīva).

sukumāra: type of six-storeyed gateway.

sukhagṛha: = *sukhālāya.*

sukhasūtra: layout line (for *sukhālaya*).

sukhāṅga: type of pavilion.

sukhālaya: principal main building in house meant for brahmins. See *sukhagṛha, saukhya.*

sukhāvaha: type of four-storeyed temple.

sukhāsana: a posture.

Sukhāsanamūrti: g.

Sugala: g. (a vāstudevatā, = Sugrīva).

Sugata: g. See Buddha.

Sugrīva: g. (a vāstudevatā). See Sukaṇṭha, Sukandhara, Sugala.

sudhā: stucco, coating, mortar.

sundara: 1. type of pavilion. 2. type of six-storeyed gateway.

supratikānta (supratīkānta): diagram with 484 squares.

subala: type of six-storeyed gateway.

Subrahmaṇya: g. (= Skanda).

subhadra: 1. type of socle. 2. type of four-storeyed temple. 3. type of seven-storeyed gateway.

subhūṣaṇa: type of pavilion.

sumaṅgala: 1. type of temple with two-storeys. 2. type of temple with three storeys. 3. type of two storeyed gateway.

Surapati: g.

suragaṇārcitaliṅga: type of Liṅga.

Surapriya: g. (= Śāstā).

Surabhāvin: g. (= Śāstā).

surārcitaliṅga: type of Liṅga.

suruṅga: side door, small

door (= *upadvāra*?).

Surendra: 1. g. 2. g. (a vāstudevatā, = Mahendra).

susaṃhita: diagram with 441 squares.

sūkaraghrāṇa: type of assembly (ref. joinery).

Sūkṣma: g. (a vidyeśvara).

sūtigṛha: confinement room. See *prasūtigṛha*.

sūtra: 1. layout line. 2. characteristic line (ref. Liṅga).

sūtragrāhin: an assistant to *sthapati*.

Sūrya: 1. g. 2. g. (a vāstudevatā). 3. twelve. See Arka, Āditya, Dinakara, Dineśa, Bhānu, Bhāskara, Ravi.

sūryaviśāla: diagram with 400 squares.

setubandha: bridge.

senāmukha: type of fortified city.

senālokaharmya: rostrum for military review.

senāveśanaharmya: entrance building with a guard.

sopāna: stair, stairway.

Soma: 1. g. (= Candra). 2. g. (a Vasu). 3. g. (a vāstudevatā, = Candra).

somavṛtta: type of hall.

saukhya: 1. = *sukhālaya*. 2. types of pavilion.

saudha: building, edifice.

saubala: type of palace.

saubhadra: 1. type of assembly (ref. joinery). 2. type of pavilion.

saumukhya: type of bell capital.

saumya: 1. type of pillar. 2. type of pedestal.

sauṣṭhika: square aedicula (= *kūṭa*).

Skanda: g. See Guha, Ṣaṇmukha, Subrahmaṇya.

skandakānta: type of single-storeyed temple.

skandha: 1. element of the pillar (placed below the bell-capital). 2. recessed part of the finial (= valagna).

skandhapaṭṭikā: rabbet bar (of door).

skandhāvāra: type of town.

stambha: 1. pillar, pilaster. 2. level of pillars (= *jaṅghāvarga*). 3. door jamb. 4. window jamb. 5. *ālāna*. See *aṅghri, kampa, gātra, caraṇa, talipa, pād, pāda, sthāṇu, sthuṇā*.

stambhakumbhalatā: a wall ornament.

stambhatoraṇa: type of arcature.

stambhāntara: intercolumniation.

stūpikā, stūpī (sthūpikā, sthūpī): finial. See *kuḍmala, kumbha, ghaṭa, cūlī.*

stūpikākīla: axis of finial.

stūpīkumbha: vase (moulding of finial).

strī: female (ref. buildings, materials).

sthaṇḍila: 1. area of ground prepared for a ritual, sacrificial area. 2. diagram with 49 squares.

sthapati: 1. architect. 2. craftsman (?).

sthala: floor, storey (= *tala*).

sthavira: aged (ref. stone, = *vṛddha*).

sthāṇu: pillar.

sthāna: building, edifice.

sthānamaṇḍapa: audience pavilion.

sthānaharmya: audience pavilion (= *sthānamaṇḍapa*).

sthānīya: 1. type of royal city. 2. diagram with 121 squares.

sthāpaka: officiating priest in construction rites.

sthūṇa: pillar, pilaster.

sthūpikā, sthūpī: see *stūpikā, stūpī.*

sthūla: peg (ref. joinery) (?).

snānamaṇḍapa: 1. pavilion for bath of images. 2. baths.

snehabhāra, snehavāri: rim (at top of pedestal).

sphaṭikaliṅga: crystal Liṅga.

Smara: g. (= Kāma).

syandana: 1. war chariot. 2. litter (for carrying timber).

sruk: spoon (attribute).

srugaka: type of pavilion.

sruva: laddle (attribute).

Svayambhu: g. (= Brahmā).

svayambhuliṅga: type of Liṅga.

svara: seven

svasti: = *svastipuccha*(?).

svastika: 1. type of house with a single main building. 2. type of house with four main buildings. 3. type of palace. 4. types of village and town. 5. type of entablature. 6. type of window. 7. type of false-dormer window. 8. type of temple with two-storeys. 9. type of temple with three-storey. 10. type of walls arrangement (ref. fort, town). 11. type of Liṅga.

svastipuccha: window, or false dormer window (ref. *sabhā*).

svastibandha: 1. type of temple with one-storey. 2. type of temple with two-storeys.

svastibandhana: 1. type of assembly (ref. joinery). 2. type of false-dormer window(?).
svastibhadra: type of plan for pavilions.
svastivalakṣa: = *valakṣa* (?).
svāmivāsa: chamber of housemaster (in principal main building of *catuśśāla*).
svāmisthāna, svāmyāvāsa: = *svāmivāsa.*
Svāhā: g.

H

hayasadana: = *aśvaśālā.*
harabhāga: = *śivabhāga.*
Hari: g. (= Viṣṇu).
haribhāga: = *viṣṇubhāga.*
haricaraṇa: lion foot leg (ref. seat).
haritāla: orpiment.
Harihara: g. See Viṣṇvardha.
harmya: 1. building, edifice. 2. flat-roof edifice.
hala: ploughshare (attribute).
havyakoṣṭha: pavilion for oblations.
hasta: 1. regular cubit (= 24 *aṅgula*). 2. string (ref. stairs). 3. handrail (ref. palanquin).
hastin: elephant (a 'matrice' in *āyādi* system).
hastipṛṣṭha: apsidal (ref. temple). See *gajapṛsṭha, dvyaśravṛtta.*
hastiśālā: elephant's stable. See *ibhasadana, nāgavāsa, nāgaśālā.*
hastihasta: 1. handrail (ref. stairway). 2. hinge pin (ref. door) (?).
hāra: 1. dwarf-gallery (on entablature, between aediculae). 2. exterior wall of aisle. 3. ? (perhaps w.r. for *harmya*). 4. frame (ref. vehicle). 5. necklace.
hālāṅgavatkuḍya: = *lāṅgalākārakuḍya.*
hīra, hīraka: a moulding of bell capital.
hṛt: plinth (= *jagatī*).
hṛdaya: heart of Vāstupuruṣa (and centre of diagram, building, settlement).
hemagarbha: ceremony of golden embryo.
Hemamālā: g. (?).
Haima: g.
homa: 1. adjustments slab (?). 2. a tree (used for pillars).
homastambha: type of pillar.
hrasvapāda, hrasvāṅghṛi: bannister.

Books of Related Interest

- **The Art of Ancient India :** Buddhist, Hindu and Jain
  —*Susan L. Huntington* [978-81-208-3617-4]

- **The Art of India Through the Ages :** Traditions of Indian Sculpture, Painting and Architecture
  —*Stella Kramrisch* [978-81-208-0182-0]

- **Art of Indian Asia (2 Vols.)** *:* Its Mythology and Transformation —*Heinrich Zimmer*, Comp. & Ed. *Joseph Campbell* [978-81-208-1630-5]

- ***The Hindu Temple (2 Vols.)*** —*Stella Kramrisch*
  [978-81-208-0222-3]

- **Indian Sculpure :** Ancient Classical and Medieval
  —*Stella Kramrisch* [978-81-208-3614-3]

- **Indian Temple :** Mirror of the World —*Bruno Dagens*
  [978-81-7822-985-5]

- **Mayamatam (2 Vols.) :** Treatise of Housing Architecture and Iconography (Sanskrit Text and Translation)
  —Ed. & Tr. *Bruno Dagens* [978-81-208-1226-0]

- **Myths and Symbols in Indian Art and Civilization** —*Heinrich Zimmer*, Ed. *Joseph Campbell* [978-81-208-0751-8]

- **Residential Architecture in Bhoja's Samaranganasutradhara** —*Felix Otter* [978-81-208-3447-7]

- **Sthapatya Ved-Vastu Sastra :** Ideal Homes, Colony and Town Planning —*Niketan Anand Gaur* [978-81-7822-042-0]

- **Vastumandaṇa of Sutradharamandana :** A Treatise on Medieval Western Indian Architecture —Critically Ed. and Tr. by *Anasuya Bhowmick* [978-81-208-4019-5]

- **Vastu Science for 21st Century :** To Enjoy the Gift of Nature —*Prof. B.B. Puri* [978-81-7822-107-6]